Contents

HARPERCOLLINS COLLEGE OUTLINE

College Algebra

Bill Orr, Ed.D.
Crafton Hills College

 HarperPerennial

A Division of HarperCollins*Publishers*

An American BookWorks Corporation Production

Project Manager: William Hamill
Editor: Swasey Editorial

Library of Congress Catalog Card Number: 91-55381
ISBN: 0-06-467140-2

92 93 94 95 96 ABW/RRD 10 9 8 7 6 5 4 3 2 1

Preface

This book was written to help students learn how to do the algebraic manipulations necessary to study higher levels of mathematics. Most of the difficulties that students have in mathematics are difficulties with algebra. A solid understanding of algebra is a key to success in higher level courses. It is mandatory that students take the time necessary to become proficient in algebraic skills.

This book was written with the student in mind. As a student of mathematics myself, my motto is "learn by doing." I believe that most students learn mathematics by doing problems. In each section of the book there are numerous examples and explanations. Definitions, theorems, and rules should be read with a good understanding, but memorization is not intended. Through the examples and problems, the students should be able to understand the techniques of solving problems.

Completed solutions to all examples are provided. Remember, most algebraic answers have many different forms. If your answer is not exactly the same as the answer in the book, it may be an equivalent answer.

When studying the examples in this book, warnings are given regarding common mistakes. Students need to take note of these warnings because mistakes are easily made and may be overlooked.

I would like to thank all of the people who have helped me in writing this book. Family, friends, colleagues, and students have given their time and understanding to help me in this endeavor. To all of them I give a sincere thank you.

Bill Orr

1

Properties of Real Numbers

SECTION 1.1 THE REAL NUMBER SYSTEM

Sets

    A **set** is a collection or group of objects. Sets are represented using braces { } and are denoted by capital letters like A, B, C, ... The objects inside the set are called the **members** or **elements** of the set. The real numbers, denoted with the letter R, is a collection of the sets below:

1. **Natural Numbers**: The set $N = \{1, 2, 3, 4, \ldots\}$. The three dots indicate that the set continues indefinitely. When a set is written by listing the members of the set, the set is said to be in **roster notation**.

2. **Whole Numbers**: The set $W = \{0, 1, 2, 3, 4, \ldots\}$.

3. **Integers**: The set $Z = \{\ldots, -3, -2, -1, 0, 1, 2, 3, \ldots\}$. The set of integers includes the set of natural numbers, their negatives, and zero.

4. **Rational Numbers**: The set $Q = \{\frac{a}{b} \mid a$ and b are integers and $b \neq 0\}$. This statement is read "Q is the set of all numbers in the form of $\frac{a}{b}$ such that a and b are integers and $b \neq 0$." The set of rational numbers is the set of all numbers which can be written in the form of $\frac{a}{b}$ where a is an integer and b is a non-zero integer. The set Q cannot be listed in roster form and is usually written in **set builder** notation, which describes the elements of a set. Set Q contains all of the integers, along with all fractions which are not integers. All numbers in the form of $\frac{a}{b}$ when written in decimal form will either terminate or repeat. Therefore, the set Q contains all terminating and repeating decimals.

5. **Irrational Numbers**: The set of irrational numbers, set I, are numbers with decimal notations that are non-terminating and non-repeating. The set of irrational numbers is the set of all numbers which cannot be written as fractions. Irrational numbers include numbers like $\sqrt{2}$, π and e.

6. **Real Numbers**: The set of real numbers, set R, is the set of all rational and all irrational numbers.

Properties of Real Numbers

ADDITION PROPERTIES

> **Addition Properties** Let a, b, and c be real numbers, then
> **Closure**: $a + b$ is a unique real number.
> **Commutative**: $a + b = b + a$
> **Associative**: $a + (b + c) = (a + b) + c$
> **Identity**: Zero is the additive identity. That is, $a + 0 = 0 + a = a$.
> **Additive Inverse**: For every real number a there is a unique
> $\qquad$ number $(-a)$ such that $a + (-a) = (-a) + a = 0$.
> $(-a)$ is called the **negative** (or **additive inverse**) of a.

MULTIPLICATION PROPERTIES

> **Multiplication Properties** Let a, b, and c be real numbers, then
> **Closure**: $a \cdot b$ is a unique real number.
> **Commutative**: $a \cdot b = b \cdot a$
> **Associative**: $a \cdot (b \cdot c) = (a \cdot b) \cdot c$
> **Identity**: 1 is the multiplicative identity. $a \cdot 1 = 1 \cdot a = a$.
> **Multiplicative Inverse**: For all $a \neq 0$, there exists a unique
>
> $$\text{number } \frac{1}{a} \text{ such that, } a \cdot \frac{1}{a} = \frac{1}{a} \cdot a = 1.$$
>
> $\frac{1}{a}$ is called the **reciprocal** (or **multiplicative inverse**) of a.

DISTRIBUTIVE PROPERTY

> **Distributive Property of Multiplication Over Addition**:
> Let a, b, and c be real numbers, then $a \cdot (b + c) = a \cdot b + a \cdot c$.

SUBTRACTION AND DIVISION

> **Definition**
> For all real numbers a and b:
> **Subtraction**: $a - b = a + (-b)$
>
> **Division**: $a \div b = a \cdot \frac{1}{b} = \frac{a}{b}$ where $b \neq 0$.

PROPERTIES OF NEGATIVE NUMBERS

In these definitions, $(-b)$ is called the **negative** (additive inverse) of b, and $\frac{1}{b}$ is called the **reciprocal** (multiplicative inverse) of b. In fractional form, a is called the **numerator** of the fraction and b is called the **denominator** of the fraction.

Properties of Negation

For all real numbers a and b:

1) $-a = -1 \cdot a$
2) $-(-a) = a$
3) $(-a) \cdot b = -(ab) = a \cdot (-b) = -ab$
4) $(-a) \cdot (-b) = ab$
5) $-(a+b) = (-a) + (-b)$
6) $-(a-b) = (-a) + b$
7) $-(-a+b) = a + (-b)$
8) $-(-a-b) = a + b$

PROPERTIES OF ZERO

Properties of Zero

For all real numbers a and b:

1) $a + 0 = a$

2) $a - 0 = a$

3) $a \cdot 0 = 0 \cdot a = 0$ **Zero Factor Property**

4) $\dfrac{0}{a} = 0, a \neq 0$

5) $\dfrac{a}{0}$ is undefined

6) If $ab = 0$, then $a = 0$ or $b = 0$ or both. **Factorization Property of Zero**.

PROPERTIES OF FRACTIONS

Properties of Fractions
For all real numbers a, b, c, and d where b and $d \neq 0$,

1) **Equivalent Fractions:** $\dfrac{a}{b} = \dfrac{c}{d}$ if and only if $ad = bc$.

2) **Positive Fractions:** $+\dfrac{+a}{+b} = +\dfrac{-a}{-b} = -\dfrac{-a}{+b} = -\dfrac{+a}{-b}$

3) **Negative Fractions:** $-\dfrac{+a}{+b} = +\dfrac{-a}{+b} = +\dfrac{+a}{-b} = -\dfrac{-a}{-b}$

4) **Fundamental Principle of Fractions:** $\dfrac{a}{b} = \dfrac{ac}{bc}, c \neq 0$

5) **Adding Fractions with Like Denominators:** $\dfrac{a}{b} + \dfrac{c}{b} = \dfrac{a+c}{b}$

6) **Subtracting Fractions with Like Denominators:** $\dfrac{a}{b} - \dfrac{c}{b} = \dfrac{a-c}{b}$

7) **Adding Fractions with Unlike Denominators:** $\dfrac{a}{b} + \dfrac{c}{d} = \dfrac{ad+bc}{bd}$

8) **Subtracting Fractions with Unlike Denominators:** $\dfrac{a}{b} - \dfrac{c}{d} = \dfrac{ad-bc}{bd}$

9) **Multiplying Fractions:** $\dfrac{a}{b} \cdot \dfrac{c}{d} = \dfrac{ac}{bd}$

10) **Dividing Fractions:** $\dfrac{a}{b} \div \dfrac{c}{d} = \dfrac{a}{b} \cdot \dfrac{d}{c} = \dfrac{ad}{bc}, c \neq 0$

Prime Numbers and Least Common Denominators

PRIME AND COMPOSITE NUMBERS

If a, b, and c are integers and $ab = c$, then a and b are called **factors** of c. If c has exactly two factors, then c is called a **prime number**. Examples of prime numbers include 2, 3, 5, 7, 11, ... These numbers are prime because they have exactly two factors: 1 and the number itself.

The number c is said to be **prime factored** if $ab = c$ and a and b are prime numbers. The **Fundamental Theorem of Arithmetic** states that every positive integer greater than 1, which is not prime, can be written as a product of two or more prime numbers in exactly one way when order is not taken into account. Any positive integer greater than one which is not prime is called **composite**. Examples of composite numbers are 4, 6, 8, 9, 10, ... The number one (1) is neither prime nor composite.

EXAMPLE 1.1

Prime factor the following numbers:
a) 15
b) 18
c) 24
d) 150
e) 450

SOLUTION 1.1

a) $15 = 3 \cdot 5$
b) $18 = 2 \cdot 9 = 2 \cdot 3 \cdot 3 = 2 \cdot 3^2$
c) $24 = 4 \cdot 6 = 2 \cdot 2 \cdot 2 \cdot 3 = 2^3 \cdot 3$
d) $150 = 15 \cdot 10 = 3 \cdot 5 \cdot 2 \cdot 5 = 2 \cdot 3 \cdot 5 \cdot 5 = 2 \cdot 3 \cdot 5^2$
e) $450 = 45 \cdot 10 = 5 \cdot 9 \cdot 2 \cdot 5 = 5 \cdot 3 \cdot 2 \cdot 5 = 2 \cdot 3 \cdot 3 \cdot 5 \cdot 5$
       $= 2 \cdot 3^2 \cdot 5^2$

REDUCING FRACTIONS

Prime factoring is useful in reducing fractions (rational numbers).

EXAMPLE 1.2

Use prime factoring to reduce the following fractions:

a) $\dfrac{6}{8}$

b) $\dfrac{26}{48}$

SOLUTION 1.2

a) $\dfrac{6}{8} = \dfrac{2 \cdot 3}{2 \cdot 2 \cdot 2} = \dfrac{\cancel{2} \cdot 3}{\cancel{2} \cdot 2 \cdot 2} = \dfrac{3}{2 \cdot 2} = \dfrac{3}{4}$

b) $\dfrac{26}{48} = \dfrac{2 \cdot 13}{2 \cdot 2 \cdot 2 \cdot 2 \cdot 3} = \dfrac{\cancel{2} \cdot 13}{\cancel{2} \cdot 2 \cdot 2 \cdot 2 \cdot 3} = \dfrac{13}{2 \cdot 2 \cdot 2 \cdot 3} = \dfrac{13}{24}$

LEAST COMMON DENOMINATORS

Prime factoring also helps us add and subtract unlike fractions by finding the least common denominator (LCD). The **Least Common Denominator** is the smallest denominator that all denominators will divide evenly into. To add (or subtract) two or more fractions, find the LCD, change the fractions to be added (or subtracted) into equivalent fractions which have the LCD, and then add (or subtract) the fractions using the rule for adding (or subtracting) fractions with like denominators.

To add $\frac{3}{8} + \frac{1}{6}$, find the LCD of the denominators of 8 and 6. Prime factor the denominators. Find all of the different prime factors of the denominators. The LCD is the product of these factors.

$8 = 2 \cdot 2 \cdot 2$
$6 = 2 \cdot 3$
$LCD = 2 \cdot 2 \cdot 2 \cdot 3 = 24$

Now change $\frac{3}{8}$ and $\frac{1}{6}$ into equivalent fractions with denominators of 24.

$$\frac{3}{8} + \frac{1}{6} = \frac{3 \cdot 3}{8 \cdot 3} + \frac{1 \cdot 4}{6 \cdot 4} = \frac{9}{24} + \frac{4}{24}$$

Now add using the rule for adding fractions with like denominators.

$$\frac{9}{24} + \frac{4}{24} = \frac{13}{24}$$

EXAMPLE 1.3

Add or subtract the following fractions by using the LCD.

a) $\frac{5}{8} + \frac{7}{12}$

b) $\frac{7}{12} + \frac{1}{6} + \frac{4}{9}$

c) $\frac{11}{12} - \frac{3}{8}$

d) $\frac{17}{24} + \frac{3}{8} - \frac{5}{16}$

SOLUTION 1.3

a) $\frac{5}{8} + \frac{7}{12}$

First find the LCD.

$$8 = 2 \cdot 2 \cdot 2$$
$$12 = 2 \cdot 2 \cdot 3$$
$$LCD = 2 \cdot 2 \cdot 2 \cdot 3 = 24$$

Change $\frac{5}{8}$ and $\frac{7}{12}$ to equivalent fractions with the LCD of 24, then add.

$$\frac{5 \cdot 3}{8 \cdot 3} + \frac{7 \cdot 2}{12 \cdot 2} = \frac{15}{24} + \frac{14}{24} = \frac{29}{24} = 1\frac{5}{24}$$

b) $\frac{7}{12} + \frac{1}{6} + \frac{4}{9}$

Find the LCD.

$$12 = 2 \cdot 2 \cdot 3$$
$$6 = 2 \cdot 3$$
$$9 = 3 \cdot 3$$
$$\text{LCD} = 2 \cdot 2 \cdot 3 \cdot 3 = 36$$

Change $\dfrac{7}{12}, \dfrac{1}{6}$ and $\dfrac{4}{9}$ into equivalent fractions with the LCD, then add.

$$\frac{7 \cdot 3}{12 \cdot 3} + \frac{1 \cdot 6}{6 \cdot 6} + \frac{4 \cdot 4}{9 \cdot 4} = \frac{21}{36} + \frac{6}{36} + \frac{16}{36} = \frac{43}{36} \text{ or } 1\frac{7}{36}$$

c) $\dfrac{11}{12} - \dfrac{3}{8}$

Find the LCD.

$$12 = 2 \cdot 2 \cdot 3$$
$$8 = 2 \cdot 2 \cdot 2$$
$$\text{LCD} = 2 \cdot 2 \cdot 2 \cdot 3 = 24$$

Change $\dfrac{11}{12}$ and $\dfrac{3}{8}$ into equivalent fractions with LCD of 24, then subtract.

$$\frac{11 \cdot 2}{12 \cdot 2} - \frac{3 \cdot 3}{8 \cdot 3} = \frac{22}{24} - \frac{9}{24} = \frac{13}{24}$$

d) $\dfrac{17}{24} + \dfrac{3}{8} - \dfrac{5}{16}$

Find the LCD.

$$24 = 2 \cdot 2 \cdot 2 \cdot 3$$
$$8 = 2 \cdot 2 \cdot 2$$
$$16 = 2 \cdot 2 \cdot 2 \cdot 2$$
$$\text{LCD} = 2 \cdot 2 \cdot 2 \cdot 2 \cdot 3 = 48$$

Change $\dfrac{17}{24}, \dfrac{3}{8}$ and $\dfrac{5}{16}$ into equivalent fractions with the LCD, then add or subtract.

$$\frac{17 \cdot 2}{24 \cdot 2} + \frac{3 \cdot 6}{8 \cdot 6} - \frac{5 \cdot 3}{16 \cdot 3} = \frac{34}{48} + \frac{18}{48} - \frac{15}{48} = \frac{37}{48}$$

The Number Line

A **number line** is a line in which the points on the line correspond to the real numbers. There is a **one-to-one correspondence** between the real numbers and the points on the line: for each real number there is one and only one point on the number line that corresponds to that number and for each point on the number line there is one and only one number in the set of real numbers that corresponds to that point.

The location for zero is called the origin of the number line. The numbers to the right of zero are called **positive numbers** and the numbers to the left of zero are called **negative numbers**. We use the term **non-nega-**

tive to describe a number which is either positive or zero. The term **non-positive** means negative or zero. Positive and negative numbers have both a magnitude (a value) and a direction (+ or –).

EXAMPLE 1.4

Graph the following sets of numbers on the number line:
a) {1, 2, 3, 5}
b) {–3, –1, 0, 2}
c) {–5, –2, 1, 5}
d) {–4, –2, 0, 1, 2, 5}

SOLUTION 1.4

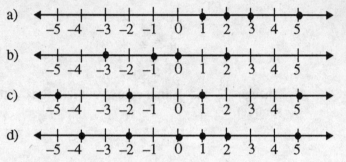

SECTION 1.2 POLYNOMIALS AND SPECIAL PRODUCTS

Evaluating Expressions

To **evaluate** expressions, we replace variables with specific numerical values and then compute the numerical answer for the expression. The set of possible numerical replacements for the variables is called the **domain** of the variable. Two algebraic expressions are said to be **equivalent** if they have the same domain and the same numeric value for all replacements of the variables within the domain.

EXAMPLE 1.5

Evaluate the following expressions for the given replacements of the variables.
a) $12x^2y^3$ if $x = -2$ and $y = 5$.
b) $7x^3y + 6x^2y^2$ if $x = 4$ and $y = 3$
c) $2x^4y^7 - 8x^3y^4$ if $x = -3$ and $y = 2$
d) $-x^3y^2 - 2x - 5y$ if $x = -2$ and $y = -3$

SOLUTION 1.5

a) $12x^2y^3$ if $x = -2$ and $y = 5$.

Replace x with (-2) and y with 5.

$12x^2y^3 = 12(-2)^2(5)^3 = 12(4)(125) = 6000$

b) $7x^3y + 6x^2y^2$ if $x = 4$ and $y = 3$.

Replace x with 4 and y with 3.

$7x^3y + 6x^2y^2 = 7(4)^3(3) + 6(4)^2(3)^2$

$= 7(64)(3) + 6(16)(9) = 1344 + 864 = 2208$

c) $2x^4y^7 - 8x^3y^4$ if $x = -3$ and $y = 2$.

Replace x with (-3) and y with 2..

$2x^4y^7 - 8x^3y^4 = 2(-3)^4(2)^7 - 8(-3)^3(2)^4$

$= 2(81)(128) - 8(-27)(16) = 20736 + 3456 = 24192$

d) $-x^3y^2 - 2x - 5y$ if $x = -2$ and $y = -3$.

Replace x with (-2) and y with (-3).

$-x^3y^2 - 2x - 5y = -(-2)^3(-3)^2 - 2(-2) - 5(-3)$

$= -(-8)(9) + 4 + 15 = 72 + 4 + 15 = 91$

Simplifying Terms

A **variable** is a letter or symbol used to represent a number or set of numbers. A **term** is a number or a number and one or more variables raised to powers. In a term, the numbers and variables are multiplied or divided. An **expression** is any mathematical statement. Numbers, variables, terms and expressions can be added, subtracted, multiplied, or divided.

Adding Terms

Only like terms can be added to form a more simplified expression. **Like terms** are terms with identically the same variables and exponents (powers). To add like terms, we use the distributive property.

$4 + 3 = 7 \qquad 4x + 3x = (4 + 3)x = 7x$

$4x^2 + 3x^2 = (4 + 3)x^2 = 7x^2$

We add like terms by adding the numerical **coefficients** (the numbers in front of the variable) and keeping the variable(s).

$4xy^3 + 3xy^3 = (4 + 3)xy^3 = 7xy^3$

Subtracting Terms

Only like terms can be subtracted. We also use the distributive property to subtract like terms.

$$4 - 3 = 1 \qquad 4x - 3x = (4 - 3)x = 1x = x$$
$$4x^2 - 3x^2 = (4 - 3)x^2 = 1x^2 = x^2$$

We subtract like terms by subtracting the numerical coefficients and keeping the variable(s).

$$4xy^3 - 3xy^3 = (4 - 3)xy^3 = 1xy^3 = xy^3$$

Adding and subtracting like terms is called **combining like terms**.

Multiplying Terms

The terms (numbers and variables) used in a multiplication problem are called factors. To multiply terms we need to consider definition of powers and the rule for multiplication of powers.

Definition: $x^n = \underbrace{x \cdot x \cdot x \cdots x}_{n \text{ factors of } x}$ where n is a natural number ≥ 2.

$$x^0 = 1$$

$$x^1 = x$$

Product Rule of Exponents:

$$x^m \cdot x^n = x^{m+n}$$

$$x^3 \cdot x^5 = x^{3+5} = x^8 \qquad x^4 \cdot x^7 = x^{4+7} = x^{11}$$

Any terms may be multiplied. To multiply terms, first multiply the numerical coefficients and then multiply the variables by using the product rule of exponents.

$$3 \cdot 4 = 12$$

$$3x \cdot 4x = 3 \cdot 4 \cdot x \cdot x = 12x^{1+1} = 12x^2$$

$$3x \cdot 4x^3 = 3 \cdot 4 \cdot x^1 \cdot x^3 = 12x^{1+3} = 12x^4$$

$$5x^2y^5 \cdot 7x^3y^4 = 5 \cdot 7 \cdot x^2 \cdot x^3 \cdot y^5 \cdot y^4 = 35 \cdot x^{2+3} \cdot y^{5+4} = 35x^5y^9$$

Dividing Terms

To divide terms, we need the definition for the division of powers.

> **Division Rule of Exponents:**
> $$x^m \div x^n = x^{m-n}$$
> or
> $$\frac{x^m}{x^n} = x^{m-n}$$
>
> The definition assumes that $m \geq n$. If $n > m$, then
> $$\frac{x^m}{x^n} = \frac{1}{x^{n-m}}$$

$$x^5 \div x^3 = x^{5-3} = x^2 \qquad \frac{x^7}{x^3} = x^{7-3} = x^4 \qquad \frac{x^5}{x^{11}} = \frac{1}{x^{11-5}} = \frac{1}{x^6}$$

Any terms can be divided. We divide terms by dividing the numerical coefficients and dividing the variables by using the division rule of exponents.

$$12 \div 4 = 3$$

$$12x^4 \div 4x = \frac{12x^4}{3x^1} = 4x^{4-1} = 4x^3$$

$$36x^7 \div 6x^3 = \frac{36x^7}{6x^3} = 6x^{7-3} = 6x^4$$

Polynomials

The simplest and most common type of mathematical expression is a **polynomial**.

> **Definition of a Polynomial:** A polynomial is any expression in the form of
> $$a_k x^k + a_{k-1} x^{k-1} + a_{k-2} x^{k-2} + \ldots + a_2 x^2 + a_1 x + a_0$$
> where k is a whole number.

Polynomial expressions include:
$$3, \quad 5x - 4, \quad x^2 - 4x + 7 \quad \text{and} \quad 5x^3 + 8x^9$$

The individual terms of a polynomial in the variable x have the form of $a_k x^k$. a_k is called the **numerical coefficient** of x^k and k is called the **degree** of the term $a_k x^k$. The highest power of x in the polynomial is called the **degree of the polynomial**.

Polynomials with only one term are called **monomials**, polynomials with two terms are called **binomials** and polynomials with three terms are called **trinomials**. Polynomials with more than three terms are referred to as polynomials. Polynomials are said to be in **standard form** when the terms are written in descending order so that the term with the highest power of the variable is written first and the term with the lowest power of the variable is written last.

EXAMPLE 1.6

Name the number of terms and the degree in each polynomial. Put the polynomial into standard form.

a) $3x^3 + 2x^2 - 3$
b) $3 - x^7 + 6x^{11} + 13x^3 - 15x^2$
c) $3x^2 + 7x^5 - (4x^3 + 2x^4)$
d) $3x^8$

SOLUTION 1.6

a) $3x^3 + 2x^2 - 3$ is a three-term polynomial or trinomial. The degree of the polynomial is three since the highest power of the variable is 3. The polynomial is already in standard form; the term with the highest exponent $(3x^3)$ is first, the second highest exponent $(2x^2)$ is second and the lowest exponent $(3 = 3x^0)$ is last.

b) $3 - x^7 + 6x^{11} + 13x^3 - 15x^2$ has five terms. The degree of the polynomial is eleven since the highest power of the variable is 11. The polynomial in standard form is written
$$6x^{11} - x^7 + 13x^3 - 15x^2 + 3,$$
where the exponents of the terms are written in descending order.

c) $3x^2 + 7x^5 - (4x^3 + 2x^4)$ is a three-term polynomial or trinomial. Because $(4x^3 + 2x^4)$ is in parentheses, it is one term, not two. The degree of the polynomial is five since the highest power of the variable outside of parentheses is 5. The polynomial in standard form is written
$$7x^5 + 3x^2 - (4x^3 + 2x^4).$$

In standard form the term $(4x^3 + 2x^4)$ is to the first power. So the $7x^5$ is the highest power term and $3x^2$ is the second highest power.

d) $3x^8$ is a one-term polynomial or a monomial. The degree of the polynomial is 8. The polynomial is in standard form.

SIMPLIFICATION OF POLYNOMIALS

Simplification is the process of removing parentheses and combining like terms.

ADDING AND SUBTRACTING POLYNOMIALS

To add or subtract polynomials, we can use the commutative and associative properties of addition.

(Recall that $a - b = a + (-b)$.)

EXAMPLE 1.7

Add and subtract the following polynomials, as indicated.

a) $(4x^2 + 3x + 5) + (5x^2 + 4x + 7)$

b) $(9x^2 + 4x + 15) + (3x^2 + 6x + 17) + (11x^2 + 3x + 8)$

c) $(4x^2 - 7x - 9) - (3x^2 - 5x - 12)$

d) $(5x^2 + 7x - 2) - (4x^2 - 8x - 15) - (13x^2 - 19x + 5)$

e) $(2x^2 + 9x + 7) + (8x^2 - 13x - 5) - (2x^2 + 7x - 9)$

SOLUTION 1.7

a) $(4x^2 + 3x + 5) + (5x^2 + 4x + 7)$ Remove parentheses (no sign changes are needed).

$= 4x^2 + 3x + 5 + 5x^2 + 4x + 7$ Use the commutative property to rearrange terms.

$= 4x^2 + 5x^2 + 3x + 4x + 5 + 7$ Combine like terms.

$= 9x^2 + 7x + 12$

b) $(9x^2 + 4x + 15) + (3x^2 + 6x + 17) + (11x^2 + 3x + 8)$

    Remove parentheses.

$= 9x^2 + 4x + 15 + 3x^2 + 6x + 17 + 11x^2 + 3x + 8$

    Rearrange terms.

$= 9x^2 + 3x^2 + 11x^2 + 4x + 6x + 3x + 15 + 17 + 8$

    Combine like terms.

$= 23x^2 + 13x + 40$

c) $(4x^2 - 7x - 9) - (3x^2 - 5x - 12)$ Remove parentheses. (Remember to change signs when removing parentheses with a negative sign in front.)

$= 4x^2 - 7x - 9 - 3x^2 + 5x + 12$ Rearrange terms.

$= 4x^2 - 3x^2 - 7x + 5x - 9 + 12$ Combine like terms.

$$= x^2 - 2x + 3$$

d) $(5x^2 + 7x - 2) - (4x^2 - 8x - 15) - (13x^2 - 19x + 5)$

Remove parentheses.

$$= 5x^2 + 7x - 2 - 4x^2 + 8x + 15 - 13x^2 + 19x - 5$$

Rearrange terms.

$$= 5x^2 - 4x^2 - 13x^2 + 7x + 8x + 19x - 5 - 2 + 15 - 5$$

Combine like terms.

$$= -12x^2 + 34x + 8$$

e) $(2x^2 + 9x + 7) + (8x^2 - 13x - 5) - (2x^2 + 7x - 9)$

Remove parentheses.

$$= 2x^2 + 9x + 7 + 8x^2 - 13x - 5 - 2x^2 - 7x + 9$$

Rearrange terms.

$$= 2x^2 + 8x^2 - 2x^2 + 9x - 13x - 7x + 7 - 5 + 9$$

Combine like terms.

$$= 8x^2 - 11x + 11$$

Multiplying Polynomials

MONOMIAL × POLYNOMIAL

To multiply a monomial times a polynomial, we use the distributive property of multiplication over addition and the rules for multiplying terms.

EXAMPLE 1.8

Simplify the following:
a) $4x(3x^2 - 5x - 7)$
b) $5x^2y^3(4x^3y^2 - 7x^2y + 9x^5y^4)$
c) $2x(5x^2 - 3x + 4) + 4x(6x^2 + 2x - 3) - 5x(7x^2 + 2x - 6)$
d) $3xy(4x^2 - 4x - 7) - 4xy(5x^2 - 7x - 5) + 2xy(4x^2 - 8x + 3)$

SOLUTION 1.8

a) $4x(3x^2 - 5x - 7) =$ Distribute $4x$.

$$= 4x \cdot 3x^2 - 4x \cdot 5x - 4x \cdot 7$$ Multiply terms.

$$= 12x^3 - 20x^2 - 28x$$

b) $5x^2y^3(4x^3y^2 - 7x^2y + 9x^5y^4)$ Distribute $5x^2y^3$.

$$= 5x^2y^3 \cdot 4x^3y^2 - 5x^2y^3 \cdot 7x^2y + 5x^2y^3 \cdot 9x^5y^4$$

Multiply terms.

$$= 20x^5y^5 - 35x^4y^4 + 45x^7y^7$$ Put into standard form.

$$= 45x^7y^7 + 20x^5y^5 - 35x^4y^4$$

c) $2x(5x^2 - 3x + 4) + 4x(6x^2 + 2x - 3) - 5x(7x^2 + 2x - 6)$

                            Distribute terms.

$$= 2x \cdot 5x^2 - 2x \cdot 3x + 2x \cdot 4 + 4x \cdot 6x^2 + 4x \cdot 2x - 4x \cdot 3 - 5x \cdot 7x^2 - 5x \cdot 2x + 5x \cdot 6$$

                            Multiply terms.

$$= 10x^3 - 6x^2 + 8x + 24x^3 + 8x^2 - 12x - 35x^3 - 10x^2 + 30x$$

                            Combine like terms.

$$= -x^3 - 8x^2 + 26x$$

d) $3xy(4x^2 - 4x - 7) - 4xy(5x^2 - 7x - 5) + 2xy(4x^2 - 8x + 3)$

                            Distribute.

$$= 3xy \cdot 4x^2 - 3xy \cdot 4x - 3xy \cdot 7 - 4xy \cdot 5x^2 + 4xy \cdot 7x$$
$$+ 4xy \cdot 5 + 2xy \cdot 4x^2 - 2xy \cdot 8x + 2xy \cdot 3$$

                            Multiply terms.

$$= 12x^3y - 12x^2y - 21xy - 20x^3y + 28x^2y + 20xy + 8x^3y - 16x^2y + 6xy$$

                            Combine like terms.

$$= 0x^3y + 0x^2y + 5xy$$

                            Remove terms with
                            coefficients of 0.

$$= 5xy$$

POLYNOMIAL $\times$ POLYNOMIAL

To multiply a polynomial times a polynomial, we use the distributive property.

EXAMPLE 1.9

Multiply the following.

a) $(6x + 7)(2x^2 + 4x + 3)$

b) $(2x^2 - 5x + 4)(3x^2 - 2x - 7)$

SOLUTION 1.9

a) $(6x + 7)(2x^2 + 4x + 3)$

Distribute $(6x + 7)$ into the trinomial $(2x^2 + 4x + 3)$. Treat $(6x + 7)$ like a single term.

$(6x + 7)(2x^2 + 4x + 3) =$

$= (6x + 7) \cdot 2x^2 + (6x + 7) \cdot 4x + (6x + 7) \cdot 3$

Now distribute the monomials $2x^2$, $4x$ and 3.

$= 6x \cdot 2x^2 + 7 \cdot 2x^2 + 6x \cdot 4x + 7 \cdot 4x + 6x \cdot 3 + 7 \cdot 3$

$$= 12x^3 + 14x^2 + 24x^2 + 28x + 18x + 21 \quad \text{Combine like terms.}$$
$$= 12x^3 + 38x^2 + 46x + 21.$$

b) $(2x^2 - 5x + 4)(3x^2 - 2x - 7)$

Distribute $(2x^2 - 5x + 4)$ into the trinomial $(3x^2 - 2x - 7)$. Treat $(2x^2 - 5x + 4)$ like a single term.

$$(2x^2 - 5x + 4)(3x^2 - 2x - 7) =$$
$$(2x^2 - 5x + 4) \cdot 3x^2 + (2x^2 - 5x + 4)$$
$$+ (-2x) + (2x^2 - 5x + 4) \cdot (-7)$$

Now distribute the monomials $2x^2$, $-5x$ and 4.

$$2x^2 \cdot 3x^2 - 5x \cdot 3x^2 + 4 \cdot 3x^2 + 2x^2 \cdot (-2x) - 5x \cdot (-2x)$$
$$+ 4 \cdot (-2x) + (2)x^2 \cdot (-7) - 5x \cdot (-7) + 4 \cdot (-7)$$
$$= 6x^4 - 15x^3 + 12x^2 - 4x^3 + 10x^2 - 8x - 14x^2 + 35x - 28$$

Combine like terms.

$$= 6x^4 - 19x^3 + 8x^2 + 27x - 28.$$

FOIL METHOD OF MULTIPLICATION

If we are multiplying two binomials, we can use the FOIL method. The letters FOIL stand for multiplying the first term times the first term (F), the outer term times the outer term (O), the inner term times the inner term (I), and the last term times the last term (L).

EXAMPLE 1.10

Multiply the following binomials using the FOIL method.

a) $(6x + 7)(4x + 3)$

b) $(6x + 5)(2x + 3)$

c) $(2x - 7)(5x + 4)$

d) $(4x - 5)(2x - 11)$

SOLUTION 1.10

a) $(6x + 7)(4x + 3)$ Multiply first terms (F).

$= (6x \cdot 4x) = 24x^2$ Multiply the outer terms (O).

$= (6x \cdot 3) = 18x$ Multiply the inner terms (I).

$= (7 \cdot 4x) = 28x$ Multiply the last terms (L).

$= (7 \cdot 3) = 21$ Add these products and combine like terms.

$= 24x^2 + 18x + 28x + 21 = 24x^2 + 46x + 21$

b) $(6x+5)(2x+3)$

       F   O   I   L

$= 6x \cdot 2x + 6x \cdot 3 + 5 \cdot 2x + 5 \cdot 3$ Multiply using FOIL.

$= 12x^2 + 18x + 10x + 15$ Combine like terms.

$= 12x^2 + 28x + 15$

c) $(2x-7)(5x+4)$ Multiply using FOIL.

$= 2x \cdot 5x + 2x \cdot 4 - 7 \cdot 5x - 7 \cdot 4$

$= 10x^2 + 8x - 35x - 28$ Combine like terms.

$= 10x^2 - 27x - 28$

d) $(4x-5)(2x-11)$ Multiply using FOIL.

$= 4x \cdot 2x + 4x \cdot (-11) - 5 \cdot 2x - 5 \cdot (-11)$

$= 8x^2 - 44x - 10x + 55$ Combine like terms.

$= 8x^2 - 54x + 55$

Special Products

There are **Special Products of Binomials** which should be memorized.

Multiplication of Conjugate Pairs	$(a+b)(a-b) = a^2 - b^2$
Binomial Squared	$(a+b)^2 = a^2 + 2ab + b^2$
	$(a-b)^2 = a^2 - 2ab + b^2$
Binomial Cubed	$(a+b)^3 = a^3 + 3a^2b + 3ab^2 + b^3$
	$(a-b)^3 = a^3 - 3a^2b + 3ab^2 - b^3$

EXAMPLE 1.11

Multiply the following special products:
a) $(2x+3)(2x-3)$
b) $(3x+5)^2$
c) $(6x-7)^2$
d) $(2x+5)^3$
e) $(x-7)^3$

SOLUTION 1.11

a) $(2x+3)(2x-3)$ These two binomials are called conjugate pairs. The two binomials have identically the same terms except one binomial is the sum of the terms and the other is the difference of the terms. In the multiplication of conjugate pairs, the outer and inner products drop out. Therefore, the product is strictly the first term squared minus the second term squared.

$$(2x)^2 - (3)^2 = 4x^2 - 9$$

Check by using FOIL.

$$(2x+3)(2x-3) = 2x \cdot 2x + 2x \cdot (-3) + 3 \cdot 2x + 3 \cdot (-3)$$
$$= 4x^2 - 6x + 6x - 9 \qquad\qquad \text{Combine like terms.}$$
$$= 4x^2 - 9$$

b) $(3x+5)^2$ To square the sum of two terms, we square the first term, add two times the first term times the second term, and add the last term squared.

$$(3x)^2 + 2(3x)(5) + (5)^2 = 9x^2 + 30x + 25$$

Check by using FOIL.

$$(3x+5)(3x+5) = 3x \cdot 3x + 3x \cdot 5 + 5 \cdot 3x + 5 \cdot 5$$
$$= 9x^2 + 15x + 15x + 25 \qquad\qquad \text{Combine like terms.}$$
$$= 9x^2 + 30x + 25$$

c) $(6x-7)^2$ To square the difference of two terms, we square the first term, subtract two times the first term times the second term, and add the last term squared.

$$(6x)^2 - 2(6x)(7) + (7)^2 = 36x^2 - 84x + 49$$

Check by using FOIL.

$$(6x-7)(6x-7) = 6x \cdot 6x + 6x \cdot (-7) + (-7) \cdot 6x + (-7) \cdot (-7)$$
$$= 36x^2 - 42x - 42x + 49 \qquad\qquad \text{Combine like terms.}$$
$$= 36x^2 - 84x + 49$$

d) $(2x+5)^3$ To cube the sum of two terms, we cube the first term, add three times the first term squared times the second term, add three times the first term times the second term squared, and add the second term cubed.

$(2x)^3 = 8x^3$	First term squared
$3 \cdot (2x)^2 \cdot (5) = 60x^2$	3 • first term squared • second term
$3 \cdot (2x) \cdot (5)^2 = 150x$	3 • first term • second term squared
$(5)^3 = 125$	Second term cubed

Add the terms together.

$$(2x)^3 + 3 \cdot (2x)^2 \cdot (5) + 3 \cdot (2x) \cdot (5)^2 + (5)^3$$

Notice the pattern for cubing a binomial. The first term, $2x$, has powers of $(2x)^3$, $(2x)^2$, $(2x)^1$ and then $(2x)^0$. The second term, 5, has powers in reverse, $(5)^0$, $(5)^1$, $(5)^2$, $(5)^3$. The two middle terms are multiplied by 3.

$$= (2x)^3 + 3(2x)^2(5) + 3(2x)(5)^2 + (5)^3$$
$$= 8x^3 + 60x^2 + 150x + 125$$

e) $(x-7)^3$ To cube the difference of two terms, we cube the first term, subtract three times the first term squared times the second term, add three times the first term times the second term squared, and subtract the second term cubed.

$$(x-7)^3 = (x)^3 - 3(x)^2(7) + 3(x)(7)^2 - (7)^3$$
$$= x^3 - 21x^2 + 147x - 343$$

Combined Operations

Simplification is the process of removing parentheses and combining like terms. The order of operations is to remove parentheses according to the operation and combine like terms.

EXAMPLE 1.12

Simplify each of the following:

a) $5(3x^2 - 5x + 6) - (4x^2 - 3x + 7) - 3(4x^2 - 7x + 3)$

b) $(2x - 5)(3x + 2)$

c) $3(3x^2 - 5)(4x^2 - 5) - (5x^2 + 7)(2x^2 - 3)$

d) $(4x - 3)^2 + (2x + 5)^2$

e) $(x + 3)^3 - (x - 4)^3$

SOLUTION 1.12

a) $5(3x^2 - 5x + 6) - (4x^2 - 3x + 7) - 3(4x^2 - 7x + 3)$

Remove parentheses by use of the distributive property.

$$= 15x^2 - 25x + 30 - 4x^2 + 3x - 7 - 12x^2 + 21x - 9$$

Combine like terms.

$$= -x^2 - x + 14$$

b) $(2x - 5)(3x + 2)$

Remove parentheses by using FOIL.

$$= 6x^2 + 4x - 15x - 10$$

Combine like terms.

$$= 6x^2 - 11x - 10$$

c) $3(3x^2-5)(4x^2-5)-(5x^2+7)(2x^2-3)$

Remove parentheses by using FOIL.

$= 3(12x^4-15x^2-20x^2+25)-(10x^4-15x^2+14x^2-21)$

Combine like terms.

$= 3(12x^4-35x^2+25)-(10x^4-x^2-21)$

Remove parentheses.

$= 36x^4-105x^2+75-10x^4+x^2+21$ Combine like terms.

$= 26x^4-104x^2+96$

d) $(4x-3)^2+(2x+5)^2$

Square using the special products for squaring.

$= [(4x)^2-2(4x)(3)+(3)^2]+[(2x)^2+2(2x)(5)+(5)^2]$

$= (16x^2-24x+9)+(4x^2+20x+25)$ Remove parentheses.

$= 16x^2-24x+9+4x^2+20x+25$ Combine like terms.

$= 20x^2-4x+34$

e) $(x+3)^3-(x-4)^3$

Cube using the special products for cubing.

$= [(x)^3+3(x)^2(3)+3(x)(3)^2+(3)^3]$
$\qquad - [(x)^3-3(x)^2(4)+3(x)(4)^2-(4)^3]$

$= (x^3+9x^2+27x+27)-(x^3-12x^2+48x-64)$

Remove parentheses.

$= x^3+9x^2+27x+27-x^3+12x^2-48x+64$

Combine like terms.

$= 0x^3+21x^2-21x+91$

$= 21x^2-21x+91$

SECTION 1.3 FACTORING

Factoring means to rewrite an expression as a multiplication problem. Simplification means to remove parentheses and combine like terms. Factoring requires that the expression be written so that all addition and subtraction signs are contained inside of parentheses. The most common techniques of factoring are listed below:

Special Forms for Factoring

Common Monomial Factors: $ab + ac = a(b + c)$

Common Polynomial Factors: $a(c + d) + b(c + d) = (a + b)(c + d)$

Difference of Perfect Squares: $a^2 - b^2 = (a + b)(a - b)$

Sum of Perfect Cubes: $a^3 + b^3 = (a + b)(a^2 - ab + b^2)$

Difference of Perfect Cubes: $a^3 - b^3 = (a - b)(a^2 + ab + b^2)$

Perfect Square: $a^2 + 2ab + b^2 = (a + b)^2$

$a^2 - 2ab + b^2 = (a - b)^2$

Simple Trinomials: $x^2 + (a + b)x + ab = (x + a)(x + b)$

General Trinomials: $acx^2 + (ad + bc)x + bd$
$$= (ax + b)(cx + d)$$

2 by 2 Grouping: $ac + ad + bc + bd$
$$= (ac + ad) + (bc + bd)$$
$$= a(c + d) + b(c + d)$$
$$= (a + b)(c + d)$$

3 by 1 Grouping: $a^2 + 2ab + b^2 - c^2 = (a^2 + 2ab + b^2) - c^2$
$$= (a + b)^2 - c^2$$
$$= (a + b + c)(a + b - c)$$

1 by 3 Grouping: $a^2 - b^2 - 2bc - c^2 = a^2 - (b^2 + 2bc + c^2)$
$$= a^2 - (b + c)^2$$
$$= (a + b + c)(a - b - c)$$

Common Monomial Factors

EXAMPLE 1.13

Factor by removing the common monomial factors from each term:
a) $15x + 25$
b) $2x^3 - 8x^2$
c) $36x^4 - 18x^3 + 15x^2$
d) $35x^2y^3 - 42xy^4$

SOLUTION 1.13

a) $15x + 25$ Factor out 5.
   $= 5 \cdot 3x + 5 \cdot 5$
   $= 5(3x + 5)$ Check your answer by multiplying.

b) $2x^3 - 8x^2$ Factor out $2x^2$.
   $= 2x^2 \cdot x - 2x^2 \cdot 4$
   $= 2x^2(x - 4)$ Check your answer.

c) $36x^4 - 18x^3 + 15x^2$ Common factor of $3x^2$.
   $= 3x^2 \cdot 12x^2 - 3x^2 \cdot 6x + 3x^2 \cdot 5$
   $= 3x^2(12x^2 - 6x + 5)$

d) $35x^2y^3 - 42xy^4$ Common factor of $7xy^3$.
   $= 7xy^3 \cdot 5x - 7xy^3 \cdot 6y$
   $= 7xy^3(5x - 6y)$

Common Polynomial Factors

In a case like: $x(a+b) + y(a+b)$
the polynomial factor $(a+b)$ is common to both terms. We can factor out the common binomial factor $(a+b)$.
$$(x + y)(a + b)$$

EXAMPLE 1.14

Factor each of the following:
a) $3x(2x - 3y) + 5(2x - 3y)$
b) $4a(2x - 3y)^2 + 7b(2x - 3y)^2$
c) $5x(x + y)^2 + 3(x + y)$
d) $3x(2x + y) - 6y(2x + y)$
e) $12x^2y^3(3x - 4)^3 + 18xy^2(3x - 4)^3$

SOLUTION 1.14

a) $3x(2x - 3y) + 5(2x - 3y)$ $(2x - 3y)$ is common to both terms.

$$= (3x+5)(2x-3y)$$

b) $4a(2x-3y)^2 + 7b(2x-3y)^2$

The binomial $(2x-3y)^2$ is common to both terms and may be factored out.

$$= (4a+7b)(2x-3y)^2$$

c) $5x(x+y)^2 + 3(x+y)$

Both terms have the binomial $(x+y)$. The first term has $(x+y)^2$ and the second term has $(x+y)$. Only one factor of $(x+y)$ may be distributed out.

$$= (x+y)[5x(x+y)+3]$$

Remove inner parentheses.

$$= (x+y)(5x^2+5xy+3)$$

d) $3x(2x+y) - 6y(2x+y)$

Remove common factors of 3 and $(2x+y)$.

$$= 3(2x+y)(x-2y)$$

e) $12x^2y^3(3x-4)^3 + 18xy^2(3x-4)^3$

Remove common factors of $6xy^2$ and $(3x-4)^3$.

$$= 6xy^2(3x-4)^3(2xy+3)$$

Difference of Two Perfect Squares

The **difference of two perfect squares** is a mathematical expression in which:
1. There are two terms (binomial).
2. One term is subtracted from the other.
3. Both terms have perfect square roots.

$x^2 - 4$ is a difference of perfect squares. It is a binomial, one term is subtracted from the other and both terms have perfect square roots

$\sqrt{x^2} = x$ and $\sqrt{4} = 2$. The difference of two perfect squares factors into the sum and difference of the square roots of the two terms.

$$x^2 - 4 = (x)^2 - (2)^2 = (x+2)(x-2)$$

The expressions $(x+2)(x-2)$ are called conjugate pairs. The product of conjugate pairs is the first term squared minus the second term squared. Only the difference (subtraction) of perfect squares will factor. The addition of perfect squares will not factor using real numbers.

EXAMPLE 1.15

Factor each of the following:

a) $25a^2 - 49b^2$

b) $121a^2b^4 - 64c^2d^4$

c) $81x^6y^8 - 121z^{16}$

d) $16x^2 - 36y^2$

SOLUTION 1.15

a) $25a^2 - 49b^2$

$5a$ is the square root of $25a^2$
$7b$ is the square root of $49b^2$

$$= (5a)^2 - (7b)^2$$

The difference of two perfect squares factors into the sum of the roots times the difference of the roots.

$$= (5a + 7b)(5a - 7b)$$

b) $121a^2b^4 - 64c^2d^4$

Find the roots.

$$= (11ab^2)^2 - (8cd^2)^2$$

Factor into the sum and difference of the roots.

$$= (11ab^2 + 8cd^2)(11ab^2 - 8cd^2)$$

c) $81x^6y^8 - 121z^{16}$

Find the roots.

$$= (9x^3y^4)^2 - (11z^8)^2$$

Factor into the sum and difference of the roots.

$$= (9x^3y^4 - 11z^8)(9x^3y^4 - 11z^8)$$

d) $16x^2 - 36y^2$

Both terms have a common factor of 4. Factor out the common factor of 4 first. Find the roots.

$$= 4(4x^2 - 9y^2)$$

$$= 4[(2x)^2 - (3y)^2]$$

Factor into the sum and difference of the roots.

$$= 4(2x + 3y)(2x - 3y)$$

Sum or Difference of Two Perfect Cubes

The sum or difference of two perfect cubes is a mathematical expression in which:

1. There are two terms (binomial).
2. Both terms have perfect cubic roots.

$$8x^3 - 27y^3 = (2x)^3 - (3y)^3 = (2x - 3y)(4x^2 + 6xy + 9y^2)$$

$$8x^3 + 27y^3 = (2x)^3 + (3y)^3 = (2x + 3y)(4x^2 - 6xy + 9y^2)$$

The sum or difference of two perfect cubes factor into a binomial multiplied by a trinomial. The binomial is obtained by taking the cubic root of each of the two terms. If the original expression is the sum of two perfect cubes, then the binomial is the sum of their cubic roots. If the original expression is the difference of two perfect cubes, then the binomial is the difference of their cubic roots. The three terms of the trinomial can be found by multiplying the first cubic root by itself, the first cubic root by the second cubic root, and the second cubic root by itself. The signs of the first and third term of the trinomial are always positive. The sign of the second term of the trinomial is negative for the sum of cubes and positive for the difference of cubes.

To factor either $8x^3 + 27y^3$ or $8x^3 - 27y^3$, we take the cubic roots of $8x^3$ and $27y^3$. The cubic root of $8x^3$ is $2x$ and of $27y^3$ is $3y$. These cubic roots are put into the binomial $(2x + 3y)$ for the sum of cubes and $(2x - 3y)$ for the difference of cubes. The trinomial is obtained by multiplying the cubic roots $2x$ and $3y$ together. The first term is $2x$ times itself $(2x \cdot 2x = 4x^2)$. The second term is $2x$ times $3y$ $(2x \cdot 3y = 6xy)$ and the third term is $3y$ times itself $(3y \cdot 3y = 9y^2)$. Put these terms into a trinomial $(4x^2 \quad 6xy \quad 9y^2)$. The sign of the binomial is the same as the sign of the problem. The sign of the first term of the trinomial is always plus (+). The middle term of the trinomial has the opposite sign of the original problem. The last term of the trinomial is always plus (+).

EXAMPLE 1.16

Factor the following sums and differences of cubes:
a) $x^3 - 125y^3$
b) $27x^3 + 125$

SOLUTION 1.16

a) $x^3 - 125y^3$ — Put the cubic root of both x^3 and $125y^3$ into a binomial.

$(x \quad 5y)$ — Multiply x times x $(x \cdot x = x^2)$, multiply x times $5y$ $(x \cdot 5y = 5xy)$, and multiply $5y$ times $5y$ $(5y \cdot 5y = 25y^2)$. Put these products into a trinomial.

$(x^2 \quad 5xy \quad 25y^2)$ — Multiply the binomial times the trinomial.

$\Rightarrow (x \quad 5y)(x^2 \quad 5xy \quad 25y^2)$ — The sign of the binomial is the same as the problem.

$\Rightarrow (x - 5y)(x^2 \quad 5xy \quad 25y^2)$ — The first and last term of the

$$= (x - 5y)(x^2 + 5xy + 25y^2)$$

trinomial are always positive. The sign of the second term is the opposite sign of that in the problem.

b) $27x^3 + 125 = (3x)^3 + (5)^3$

Take cubic roots of the two terms and put them into a binomial. Multiply the first cubic root times itself, the first cubic root times the second cubic root, and the second cubic root times itself.

$$\Rightarrow (3x \quad 5)(9x^2 \quad 15x \quad 25)$$

The binomial has the same sign as the problem. In the trinomial, the first and last terms are always positive and the second term has the opposite sign of the original problem.

$$= (3x + 5)(9x^2 - 15x + 25)$$

Perfect Squares

$$a^2 + 2ab + b^2 = (a + b)^2$$

$$a^2 - 2ab + b^2 = (a - b)^2$$

Trinomials that are formed by the square of a binomial are called **perfect squares**. A perfect square is a number, variable or expression which came from the product of a number, variable, or expression times itself. Examples of perfect squares are 4 (2 · 2), $16x^2y^2$ ($(4xy^2)^2$), and $9x^2 + 12x + 4$ ($(3x + 2)^2$). Note that in the perfect square $a^2 + 2ab + b^2$ both the first and last terms are perfect squares. The middle term of the trinomial is $2ab$ where a is the square root of a^2 (the first term of the trinomial) and b is the square root of b^2 (the last term of the trinomial).

If the first term of a trinomial has a perfect square root, the last term of the trinomial has a perfect square root and the middle term of the trinomial is two times the product of those square roots, then the trinomial is a perfect square. When factoring a perfect square trinomial, take the square roots of first and last terms and put them into a binomial squared [( )^2] with the same sign as the middle term in the trinomial.

EXAMPLE 1.17

Verify if the following are perfect squares. If so, factor completely.
a) $x^2 + 4x + 4$
b) $x^2 - 6x - 16$
c) $25x^2 - 20x + 4$
d) $81x^2 - 72x^2 + 16$

SOLUTION 1.17

a) $x^2 + 4x + 4$

Verify the trinomial is a perfect square. Take the square roots of the first and last terms.

$\sqrt{x^2} = x$ and $\sqrt{4} = 2$

Verify that the middle term is $2(x)(2) = 4x$.

$(x)^2 + 2(x)(2) + (2)^2 = x^2 + 4x + 4$

Since the trinomial is a perfect square, it factors into a binomial squared. The sign of the binomial is the same as the second term of the original trinomial.

$(x + 2)^2$.

b) $x^2 - 6x - 16$

Verify the trinomial is a perfect square.

$\sqrt{x^2} = x$ and $\sqrt{16} = 4$

$2(x)(4) = 8x$

Check to see if the middle term is $2(x)(4)$.

$2(x)(4) \neq 6x$

The trinomial is not a perfect square. Trinomials of this type will be discussed in the next section.

c) $25x^2 - 20x + 4$

Verify the trinomial is a perfect square.

$\sqrt{25x^2} = 5x$ and $\sqrt{4} = 2$

Verify that the middle term is $2(5x)(2) = 20x$.

$(5x)^2 - 2(5x)(2) + (2)^2 = 25x^2 - 20x + 4$

Since the trinomial is a perfect square, it factors into

$(5x - 2)^2$.

Note that this time the sign is minus, not plus.

d) $81x^2 - 72x^2 + 16$

Verify the trinomial is a perfect square.

$\sqrt{81x^4} = 9x^2$ and $\sqrt{16} = 4$

Verify that the middle term is $2(9x^2)(4) = 72x^2$.

$(9x^2)^2 - 2(9x^2)(4) + (4)^2 = 81x^4 - 72x^2 + 16$

Since the trinomial is a perfect square, it factors into $(9x^2 - 4)^2$.

This expression, however, is not completely factored. $9x^2 - 4$ is a difference of perfect squares and factors into $(3x + 2)(3x - 2)$. When we factor completely the expression becomes

$$[(3x + 2)(3x - 2)]^2 = (3x + 2)^2(3x - 2)^2$$

Simple and General Trinomials

Simple trinomials are trinomials whose first term has a coefficient of one (1).

$$x^2 - 2xy - 3y^2$$

General trinomials have a coefficient other than one in the first term.

$$3x^2 - 5x - 2$$

SIMPLE TRINOMIALS

EXAMPLE 1.18

Factor completely the following simple trinomial: $x^2 + 5x + 6$.

SOLUTION 1.18

Simple trinomials factor into the product of two binomials. To multiply a binomial times a binomial we use the FOIL method. To factor a simple trinomial we use the FOIL method of multiplication in reverse.

$x^2 + 5x + 6$ factors into two binomials.
$$x^2 + 5x + 6 = (\Box \ \ \Box)(\Box \ \ \Box)$$

The product of the first terms (F) must equal the first term of the trinomial (x^2).
$$x^2 + 5x + 6 = \underbrace{(\Box \ \ \Box)(\Box}_{x^2} \ \ \Box)$$

In this case, the only factors are x and x. Put an x as the first term in both binomials.
$$x^2 + 5x + 6 = \underbrace{(\boxed{x} \ \ \Box)(\boxed{x}}_{x^2} \ \ \Box)$$

The product of the last terms (L) must equal the last term of the trinomial (+6). The choice of factors are $(1 \cdot 6)$, $(6 \cdot 1)$, $(2 \cdot 3)$, and $(3 \cdot 2)$. These could also be negative integers, i.e. $(-1) \cdot (-6)$.
$$x^2 + 5x + 6 = (\boxed{x} \ \ \underbrace{\Box)(\boxed{x} \ \ \Box)}_{6}$$

The outer product (O) and the inner product (I) must combine to give the value of the second term of the trinomial (+5x). In this case, what pair of factors have +6 as their product and +5 as their sum?

$$x^2 + 5x + 6 = (\boxed{x}\ \overbrace{\underbrace{\boxed{a})(\boxed{x}}_{ax}}^{bx}\ \boxed{b}) \qquad ax + bx = +5x.$$
$$a \cdot b = +6$$

We find that $(+3) \cdot (+2) = 6$ and $(+3) + (+2) = 5$

$$x^2 + 5x + 6 = (\boxed{x} + \overbrace{\underbrace{\boxed{3})(\boxed{x}}_{3x}}^{2x} + \boxed{2})$$

Use the FOIL method to check your results.

$$(x+3)\,(x+2) = x^2 + 5x + 6$$

GENERAL TRINOMIALS

EXAMPLE 1.19

Factor completely the following general trinomial: $3x^2 + 5x + 2$.

SOLUTION 1.19

General trinomials factor into the product of two binomials. To factor a general trinomial, we use the FOIL method in reverse.

$3x^2 + 5x + 2$ factors into two binomials.
$$3x^2 + 5x + 2 = (\square\ \ \square)(\square\ \ \square)$$

The product of the first terms (F) must equal the first term of the trinomial $(3x^2)$.
$$3x^2 + 5x + 2 = \underbrace{(\square\ \ \square)(\square}_{3x^2}\ \ \square)$$

In this case, start with $3x$ and x.
$$3x^2 + 5x + 2 = \underbrace{(\boxed{3x}\ \square)(\boxed{x}}_{3x^2}\ \square)$$

The product of the last terms (L) must equal the last term of the trinomial (+2).
$$3x^2 + 5x + 2 = (\boxed{3x}\ \underbrace{\square)(\boxed{x}\ \square}_{+2})$$

The outer product and the inner product must combine to give the value of the second term of the trinomial (+5x).

$$3x^2 + 5x + 2 = (\boxed{3x}\ \overbrace{\underbrace{\boxed{a})(\boxed{x}}_{ax}}^{3bx}\ \boxed{b}) \qquad ax + 3bx = +5x.$$
$$a \cdot b = +2$$

The only choices are $1 \cdot 2$ and $2 \cdot 1$. Negative integers might be tried, i.e.

$(-1) \cdot (-2)$. Try 2 and 1.

$$3x^2 + 5x + 2 = \;\overbrace{(\underbrace{\boxed{3x} + \boxed{2})(\boxed{x}}_{2x} \quad \boxed{1})}^{3x} \qquad 2x + 3x = 5x.$$

Use the FOIL method to check your results.

$(3x + 2)\,(x + 1) \;=\; 3x^2 + 5x + 2$

Note: When x^2 has a coefficient other than 1, the order of the factors is very important. Use the FOIL method to check the results. The binomial factors would not have been correct if we had chosen $1 \cdot 2$ instead of $2 \cdot 1$. $(3x + 1)(x + 2) \neq 3x^2 + 5x + 2$.

Grouping

For algebraic expressions containing more than three terms, we must group the expressions into expressions containing two or three terms. A four-termed expression may be grouped into two binomials or into a trinomial and a single term.

2 BY 2 GROUPING

A **2 by 2** grouping occurs when we group a four-termed expression into two binomial expressions. Follow the steps in the following 2 by 2 grouping:

$ax + ay + bx + by$	1. First group into two pairs. Use parentheses.
$(ax + ay) + (bx + by)$	2. Factor both pairs.
$a(x + y) + b(x + y)$	3. In a 2 by 2 grouping you must get a common binomial factor.
$(x + y)\,(a + b)$	4. Factor out the common binomial.
	5. Check to see if either binomial will factor again.

Be careful with the signs in any type of grouping problem. Remember addition is commutative and associative; subtraction is not. When grouping subtraction problems, negatives must often be factored out of the expression. Notice how the signs change in the last two terms of the next problem.

$ax + ay - bx - by$	Group into two pairs. Use parentheses.
$(ax + ay) - (bx + by)$	Notice how the signs changed in the last two terms when the negative was placed on the outside of the parentheses. Factor both pairs. Must get a common binomial factor.

$$a(x+y) - b(x+y)$$ Factor out the common binomial.

$$(x+y)(a-b)$$ Check to see if either binomial will factor again.

With the expression
$$ax + ay - bx - by,$$
avoid errors like this:
$$(ax + ay) - (bx - by)$$
Here parentheses were inserted incorrectly.

EXAMPLE 1.20

Factor each using a 2 by 2 grouping.

a) $3x^3 - 6x^2 + 5x - 10$
b) $5x^3 + 6x + 5x^2 + 6$

SOLUTION 1.20

a) $3x^3 - 6x^2 + 5x - 10$ Group into two pairs using parentheses.

$= (3x^3 - 6x^2) + (5x - 10)$ Factor each pair.
$= 3x^2(x - 2) + 5(x - 2)$ Factor out the common binomial.

$= (3x^2 + 5)(x - 2)$ Check to see if either binomial will factor again. Check your answer using FOIL multiplication.

$$(3x^2 + 5)(x - 2) = 3x^3 - 6x^2 + 5x - 10$$

b) $5x^3 + 6x + 5x^2 + 6$
$= 5x^3 + 5x^2 + 6x + 6$ Group into two pairs.
$= (5x^3 + 5x^2) + (6x + 6)$ Factor each pair.
$= 5x^2(x + 1) + 6(x + 1)$ Factor out the common binomial.

$= (5x^2 + 6)(x + 1)$ Check to see if either binomial will factor again. Check your answer.

$$(5x^2 + 6)(x + 1) = 5x^3 + 5x^2 + 6x + 6$$

3 BY 1 OR 1 BY 3 GROUPING

3 by 1 or 1 by 3 grouping separates a four-termed polynomial into a trinomial and a single term. The polynomial may need to be rearranged to get a factorable trinomial in the first or last three terms.

EXAMPLE 1.21

a) $x^2 + 4x + 4 - y^2$

b) $9 - x^2 - 2xy - y^2$

SOLUTION 1.21

a) $x^2 + 4x + 4 - y^2$ — Group into a trinomial and a single term using parentheses. The trinomial must factor into a quantity squared $[(\quad)^2]$.

$= (x^2 + 4x + 4) - y^2$ — The single term must be a perfect square. Factor the trinomial.

$= (x + 2)(x + 2) - y^2$ — Put $(x + 2)(x + 2)$ into power notation. $(x + 2)^2$

$= (x + 2)^2 - y^2$ — Factor as a difference of squares.

$= [(x + 2) + y][(x + 2) - y]$ — Remove the innter parentheses and simplify.

$= (x + 2 + y)(x + 2 - y)$ — Write in standard form.

$= (x + y + 2)(x - y + 2)$

b) $9 - x^2 - 2xy - y^2$ — Group into a trinomial and a single term using parentheses. Be careful with negative signs. The trinomial must factor into a quantity squared $[(\quad)^2]$.

$= 9 - (x^2 + 2xy + y^2)$ — Factor the trinomial.

$= 9 - (x + y)(x + y)$ — Put 9 and $(x + y)(x + y)$ into power notation.

$= 3^2 - (x + y)^2$ — Factor as a difference of squares.

$= [3 + (x + y)][3 - (x + y)]$ — Remove the innter parentheses and simplify.

$= (3 + x + y)(3 - x - y)$ — Do not put this into standard form because the factor $(3 - x - y)$ would begin with a negative term.

Factoring skills are extremely important to the mathematician. Mathematics students should be able to factor quickly and accurately. Take some time to work the following exercises.

SECTION 1.4 RATIONAL EXPRESSIONS

Rational expressions are fractional expressions in which both the numerator and the denominator are polynomials.

Standard Form

There are three locations where + and – signs may be placed in a rational expression:

1) the sign in front of the fraction $+\dfrac{a}{b}$ or $-\dfrac{a}{b}$

2) the sign of the leading coefficient of the numerator, $\dfrac{+a}{b}$ or $\dfrac{-a}{b}$

3) the sign of the leading coefficient of the denominator. $\dfrac{a}{+b}$ or $\dfrac{a}{-b}$

Note that the fraction $-\dfrac{a+b}{c}$ is the same as $-\dfrac{(a+b)}{(c)}$. It is also the same

as $\dfrac{-(a+b)}{(c)}$. It is not the same as $\dfrac{-a+b}{c}$. That is:

$$\frac{-(a+b)}{(c)} \neq \frac{-a+b}{c}.$$

The standard forms for the positive and negative fractions are given below.

Positive fraction:

$$+\boxed{\frac{+a}{+b}} = +\frac{-a}{-b} = -\frac{-a}{+b} = -\frac{+a}{-b}$$

Negative fraction:

$$-\frac{+a}{+b} = \boxed{+\frac{-a}{+b}} = +\frac{+a}{-b} = -\frac{-a}{-b}$$

The boxed fractions are the positive and negative fractions in standard form. The standard form of a fraction requires that the sign in front of the fraction be positive and the denominator of the fraction begins with a leading coefficient that is positive. Anytime you want to change a sign, you must change two of the three signs (numerator and denominator, numerator and sign in front, or denominator and sign in front).

EXAMPLE 1.22

Put the following fractions into standard form:

a) $\dfrac{x-3}{-2}$

b) $-\dfrac{2x+5}{-6}$

c) $-\dfrac{4x-3}{-x-2}$

SOLUTION 1.22

a) $\dfrac{x-3}{-2}$

$= \dfrac{(x-3)}{(-2)}$

Put parentheses around the numerator and the denominator.
The sign in front of the fraction is positive. It does not need to be changed. The sign in the denominator is negative. It must changed to positive. Since the sign in front is already positive, change the sign of the denominator and the sign of the numerator.

$= \dfrac{-(x-3)}{-(-2)} = \dfrac{-x+3}{2}$ or $\dfrac{3-x}{2}$

b) $-\dfrac{2x+5}{-6} =$

$-\dfrac{(2x+5)}{(-6)} =$

Put parentheses around the numerator and the denominator.
The sign in front of the fraction is negative. It needs to be changed to positive. The sign in the denominator is negative. It must also be changed to positive. Change the signs in front of the fraction and the denominator.

$-\dfrac{(2x+5)}{(-6)} = +\dfrac{(2x+5)}{-(-6)} = +\dfrac{2x+5}{+6} = \dfrac{2x+5}{6}$

c) $-\dfrac{4x-3}{-x-2} =$

$-\dfrac{(4x-3)}{(-x-2)} =$

Put parentheses around the numerator and the denominator.
The sign in front of the fraction is negative. It needs to be changed to positive. The sign of the leading coefficient in the denominator is negative. It must also be changed to positive. Change the signs in front of the fraction and the denominator.

$$-\dfrac{(4x-3)}{(-x-2)} = +\dfrac{(4x-3)}{-(-x-2)} = \dfrac{4x-3}{x+2}$$

Reducing Rational Expressions to Lowest Terms

Reducing fractions requires the use of the *Fundamental Theorem of Fractions*.

$$\dfrac{a \cdot c}{b \cdot c} = \dfrac{a}{b} \qquad (b, c \neq 0)$$

The **Fundamental Theorem of Fractions** states that when the numerator is factored and the denominator is factored, you may divide any common factor from both the numerator and the denominator without affecting the value of the fraction. Notice that in the fundamental theorem of fractions, $\frac{c}{c}$ equals 1. The property of multiplication by one (Multiplicative Identity) guarantees that $x \cdot 1 = x$.

EXAMPLE 1.23

Reduce the following fractions and indicate for what values of x the fraction is undefined:

a) $\dfrac{x^2-4}{x^2+4x+4}$

b) $\dfrac{5x^2-4xy}{16xy^2-25x^3}$

SOLUTION 1.23

a) $\dfrac{x^2-4}{x^2+4x+4}$ Factor completely both
                                              numerator and denominator.

$= \dfrac{(x+2)\,(x-2)}{(x+2)\,(x+2)}$ Divide any common factors
                                              from numerator and
                                              denominator.

$= \dfrac{(x-2)}{(x+2)} = \dfrac{x-2}{x+2}$

The parentheses around the numerator and the denominator may be removed. The parentheses, however, are sometimes are helpful to avoid mistakes. Note that,

$\dfrac{x^2-4}{x^2+4x+4} = \dfrac{x-2}{x+2}$ for all x except $x \neq -2$. If $x = -2$ the
                                              denominator of both fractions equals 0 and
                                              the fractions are undefined.

b) $\dfrac{5x^2-4xy}{16xy^2-25x^3}$ Factor completely both
                                              numerator and
                                              denominator. Begin with
                                              common factors.

$= \dfrac{x\,(5x-4y)}{x\,(16y^2-25x^2)}$ Continue factoring the
                                              denominator as a difference
                                              of squares.

$= \dfrac{x\,(5x-4y)}{x\,(4y+5x)\,(4y-5x)}$ We have a common factor of
                                              x. If we factor -1 out of the
                                              numerator we get another
                                              common factor.

$= \dfrac{-1x\,(4y-5x)}{x\,(4y+5x)\,(4y-5x)}$ Divide the common factors
                                              of $(4y-5x)$ and x.

$= \dfrac{-1}{(4y+5x)}$ Note, $16xy^2-25x^3 \neq 0$.

Fractions are in lowest terms when both the numerator and the denominator are completely factored and there are no common factors.

Multiplying and Dividing Rational Expressions

To multiply rational expressions, use the following theorem:

$$\frac{a}{b} \cdot \frac{c}{d} = \frac{ac}{bd} \qquad (b, d \neq 0)$$

Multiplying rational expressions is very much like reducing rational expressions. To multiply, use the following rules:

1. Completely factor all numerators and all denominators.

2. Multiply numerator times numerator and denominator times denominator (multiply straight across).

3. Divide any common factors between the numerator and denominator.

4. Factor our −1 if necessary to get common factors. Divide again any common factors.

5. Simplify if possible.

Division is the inverse operation of multiplication. To divide rational expressions, we multiply by the reciprocal of the divisor.

$$\frac{a}{b} \div \frac{c}{d} = \frac{a}{b} \cdot \frac{d}{c} = \frac{ad}{bc} \quad (b, c, \text{ and } d \neq 0)$$

EXAMPLE 1.24

Multiply and divide the following fractions.

a) $\dfrac{x^2 - 5xy - 14y^2}{x^2 - 6xy - 7y^2} \cdot \dfrac{x^2 - 4xy + 4y^2}{x^2 - 4y^2}$

b) $\dfrac{x^2 - 1}{2x - 2} \div \dfrac{3x^2 + x - 2}{9x^2 - 4}$

SOLUTION 1.24

a) $\dfrac{x^2 - 5xy - 14y^2}{x^2 - 6xy - 7y^2} \cdot \dfrac{x^2 - 4xy + 4y^2}{x^2 - 4y^2}$

Factor completely all numerators and denominators.

$= \dfrac{(x - 7y)\,(x + 2y)}{(x + y)\,(x - 7y)} \cdot \dfrac{(x - 2y)\,(x - 2y)}{(x + 2y)\,(x - 2y)}$

Multiply all numerators and denominators.

$= \dfrac{(x - 7y)\,(x + 2y)\,(x - 2y)\,(x - 2y)}{(x + y)\,(x - 7y)\,(x + 2y)\,(x - 2y)}$

Divide any common factors between the numerator and denominator.

$= \dfrac{(x - 2y)}{(x + y)}$

Remember the denominators $\neq 0$.

b) $\dfrac{x^2 - 1}{2x - 2} \div \dfrac{3x^2 + x - 2}{9x^2 - 4}$ Change the division to multiplication.

$= \dfrac{x^2 - 1}{2x - 2} \cdot \dfrac{9x^2 - 4}{3x^2 + x - 2}$ Factor completely all numerators and denominators.

$= \dfrac{(x + 1)\,(x - 1)}{2\,(x - 1)} \cdot \dfrac{(3x + 2)\,(3x - 2)}{(3x - 2)\,(x + 1)}$ Multiply straight across.

$= \dfrac{\cancel{(x+1)}\,\cancel{(x-1)}\,(3x + 2)\,\cancel{(3x-2)}}{2\,\cancel{(x-1)}\,(\,\cancel{(3x-2)}\,\cancel{(x+1)}\,)}$ Divide any common factors.

$= \dfrac{(3x + 2)}{2}$ No denominator can equal 0.

Adding and Subtracting Fractions

Adding and subtracting fractions requires that all fractions have a common denominator. Changing fractions from the original denominator to the common denominator is accomplished by the **Fundamental Theorem of Fractions**. The theorem states:

$$\frac{a}{b} = \frac{a \cdot c}{b \cdot c} \quad (b, c \neq 0)$$

This theorem indicates that we may multiply both the numerator and the denominator of any fraction by any non-zero number and the value of the fraction does not change. The basic theorems for adding and subtracting fractions are:

$$\frac{a}{b} + \frac{c}{b} = \frac{a + c}{b} \quad \text{and} \quad \frac{a}{b} - \frac{c}{b} = \frac{a - c}{b}$$

To add or subtract fractions, you must have a common denominator. Once you have a common denominator, add the fractions by adding the numerators and keeping the denominator or subtract the fractions by subtracting the numerators and keeping the denominators. Follow the rules below to add or subtract fractions.

1. Find the Least Common Denominator (LCD).

2. Raise each fraction to higher terms (change to LCD).

3. Simplify all numerators (remove parentheses).

4. Add or subtract all of the numerators and keep the common denominator.

5. Reduce the final answer if possible.

a) Factor both the numerator and denominator.
b) Factor out −1 if necessary.
c) Divide any common factors from the numerator and denominator.
d) Simplify final answer.

EXAMPLE 1.25

Add or subtract the following fractions:

a) $\dfrac{x+2}{2x} + \dfrac{2x+3}{2x}$

b) $\dfrac{3}{x^2 - 2z - 3} + \dfrac{2}{x^2 - 9}$

c) $\dfrac{x-5}{x^2 - 4x - 5} - \dfrac{x+6}{x^2 - 3x - 4}$

SOLUTION 1.25

a) $\dfrac{x+2}{2x} + \dfrac{2x+3}{2x}$

$= \dfrac{(x+2) + (2x+3)}{2x}$

$= \dfrac{x+2+2x+3}{2x} = \dfrac{3x+5}{2x}$

The fractions already have a common denominator. Add the numerators and keep the denominator.
Notice when adding numerators, parentheses are used to separate the two numerators.
Neither numerator nor the denominator are factorable so the fraction cannot reduce.

b) $\dfrac{3}{x^2 - 2z - 3} + \dfrac{2}{x^2 - 9}$

Find the LCD. Factor all denominators.

$= \dfrac{3}{(x-3)(x+1)} + \dfrac{2}{(x+3)(x-3)}$

The denominators are in power notation. The LCD is $(x-3)(x+1)(x-3)$.
Raise the fractions to higher terms by multiplying both the numerator and the denominator by missing factors.

$= \dfrac{3 \cdot (x+3)}{(x-3)(x+2) \cdot (x+3)} + \dfrac{2 \cdot (x+1)}{(x-3)(x+3) \cdot (x+2)}$

Simplify the numerators.

$= \dfrac{3x+9}{(x-3)(x+2)(x+3)} + \dfrac{2x+2}{(x-3)(x+2)(x+3)}$

$$= \frac{(3x+9) + (2x+2)}{(x-3)(x+2)(x+3)}$$

Add numerators and keep the denominator.
Remove parentheses in the numerator and combine like terms.

$$= \frac{5x+11}{(x-3)(x+2)(x+3)}$$

$5x + 11$ will not factor, so the fraction cannot reduce.

c) $\dfrac{x-5}{x^2-4x-5} - \dfrac{x+6}{x^2-3x-4}$

Find the LCD. Factor all denominators.

$$= \frac{x-5}{(x-5)(x+1)} - \frac{x+6}{(x-4)(x+1)}$$

Notice that the first fraction will reduce. Reduce before finding LCD.

$$= \frac{1}{(x+1)} - \frac{x+6}{(x-4)(x+1)}$$

Find the LCD. The LCD is $(x+1)(x-4)$. Raise all fractions to LCD.

$$= \frac{1 \cdot (x-4)}{(x+1) \cdot (x-4)} - \frac{(x+6)}{(x-4)(x+1)}$$

Subtract the numerators and keep the denominator.

$$= \frac{(x-4) - (x+6)}{(x+1)(x-4)}$$

Remove parentheses.

$$= \frac{x-4-x-6}{(x+1)(x-4)}$$

Combine like terms.

$$= \frac{-10}{(x+1)(x-4)}$$

Complex Fractions

Remember that the definition of a fraction is any expression that can be written in the form of $\dfrac{a}{b}$ where $b \neq 0$. When either a or b contains a fractional expression, then the fraction $\dfrac{a}{b}$ is called a **complex fraction** or **compound fraction**. Some examples of complex fractions are

$$\frac{\dfrac{2x}{5}}{\dfrac{3x}{7}}, \qquad \frac{\dfrac{2x+3}{5x-2}}{\dfrac{5x}{2}+2}, \qquad \text{and} \qquad \frac{\dfrac{x}{2}-\dfrac{2x}{3}}{\dfrac{x}{2}+\dfrac{2x}{3}}$$

Remember that $\dfrac{a}{b}$ is a division problem. $\dfrac{a}{b}$ means to take $a \div b$ or $a \cdot \dfrac{1}{b}$. One way to simplify complex fractions is to write both the numerator of the complex fraction and its denominator as single fractions and solve as a division problem (invert the denominator and multiply).

EXAMPLE 1.26

Simplify the following complex fractions:

a) $\dfrac{\dfrac{2x}{5}}{\dfrac{3x}{7}}$

b) $\dfrac{\dfrac{2x}{3} + \dfrac{x}{2}}{\dfrac{5x}{6} - \dfrac{x}{3}}$

c) $\dfrac{\dfrac{3}{x} - 2}{\dfrac{x}{x-1} + 1}$

SOLUTION 1.26

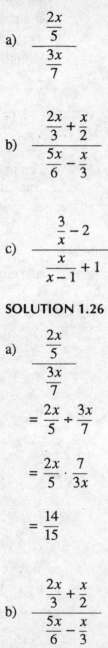

a) $\dfrac{\dfrac{2x}{5}}{\dfrac{3x}{7}}$

$= \dfrac{2x}{5} \div \dfrac{3x}{7}$

$= \dfrac{2x}{5} \cdot \dfrac{7}{3x}$

$= \dfrac{14}{15}$

Both the numerator and the denominator are single fractions. Change to division.
Invert and multiply.

Divide common factor of x and simplify.

b) $\dfrac{\dfrac{2x}{3} + \dfrac{x}{2}}{\dfrac{5x}{6} - \dfrac{x}{3}}$

Combine the fractions in the numerator and in the denominator.

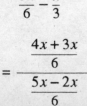

$= \dfrac{\dfrac{4x + 3x}{6}}{\dfrac{5x - 2x}{6}}$

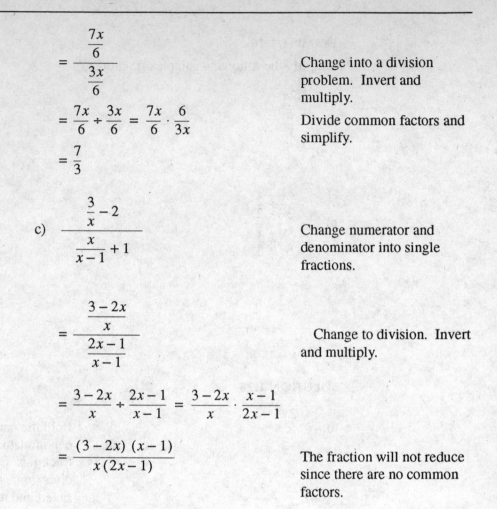

$$= \frac{\dfrac{7x}{6}}{\dfrac{3x}{6}}$$

Change into a division problem. Invert and multiply.

$$= \frac{7x}{6} \div \frac{3x}{6} = \frac{7x}{6} \cdot \frac{6}{3x}$$

Divide common factors and simplify.

$$= \frac{7}{3}$$

c) $$\frac{\dfrac{3}{x} - 2}{\dfrac{x}{x-1} + 1}$$

Change numerator and denominator into single fractions.

$$= \frac{\dfrac{3-2x}{x}}{\dfrac{2x-1}{x-1}}$$

Change to division. Invert and multiply.

$$= \frac{3-2x}{x} \div \frac{2x-1}{x-1} = \frac{3-2x}{x} \cdot \frac{x-1}{2x-1}$$

$$= \frac{(3-2x)(x-1)}{x(2x-1)}$$

The fraction will not reduce since there are no common factors.

SECTION 1.5 REVIEW EXERCISES

Name the following properties:

1. $a + b = b + a$

2. $1 \cdot a = a$

3. $x + y \cdot 0 = y \cdot 0 + x$

4. $a \cdot (b + c) = a \cdot (c + b)$

5. $a + (b + c) = a \cdot b + a \cdot c$

6. $x \cdot 1 + 0 = x \cdot 1$

Compute the following:

7. $\dfrac{2x}{5} + \dfrac{5x}{6}$

8. $\dfrac{3x}{5} - \dfrac{4x}{7}$

9. $\dfrac{3x}{4y} \cdot \dfrac{5y}{2}$

10. $\dfrac{4x}{6y} \div \dfrac{8x}{6y^2}$

Evaluate each of the following expressions:

11. $4x^2y$ if $x = 2$ and $y = -3$.

12. $7x^2y^2 - 4xy + 3$ if $x = -5$ and $y = 2$.

Simplify the following polynomials:

13. $-(3x^2 + 7x - 13) - (4x^2 + 5x - 7)$

14. $(5x^2 + 7x + 5) - (6x^2 - 17x - 11) - (12x^2 + 4x - 19)$

15. $(3x^2 - 7x + 12) - (4x^2 - 19x + 18) + (16x^2 + 15x - 3)$

16. $6(3x^2 + 2x + 15) - 4(3x^2 - 7x - 14) - (2x^2 + 14x - 9)$

17. $(x + 9)(2x + 7)$

18. $(8x - 13)(x - 5)$

19. $(2x + 3)^2$

20. $(4x - 9)^2$

21. $(2x + 5y)(3x^2 - 2xy - 5y^2) - (4x - 3y)(5x^2 + 3xy - 2y^2)$

Factor each of the following:

22. $3x^3 - 6x^7$

23. $34a^2b^3c^4 - 51ab^2c^3$

24. $120x^3y^2 + 48x^2y^3 - 96x^4y^4$

25. $x(2x + 3y) - y(2x + 3y)$

26. $3x(3x - 4y) - 4y(3x - 4y)$

27. $2(x - y)^3 - 6(x - y)^2$

28. $(a + b)^2 + 2(a + b)$

29. $25x^2 - 36$

30. $32x^4 - 2$

31. $8x^3 + 125y^3$

32. $x^6 - 64y^6$

33. $16x^2 + 72x + 81$

34. $16x^2 - 24xy + 9y^2$

35. $x^2 - 2xy - 3y^2$

36. $x^2 - 6x - 16$

37. $4x^2 + 10x - 6$

38. $2x^3 - 3x^2 - 8x + 12$

39. $2x^3 + 3x^2 - 8x - 12$

40. $5x^2 - a^2 - 6ab - 9b^2$

Put the following fractions into standard form:

41. $-\dfrac{-4x - 3}{-2}$

42. $\dfrac{4x - 3}{-x^2 + 2x + 2}$

Reduce the following fractions:

43. $\dfrac{2x^2 - 3x - 2}{x^2 - x - 2}$

44. $\dfrac{x^3 - 4x^2 - 4x + 16}{4 - x^2}$

45. $\dfrac{6x^2 - x - 12}{2x^2 + 15x - 27} \cdot \dfrac{9 - 17x - 2x^2}{6x^2 + 11x + 4}$

46. $\dfrac{2x^2 + 7x + 6}{2x^2 - x - 6} \cdot \dfrac{x^2 - 5x + 6}{x^2 + 7x + 10} \cdot \dfrac{2x^2 + 17x + 35}{4x^2 + 2x - 42}$

Find the LCD for the following:

47. $\dfrac{4}{x^2 - 2x - 15} ; \dfrac{5}{x^2 + x - 6}$

Find the common denominator and raise the fractions to that denominator:

48. $\dfrac{1}{x^3 + 1} ; \dfrac{2}{x^2 - x + 1} ; \dfrac{-1}{x + 1}$

Add or subtract the following fractions:

49. $\dfrac{x^2 - 2x + 3}{x^3 + 1} + \dfrac{x - 2}{x^2 - x + 1} - \dfrac{1}{x + 1}$

Simplify the following complex fraction:

50. $\dfrac{1 - \dfrac{2}{x} - \dfrac{3}{x^3}}{1 - \dfrac{9}{x^2}}$

Answers to Review Exercises 1.5

1. {Commutative Property of Addition}
2. {Multiplicative Identity}
3. {Commutative Property of Addition}
4. {Commutative Property of Addition}
5. {Distributive Property of Multiplication over Addition}
6. {Additive Identity}

7. $\{\dfrac{37x}{30}\}$

8. $\{\dfrac{21x - 20y}{35}\}$

9. $\{\dfrac{15x}{8}\}$

10. $\{\dfrac{y}{2}\}$

11. $\{-48\}$

12. $\{743\}$

13. $\{-7x^2 - 12x + 20\}$

14. $\{-13x^2 + 20x + 35\}$

15. $\{15x^2 + 28x - 9\}$

16. $\{4x^2 + 26x + 155\}$

17. $\{2x^2 + 25x + 63\}$

18. $\{8x^2 - 53x + 65\}$

19. $\{4x^2 + 12x + 9\}$

20. $\{16x^2 - 72x + 81\}$

21. $\{-14x^3 + 14x^2y - 3xy^2 - 31y^3\}$ 22. $\{3x(1 - 2x^4)\}$

23. $\{17ab^2c^3(2abc - 3)\}$

24. $\{24x^2y^2(5x + 2y - 4x^2y^2)\}$

25. $\{(x - y)(2x + 3y)\}$

26. $\{(3x - 4y)^2\}$

27. $\{2(x - y - 3)(x - y)^2\}$

28. $\{(a + b)(a + b + 2)\}$

29. $\{(5x + 6)(5x - 6)\}$

30. $\{2(4x^2 + 1)(2x + 1)(2x - 1)\}$

31. $\{(2x + 5y)(4x^2 - 10xy + 25y^2)\}$

32. $\{(x + 2y)(x^2 - 2xy + 4y^2)(x - 2y)(x^2 + 2xy + 4y^2)\}$

33. $\{(4x + 9)^2\}$

34. $\{(4x - 3y)^2\}$

35. $\{(x - 3y)(x + y)\}$

36. $\{(x - 8)(x + 2)\}$

37. $\{2(2x - 1)(x + 3)\}$

38. $\{(x + 2)(x - 2)(2x - 3)\}$

39. $\{(x + 2)(x - 2)(2x + 3)\}$

40. $\{(5x + a + 3b)(5x - a - 3b)\}$

41. $\{\dfrac{-4x - 3}{2}\}$ 42. $\{\dfrac{-4x + 3}{x^2 - 2x - 2}\}$

43. $\{\dfrac{2x + 1}{x + 1}\}$ 44. $\{4 - x\}$

45. $\{\dfrac{1 - 2x}{2x + 1}\}$ 46. $\{\dfrac{1}{2}\}$

47. $\{(x - 5)(x + 3)(x - 2)\}$

48. $\{\dfrac{1}{(x + 1)(x^2 - x + 1)}; \dfrac{2(x + 1)}{(x + 1)(x^2 - x + 1)}; \dfrac{-1(x^2 - x + 1)}{(x + 1)(x^2 - x + 1)}\}$

49. $\{\dfrac{x(x - 2)}{(x + 1)(x^2 - x + 1)}\}$

50. $\{\dfrac{x + 1}{x + 3}\}$

2

Exponents and Radicals

SECTION 2.1 INTEGER EXPONENTS

The expression x^n is called a power expression or an exponential expression. The x is the base of the exponential expression; n is the power or the exponent. The definition of x^n is:

Definitions

$$x^n = \underbrace{x \cdot x \cdot x \cdot \ldots \cdot x}_{n \text{ times}} \qquad \text{if } n \text{ is a natural number} \geq 2.$$

$$x^0 = 1 \quad (x \neq 0) \qquad x^1 = x$$

Theorems of Exponents

The simplification of exponential expressions is accomplished using the following theorems:

Theorems of Exponents

1. $x^m \cdot x^n = x^{m+n}$	2. $\dfrac{x^m}{x^n} = x^{m-n}$
3. $\dfrac{x^m}{x^n} = \dfrac{1}{x^{n-m}}$	4. $(x^m)^n = x^{mn}$
5. $(x^m y^n)^p = x^{mp} y^{np}$	6. $\left(\dfrac{x^m}{x^n}\right)^p = \dfrac{x^{mp}}{x^{np}}$
7. $x^{-n} = \dfrac{1}{x^n}$	8. $\left(\dfrac{a}{b}\right)^{-n} = \dfrac{b^n}{a^n}$
9. $\dfrac{a^{-m}}{b^{-n}} = \dfrac{b^n}{a^m}$	10. $\left(\dfrac{a^{-m}}{b^{-n}}\right)^{-p} = \dfrac{a^{mp}}{b^{np}}$

Multiplying and Dividing with Positive Exponents

Only expressions with like bases can be simplified. To multiply two exponential expressions with like bases, keep the base and add the exponents. (Theorem 2.1) To divide two exponential expressions with like bases, apply either Theorem 2 or 3. If the exponent in the numerator is larger than that in the denominator, apply Theorem 2. If the exponent in the denominator is larger, apply Theorem 3. In both cases, keep the same base. To raise an exponential expression to a power, keep the base and multiply the powers.

EXAMPLE 2.1

Simplify the following expressions. Write answers using only positive powers.

a) $\dfrac{a^6 b^3 c^7}{a^5 b^{11} c^4}$

b) $\left(\dfrac{a^3}{b^5}\right)^7$

c) $\left(\dfrac{a^3 b^4}{a^5 b^7}\right)^2$

d) $\left(\dfrac{a^8 b^2 c^9}{a^3 b^7 c^5}\right)^4$

SOLUTION 2.1

a) $\dfrac{a^6 b^3 c^7}{a^5 b^{11} c^4} = \dfrac{a^{(6-5)} c^{(7-3)}}{b^{(11-3)}} = \dfrac{a^1 c^4}{b^8} = \dfrac{ac^4}{b^8}$

When dividing powers, keep the base and subtract the smaller power from the larger power. Keep the base in the numerator or denominator depending on which has the larger power.

b) $\left(\dfrac{a^3}{b^5}\right)^7$ Distribute the power of 7 to both the numerator and denominator.

$= \dfrac{a^{3 \cdot 7}}{b^{5 \cdot 7}}$ Simplify.

$= \dfrac{a^{21}}{b^{35}}$

c) $\left(\dfrac{a^3 b^4}{a^5 b^7}\right)^2$ Distribute the power of 2.

$= \dfrac{a^{3 \cdot 2} b^{4 \cdot 2}}{a^{5 \cdot 2} b^{7 \cdot 2}}$ Simplify.

$= \dfrac{a^6 b^8}{a^{10} b^{14}}$ Divide the variables by keeping the base and subtracting the powers.

$= \dfrac{1}{a^{10-6} b^{14-8}}$ Simplify.

$= \dfrac{1}{a^4 b^6}$

This problem could also be solved by first simplifying inside the parentheses.

d) $\left(\dfrac{a^8 b^2 c^9}{a^3 b^7 c^5}\right)^4$ Distribute the power of 4.

$= \dfrac{a^{8 \cdot 4} b^{2 \cdot 4} c^{9 \cdot 4}}{a^{3 \cdot 4} b^{7 \cdot 4} c^{5 \cdot 4}}$ Simplify.

$= \dfrac{a^{32} b^8 c^{36}}{a^{12} b^{28} c^{20}}$ Divide the powers by keeping the base and subtracting the powers.

$= \dfrac{a^{32-12} c^{36-20}}{b^{28-8}}$ Simplify.

$= \dfrac{a^{20} c^{16}}{b^{20}}$

Like example c) this problem can also be solved by first simplifying inside the parentheses.

Multiplying and Dividing with Negative Exponents

Theorems 7 through 10 involve negative powers. Negative powers do not represent negative numbers. Negative powers indicate reciprocals.

x^{-1} means $\dfrac{1}{x}$. $\left(\tfrac{1}{x}\right)^{-1}$ means $\dfrac{x}{1} = x$.

$$2^{-1} \neq -2$$

$$2^{-1} = \dfrac{1}{2}$$

EXAMPLE 2.2

Simplify the following. Write answers using only positive exponents.

a) $\dfrac{a^{-3}b^7c^{-2}}{a^4b^{-11}c^{-5}}$

b) $\left(\dfrac{a^{-3}}{b^6}\right)^{-3}$

c) $\left(\dfrac{a^3b^{-4}}{a^{-5}b^7}\right)^{-2}$

d) $\left(\dfrac{a^6b^{-5}c^{-8}}{a^{-5}b^{13}c^2}\right)^4$

SOLUTION 2.2

a) $\dfrac{a^{-3}b^7c^{-2}}{a^4b^{-11}c^{-5}}$ Apply Theorem 7 to change all exponents to positive integers.
Simplify.

$= \dfrac{b^7b^{11}c^5}{a^4a^3c^2}$

$= \dfrac{b^{7+11}c^{5-2}}{a^{4+3}}$

$= \dfrac{b^{18}c^3}{a^7}$

Theorems 7 and 8 indicate that negative powers in the numerator of a fraction become positive powers in the denominator $(x^{-n} = \dfrac{1}{x^n})$ and negative powers in the denominator of a fraction become positive powers in the numerator $(\dfrac{1}{x^{-n}} = x^n)$. This movement can only be accomplished when there is no addition or subtraction outside of parentheses in the numerator or denominator containing the negative powers.

b) $\left(\dfrac{a^{-3}}{b^6}\right)^{-3}$ Simplify inside the parentheses first. Move the negative power to the denominator.
Distribute the power outside of parentheses.

$= \left(\dfrac{1}{a^3b^6}\right)^{-3}$

$$= \frac{1}{a^{-9}b^{-18}}$$

Move the negative powers to the numerator of the fraction.

$$= a^9 b^{18}$$

This problem can also be solved by distributing the power first.

$$\left(\frac{a^{-3}}{b^6}\right)^{-3}$$

Distribute the power inside the parentheses.

$$= \frac{a^{(-3)(-3)}}{b^{6(-3)}}$$

Simplify the powers.

$$= \frac{a^9}{b^{-18}}$$

Move the negative power to the numerator of the fraction.

$$= \frac{a^9 b^{18}}{1} = a^9 b^{18}$$

c) $\left(\dfrac{a^3 b^{-4}}{a^{-5} b^7}\right)^{-2}$

Change negative powers to positive.

$$= \left(\frac{a^3 a^5}{b^4 b^7}\right)^{-2}$$

Simplify inside the parentheses.

$$= \left(\frac{a^8}{b^{11}}\right)^{-2}$$

Distribute the powers and change to positive powers.

$$= \frac{a^{-16}}{b^{-22}} = \frac{b^{22}}{a^{16}}$$

d) $\left(\dfrac{a^6 b^{-5} c^{-8}}{a^{-5} b^{13} c^2}\right)^4$

Simplify inside parentheses.

$$= \left(\frac{a^6 a^5}{b^5 b^{13} c^2 c^8}\right)^4$$

Continue simplifying.

$$= \left(\frac{a^{11}}{b^{18} c^{10}}\right)^4$$

Distribute the power of 4.

$$= \frac{a^{44}}{b^{72} c^{40}}$$

Simplifying Integer Exponents That Include Addition and Subtraction   Negative powers may not be moved from numerator to denominator when there is addition or subtraction outside of parentheses in the fraction. To clear the fraction of negative powers, treat the negative powers as reciprocals and simplify the fractions.

EXAMPLE 2.3

Simplify the following. Write your answers using only positive powers.

a) $a^{-2} + a^{-1}$

b) $2a^{-1} - a^{-2}$

c) $(2x)^{-2} + 2x^{-2}$

d) $\dfrac{a^{-3} + b^{-2}}{b^{-1}}$

e) $\dfrac{a^{-2} - a^2}{a^{-1}}$

SOLUTION 2.3

a) $a^{-2} + a^{-1}$ Rewrite the negative powers as reciprocals.

$= \dfrac{1}{a^2} + \dfrac{1}{a}$ Simplify using the LCD.

$= \dfrac{1}{a^2} + (\dfrac{1}{a} \cdot \dfrac{a}{a})$

$= \dfrac{1}{a^2} + \dfrac{a}{a^2} = \dfrac{1+a}{a^2}$

b) $2a^{-1} - a^{-2}$ Rewrite the negative powers as reciprocals.

$= \dfrac{2}{a} - \dfrac{1}{a^2}$ Simplify using the LCD.

$= (\dfrac{2}{a} \cdot \dfrac{a}{a}) \cdot \dfrac{1}{a^2}$

$= \dfrac{2a}{a^2} - \dfrac{1}{a^2} = \dfrac{2a-1}{a^2}$

c) $(2x)^{-2} + 2x^{-2}$ Rewrite the negative powers as reciprocals.

$= \dfrac{1}{(2x)^2} + \dfrac{2}{x^2}$ Simplify.

$= \dfrac{1}{4x^2} + \dfrac{2}{x^2}$ Combine, using the LCD of

$$4x^2.$$

$$= \frac{1}{4x^2} + \left(\frac{2}{x^2} \cdot \frac{4}{4}\right)$$

$$= \frac{1}{4x^2} + \frac{8}{4x^2} = \frac{9}{4x^2}$$

d) $\dfrac{a^{-3} + b^{-2}}{b^{-1}}$

Rewrite the negative powers as reciprocals.

$$= \frac{\dfrac{1}{a^3} + \dfrac{1}{b^2}}{\dfrac{1}{b}}$$

Simplify the numerator using the LCD.

$$= \frac{\dfrac{1}{a^3}\left(\dfrac{b^2}{b^2}\right) + \dfrac{1}{b^2}\left(\dfrac{a^3}{a^3}\right)}{\dfrac{1}{b}} = \frac{\dfrac{b^2 + a^3}{a^3 b^2}}{\dfrac{1}{b}}$$

Simplify the complex fraction.

$$= \frac{b^2 + a^3}{a^3 b^2} \div \frac{1}{b} = \frac{b^2 + a^3}{a^3 b^2} \cdot \frac{b}{1} = \frac{(b^2 + a^3)b}{a^3 b^2} = \frac{b^2 + a^3}{a^3 b}$$

e) Another way to clear negative exponents is to multiply both the numerator and denominator by positive powers.

$$\frac{a^{-2} - a^2}{a^{-1}}$$

Multiply both numerator and denominator by a^2.

$$= \frac{(a^{-2} - a^2) \cdot a^2}{(a^{-1}) \cdot a^2}$$

Distribute a^2.

$$= \frac{a^{-2} \cdot a^2 - a^2 \cdot a^2}{a^{-1} \cdot a^2}$$

Simplify.

$$= \frac{1 - a^4}{a}$$

SECTION 2.2 RATIONAL EXPONENTS

In the last section, we studied integer exponents. In this section we study rational exponents.

N^{th} Roots

Definition

If n is an even natural number and $a > 0$, then $a^{\frac{1}{n}}$ is the positive number such that

$$\left(a^{\frac{1}{n}}\right)^n = a^{\frac{n}{n}} = a.$$

The number $a^{\frac{1}{n}}$ is called the **positive nth root of a.**
The restriction of $a > 0$ is not necessary if n is odd.

Definition

If n is an odd natural number, then $a^{\frac{1}{n}}$ is the number such that

$$\left(a^{\frac{1}{n}}\right)^n = a^{\frac{n}{n}} = a$$

.

Definition

For a natural number, $0^{\frac{1}{n}} = 0$.

The next definition allows us to work with rational exponents that have numerators other than one.

Definition

$a^{\frac{m}{n}} = \left(a^{\frac{1}{n}}\right)^m = (a^m)^{\frac{1}{n}}$ where $a^{\frac{1}{n}}$ is a real number.

If we put this together with negative exponents, we get:

Definition

$a^{-\frac{m}{n}} = \dfrac{1}{a^{\frac{m}{n}}}$ where $a^{\frac{1}{n}}$ is a real number and $a \neq 0$.

A rational exponent presents both a power and a root. A negative rational represents a power, a root and a reciprocal. Notice how the numerator of the fraction is the power and the denominator is the root.

$$x^{\frac{m\,(\text{power})}{n\,(\text{root})}}$$

EXAMPLE 2.4

Write the following without the rational power.

a) $(9)^{\frac{3}{2}}$

b) $(8)^{\frac{2}{3}}$

c) $(16)^{-\frac{3}{2}}$

d) $(64)^{-\frac{3}{2}}$

e) $(-64)^{-\frac{2}{3}}$

SOLUTION 2.4

a) $(9)^{\frac{3}{2}}$ The fraction $\frac{3}{2}$ means to take the square root of 9 and cube it.

$$(\sqrt{9})^3 = 3^3 = 27$$

The fraction $\frac{3}{2}$ also means to cube 9 and then take the square root.

$$(9)^{\frac{3}{2}} = \sqrt{(9^3)} = \sqrt{729} = 27$$

b) $(8)^{\frac{2}{3}}$ Take the cubic root of 8 and square it.

$$(\sqrt[3]{8})^2 = (2)^2 = 4$$

c) $(16)^{-\frac{3}{2}}$

The $-\frac{3}{2}$ power means to perform three operations (take the square root, raise to the third power and take the reciprocal). The order in which these operations are performed is unimportant. Let's first take the square root of 16, invert that number and then cube the result.

$$(\sqrt{16})^{-3} = 4^{-3} = \frac{1}{4^3} = \frac{1}{64}$$

We could take 16 and cube it, take the square root of that number, and then take its reciprocal.

$$(\sqrt{16})^{-1} = (\sqrt{4096})^{-1} = 64^{-1} = \frac{1}{64}$$

We could also take the square root of 16, cube it and then take its reciprocal.

$$(\sqrt{16})^{-3} = (4^3)^{-1} = 64^{-1} = \frac{1}{64}$$

The important point is that with a fractional power, the power, root or reciprocal can be done in any order without affecting the final answer.

d) $(64)^{-\frac{3}{2}}$ Take the square root, invert it, and cube.

$$(\sqrt{64})^{-3} = 8^{-3} = \frac{1}{8^3} = \frac{1}{512}$$

e) $(-64)^{-\frac{2}{3}}$ Take the cubic root, invert it, and square the result.

$$(\sqrt[3]{-64})^{-2} = (-4)^{-2} = \frac{1}{(-4)^2} = \frac{1}{16}$$

EXAMPLE 2.5

Simplify the following exponential expressions using the basic theorems of exponents:

a) $x^{1.2} \cdot x^{1.3}$

b) $\left(\dfrac{a^{2.4}}{b^{3.2}}\right)^{-2}$

c) $\left(\dfrac{a^{\frac{2}{3}}}{b^{\frac{5}{6}}}\right)^{6}$

d) $\left(\dfrac{a^{\frac{1}{2}}}{b^{\frac{3}{4}}}\right)^{-8}$

e) $\left(\dfrac{a^{\frac{1}{2}}b^{\frac{2}{3}}}{a^{\frac{5}{6}}b^{\frac{3}{4}}}\right)^{8}$

SOLUTION 2.5

a) $x^{1.2} \cdot x^{1.3}$

To multiply a power times a power, keep the base and add the exponents.

$= x^{1.2+1.3} = x^{2.5}$

b) $\left(\dfrac{a^{2.4}}{b^{3.2}}\right)^{-2}$

To raise a power to a power, keep the base and multiply the exponents.
Now remove negative powers by inverting the numerator and denominator.

$= \dfrac{a^{-4.8}}{b^{-6.4}}$

$= \dfrac{b^{6.4}}{a^{4.8}}$

c) $\left(\dfrac{a^{\frac{2}{3}}}{b^{\frac{5}{6}}}\right)^{6}$

Distribute the power of 6 by keeping the base and multiplying the exponents.

$= \dfrac{a^{\frac{2}{3}\cdot 6}}{b^{\frac{5}{6}\cdot 6}}$

Simplify.

$= \dfrac{a^{4}}{b^{5}}$

d) $\left(\dfrac{a^{\frac{1}{2}}}{b^{\frac{3}{4}}}\right)^{-8}$

Distribute the power of (–8). The base stays the same and the powers are multiplied.

$= \dfrac{a^{\frac{1}{2}\cdot(-8)}}{b^{\frac{3}{4}\cdot(-8)}} = \dfrac{a^{-4}}{b^{-6}}$

Invert negative powers.

$= \dfrac{b^{6}}{a^{4}}$

e) $$\left(\dfrac{a^{\frac{1}{2}}b^{\frac{2}{3}}}{a^{\frac{5}{6}}b^{\frac{3}{4}}}\right)^{8}$$

To raise a power to a power, keep the base and multiply the exponents.

$$= \dfrac{a^{\frac{1}{2}\cdot 8}\, b^{\frac{2}{3}\cdot 8}}{a^{\frac{5}{6}\cdot 8}\, b^{\frac{3}{4}\cdot 8}} = \dfrac{a^{4}b^{\frac{16}{3}}}{a^{\frac{20}{3}}b^{6}}$$

To divide a power by a power, keep the base and subtract exponents.

$$= \dfrac{1}{a^{\frac{20}{3}-4}\, b^{6-\frac{16}{3}}}$$

Simplify.

$$= \dfrac{1}{a^{\frac{8}{3}}b^{\frac{2}{3}}}$$

EXAMPLE 2.6

Simplify the following products:

a) $x^{\frac{1}{2}}\left(x^{\frac{2}{3}}+x^{\frac{1}{2}}\right)$

b) $x^{\frac{3}{4}}\left(x^{\frac{1}{2}}-x^{\frac{1}{3}}\right)$

c) $\left(x^{\frac{1}{2}}-x^{-\frac{1}{2}}\right)^{2}$

d) $\left(x^{\frac{1}{2}}+3\right)\left(x^{\frac{1}{2}}-4\right)$

SOLUTION 2.6

a) $x^{\frac{1}{2}}\left(x^{\frac{2}{3}}+x^{\frac{1}{2}}\right)$

Distribute $x^{\frac{1}{2}}$.

$$= x^{\frac{1}{2}}\cdot x^{\frac{2}{3}} + x^{\frac{1}{2}}\cdot x^{\frac{1}{2}}$$

Keep the base and add the exponents.

$$= x^{\frac{1}{2}+\frac{2}{3}} + x^{\frac{1}{2}+\frac{1}{2}}$$

Simplify.

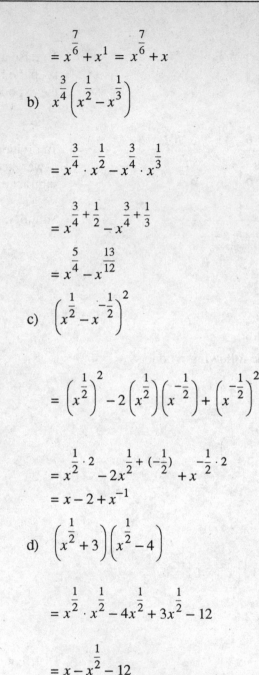

$$= x^{\frac{7}{6}} + x^1 = x^{\frac{7}{6}} + x$$

b) $x^{\frac{3}{4}}\left(x^{\frac{1}{2}} - x^{\frac{1}{3}}\right)$ Distribute $x^{\frac{3}{4}}$.

$$= x^{\frac{3}{4}} \cdot x^{\frac{1}{2}} - x^{\frac{3}{4}} \cdot x^{\frac{1}{3}}$$ Keep the base and add the powers.

$$= x^{\frac{3}{4} + \frac{1}{2}} - x^{\frac{3}{4} + \frac{1}{3}}$$ Simplify.

$$= x^{\frac{5}{4}} - x^{\frac{13}{12}}$$

c) $\left(x^{\frac{1}{2}} - x^{-\frac{1}{2}}\right)^2$ Use the rule of raising a binomial to a power.
$[(a-b)^2 = (a)^2 - 2(a)(b) + (b)^2]$

$$= \left(x^{\frac{1}{2}}\right)^2 - 2\left(x^{\frac{1}{2}}\right)\left(x^{-\frac{1}{2}}\right) + \left(x^{-\frac{1}{2}}\right)^2$$ To raise a power to a power, keep the base and multiply the powers.

$$= x^{\frac{1}{2} \cdot 2} - 2x^{\frac{1}{2} + (-\frac{1}{2})} + x^{-\frac{1}{2} \cdot 2}$$ Simplify.

$$= x - 2 + x^{-1}$$

d) $\left(x^{\frac{1}{2}} + 3\right)\left(x^{\frac{1}{2}} - 4\right)$ Multiply using FOIL.

$$= x^{\frac{1}{2}} \cdot x^{\frac{1}{2}} - 4x^{\frac{1}{2}} + 3x^{\frac{1}{2}} - 12$$ Multiply the variables and combine like terms.

$$= x - x^{\frac{1}{2}} - 12$$

EXAMPLE 2.7

Simplify the following exponential expressions using the basic theorems of exponents:

a) $\left(\dfrac{a^{\frac{n}{2}}}{b^{\frac{n}{6}}}\right)^{6}$

b) $\left(\dfrac{a^{\frac{n}{4}}}{a^{\frac{3n}{4}}}\right)^{8}$

c) $\left(\dfrac{a^{\frac{n}{2}}b^{\frac{2n}{3}}}{a^{\frac{n}{6}}b^{\frac{3n}{4}}}\right)^{12}$

SOLUTION 2.7

a) $\left(\dfrac{a^{\frac{n}{2}}}{b^{\frac{n}{6}}}\right)^{6}$ Distribute the power.

$= \dfrac{a^{\frac{n}{2}\cdot 6}}{b^{\frac{n}{6}\cdot 6}}$ Simplify.

$= \dfrac{a^{3n}}{b^{n}}$

b) $\left(\dfrac{a^{\frac{n}{4}}}{a^{\frac{3n}{4}}}\right)^{8}$ Simplify inside the parentheses.

$= \left(\dfrac{1}{a^{\frac{3n}{4}-\frac{n}{4}}}\right)^{8}$ Simplify.

$= \left(\dfrac{1}{a^{\frac{n}{2}}}\right)^{8}$ Distribute the power.

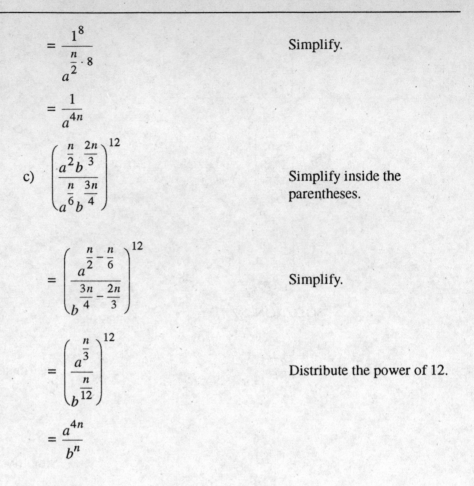

$$= \frac{1^8}{a^{\frac{n}{2} \cdot 8}}$$ Simplify.

$$= \frac{1}{a^{4n}}$$

c) $$\left(\frac{a^{\frac{n}{2}} b^{\frac{2n}{3}}}{a^{\frac{n}{6}} b^{\frac{3n}{4}}} \right)^{12}$$ Simplify inside the parentheses.

$$= \left(\frac{a^{\frac{n}{2} - \frac{n}{6}}}{b^{\frac{3n}{4} - \frac{2n}{3}}} \right)^{12}$$ Simplify.

$$= \left(\frac{a^{\frac{n}{3}}}{b^{\frac{n}{12}}} \right)^{12}$$ Distribute the power of 12.

$$= \frac{a^{4n}}{b^{n}}$$

EXERCISE 2.1

Simplify the following exponential expressions using the basic theorems of exponents:

1. $$\left(\frac{a^{\frac{2n}{3}}}{b^{\frac{3n}{2}}} \right)^{6}$$

2. $$\left(\frac{a^{\frac{5n}{6}}}{a^{\frac{3n}{4}}} \right)^{12}$$

3. $$\left(\frac{a^{\frac{5n}{12}} b^{\frac{7n}{3}}}{a^{\frac{5n}{6}} b^{\frac{5n}{8}}} \right)^{24}$$

ANSWERS TO EXERCISE 2.1

1. $\{\dfrac{a^{4n}}{b^{9n}}\}$

2. $\{a^n\}$

3. $\{\dfrac{b^{41n}}{a^{10n}}\}$

SECTION 2.3 RADICAL EXPRESSIONS

Radical expressions are expressions which contain roots. Square roots, cubic roots and other roots are important when solving higher degree equations. Simplification of radical expressions are necessary when solving equations which have irrational roots.

Radical Notation

In the radical expression $\sqrt[n]{x}$ the n is called the index, the symbol $\sqrt{}$ is called the radical or radical sign and the expression x is called the radicand. If no index is written, the index is assumed to be 2.

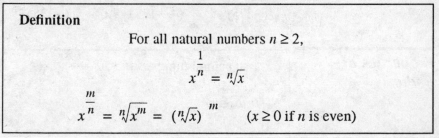

> **Definition**
>
> For all natural numbers $n \geq 2$,
>
> $$x^{\frac{1}{n}} = \sqrt[n]{x}$$
>
> $$x^{\frac{m}{n}} = \sqrt[n]{x^m} = \left(\sqrt[n]{x}\right)^m \qquad (x \geq 0 \text{ if } n \text{ is even})$$

EXAMPLE 2.8

Rewrite the following as radical expressions. Do not simplify.

a) $9^{\frac{1}{2}}$

b) $2x^{\frac{1}{2}}$

c) $4x^{\frac{1}{3}}$

d) $(8x)^{\frac{1}{3}}$

e) $9^{\frac{3}{2}}$

f) $64^{-\frac{2}{3}}$

g) $(-125)^{-\frac{5}{3}}$

SOLUTION 2.8

a) $9^{\frac{1}{2}} = \sqrt{9}$

b) $2x^{\frac{1}{2}} = 2 \cdot x^{\frac{1}{2}} = 2\sqrt{x}$

c) $4x^{\frac{1}{3}} = 4 \cdot x^{\frac{1}{3}} = 4 \cdot \sqrt[3]{x}$

d) $(8x)^{\frac{1}{3}} = \sqrt[3]{8x}$

e) $9^{\frac{3}{2}} = (\sqrt{9})^3$ or $\sqrt{9^3}$

f) $64^{-\frac{2}{3}} = (\sqrt[3]{64})^{-2}$ or $\sqrt[3]{(64)^{-2}}$

g) $(-125)^{-\frac{5}{3}} = (\sqrt[3]{-125})^5$ or $\sqrt[3]{(-125)^{-5}}$

Properties of Radicals	For all natural numbers $n \geq 2$.
	1. $\sqrt[n]{0} = 0$
	2. $\sqrt[n]{1} = 1$
	3. $\sqrt[n]{-1} = \begin{cases} \text{Is not a real number if } n \text{ is even.} \\ -1 \text{ if } n \text{ is odd} \end{cases}$

While there are no real even roots of negative one, there are odd roots. Let $r = \sqrt[3]{-1}$. Then we are looking for a real number r, such that

$r^3 = -1$. If $r = -1$, then $r^3 = -1$. Hence $\sqrt[3]{-1} = -1$.

---

4. For n an even natural number and $x \geq 0$, $\sqrt[n]{x}$ is a nonnegative number a, such that $a^n = x$.
5. For n an odd natural number, $\sqrt[n]{x}$ is a number a, such that $a^n = x$.

EXAMPLE 2.9

Simplify the following radical expressions:

a) $\sqrt{16}$

b) $\sqrt[6]{64}$

c) $\sqrt[3]{125}$

d) $\sqrt[3]{-8}$

SOLUTION 2.9

a) $\sqrt{16} = 4$, since $4^2 = 16$.

b) $\sqrt[6]{64} = 2$ since $2^6 = 64$.

c) $\sqrt[3]{125} = 5$, since $5^3 = 125$.

d) $\sqrt[3]{-8} = -2$, since $(-2)^3 = -8$.

---

6. $\sqrt[n]{x^n} = \begin{cases} x & \text{if n is odd} \\ |x| & \text{if } n \text{ is even} \end{cases}$

7. $\left(\sqrt[n]{x}\right)^n = x$ if $x \geq 0$

Remember that $\sqrt[n]{x}$ is a positive number, if n is even.

Theorems: For a and $b > 0$ and n a natural number,

8. $\sqrt[n]{ab} = \sqrt[n]{a} \cdot \sqrt[n]{b}$

9. $\sqrt[n]{\dfrac{a}{b}} = \dfrac{\sqrt[n]{a}}{\sqrt[n]{b}}$

10. $\sqrt[cn]{x^{cm}} = \sqrt[n]{x^m}$

EXAMPLE 2.10

Simplify the following radical expressions:

a) $\sqrt{1296}$

b) $\sqrt[3]{216}$

c) $\sqrt{1225}$

SOLUTION 2.10

a) $\sqrt{1296}$

Write 1296 as a product of factors which have perfect roots.

$= \sqrt{4 \cdot 324}$

$= \sqrt{4 \cdot 4 \cdot 81}$ 　　　　　Simplify using Property 8.

$= \sqrt{4} \cdot \sqrt{4} \cdot \sqrt{81}$

$= 2 \cdot 2 \cdot 9 = 36$

b) $\sqrt[3]{216}$

Write 216 as a product of factors which have perfect cubic roots.

$= \sqrt[3]{8 \cdot 27}$ 　　　　　Simplify using Property 8.

$= \sqrt[3]{8} \cdot \sqrt[3]{27}$

$= 2 \cdot 3 = 6$

c) $\sqrt{1225}$

Write 1225 as a product of factors which have perfect roots.

$= \sqrt{25 \cdot 49}$ 　　　　　Simplify using Property 8.

$= \sqrt{25} \cdot \sqrt{49}$

$= 5 \cdot 7 = 35$

EXAMPLE 2.11

Simplify the following radical expressions:

a) $\sqrt{\dfrac{4}{9}}$

b) $\sqrt{\dfrac{36}{49}}$

c) $\sqrt{\dfrac{400}{441}}$

SOLUTION 2.11

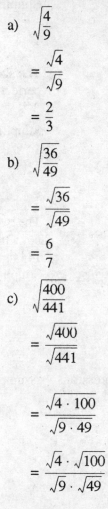

a) $\sqrt{\dfrac{4}{9}}$ · Simplify using Property 9.

$= \dfrac{\sqrt{4}}{\sqrt{9}}$

$= \dfrac{2}{3}$

b) $\sqrt{\dfrac{36}{49}}$ · Simplify using Property 9.

$= \dfrac{\sqrt{36}}{\sqrt{49}}$

$= \dfrac{6}{7}$

c) $\sqrt{\dfrac{400}{441}}$ · Simplify using Property 9.

$= \dfrac{\sqrt{400}}{\sqrt{441}}$ · · · · · · · · · · · · · · · Write the numerator and the denominator as products of factors which are perfect square roots.

$= \dfrac{\sqrt{4 \cdot 100}}{\sqrt{9 \cdot 49}}$ · · · · · · · · · · · · Simplify using Property 8.

$= \dfrac{\sqrt{4} \cdot \sqrt{100}}{\sqrt{9} \cdot \sqrt{49}}$

$= \dfrac{2 \cdot 10}{3 \cdot 7} = \dfrac{20}{21}$

EXAMPLE 2.12

Simplify the following radical expressions:

a) $\sqrt[4]{4}$

b) $\sqrt[6]{9}$

c) $\sqrt[12]{144}$

SOLUTION 2.12

a) $\sqrt[4]{4}$ · The fourth root of 4 is not a perfect root. Rewrite 4 as

2^2.

$$= \sqrt[4]{2^2}$$

Simplify using Property 10.

$$= {}^{2 \cdot 2}\!\!\sqrt{2^{1 \cdot 2}}$$

$$= \sqrt{2}$$

b) $\sqrt[6]{9}$

The sixth root of 9 is not a perfect root. Rewrite 9 as 3^2.

$$= \sqrt[6]{3^2}$$

Simplify using Property 10.

$$= {}^{3 \cdot 2}\!\!\sqrt{3^{1 \cdot 2}}$$

$$= \sqrt[3]{3}$$

c) $\sqrt[12]{144}$

The twelfth root of 144 is not a perfect root. Rewrite 144 as $2^4 \cdot 3^2$.

$$= \sqrt[12]{2^4 \cdot 3^2}$$

Simplify using Property 10.

$$= {}^{2 \cdot 2 \cdot 3}\!\!\sqrt{2^{2 \cdot 2} \cdot 3^{1 \cdot 2}}$$

$$= \sqrt[6]{2^2 \cdot 3^1} = \sqrt[6]{12}$$

EXAMPLE 2.13

Simplify the following radical expressions. Assume all variables to have positive values:

a) $\sqrt[3]{27x^3y^9}$

b) $\sqrt{\dfrac{36x^2}{25y^4}}$

c) $\sqrt[12]{x^6y^3z^9}$

SOLUTION 2.13

a) $\sqrt[3]{27x^3y^9}$

Simplify using Property 8.

$$= \sqrt[3]{27} \cdot \sqrt[3]{x^3} \cdot \sqrt[3]{y^9}$$

$$= 3 \cdot x \cdot y^3 = 3xy^3$$

b) $\sqrt{\dfrac{36x^2}{25y^4}}$

Simplify using Property 9.

$$= \dfrac{\sqrt{36x^2}}{\sqrt{25y^4}}$$

Simplify using Property 8.

$$= \frac{\sqrt{36} \cdot \sqrt{x^2}}{\sqrt{25} \cdot \sqrt{y^4}} = \frac{6x}{5y^2}$$

c) $\sqrt[12]{x^6 y^3 z^9}$

Rewrite $x^6 y^3 2^9$ as
$x^{2 \cdot 3} y^{1 \cdot 3} z^{3 \cdot 3}$.

$$= \sqrt[2 \cdot 2 \cdot 3]{x^{2 \cdot 3} y^{1 \cdot 3} z^{3 \cdot 3}}$$

Simplify using Property 10.

$$= \sqrt[4]{x^2 y z^3}$$

Simplifying Radicals

Like all mathematical expressions, radical expressions must be simplified whenever possible. Simplifying radicals is often referred to as **standardizing radicals**. To simplify radical expressions we use the theorems of radicals and the following rules:

RULES FOR SIMPLIFYING RADICAL EXPRESSIONS

1. All perfect roots which are factors of the radicand must be removed.
2. All powers of any factors must be less than the index.
3. No fractions may be left under the radical sign.
4. No radical may appear in the denominator of a fraction.
5. Reduce the order of each radical by dividing common factors between the index and all of the powers.

EXAMPLE 2.14

Simplify the following radical expressions. Apply the rules for simplifying.

a) $\sqrt{45}$

b) $\sqrt{150}$

c) $\sqrt{x^9}$

d) $\sqrt[3]{x^3 y^7 z^{14}}$

e) $\sqrt{50x^2 y^3}$

f) $\sqrt[3]{16x^4 y^8 z^9}$

SOLUTION 2.14

a) $\sqrt{45}$ See if 45 contains any perfect roots among its factors.

$= \sqrt{9 \cdot 5}$ Simplify using Property 8.

$= \sqrt{9} \cdot \sqrt{5}$

$= 3\sqrt{5}$

b) $\sqrt{150}$ Find all perfect roots which are factors of 150.

$= \sqrt{25 \cdot 6}$ Simplify using Property 8.

$= \sqrt{25} \cdot \sqrt{6}$

$= 5\sqrt{6}$

c) $\sqrt{x^9}$ Factor x^9 into $x^8 \cdot x$.

$= \sqrt{x^8 x^1}$ Simplify using Property 8.

$= \sqrt{x^8} \cdot \sqrt{x^1}$

$= x^4 \sqrt{x}$

d) $\sqrt[3]{x^3 y^7 z^{14}}$ Factor $x^3 y^7 z^{14}$ to find perfect roots.

$= \sqrt[3]{x^3} \cdot \sqrt[3]{y^6 \cdot y} \cdot \sqrt[3]{z^{12} \cdot z^2} = \sqrt[3]{x^3} \cdot \sqrt[3]{y^6} \cdot \sqrt[3]{y} \cdot \sqrt[3]{z^{12}} \cdot \sqrt[3]{z^2}$

$= x \cdot y^2 \sqrt[3]{y} \cdot z^4 \cdot \sqrt[3]{z^2} = xy^2 z^4 \sqrt[3]{yz^2}$

$= \sqrt[3]{x^3 y^6 y^1 z^{12} z^2}$ Simplify using Property 8.

$= \sqrt[3]{x^3} \cdot \sqrt[3]{y^6} \cdot \sqrt[3]{y} \cdot \sqrt[3]{z^{12}} \cdot \sqrt[3]{z^2}$

$= xy^2 z^4 \sqrt[3]{y} \cdot \sqrt{z^2}$

$= xy^2 z^4 \sqrt[3]{yz^2}$

e) $\sqrt{50x^2y^3}$ Factor $50x^2y^3$ to find factors which are perfect roots.

$= \sqrt{25 \cdot 2 \cdot x^2 \cdot y^2 \cdot y}$ Simplify using Property 8.

$= \sqrt{25} \cdot \sqrt{2} \cdot \sqrt{x^2} \cdot \sqrt{y^2} \cdot \sqrt{y}$

$= 5xy \cdot \sqrt{2} \cdot \sqrt{y}$

$= 5xy\sqrt{2y}$

f) $\sqrt[3]{16x^4y^8z^9}$ Factor to find perfect cubes.

$= \sqrt[3]{8 \cdot 2 \cdot x^3 \cdot x \cdot y^6 \cdot y^2 \cdot z^9}$ Simplify using Property 8.

$= \sqrt[3]{8} \cdot \sqrt[3]{2} \cdot \sqrt[3]{x^3} \cdot \sqrt[3]{x} \cdot \sqrt[3]{y^6} \cdot \sqrt[3]{y^2} \cdot \sqrt[3]{z^9}$

$= 2 \cdot \sqrt[3]{2} \cdot x \cdot \sqrt[3]{x} \cdot y^2 \cdot \sqrt[3]{y^2} \cdot z^3$

$= 2xy^2z^3 \sqrt[3]{2xy^2}$

A radical expression such as $\sqrt{\dfrac{3}{5}}$ is not in simplified form. Rule 3 above states that we may not leave a fraction under a radical sign. We can change $\sqrt{\dfrac{3}{5}}$ to $\dfrac{\sqrt{3}}{\sqrt{5}}$ using Property 8, but this still leaves us with a problem: according to Rule 4, no radical may appear in the denominator. We solve this by converting $\dfrac{3}{5}$ to an equivalent fraction in which the denominator is a perfect root.

In this case $\sqrt{\dfrac{3}{5}} = \sqrt{\dfrac{3 \cdot 5}{5 \cdot 5}} = \dfrac{\sqrt{15}}{\sqrt{25}} = \dfrac{\sqrt{15}}{5}$. Thus $\dfrac{\sqrt{15}}{5}$ is the simplified form of $\sqrt{\dfrac{3}{5}}$.

EXAMPLE 2.15

Simplify the following. All variables are assumed to be positive.

a) $\sqrt{\dfrac{2a}{b}}$

b) $\sqrt{\dfrac{2a}{3c^3}}$

c) $\sqrt[3]{\dfrac{3a}{2b^2}}$

d) $\sqrt[5]{\dfrac{2a^3b^7c^3}{9a^4c^2}}$

e) $\sqrt{\dfrac{8a^3}{3b}}$

f) $\sqrt[3]{\dfrac{27a^5b^9}{200c^2}}$

SOLUTION 2.15

a) $\sqrt{\dfrac{2a}{b}}$ Convert this expression to an equivalent one in which the denominator is a perfect root. Multiply both the numerator and the denominator by b.

$= \sqrt{\dfrac{2a \cdot b}{b \cdot b}}$ Simplify.

$= \sqrt{\dfrac{2ab}{b^2}}$ Simplify using Property 9.

$= \dfrac{\sqrt{2ab}}{\sqrt{b^2}} = \dfrac{\sqrt{2ab}}{b}$

b) $\sqrt{\dfrac{2a}{3c^3}}$ Convert to an equivalent expression in which the denominator is a perfect square. $3c^3$ is not a perfect square, but 3^2c^4 is a perfect square. Multiply the numerator and denominator by $3c$ to get 3^2c^4.

$= \sqrt{\dfrac{2a \cdot 3c}{3c^3 \cdot 3c}}$ Simplify.

$= \sqrt{\dfrac{6ac}{9c^4}}$ Simplify using Property 9.

$= \dfrac{\sqrt{6ac}}{\sqrt{9c^4}} = \dfrac{\sqrt{6ac}}{3c^2}$

c) $\sqrt[3]{\dfrac{3a}{2b^2}}$

To find the cubic root of a fraction, we need to have the denominator written as a perfect cube. $2b^2$ is not a perfect cube, but $2^3 b^3$ is a perfect cube. Multiply the numerator and the denominator by $2^2 b$ to get $2^3 b^3$ in the denominator. Simplify.

$= \sqrt[3]{\dfrac{3a \cdot 2^2 b}{2b^2 \cdot 2^2 b}}$

$= \sqrt[3]{\dfrac{12ab}{2^3 b^3}}$

Simplify using Property 9.

$= \dfrac{\sqrt[3]{12ab}}{\sqrt[3]{2^3 b^3}}$

$= \dfrac{\sqrt[3]{12ab}}{2b}$

d) $\sqrt[5]{\dfrac{2a^3 b^7 c^3}{9a^4 c^2}}$

Before trying to standardize the radical, reduce the fraction under the radical.

$= \sqrt[5]{\dfrac{2b^7 c}{9a}}$

To find the fifth root of a fraction, we need to have the denominator written as a perfect fifth. Neither $9a$, nor its equivalent $3^2 a$, are perfect fifths. But $3^5 a^5$ is a perfect fifth. Multiply both the numerator and the denominator by $3^3 a^4$ to get $3^5 a^5$. Simplify.

$= \sqrt[5]{\dfrac{2b^7 c \cdot (3^3 a^4)}{3^2 a \cdot (3^3 a^4)}}$

$= \sqrt[5]{\dfrac{54 a^4 b^7 c}{3^5 c^5}}$

Simplify using Property 9.

$= \dfrac{\sqrt[5]{54 a^4 b^7 c}}{\sqrt[5]{3^5 c^5}}$

$$= \frac{\sqrt[5]{54a^4b^7c}}{3c}$$

The power of b is greater than the index. Therefore simplify further by factoring out b^5 using Property 8.

$$= \frac{\sqrt[5]{54a^4b^5b^2c}}{3c}$$

$$= \frac{b\,\sqrt[5]{54a^4b^2c}}{3c}$$

e) $\sqrt{\dfrac{8a^3}{3b}}$

Convert to an equivalent expression in which the denominator is a perfect square. Multiply the numerator and the denominator by $3b$.

$$= \sqrt{\frac{8a^3 \cdot 3b}{3b \cdot 3b}}$$

$$= \sqrt{\frac{2^2 \cdot 2 \cdot 3 \cdot a^2 \cdot b}{3^2 b^2}}$$

Simplify using Properties 8 and 9.

$$= \frac{\sqrt{2^2} \cdot \sqrt{a^2} \cdot \sqrt{2 \cdot 3 \cdot b}}{\sqrt{3^2} \cdot \sqrt{b^2}}$$

$$= \frac{2a\sqrt{6b}}{3b}$$

f) $\sqrt[3]{\dfrac{27a^5b^9}{200c^2}}$

Factor the numerator and denominator and put into power notation.

$$= \sqrt[3]{\frac{3^3 a^3 a^2 b^9}{2^3 5^2 c^2}}$$

Multiply both the numerator and the denominator by $5c$ so that the denominator of the equivalent expression is a perfect cube.
Simplify using Properties 8 and 9.

$$= \sqrt[3]{\frac{3^3 a^3 a^2 b^9 \cdot 5c}{2^3 5^2 c^2 \cdot 5c}}$$

$$= \frac{\sqrt[3]{3^3} \cdot \sqrt[3]{a^3} \cdot \sqrt[3]{b^9} \cdot \sqrt[3]{5a^2c}}{\sqrt[3]{2^3} \cdot \sqrt[3]{5^2} \cdot \sqrt[3]{c^2}} \qquad \text{Simplify.}$$

$$= \frac{3ab^3 \sqrt[3]{5a^2c}}{10c}$$

EXAMPLE 2.16

Simplify the following radical expressions. Assume all variables are positive.

a) $\dfrac{1}{\sqrt{2}}$

b) $\dfrac{1}{\sqrt{12}}$

c) $\dfrac{1}{\sqrt{18ab^2}}$

d) $\dfrac{\sqrt{3}}{\sqrt{2}}$

SOLUTION 2.16

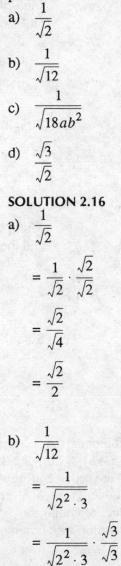

a) $\dfrac{1}{\sqrt{2}}$ Multiply the numerator and the denominator by $\dfrac{\sqrt{2}}{\sqrt{2}}$.

$$= \frac{1}{\sqrt{2}} \cdot \frac{\sqrt{2}}{\sqrt{2}} \qquad \text{Simplify.}$$

$$= \frac{\sqrt{2}}{\sqrt{4}}$$

$$= \frac{\sqrt{2}}{2}$$

b) $\dfrac{1}{\sqrt{12}}$ Factor the denominator.

$$= \frac{1}{\sqrt{2^2 \cdot 3}} \qquad \text{Multiply the numerator and the denominator by } \dfrac{\sqrt{3}}{\sqrt{3}}.$$

$$= \frac{1}{\sqrt{2^2 \cdot 3}} \cdot \frac{\sqrt{3}}{\sqrt{3}}$$

$$= \frac{\sqrt{3}}{\sqrt{2^2 \cdot 3^2}}$$ Simplify.

$$= \frac{\sqrt{3}}{6}$$

c) $$\frac{1}{\sqrt{18ab^2}}$$ Factor the denominator.

$$= \frac{1}{\sqrt{2 \cdot 3^2 \cdot ab^2}}$$ Multiply the numerator $\frac{\sqrt{2a}}{\sqrt{2a}}$ and denominator by $\frac{\sqrt{2a}}{\sqrt{2a}}$.

$$= \frac{1}{\sqrt{2 \cdot 3^2 \cdot ab^2}} \cdot \frac{\sqrt{2a}}{\sqrt{2a}}$$

$$= \frac{\sqrt{2a}}{\sqrt{2^2 \cdot 3^2 \cdot a^2 \cdot b^2}}$$ Simplify.

$$= \frac{\sqrt{2a}}{2 \cdot 3ab} = \frac{\sqrt{2a}}{6ab}$$

d) $$\frac{\sqrt{3}}{\sqrt{2}}$$ Multiply the numerator and the denominator by $\frac{\sqrt{2}}{\sqrt{2}}$.

$$= \frac{\sqrt{3}}{\sqrt{2}} \cdot \frac{\sqrt{2}}{\sqrt{2}}$$

$$= \frac{\sqrt{6}}{\sqrt{4}}$$ Simplify.

$$= \frac{\sqrt{6}}{2}$$

CONJUGATES

To eliminate a radical from a binomial expression, recall that
$$(a + b)(a - b) = a^2 - b^2$$
The binomials $a + b$) and $(a - b)$ are called **conjugates**. When conjugates are multiplied together, their product is the first term squared minus the second term squared. The product of conjugates helps to eliminate radicals from the denominator of a fraction with binomials involving radicals.

EXAMPLE 2.17

Simplify the following radical expressions. All variables are assumed to be positive.

a) $\dfrac{1}{1+\sqrt{2}}$

b) $\dfrac{3}{\sqrt{3}-\sqrt{2}}$

c) $\dfrac{\sqrt{x}}{\sqrt{x}-\sqrt{y}}$

SOLUTION 2.17

a) $\dfrac{1}{1+\sqrt{2}}$

Multiply the numerator and the denominator by the conjugate of the denominator. The conjugate of $(1+\sqrt{2})$ is $(1-\sqrt{2})$.

$$= \dfrac{1}{(1+\sqrt{2})} \cdot \dfrac{(1-\sqrt{2})}{(1-\sqrt{2})}$$

Simplify. Remember that $(a+b)(a-b) = a^2 - b^2$.

$$= \dfrac{(1-\sqrt{2})}{1^2 - (\sqrt{2})^2}$$

$$= \dfrac{(1-\sqrt{2})}{-1}$$

Remove the negative from the denominator of the fraction and simplify.

$$= \dfrac{-1+\sqrt{2}}{1} = -1+\sqrt{2}$$

b) $\dfrac{3}{\sqrt{3}-\sqrt{2}}$

Multiply the numerator and the denominator by the conjugate of the denominator. The conjugate of the denominator is $(\sqrt{3}+\sqrt{2})$.

$$= \dfrac{3}{\sqrt{3}-\sqrt{2}} \cdot \dfrac{(\sqrt{3}+\sqrt{2})}{(\sqrt{3}+\sqrt{2})}$$

$$= \dfrac{3(\sqrt{3}+\sqrt{2})}{(\sqrt{3})^2 - (\sqrt{2})^2}$$

Simplify.

$$= \frac{3\sqrt{3} + 3\sqrt{2}}{3 - 2}$$

$$= \frac{3\sqrt{3} + 3\sqrt{2}}{1}$$

$$= 3\sqrt{3} + 3\sqrt{2}$$

c) $\dfrac{\sqrt{x}}{\sqrt{x} - \sqrt{y}}$

Multiply the numerator and the denominator by the conjugate of the denominator.

$$= \frac{\sqrt{x}}{\sqrt{x} - \sqrt{y}} \cdot \frac{(\sqrt{x} + \sqrt{y})}{(\sqrt{x} + \sqrt{y})}$$

$$= \frac{\sqrt{x}(\sqrt{x} + \sqrt{y})}{(\sqrt{x})^2 - (\sqrt{y})^2}$$

Simplify.

$$= \frac{\sqrt{x^2} + \sqrt{xy}}{x - y} = \frac{x + \sqrt{xy}}{x - y}$$

Addition and Subtraction of Radicals

The theorems we've used thus far for radical expressions apply to the operations of multiplication, division, and powers. They do not apply to addition or subtraction.

Addition under radical signs cannot be separated by terms.

$$\sqrt{9 + 16} \qquad\qquad (\sqrt{9} + \sqrt{16})$$

$$= \sqrt{25} \qquad\qquad = \sqrt{9} + \sqrt{16}$$

$$= 5 \qquad\qquad\qquad = 3 + 4 = 7$$
$$5 \qquad\qquad \ne \qquad\qquad 7$$

Radical expressions can be added and subtracted only if they are alike. **Like radical expressions** are those with exactly the same radicand. Addition and subtraction of radical expressions is similar to addition and subtraction of terms. Only like terms may be added or subtracted. To add or subtract like terms, we add or subtract their numerical coefficients and keep the variable. To add or subtract radical expressions, we add or subtract their numerical coefficients and keep the radicand.

EXAMPLE 2.18

Add or subtract the following radical expressions. Assume all variables are positive.

a) $2\sqrt{3} + 3\sqrt{3}$

b) $5\sqrt{12} + 2\sqrt{27} - 3\sqrt{75}$

c) $\sqrt{8x^3} + 4x\sqrt{50x} - \sqrt{72x^3}$

SOLUTION 2.18

a) $2\sqrt{3} + 3\sqrt{3}$ These are like expressions. Apply the distributive property.

$$= (2+3)\sqrt{3}$$
$$= 5\sqrt{3}$$

b) $5\sqrt{12} + 2\sqrt{27} - 3\sqrt{75}$ These radical expressions cannot be added or subtracted as is. However, they can be standardized. First, factor the radicands.

$$= 5\sqrt{4 \cdot 3} + 2\sqrt{9 \cdot 3} - 3\sqrt{25 \cdot 3}$$ Simplify using Property 8.

$$= 5\sqrt{4} \cdot \sqrt{3} + 2\sqrt{9} \cdot \sqrt{3} - 3\sqrt{25} \cdot \sqrt{3}$$ Standardize perfect roots.

$$= 5 \cdot 2\sqrt{3} + 2 \cdot 3\sqrt{3} - 3 \cdot 5\sqrt{3}$$ Simplify.

$$= 10\sqrt{3} + 6\sqrt{3} - 15\sqrt{3}$$ Apply the distributive property.

$$= (10 + 6 - 15)\sqrt{3}$$

$$= \sqrt{3}$$

c) $\sqrt{8x^3} + 4x\sqrt{50x} - \sqrt{72x^3}$ These radical expressions are not alike. Factor the radicands.

$$= \sqrt{4 \cdot 2 \cdot x^2 \cdot x} + 4x\sqrt{25 \cdot 2 \cdot x} - \sqrt{36 \cdot 2 \cdot x^2 \cdot x}$$

Simplify using Property 8.

$$= \sqrt{4} \cdot \sqrt{x^2} \cdot \sqrt{2x} + 4x\sqrt{25} \cdot \sqrt{2x} - \sqrt{36} \cdot \sqrt{x^2} \cdot \sqrt{2x}$$

Remove perfect roots.

$$= 2x\sqrt{2x} + 4x \cdot 5\sqrt{2x} - 6x\sqrt{2x}$$ Simplify.

$$= 2x\sqrt{2x} + 20x\sqrt{2x} - 6x\sqrt{2x}$$ Apply the distributive property. Add coefficients and keep the radicals.

$$= 16x\sqrt{2x}$$

EXAMPLE 2.19

Simplify the following radical expressions. Perform the indicated operations and simplify your final answer. Assume all variables are positive.

a) $(\sqrt{3} + \sqrt{2})\,(2\sqrt{3} - 3\sqrt{2})$

b) $(2\sqrt{5} + 3\sqrt{2})\,(2\sqrt{5} - 4\sqrt{2})$

c) $(2\sqrt{6} + 3\sqrt{2})^2$

SOLUTION 2.19

a) $(\sqrt{3} + \sqrt{2})\,(2\sqrt{3} - 3\sqrt{2})$ Multiply by using FOIL.

$= \sqrt{3}\cdot 2\sqrt{3} - \sqrt{3}\cdot 3\sqrt{2} + \sqrt{2}\cdot 2\sqrt{3} - \sqrt{2}\cdot 3\sqrt{2}$

Simplify using Property 8.

$= 2\sqrt{3\cdot 3} - 3\sqrt{3\cdot 2} + 2\sqrt{2\cdot 3} - 3\sqrt{2\cdot 2}$ Simplify.

$= 2\sqrt{9} - 3\sqrt{6} + 2\sqrt{6} - 3\sqrt{4}$ Simplify and combine like terms.

$= (2\cdot 3) - \sqrt{6} - (3\cdot 2)$

$= 6 - 6 - \sqrt{6}$

$= -\sqrt{6}$

b) $(2\sqrt{5} + 3\sqrt{2})\,(2\sqrt{5} - 4\sqrt{2})$ Multiply by using FOIL.

$= 2\sqrt{5}\cdot 2\sqrt{5} - 2\sqrt{5}\cdot 4\sqrt{2} + 3\sqrt{2}\cdot 2\sqrt{5} - 3\sqrt{2}\cdot 4\sqrt{2}$

Simplify using Property 8.

$= 4\sqrt{5\cdot 5} - 8\sqrt{5\cdot 2} + 6\sqrt{2\cdot 5} - 12\sqrt{2\cdot 2}$

Simplify.

$= 4\sqrt{25} - 8\sqrt{10} + 6\sqrt{10} - 12\sqrt{4}$ Simplify and add like terms.

$= (4\cdot 5) - 2\sqrt{10} - (12\cdot 2)$

$= 20 - 2\sqrt{10} - 24$

$= -4 - 2\sqrt{10}$

c) $(2\sqrt{6} + 3\sqrt{2})^2$ Recall that
$(a+b)\,(a-b) = a^2 - b^2.$

$= (2\sqrt{6})^2 + 2\cdot (2\sqrt{6})\cdot (3\sqrt{2}) + (3\sqrt{2})^2$

Remove parentheses.

$= 4\sqrt{36} + 12\sqrt{12} + 9\sqrt{4}$ Simplify.

$= (4\cdot 6) + 12\sqrt{4\cdot 3} + (9\cdot 2)$

$$= 24 + 12 \cdot 2\sqrt{3} + 18$$
$$= 42 + 24\sqrt{3}$$

EXERCISE 2.2

Simplify the following radicals.

1. $\sqrt{20} + \sqrt{45} - \sqrt{80}$
2. $2\sqrt{3} - \sqrt{48} + \sqrt{147}$
3. $(2 + \sqrt{3})(5 - \sqrt{3})$
4. $(\sqrt{2} + \sqrt{5})^2$
5. $(\sqrt{18} + \sqrt{48})(\sqrt{8} - \sqrt{27})$

ANSWERS TO EXERCISE 2.2

1. $\{\sqrt{5}\}$
2. $\{5\sqrt{3}\}$
3. $\{7 + 3\sqrt{3}\}$
4. $\{7 + 2\sqrt{10}\}$
5. $\{-24 - \sqrt{6}\}$

3

Solving Equations

SECTION 3.1 SOLVING LINEAR EQUATIONS IN ONE VARIABLE

An equality is a statement showing that two mathematical expressions are equal.

$$2 + 3 = 5 \qquad 2x - 7 = 11 \qquad x^2 - 5x - 6 = 0$$

To solve an equation in x, we need to find all the values of x that make the equation true. These values are called **solutions** or **roots** of the equation.

Types of Equations

Equations which have no solutions are called **contradictions** and equations which are true for all values of x are called **identities**. Equations which are true for a finite number of replacements for x are called **conditional** equations; the truth of the equations balances on the condition that x is replaced by a solution.

The equation $2(x + 3) = 2x + 6$ is an identity. If we remove the parenthesis from the left side of the equation, the left and right sides are identically the same: $2x + 6 = 2x + 6$. The equation $x = x + 1$ is a contradiction. The equation says that a number x is equal to itself plus 1; that is, 2 is equal to 3, 3 is equal to 4, and so forth. These statements are contradictions since they are never true. The equation $2x + 5 = 11$ is a conditional equation. It is true on the condition that $x = 3$.

Linear Equations

> **Definition**:
> An equation that can be written in the form of
> $$ax + b = 0$$
> where a and b are real numbers and $a \neq 0$, is called a **linear equation** in one variable or a **first degree equation** in one variable.

Conditional linear equations have exactly one solution. To solve a linear degree equation in one variable we must isolate the variable on one side of the equation. To do this we use the following properties of equality.

Properties of Equality

> **Properties of Equality**:
> For all real numbers a, b and c
> 1. Addition Property of Equality
>   If $a = b$ then $a + c = b + c$.
> 2. Subtraction Property of Equality
>   If $a = b$ then $a - c = b - c$.
> 3. Multiplication Property of Equality
>   If $a = b$ then $a \cdot c = b \cdot c$ $(c \neq 0)$.
> 4. Division Property of Equality
>   If $a = b$ then $a \div c = b \div c$ $(c \neq 0)$

Solving Equations

To solve the equation $ax + b = 0$ we must isolate x on one side. To do this we apply the properties of equality to write equivalent equations. By applying Property 2 to $ax + b = 0$, we subtract b from both sides of the equation.
$$ax + b - b = 0 - b$$
This leads to the equivalent equation
$$ax = -b$$
Now we apply Property 4 and divide both sides by a $(a \neq 0)$.
$$\frac{ax}{a} = \frac{-b}{a} \qquad \text{Simplify.}$$
$$x = \frac{-b}{a}$$
To solve an equation, we use the properties of equality along with the following rules.
1. Simplify both sides of the equation (remove parentheses and combine

like terms).

2. Clear all fractions by multiplying both sides of the equation by the Least Common Denominator (LCD).

3. Isolate the variable on one side of the equation by applying the properties of equality.

EXAMPLE 3.1

Solve the following linear equations for x:

a) $2x + 3 = 17$

b) $5x + 6 = -9$

c) $3(x - 1) + 2(x + 4) = 35$

d) $2(x - 3) - 4(x + 2) + 5(x + 3) = 7$

e) $4(3 - (2x + 4)) - 5(7 - (3x + 2)) = 27$

f) $3(2x + 6) - 2(3x + 4) - 5(x + 3) = 45$

SOLUTION 3.1

a) $2x + 3 = 17$ Subtract 3 from both sides of the equation.

$2x + 3 - 3 = 17 - 3$ Simplify.

$2x = 14$ Divide both sides by 2.

$$\frac{2x}{2} = \frac{14}{2}$$ Simplify your answer.

$x = 7$

The equation $x = 7$ is a conditional equation. The value 7 is the solution to the equation $x = 7$ and the original, equivalent equation $2x + 3 = 17$. We can write the solution set as $\{7\}$. The solution set is the set of all possible values for the variable that make the equation a true statement.

b) $5x + 6 = -9$ Subtract 6 from both sides.

$5x + 6 - 6 = -9 - 6$ Simplify.

$5x = -15$ Divide both sides by 5.

$$\frac{5x}{5} = \frac{-15}{5}$$ Simplify.

$x = -3$

$\{-3\}$ $\{-3\}$ represents the solution set.

c) $3(x - 1) + 2(x + 4) = 35$ Remove parentheses.

$3x - 3 + 2x + 8 = 35$ Combine like terms.

$5x + 5 = 35$ Subtract 5 from both sides of the equation.

$5x = 35 - 5$ Simplify.

$5x = 30$ Divide both sides by 5.

$$\frac{5x}{5} = \frac{30}{5}$$ Compute.

$x = 6$ Write your answer as a solution set.

$\{6\}$

d) $2(x-3) - 4(x+2) + 5(x+3) = 7$ Remove parentheses.
$2x - 6 - 4x - 8 + 5x + 15 = 7$ Combine like terms.
$3x + 1 = 7$ Subtract 1 from both sides.
$3x = 6$ Divide both sides by 3.

$$\frac{3x}{3} = \frac{6}{3}$$ Compute.

$x = 2$ Write your answer as a solution set.

$\{2\}$

e) $4(3 - (2x+4)) - 5(7 - (3x+2)) = 27$

Remove innermost parentheses.

$4(3 - 2x - 4) - 5(7 - 3x - 2) = 27$ Simplify inside of parentheses.

$4(-2x - 1) - 5(-3x + 5) = 27$ Remove parentheses again.
$-8x - 4 + 15x - 25 = 27$ Simplify.
$7x - 29 = 27$ Add 29 to both sides.
$7x = 56$ Divide both sides by 7.

$$\frac{7x}{7} = \frac{56}{7}$$ Compute.

$x = 8$ Write your answer as a solution set.

$\{8\}$

f) $3(2x+6) - 2(3x+4) - 5(x+3) = 45$

Remove parentheses.

$6x + 18 - 6x - 8 - 5x - 15 = 45$ Combine like terms.
$-5x - 5 = 45$ Add 5 to both sides.
$-5x = 50$ Divide both sides by -5.

$$\frac{-5x}{-5} = \frac{50}{-5}$$ Compute.

$x = -10$ Write your answer as a solution set.

$\{-10\}$

In all of the previous examples the variable was on only one side of the original equation. If the variable is on both sides of the equation, we must first get the variable on one side of the equation and then get everything else on the other side.

EXAMPLE 3.2

Solve the following equations for x:

a) $5(2x-3) - 3(3x-5) = 4(x-5)$

b) $4(2x+3) - 3(x+2) = 5(x-7) - 4(2x+3)$

SOLUTION 3.2

a) $5(2x-3) - 3(3x-5) = 4(x-5)$ Simplify.

$10x - 15 - 9x + 15 = 4x - 20$ Combine like terms.

$x = 4x - 20$ Subtract $4x$ from both sides

to isolate the variable.

$x - 4x = 4x - 20 - 4x$ Simplify.

$-3x = -20$ Divide both sides by -3.

$\dfrac{-3x}{-3} = \dfrac{-20}{-3}$ Simplify.

$x = \dfrac{20}{3}$ or $6\dfrac{2}{3}$ Write your answer as a

solution set.

$\{\dfrac{20}{3}\}$ or $\{6\dfrac{2}{3}\}$ Either answer is acceptable.

We could also solve this equation by isolating x on the right side. Simplify.

$x = 4x - 20$ Subtract x from both sides.

$x - x = 4x - 20 - x$ Simplify.

$0 = 3x - 20$ Add 20 to both sides.

$0 + 20 = 3x - 20 + 20$ Simplify.

$20 = 3x$ Divide both sides by 3 and

simplify.

$\dfrac{20}{3} = \dfrac{3x}{3}$

$x = \dfrac{20}{3}$ or $6\dfrac{2}{3}$

By isolating x so that the coefficient of x is positive, we often avoid careless mistakes.

b) $4(2x+3) - 3(x+2)$

$\qquad = 5(x-7) - 4(2x+3)$ Simplify.

$8x + 12 - 3x - 6 = 5x - 35 - 8x - 12$ Combine like terms.

$5x + 6 = -3x - 47$ Add $3x$ to both sides.

$5x + 6 + 3x = -3x - 47 + 3x$ Simplify.

$8x + 6 = -47$ Subtract 6 from both sides.

$8x = -53$ Divide both sides by 8.

$$\frac{8x}{8} = \frac{-53}{8}$$

$x = \dfrac{-53}{8}$ or $-6\dfrac{5}{8}$ Write your answer as a solution set.

$$\left\{\frac{-53}{8}\right\} \quad \text{or} \quad \left\{-6\frac{5}{8}\right\}$$

FRACTIONAL COEFFICIENTS

Sometimes equations contain fractional coefficients. We can clear the fractional coefficients by multiplying both sides of the equation by the least common denominator (LCD).

EXAMPLE 3.3

Solve the following equations for x:

a) $\dfrac{1}{2}x + \dfrac{2}{3} = \dfrac{3}{4}x - \dfrac{5}{6}$

b) $\dfrac{1}{2}(x+3) - \dfrac{2}{3}(6x+4) = \dfrac{5}{6}(3x-5)$

SOLUTION 3.3

a) $\dfrac{1}{2}x + \dfrac{2}{3} = \dfrac{3}{4}x - \dfrac{5}{6}$ Clear fractions by multiplying both sides by the LCD 12.

$$12\left(\frac{1}{2}x + \frac{2}{3}\right) = 12\left(\frac{3}{4}x - \frac{5}{6}\right)$$ Simplify.

$6x + 8 = 9x - 10$ Subtract $6x$ from both sides.

$6x + 8 - 6x = 9x - 10 - 6x$ Simplify.

$8 = 3x - 10$ Add 10 to both sides.

$8 + 10 = 3x - 10 + 10$ Simplify.

$18 = 3x$ Divide both sides by 3.

$6 = x$ Use the property of symmetry to rewrite the equation.

$x = 6$ The solution set is $\{6\}$.

b) $\frac{1}{2}(x+3) - \frac{2}{3}(6x+4) = \frac{5}{6}(3x-5)$ Remove the parentheses.

$\frac{1}{2}x + \frac{3}{2} - 4x + \frac{8}{3} = \frac{5}{2}x - \frac{25}{6}$ Multiply both sides by the LCD 6.

$6(\frac{1}{2}x + \frac{3}{2} - 4x + \frac{8}{3}) = 6(\frac{5}{2}x - \frac{25}{6})$ Simplify.

$3x + 9 - 24x + 16 = 15x - 25$ Combine like terms.

$-21x + 25 = 15x - 25$ Add $21x$ to both sides.

$-21x + 25 + 21x = 15x - 25 + 21x$ Simplify.

$25 = 36x - 25$ Add 25 to both sides.

$50 = 36x$ Divide both sides by 36.

$\frac{50}{36} = \frac{36x}{36}$ Reduce your answer.

$\frac{25}{18} = x$ Use the property of symmetry to rewrite your answer.

$x = \frac{25}{18}$

The solution set is $\{\frac{25}{18}\}$.

EQUATIONS THAT DON'T APPEAR TO BE FIRST DEGREE

Sometimes equations do not appear to be first degree. Higher powers of the variable may appear on both sides of the equation. While higher power equations are solved differently than first degree equations, many times the higher power will drop out when the terms involving the variable are written on the same side.

EXAMPLE 3.4

Solve the following equations for x:
a) $2(x+3) - (2x-3)(x+5) = (x+2)(x-4) - 3x^2$
b) $(5x+2)^2 - (4x-5)^2 = (3x+7)^2$

SOLUTION 3.4

a) $2(x+3) - (2x-3)(x+5) = (x+2)(x-4) - 3x^2$

                                        Simplify.

$2x + 6 - (2x^2 + 7x - 15) = x^2 - 4x + 2x - 8 - 3x^2$

$$2x + 6 - 2x^2 - 7x + 15 = -2x^2 - 2x - 8$$

$-2x^2 - 5x + 21 = -2x^2 - 2x - 8$ Add $2x^2$ and $2x$ to both sides and simplify.

$-2x^2 - 5x + 21 + 2x^2 + 2x = -2x^2 - 2x - 8 + 2x^2 + 2x$ Simplify.

$-3x + 21 = -8$ Notice the x^2 terms have been eliminated from the equation. We now have a first degree equation in x. Subtract 21 from both sides.

$-3x + 21 - 21 = -8 - 21$ Simplify.

$-5x = -29$ Divide both sides by -5.

$\dfrac{-5x}{-5} = \dfrac{-29}{-5}$ Simplify.

$x = \dfrac{29}{5}$ or $5\dfrac{4}{5}$ The solution set is $\{\dfrac{29}{5}\}$.

b) $(5x + 2)^2 - (4x - 5)^2 = (3x + 7)^2$ Simplify.

$(25x^2 + 20x + 4) - (16x^2 - 40x + 25) = 9x^2 + 42x + 49$

$25x^2 + 20x + 4 - 16x^2 + 40x - 25 = 9x^2 + 42x + 49$

$9x^2 + 60x - 21 = 9x^2 + 42x + 49$ Subtract $9x^2$ and $42x$ from both sides.

$9x^2 + 60x - 21 - 9x^2 - 42x$
$\qquad\qquad = 9x^2 + 42x + 49 - 9x^2 - 42x$

$18x - 21 = 49$ Add 21 to both sides of the equation and simplify.

$18x - 21 + 21 = 49 + 21$ Simplify.

$\dfrac{18x}{18} = \dfrac{70}{18}$ Divide both sides by 18 and reduce.

$x = \dfrac{35}{9}$ or $3\dfrac{8}{9}$

The solution set is $\{\dfrac{35}{9}\}$.

CONTRADICTIONS AND IDENTITIES

Some equations have no solutions (contradictions) and some equations have all real numbers as their solutions (identities). Determine if the following equations are contradictions or identities.

EXAMPLE 3.5

Solve the following equations for x:
a) $2(x+3) - (x-5) = x+7$
b) $3(x+5) - 2(4x+3) + (6x-5) = x+4$

SOLUTION 3.5

a) $2(x+3) - (x-5) = x+7$ Simplify.
    $2x+6-x+5 = x+7$ Combine like terms.
    $x+11 = x+7$ Subtract x from both sides.
    $x+11-x = x+7-x$ Simplify.
    $11 = 7$ Since $11 \neq 7$, this equation is a contradiction and the solution set is the empty set, $\{\ \}$.

b) $3(x+5) - 2(4x+3) + (6x-5) = x+4$

    Simplify.

    $3x+15-8x-6+6x-5 = x+4$
    $x+4 = x+4$ Subtract x from both sides.
    $x+4-x = x+4-x$ Simplify.
    $4 = 4$ The equation is an identity. The solution set is the set of all real numbers R.

    $R = \{x \mid x \text{ is a real number}\}$

EXERCISE 3.1

Solve the following equations for x:

1. $4x+3 = 2x+17$

2. $5x-6 = 2(x-3)+9$

3. $2(3x+2) - 3(4x-7) = 5$

4. $3(4x-2) -7 = 2(3x-7) -3$

5. $5x(3x-2) -5 = 2x(6x-5) + 3x(x-7)$

6. $3(x-4) -7(3x-5) +5(x-4) = 3(2x-4) -17$

7. $2(3x-5) - 3(2x-7) = 3x-6$

8. $(x-4)(2x-5) - (2x-5)(x-3) = 4$

9. $(x+2)^2 = x^2 - 3x + 5$

10. $(2x+5)^2 - x(4x-1) = 3x$

11. $(2x-3)(x-5) = 2x^2 - 13x + 15$

12. $2(x+5) - 3(4x-2) = 2(7-5x) + 3$

13. $3(x-2) + 4(x-5) = 13(x-2) - 3x$

14. $(2x-3)(x+5) - 2(x^2 + 2x - 7) = 5$

ANSWERS TO EXERCISE 3.1

1. $\{7\}$ 　　　　　　　　　　　　2. $\{3\}$

3. $\{\dfrac{10}{3}\}$ 　　　　　　　　　4. $\{-\dfrac{2}{3}\}$

5. $\{\dfrac{5}{21}\}$ 　　　　　　　　　6. $\{\dfrac{32}{19}\}$

7. $\{\dfrac{5}{3}\}$ 　　　　　　　　　8. $\{\dfrac{1}{2}\}$

9. $\{\dfrac{1}{7}\}$ 　　　　　　　　　10. $\{-\dfrac{25}{18}\}$

11. $R = \{x \mid x = x\}$ 　　　　　12. $\varnothing$

13. $\{0\}$ 　　　　　　　　　　　14. $\{2\}$

SECTION 3.2 APPLICATIONS INVOLVING LINEAR EQUATIONS

The techniques we use to solve linear equations can be applied to many practical problems. Several of these applications — number, age, distance-rate-time, money, mixture and geometry problems — are discussed in this section. While there is no one way to solve all word problems, many word problems follow similar kinds of patterns. Here are some strategies for solving word problems:

1. Read the problem carefully. Be sure you understand what is being asked. Determine the type of problem you need to solve.

2. Determine how many unknown quantities there are. Give the unknown quantities a variable name. Whenever possible, try to represent each unknown in terms of the same variable, say x.

3. List the known quantities. The known quantities may include formulas or other information you know about solving problems.

4. Construct an equation that will connect/link/relate the information that is known with the information you are trying to find.

5. Solve the equation. Answer all of the questions from the original problem.

6. Check your solution for accuracy and to see if it makes sense. For example, if you are asked to determine a person's age, the solution should not be a negative number.

Number Problems

Number problems provide us with opportunity to work with the strategies for solving word problems.

EXAMPLE 3.6

Solve the following number problems:
a) The sum of two consecutive integers is 133. Find the integers.
b) The sum of three consecutive even integers is 54. Find the integers.
c) In a two-digit number the tens' digit is 2 less than the units' digit. The number itself equals the sum of five times the tens' digit and four times the units' digit. Find the number.

SOLUTION 3.6

a) There are two unknowns in this problem: the two consecutive integers. Notice that consecutive integers like 5 and 6 differ by one unit. If we let x = the first consecutive integer x, then $x + 1$ = the second integer. The sum of the two integers is 133. So

$x + (x + 1) = 133$ Simplify.

$2x + 1 = 133$ Subtract 1 from both sides.

$2x = 132$ Divide both sides by 2.

$x = 66$

$x + 1 = 67$

If we check the result, $66 + 67 = 133$. The solution set is $\{66, 67\}$.

b) There are three unknowns. This time the unknowns are not consecutive integers, but consecutive even integers. Notice that consecutive even integers like 4, 6, and 8 differ by 2. Label the three integers so that

1st even integer $= x$
2nd even integer $= x + 2$
3rd even integer $= x + 4$

The sum of the three integers is 54. Write the equation and solve.

$x + (x + 2) + (x + 4) = 54$ Simplify.
$x + x + 2 + x + 4 = 54$
$3x + 6 = 54$ Subtract 6 from both sides.
$3x = 48$ Divide both sides by 3.
$x = 16 \quad x + 2 = 18 \quad x + 4 = 20$

If we check our answers, we find $16 + 18 + 20 = 54$. The solution set is $\{16, 18, 20\}$.

c) This problem has two unknowns: the units' digits and the tens' digit. Label the unknown values:

Units' $= x$
Tens' $= x - 2$

A two digit number has a value of 10 times the tens' digit plus 1 times the ones' digit. (For example, $7 = 4 \cdot 10 + 7 \cdot 1$.) Similarly, the value of our number is $10 \cdot (x - 2) + 1 \cdot x$. The problem also states that our number is equal to the sum of five times the tens' digit and four times the units' digit or $5 \cdot (x - 2) + 4 \cdot x$. Therefore,

$10(x - 2) + x = 5(x - 2) + 4x$ Solve.
$10x - 20 + x = 5x - 10 + 4x$ Simplify.
$11x - 20 = 9x - 10$ Subtract $9x$ from both sides.
$2x - 20 = -10$ Add 20 to both sides.
$2x = 10$ Divide both sides by 2.
$x = 5 \quad x - 2 = 3$

5 is the value of the units' digit and 3 is the value of the tens' digit. The number is 35. Now let's check our answer: $5 \cdot 3 + 4 \cdot 5 = 35$. The solution set is $\{35\}$.

Age Problems

EXAMPLE 3.7

a) The sum of the present ages of Bill and his father is 60 years. In six years his father will be twice as old as Bill will be. Find their present ages.

SOLUTION 3.7

a) This age problem has several unknowns: Bill's age and his father's age and now Bill's age and his father's age in six years. Age problems usually have too many unknowns to list them all. To solve an age problem build an age table. Make a table with the rows for Bill's age and his father's age and columns for present age and age in six years. Let x = Bill's age. Since the sum of Bill's age and his father's age is 60, let his father's age = $60 - x$. In six years, Bill's age will = $x + 6$ and his father's age will = $(60 - x) + 6$.

	Present Age	**Age in Six Years**
Bill's Age	x	$x + 6$
Father's Age	$60 - x$	$(60 - x) + 6$

The problem states that in 6 years,
Bill's father will be twice as old as Bill. Write an equation and solve.
Father's age in six years equals Bill's age in six years

$(60 - x) + 6 = 2(x + 6)$	Simplify.
$66 - x = 2x + 12$	Add x to both sides.
$66 = 3x + 12$	Subtract 12 from both sides.
$54 = 3x$	Divide both sides by 3.
$18 = x$	Bill's current age.
$60 - 18 = 42$	Bill's father's current age.

Bill is 18 years old. Since Bill's age and his father's age add to 60, Bill's father is $60 - x = 42$ years old. In 6 years Bill will be 24 years old and his father will be 48 years old. 48 is twice 24, thus the answer checks.

Distance-Rate-Time

Distance-rate-time problems make use of the formula that the distance an object travels is equal to the rate at which it travels multiplied by the time it travels at that rate. That is,

$$d = r \cdot t.$$

We will make use of this formula to solve distance-rate-time problems.

EXAMPLE 3.8

a) Two cars traveling in opposite directions were 240 miles apart at the end of 4 hours. If one car traveled 6 miles per hour faster than the other car, find the rate of each car.

b) Two bicyclists leave towns which are 301 miles apart and travel directly towards each other. One bicyclist averages 25 miles per hour, which is 7 miles per hour more than the other. When will they meet? How far will they be from the towns?

SOLUTION 3.8

a) Two cars traveling in opposite directions were 240 miles apart at the end of 4 hours. If one car traveled 6 miles per hour faster than the other car, find the rate of each car.

It is generally helpful to use a table with distance-rate-time problems to help organize information. The problem states that both cars travel for 4 hours; thus time = 4. One car travels 6 miles per hour faster than the other car. If we let x = rate for the first car (Car A), then the rate for the second car (Car B) = $x + 6$.

	Rate	Time	Distance
Car A	x	4	
Car B	$x + 6$	4	

Recalling that distance equals rate • time, we can complete the table.

	Rate •	Time	= Distance
Car A	x	4	$4x$
Car B	$x + 6$	4	$4(x + 6)$

The cars traveled opposite directions and were 240 miles apart after 4 hours. Thus, the distance the first car traveled plus the distance the second car traveled must equal the total distance apart.

$4x + 4(x + 6) = 240$	Simplify.
$4x + 4x + 24 = 240$	Combine like terms.
$8x + 24 = 240$	Subtract 24 from both sides.
$8x = 216$	Divide both sides by 8.

$x = 27$ miles per hour = rate of Car A
$x + 6 = 33$ miles per hour = rate of Car B

Checking the problem,
$4 \cdot 27 + 4 \cdot 33 = 108 + 132 = 240$.

b) Two bicyclists leave towns which are 301 miles apart and travel towards each other. If one bicyclist averages 7 miles per hour more than the other and they meet in 6 hours, find their respective rates of travel.

Build a travel table with distance problems. Put rate, time and distance along the top of the table and bicyclist 1 and 2 on the side of the table. The problem states that the two bicyclists meet in seven hours and one bicyclist travels 7 miles per hour faster than the other. If we label the rate of the first bicyclist x miles per hour, then the second one goes $x + 7$ miles per hour.

	Rate	**Time**	**Distance**
Bicyclist 1	x	7	
Bicyclist 2	$x + 7$	7	

Since distance is equal to rate times time, the product of the first two columns is equal to the third column.

	Rate	**•**	**Time**	**=**	**Distance**
Bicyclist 1	x		7		$7x$
Bicyclist 2	$x + 7$		7		$7(x + 7)$

The problem indicates that the bicyclists were traveling in the same direction and were 237 miles apart, so the distance traveled by the first bicyclist plus the distance traveled by the second bicyclist equal the total distance apart.

$7x + (x + 7)\,7 = 301$	Simplify.
$7x + 7x + 49 = 301$	Combine like terms.
$14x + 49 = 301$	Add -49 to both sides of the equation.
$14x + 49 - 49 = 301 - 49$	Simplify.
$14x = 252$	Divide both sides by 14.
$\dfrac{14x}{14} = \dfrac{252}{14}$	

$x = 18$ miles per hour.

x is the rate of the first bicyclist, so the rate of the second bicyclist is 25 miles per hour. Check the problem; $7 \cdot 18 + 7 \cdot 25 = 126 + 175 = 301$. The problem checks.

Money Problems

As with time-rate problems, using a table helps us organize information needed to solve word problems about money.

EXAMPLE 3.9

a) Barbara has $4.75 in nickels, dimes, and quarters. She has twice as many dimes as quarters and 7 more nickels than dimes. How many of each kind of coin does Barbara have?

SOLUTION 3.9

a) Let x equal the number of quarters. The number of dimes is twice the number of quarters, or $2x$, and the number of nickels is 7 more than the number of dimes, or $2x + 7$.

	Number of coins	Value of each coin	Total Value
Nickels	$2x + 7$	.05	
Dimes	$2x$	.10	
Quarters	x	.25	

Multiply the number of coins times the value of the coin to complete the total value in the table.

	Number of coins	Value of each coin	Total Value
Nickels	$2x + 7$	.05	$.05(2x + 7)$
Dimes	$2x$	.10	$.20x$
Quarters	x	.25	$.25x$

The total amount of money Barbara has is $4.75. Thus

$0.05(2x + 7) + 0.20x + 0.25x = 4.75$ Solve the equation.
$0.10x + 0.35 + 0.20x + 0.25x = 4.75$ Simplify.
$0.55x + 0.35 = 4.75$ Subtract .35 from both sides.
$0.55x = 4.40$ Divide both sides by .55.
$x = 8$ quarters

$2x = 16$ dimes

$2x + 7 = 23$ nickels

Checking our answer,

$(8 \times 0.25) + (16 \times 0.10) + (23 \times 0.05) =$

$\$2.00 + \$1.60 + \$1.15 = \$4.75.$

Mixture Problems

Mixture problems are problems where two or more quantities are mixed to equal a third quantity. Again a mixture table is helpful to solve mixture problems.

EXAMPLE 3.10

a) A chemist has two acid solutions, one is 65% acid and the other is 20% acid. How much of each should he mix in order to have 100 cc. of an acid solution which is 47% acid?

SOLUTION 3.10

a) The amount of 65% acid solution and 20% acid solution are unknown. Let $x =$ the amount of 65% solution. Since the total mixture is 100 cc., the amount of 20% acid solution = $100 - x$.

	Amount Solution	Percent Acid	Total Acid
65% Acid	x	0.65	
20% Acid	$100 - x$	0.20	
Mixture	100	0.47	

Multiply the amount of each solution by the percent of acid to complete the table.

	Amount Solution	Percent Acid	Total Acid
65% Acid	x	0.65	$0.65x$
20% Acid	$100 - x$	0.20	$0.20(100 - x)$
Mixture	100	0.47	$0.47(100)$

We need to add the total 65% acid with the total 20% acid to get the

47% mix. Our equation becomes:

$0.65x + 0.20(100 - x) = 0.47(100)$ Remove parentheses and combine like terms.

$0.65x + 20.00 - 0.20x = 47.00$

$0.45x + 20.00 = 47.00$ Subtract 20 from both sides.

$0.45x = 27$ Divide both sides by 0.45.

$x = 60$ cc. of 65% acid

$100 - x = 100 - 60 = 40$ cc. of 20% acid

Checking our answer,

$60(0.65) + 40(0.20) = 39 + 8 = 47$

which is equal to $100(0.47) = 47$.

Geometry Problems

Solving most geometry problems requires that you apply standard formulas you studied in an earlier mathematics course. Several of these are restated below.

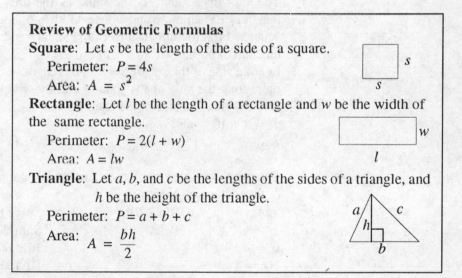

Review of Geometric Formulas

Square: Let s be the length of the side of a square.

Perimeter: $P = 4s$

Area: $A = s^2$

Rectangle: Let l be the length of a rectangle and w be the width of the same rectangle.

Perimeter: $P = 2(l + w)$

Area: $A = lw$

Triangle: Let a, b, and c be the lengths of the sides of a triangle, and h be the height of the triangle.

Perimeter: $P = a + b + c$

Area: $A = \dfrac{bh}{2}$

EXAMPLE 3.11

a) The length of a rectangle is 5 feet more than its width. If the perimeter of the rectangle is 134 feet, find its dimensions.

b) The area of a square is the same as the area of a rectangle whose length is 10 feet more and whose width is 6 feet less than a side of the square. Find the dimensions of the square and the rectangle and find the area of both.

c) The longest side of a triangle is twice the length of the shortest side. The third side of the triangle is the average of the shortest side and the longest sides. If the perimeter of the triangle is 36 inches, find the lengths of the three sides of the triangle.

SOLUTION 3.11

a) The length of a rectangle is 5 feet more than its width. If the perimeter of the rectangle is 134 feet, find its dimensions.

Let the width of the rectangle $w = x$. Then the length $l = x + 5$. The perimeter P is 134 feet. Since $P = 2(l + w)$, we have

$134 = 2((x + 5) + x)$	Solve this equation.
$134 = 2(2x + 5)$	
$134 = 4x + 10$	Subtract 10 from both sides.
$124 = 4x$	Divide both sides by 4.
$31 = x$	

$x = 31$ feet $=$ width
$x + 5 = 36$ feet $=$ length
Checking our answer,
$2(31) + 2(36) = 62 + 72 = 134$.

b) The area of a square is the same as the area of a rectangle whose length is 10 feet more and whose width is 6 feet less than a side of the square. Find the dimensions of the square and the rectangle and find the area of both.

Let one side of the square $s = x$. The length of the rectangle is 10 feet more than the side of the square, and the width of the rectangle is 6 feet less than the side of the square.

$1 = x + 10$ and $w = x - 6$. So

$$A_{\text{square}} = (x)^2 \qquad A_{\text{rectangle}} = (x + 10)(x - 6)$$

The problem states that the area of the square is the same as the area of the rectangle. Hence,

$(x)^2 = (x + 10)(x - 6)$	Solve the equation.
$x^2 = x^2 + 4x - 60$	Subtract x^2 from both sides.
$0 = 4x - 60$	Add 60 to both sides.
$60 = 4x$	Divide both sides by 4.
$15 = x$	

$x = 15$ feet $=$ side of square
$x + 10 = 25$ feet $=$ length of rectangle
$x - 6 = 9$ feet $=$ width of rectangle
Checking our answer,
$$A_{\text{square}} = (15)^2 = 225 \text{ square feet}$$
and
$$A_{\text{rectangle}} = (25)(9) = 225 \text{ square feet}.$$

c) The longest side of a triangle is twice the length of the shortest side. The third side of the triangle is the average of the shortest side and the longest sides. If the perimeter of the triangle is 36 inches, find the lengths of the three sides of the triangle.

Let a be the shortest side, and c be the longest side and let $a = x$. Then $c = 2x$. Since b is the average of a and c, then $b = \frac{1}{2}(x + 2x)$.

$$P = a + b + c = x + \frac{1}{2}(3x) + 2x$$

Since the perimeter $P = 36$ inches, then

$36 = x + \frac{3}{2}x + 2x$ Solve the equation.

$36 = \frac{9}{2}x$ Multiply both sides by 2.

$72 = 9x$ Divide both sides by 9.

$8 = x$

$a = x = 8$ in

$c = 2x = 16$ in.

$b = \frac{1}{2}(8 + 16) = 12$ in.

Checking our answer,
$8 + 16 + 12 = 36$.

EXERCISE 3.2

Solve the following word problems. Check your answers.

1. Uncle Bob is twice as old as his nephew, and eight years ago he was three times as old as his nephew. Find their present ages.

2. A goldsmith has two alloys of gold. The first alloy is 90% pure gold and the second alloy is 60% pure gold. How many ounces of each alloy must he mix to make 45 ounces of an alloy which is 72% pure gold?

3. Two sides of a triangle are equal length and the third side is 2 feet longer than the sum of the other two. If the perimeter of the triangle is 26 feet, how long is each side?

4. A hiker can climb a mountain trail at the rate of 2 miles per hour and he can descend the same trail at the rate of 5 miles per hour. If he starts up the trail at 12:00 noon and returns at 12:42 PM, how far up the trail has he gone?

5. How much pure alcohol should be mixed with 25 ounces of a 40% solution to obtain a 60% solution?

6. The area of a rectangle 64 feet long is the same as the area of a 16-foot square. Find the width of the rectangle.

ANSWERS TO EXERCISE 3.2

1. Uncle Bob is 32 years old, Nephew is 16 years old

2. 18 oz of 90% gold mixed with 27 oz of 60% gold
3. 6ft, 6 ft, 14 ft
4. 1 mile
5. 12.5 oz of pure alcohol
6. 4 ft

SECTION 3.3 LINEAR INEQUALITIES

Many of the skills that we developed to solve linear equations will also help us solve linear inequalities. Recall that if we write $a < b$, we are saying that a is less than b; there exists a real positive number c such that $a + c = b$. Similarly, $a > b$ means a is greater than b. The statement $a \leq b$ means that either a is less than b or a is equal to b, while the statement $a \geq b$ means that either a is greater than b or a is equal to b.

Properties of Inequalities

> **Properties of Inequalities:**
> For all real numbers a, b and c,
> 1. If $a < b$, then $b > a$. **Property of Symmetry**
> 2. If $a < b$ and $b < c$, then $a < c$. **Transitive Property**
> 3. If $a < b$, then $a + c < b + c$. **Addition Property**
> 4. If $a < b$, then $a - c < b - c$. **Subtraction Property**
> 5. If $a < b$ and $c > 0$, then $a \cdot c < b \cdot c$ **Multiplication Property Positive**
> 6. If $a < b$ and $c < 0$, then $a \cdot c > b \cdot c$ **Multiplication Property Negative**
> 7. If $a < b$ and $c > 0$, then $\dfrac{a}{c} < \dfrac{b}{c}$. **Division Property Positive**
> 8. If $a < b$ and $c < 0$, then $\dfrac{a}{c} > \dfrac{b}{c}$. **Division Property Negative**

Similar properties hold for $>$, $\leq$ and $\geq$. Notice that there are two properties for multiplication and two properties for division. If we multiply or divide both sides of an inequality by a negative number ($c < 0$), the sign of the inequality reverses direction, that is $<$ becomes $>$, $>$ becomes $<$, $\leq$ becomes $\geq$, and $\geq$ becomes $\leq$.

> **The order of the inequality reverses if both sides of an inequality is multiplied or divided by a negative number.**

Solving Two-Part Inequalities

EXAMPLE 3.12

Solve the following linear inequalities for x.

a) $3x - 5 > x + 7$

b) $2(3x - 7) - 5(4x - 3) > 15$

c) $\dfrac{2}{3}(4x - 6) + \dfrac{1}{2}(3x + 2) \le \dfrac{3}{4}(2x - 7)$

SOLUTION 3.12

a) $3x - 5 > x + 7$ — Subtract x from both sides.

$3x - 5 - x > x + 7 - x$ — Simplify.

$2x - 5 > 7$ — Add 5 to both sides.

$2x - 5 + 5 > 7 + 5$ — Simplify.

$2x > 12$ — Divide both sides of the inequality by 2.

$\dfrac{2x}{2} > \dfrac{12}{2}$ — Simplify.

$x > 6$ — The solution set is $\{x \mid x > 6\}$.

b) $2(3x - 7) - 5(4x - 3) > 15$ — Remove parentheses.

$6x - 14 - 20x + 15 > 15$ — Simplify.

$-14x + 1 > 15$ — Subtract 1 from both sides.

$-14x + 1 - 1 > 15 - 1$ — Simplify.

$-14x > 14$ — Divide both sides by -14. Since we are dividing by a negative number, we must reverse the inequality (from $>$ to $<$).

$\dfrac{-14x}{-14} < \dfrac{14}{-14}$ — Simplify.

$x < -1$ — The solution set is $\{x \mid x < -1\}$.

c) $\dfrac{2}{3}(4x - 6) + \dfrac{1}{2}(3x + 2) \le \dfrac{3}{4}(2x - 7)$ — Remove parentheses.

$\dfrac{8}{3}x - 4 + \dfrac{3}{2}x + 1 \le \dfrac{3}{2}x - \dfrac{21}{4}$ — Multiply both sides by the LCD 12 and simplify.

$12 \cdot \dfrac{8}{3}x - 12 \cdot 4 + 12 \cdot \dfrac{3}{2}x + 12 \cdot 1 \le 12 \cdot \dfrac{3}{2}x - 12 \cdot \dfrac{21}{4}$

$32x - 48 + 18x + 12 \le 18x - 63$

$50x - 36 \le 18x - 63$ — Subtract $18x$ from both sides.

$32x - 36 \le -63$ — Add 36 to both sides.

$$32x \leq -27$$ Divide both sides by 32.

$$x \leq \frac{-27}{32}$$ The solution set is

$$\{x \mid x \leq \frac{-27}{32}\}.$$

Solving Three-Part Inequalities

While equalities have only two parts — the right side and the left side— an inequality can have three different parts: the left side, the right side, and a middle part. Inequalities like these are called "in between" inequalities.

EXAMPLE 3.13

Solve the following linear inequalities for x.

a) $-2 \leq 2x - 8 \leq 12$

b) $4 \leq 3(2x - 4) - 2(4x - 6) < 16$

c) $7 \leq \frac{2}{3}(5x - 9) - \frac{5}{6}(9x - 2) < 15$

SOLUTION 3.13

a) $-2 \leq 2x - 8 \leq 12$ Add 8 to each part of the inequality.

$$-2 + 8 \leq 2x - 8 + 8 \leq 12 + 8$$ Simplify.
$$6 \leq 2x \leq 20$$ Divide each part of the inequality by 2.

$$\frac{6}{2} \leq \frac{2x}{2} \leq \frac{20}{2}$$ Simplify.

$$3 \leq x \leq 10$$

The solution to this inequality indicates that x falls between or equal to 3 and 10.

b) $4 \leq 3(2x - 4) - 2(4x - 6) < 16$ Remove all parentheses.
$$4 \leq 6x - 12 - 8x + 12 < 16$$ Simplify.
$$4 \leq -2x < 16$$ Divide all parts of the inequality by –2. Since we are dividing by a negative number, all inequality signs will reverse.

Simplify.

$$\frac{4}{-2} \geq \frac{-2x}{-2} > \frac{16}{-2}$$

$$-2 \geq x > 8$$
$$-8 < x \leq -2$$

c) $7 \leq \frac{2}{3}(5x - 9) - \frac{5}{6}(9x - 2) < 15$ Remove parentheses and simplify.

$7 \leq \frac{10}{3}x - 6 - \frac{15}{2}x + \frac{5}{3} < 15$ Multiply each part of the inequality by 6 and simplify.

$6 \cdot 7 \leq 6 \cdot \frac{10}{3}x - 6 \cdot 6 - 6 \cdot \frac{15}{2}x + 6 \cdot \frac{5}{3} < 6 \cdot 15$

$42 \leq 20x - 36 - 45x + 10 < 90$ Combine like terms.

$42 \leq -25x - 26 < 90$ Add 26 to all parts.

$42 + 26 \leq -25x - 26 + 26 < 90 + 26$ Simplify.

$68 \leq -25x < 116$ Divide all parts of the inequality by –25. Since we are dividing by a negative number, we must reverse all inequality signs.

$$\frac{68}{-25} \geq \frac{-25x}{-25} > \frac{116}{-25}$$

$$\frac{68}{-25} \geq x > \frac{116}{-25}$$

The solution set is $\{x| -\frac{116}{25} < x \leq -\frac{68}{25}\}$

$(\frac{116}{-25}, \frac{68}{-25}]$

EXERCISE 3.3

Solve the following inequalities for x. Write your answer in set notation.

1. $3x - 5 \geq 7$

2. $2(3x - 5) \leq 8x - 5$

3. $(x - 2)(x + 3) \leq (x - 5)(x - 8)$

4. $3 - 2x > -5$

5. $-2 \leq 3x + 4 < 13$

6. $15 \leq 3 - 6x \leq 21$

7. $-5 \leq \frac{1}{2}x - 3 < 10$

8. $\frac{3}{4} < \frac{2}{3} - \frac{5}{6}x \leq \frac{9}{4}$

ANSWERS TO EXERCISE 3.3

1. $\{x| x \geq 4\}$ 2. $\{x| x \geq -\frac{5}{2}\}$

3. $\{x|\, x \le \frac{23}{7}\}$ 4. $\{x|\, x < 4\}$

5. $\{x|\, -2 \le x < 3\}$ 6. $\{x|\, -3 \le x < -2\}$

7. $\{x|\, -4 \le x < 26\}$ 8. $\{x|\, -\frac{19}{10} \le x < \frac{1}{10}\}$

SECTION 3.4 ABSOLUTE VALUE EQUATIONS AND INEQUALITIES

From Chapter 1 we know the definition of absolute value. Let's review that definition.

Definition: Let x be any real number, then

$$|x| = \begin{cases} x & \text{if } x > 0 \\ 0 & \text{if } x = 0 \\ -x & \text{if } x < 0 \end{cases}$$

By the definition the absolute value of x is itself if x is positive, is zero if x is zero, and is the opposite of x if x is negative. The definition gives the appearance that some absolute values are negative. This is not the case. $|x| = -x$ for negative numbers. What this means is that $|\text{negative}| = -(\text{negative})$. The absolute value of a number is its distance from zero which is always considered to be non-negative.

Absolute Value Equations

To solve an absolute value equation we must eliminate the absolute value sign from the equation. To do this we need the following theorem.

Theorem: For real numbers $a \ge 0$ and all real numbers x,

$|x| = a$ if and only if $x = a$ and $x = -a$.

In using this theorem, it must be understood that the number a outside of the absolute value sign must be non-negative. If a is negative, then the equation is a contradiction (has no solutions). This theorem indicates how to remove the absolute value sign for the equation. To eliminate the absolute value sign take what is inside of the absolute value and set it equal to a and take what is inside of the absolute value sign and set it equal to the opposite of a.

EXAMPLE 3.14

Remove the absolute value sign from the following equations and find the solutions if there are any:

a) $|x| = 4$
b) $|x| = 13$
c) $|x| = -3$

SOLUTION 3.14

a) $|x| = 4$

To remove the absolute value sign from the equation, take what is inside of the absolute value sign and set it equal to 4 and –4.

$x = 4$ and $x = -4$. The solution set is $\{x \mid x = 4 \text{ and } x = -4\}$.

b) $|x| = 13$

Since the absolute value of x is equal to 13, we take x and make it equal to 13 and –13.

$x = 13$ and $x = -13$. The solution set is $\{x \mid x = 13 \text{ and } x = -13\}$.

c) $|x| = -3$

This problem is impossible. The $|x| \neq -3$. Absolute values are always non-negative.

An interesting fact about absolute value equations is the distance between two points on a number line. To find the distance between two points on a number line, we take the absolute value of their difference.

Distance Between Points A and B

Let A and B be points on the number line with coordinates of a and b, respectively. The distance from A to B is given by,

$$d(A, B) = |b - a|.$$

The notation $d(A, B)$ is called the distance from A to B. It is also called the length of the line segment $\overline{AB}$. Keep in mind, $d(A, B) = d(B, A)$. The following theorem emphasizes this fact.

Theorem of Absolute Values: Let a and b be any real number, then

$$|a - b| = |b - a|$$

Let A and B be two points on the number line with coordinates of $a = 3$ and $b = 7$. Graphically, we get.

$$d(A, B) = |b - a| = |7 - 3| = 4$$

Suppose that the coordinate of A is unknown. That is, $|7 - a| = 4$. This does not mean that a has to be 3. Remember that absolute value equations have a possibility of having two solutions. Certainly, the coordinate of a could be equal to 3. We see that from the previous example, but the coordinate of a could also be 11. This brings up an interesting way to solve absolute value equations.

EXAMPLE 3.15

Solve the following absolute value equations if possible:

a) $|x - 3| = 5$

b) $|x - 18| = 23$

SOLUTION 3.15

a) $|x - 3| = 5$

To solve the absolute value equation we must use the theorem about absolute value equations. We take what is inside the absolute value sign and set it equal to 5 and equal to –5.

$$x - 3 = 5 \quad \text{or} \quad x - 3 = -5$$

Now solve both equations. Solve the first equation.

$x - 3 = 5$	Add +3 to both sides.
$x - 3 + 3 = 5 + 3$	Simplify.
$x = 8$	

Solve the second equation.

$x - 3 = -5$	Add +3 to both sides.
$x - 3 + 3 = -5 + 3$	Simplify.
$x = -2$	

This means that both 8 and –2 are 5 units away from 3. The solution set is $\{x \mid x = 8 \text{ and } -2\}$.

b) $|x - 18| = 23$

Remove the absolute value signs.

$$x - 18 = 23 \quad \text{or} \quad x - 18 = -23$$

Solve both equations.

$x - 18 = 23$	Add +18 to both sides of the equation.
$x - 18 + 18 = 23 + 18$	Simplify.
$x = 41$	

or

$x - 18 = -23$	Add + 18 to both sides of the equation.
$x - 18 + 18 = -23 + 18$	Simplify.
$x = -5$	

41 and –5 are 23 units away from 18. The solution set is $\{x \mid x = 41 \text{ and } -5\}$.

Absolute value equations can be more complicated and yet, the same theorem is used to solve them.

EXAMPLE 3.16

Solve the following absolute value equation if possible: $|2x + 3| = 7$.

SOLUTION 3.16

$|2x + 3| = 7$

To solve this absolute value equation we take what is inside of the absolute value sign and set it equal to 7 or –7.

$$2x + 3 = 7 \quad \text{or} \quad 2x + 3 = -7$$

Solve both equations.

$2x + 3 = 7$	Add –3 to both sides of the equation.
$2x + 3 - 3 = 7 - 3$	Simplify.
$2x = 4$	Divide both sides by 2.
$\dfrac{2x}{2} = \dfrac{4}{2}$	Simplify again.
$x = 2$	

or

$2x + 3 = -7$	Add –3 to both sides of the equation.
$2x + 3 - 3 = -7 - 3$	Simplify.
$2x = -10$	Divide both sides by 2.
$\dfrac{2x}{2} = \dfrac{-10}{2}$	Simplify again.
$x = -5$	

The solution set is $\{x \mid x = 2 \text{ and } -5\}$.

Some of the following examples may not have solutions.

EXAMPLE 3.17

Solve the following absolute value equations if possible:

a) $2 \cdot |4x + 5| - 11 = 23$
b) $2 \cdot |2x - 4| + 14 = 2$

SOLUTION 3.17

a) $2 \cdot |4x + 5| - 11 = 23$

In all of the previous absolute value equations, the absolute value sign was on one side of the equation by itself. To solve an absolute value equation, we must isolate the absolute value sign on one side of the equation. In this problem, we must eliminate the –11 and the 2 before we can use the theorems on absolute value.

$2 \cdot |4x + 5| - 11 = 23$	Add +11 to both sides of the equation.
$2 \cdot |4x + 5| - 11 + 11 = 23 + 11$	Simplify.
$2 \cdot |4x + 5| = 34$	Divide both sides by 2.

$$\frac{2 \cdot |4x+5|}{2} = \frac{34}{2}$$ Simplify again.

$$|4x+5| = 17$$ Now that the absolute value sign is isolated on one side of the equation, we can use the theorem on absolute values to remove the absolute value sign. Break the equation into two equations.

$4x+5 = 17$ or $4x+5 = -17$ Solve both equations.

$4x+5 = 17$ Add –5 to both sides of the equation.

$4x+5-5 = 17-5$ Simplify.

$4x = 12$ Divide both sides by 4.

$$\frac{4x}{4} = \frac{12}{4}$$ Simplify.

$x = 3$

or

$4x+5 = -17$ Add –5 to both sides of the equation.

$4x+5-5 = -17-5$ Simplify.

$4x = -22$ Divide both sides by 4.

$$\frac{4x}{4} = \frac{-22}{4}$$ Simplify.

$$x = \frac{-11}{2}$$

The solution set is $\{x \mid x = 3 \text{ and } \frac{-11}{2}\}$.

b) $2 \cdot |2x-4| + 14 = 2$

Eliminate the 14 and the 2 to get the absolute value sign on one side of the equation by itself.

$2 \cdot |2x-4| + 14 = 2$ Add –14 to both sides of the equation.

$2 \cdot |2x-4| + 14 - 14 = 2 - 14$ Simplify.

$2 \cdot |2x-4| = -12$ Divide both sides by 2.

$$\frac{2 \cdot |2x-4|}{2} = \frac{-12}{2}$$ Simplify again.

$|2x-4| = -4$

The solution set is $\varnothing$.

This absolute value equation is impossible to solve. Absolute values cannot equal a negative number. It might have been observed back in the third step when $2 \cdot |2x - 4| = -12$ that the problem was a contradiction. Anytime you observe that the equation is a contradiction; **stop**. You are wasting your time trying to solve a contradiction.

Absolute Value Inequalities

Remember the meaning of an absolute value equation.
$$|x| = 4 \quad \text{means } x = 4 \text{ or } x = -4$$
Graphically represented by:

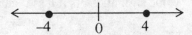

$x = 4$ and $x = -4$ are the only values of x on the number line that make the equation true. All other numbers are such that $|x| \neq 4$. Remember $|x| \neq 4$, then either $x > 4$ or $x < 4$. For all real numbers x,

1. $|x| < 4$ if $-4 < x < 4$ and
2. $|x| > 4$ if $x > 4$ or $x < -4$.

Graphically:

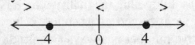

This adds new theorems on absolute value equations and inequalities:

Theorems: For real numbers $a > 0$ and all real numbers x,

1. $|x| = a$ if and only if $x = a$ and $x = -a$.
2. $|x| < a$ if and only if $-a < x < a$.
3. $|x| \leq a$ if and only if $-a \leq x \leq a$.
4. $|x| > a$ if and only if $x > a$ or $x < -a$.
5. $|x| \geq a$ if and only if $x \geq a$ or $x \leq -a$.

Notice that these theorems can only be applied for positive numbers. Theorem 1 will work for $a = 0$, but the other theorems cannot be applied for 0. These theorems allow us to solve many types of absolute value equations and inequalities.

EXAMPLE 3.18

Remove the absolute value signs by using one of the absolute value theorems. If the theorems do not apply, indicate if the problem is a contradiction or an identity.

a) $|x| < 7$
b) $|x| \geq 13$
c) $|x| \leq -5$

SOLUTION 3.18

a) $|x| < 7$

To remove the absolute value sign from the inequality use Theorem 2. Put the value of x between the positive and the negative of the number.

$$-7 < x < 7$$

The solution set is $\{x \mid -7 < x < 7\}$.

b) $|x| \geq 13$

Use Theorem 5 to remove the absolute value sign. For this problem, Theorem 5 takes what is inside of the absolute value sign and sets it greater than or equal to 13 and takes what is inside of the absolute value sign and sets it less than or equal to -13.

$$x \geq 13 \quad \text{or} \quad x \leq -13.$$

The solution set is $\{x \mid x \leq -13 \text{ or } x \geq 13\}$.

c) $|x| \leq -5$

This problem is always false. It is impossible for the $|x| \leq -5$. Absolute values are always nonnegative. If, however, the problem had asked $|x| \geq -5$, then the problem would have been true for all real numbers. Absolute values are always greater than a negative number. An absolute value inequality which is greater than a negative number is an identity and an absolute value inequality which is less than a negative number is always a contradiction.

EXERCISE 3.4

Solve the following equations and inequalities for x. Write your answers as solution sets and in interval notation:

1. $|4x + 12| = 36$

2. $|3x - 9| < 21$

3. $48 \geq |4x - 18|$

4. $24 \geq 6 \cdot |9 - 3x|$

5. $7 \leq |2x - 3|$

6. $|2x - 7| = 36$

7. $4 \cdot |3x + 5| < 16$

8. $-12 \geq |3x - 4|$

9. $14 \geq 4 \cdot |5 - 2x| - 14$

10. $-5 \le |17x + 6|$

ANSWERS TO EXERCISE 3.4

1. $\{-12, 6\}$

2. $\{(-4, 9)\}$

3. $\{\left[-\dfrac{15}{2}, \dfrac{33}{2}\right]\}$

4. $\{\left[-\dfrac{13}{3}, -\dfrac{5}{3}\right]\}$

5. $\{(-\infty, -2] \cup [5, +\infty)\}$

6. $\{-\dfrac{29}{2}, \dfrac{43}{2}\}$

7. $\{(-3, \dfrac{1}{3})\}$

8. $\varnothing$

9. $\{[-1, 6]\}$

10. $R = \{x \mid x = x\}$

SECTION 3.5 COMPLEX NUMBERS

Definitions

The real numbering system consists of positive and negative rational numbers and irrational numbers. In the real numbering system, the $x^2 = -1$ does not have a solution. To solve this equation, we must define what is called the **imaginary unit** i. The imaginary unit i is defined such that $i^2 = -1$. i is not a real number. If i were real then it would be positive or negative. Any positive or negative number squared is not equal to -1. Since $i^2 = -1$, then the $\sqrt{-1} = i$. The following definitions involving i should be memorized.

Definitions:

$$i^0 = 1$$

$$i = \sqrt{-1}$$

$$i^2 = -1$$

$$i^3 = -i$$

The definition of the imaginary unit repeats itself in cycles of 4.

$$i^4 = 1$$

$$i^5 = i^4 \cdot i = 1 \cdot i = i$$

$$i^6 = i^4 \cdot i^2 = 1 \cdot i^2 = -1$$

$$i^7 = i^4 \cdot i^3 = 1 \cdot i^3 = -i$$

$$i^8 = i^4 \cdot i^4 = 1 \cdot 1 = 1 \qquad \text{and so forth.}$$

The imaginary unit combined with real coefficients form what is called a complex number.

Definition:

A **complex number** is any number in the form of $a + bi$ where a and b are real numbers and i is the imaginary unit.

$a + bi$ is said to be in **standard form**.

Complex numbers exist in several different forms.

Forms of Complex Numbers:

i: **Imaginary Unit**

$a + bi$ where a and b are real numbers: **Standard Form Complex Number**

$a + bi$ where $b \neq 0$: **Imaginary Number**

$0 + bi = bi$ where $b \neq 0$: **Pure Imaginary Number**

$a + 0i = a$: **Pure Real Number**

$a + bi$ and $a - bi$: **Conjugate Pairs**

Complex numbers are equal only if they have the same real coefficients.

Equality Between Complex Numbers

$a + bi = c + di$ if and only if $a = c$ and $b = d$.

The complex number becomes important in working with square roots of negative numbers. By definition, $i^2 = -1$ so $\sqrt{-1} = i$. To take the square root of a negative number, we must use the properties of radicals and the imaginary unit.

EXAMPLE 3.19

Standardize the following radicals:
a) $\sqrt{-4}$
b) $(\sqrt{-2}) \cdot (\sqrt{-8})$

SOLUTION 3.19

a) $\sqrt{-4}$ To standardize radicals, we must factor and remove perfect roots.

            $= \sqrt{-4}$ Factor into perfect roots.

$$= \sqrt{-1 \cdot 4}$$ Separate the radicals.
$$= \sqrt{-1} \cdot \sqrt{4}$$ Simplify.
$$= i \cdot 2$$ Simplify again.
$$= 2i$$

b) $(\sqrt{-2}) \cdot (\sqrt{-8})$ Do not multiply the two radicals together. Radicals must be real numbers before they can be multiplied. To standardize this problem we must first remove the -1 from under the radical. Factor and remove the perfect roots.

$$= \sqrt{-1 \cdot 2} \cdot \sqrt{-1 \cdot 4 \cdot 2}$$ Remove the perfect roots.
$$= \sqrt{-1} \cdot \sqrt{2} \cdot \sqrt{-1} \cdot \sqrt{4} \cdot \sqrt{2}$$ Take the square root of each factor.
$$= i\sqrt{2} \cdot 2i\sqrt{2}$$ Multiply the results together.
$$= 2i^2 \cdot \sqrt{2 \cdot 2}$$ Simplify.
$$= 2 \left(i^2 \cdot 2 \right)$$ Simplify again.
$$= 4i^2$$ Remember, $i^2 = -1$
$$= 4 (-1) = -4$$

When standardizing radicals, we must remove all perfect roots. With the introduction of the imaginary unit, we must remove all negative signs from under a square root.

Operations with Complex Numbers

The operations with complex numbers are much like the simplification of algebraic expressions. The imaginary unit i works like any other variable x with the exception that powers of i greater than the first power must be replaced by their equivalent expression.

EXAMPLE 3.20

Simplify the following complex number:
$(2 + 3i) + (5 - 5i) + (7 - 3i)$.

SOLUTION 3.20

Addition and subtraction of complex numbers is like addition and subtraction of variable expressions. Remember, however, that all powers of i in the final answer must be less than or equal to 1.

$(2 + 3i) + (5 - 5i) + (7 - 3i)$ Remove parentheses. Parentheses may be removed by use of the associative property of addition.

$= 2 + 3i + 5 - 5i + 7 - 3i$ Combine like terms.

$$= 14 - 5i$$

To multiply complex numbers we make use of the FOIL method of multiplication.

EXAMPLE 3.21

Simplify the following multiplication problem. Remember, all powers of i must be less than two.

$$(4 + 3i) \ (2 + 7i)$$

SOLUTION 3.21

$(4 + 3i) \ (2 + 7i)$	Remove parentheses by use of FOIL multiplication.
$= 4 \cdot 2 + 4 \cdot 7i + 3i \cdot 2 + 3i \cdot 7i$	Simplify.
$= 8 + 28i + 6i + 21i^2$	Combine like terms and replace i^2 with -1.
$= 8 + 34i + 21 \ (-1)$	Simplify again.
$= 8 + 34i - 21$	Combine like terms.
$= -13 + 34i$	

Notice how the multiplication of two complex numbers gives an answer which is a complex number.

To clear imaginary numbers in the denominators of a fraction or when imaginary numbers are used in division problems, we use the techniques of radicals to clear the radical from the denominator of a fraction.

EXAMPLE 3.22

Simplify the following problems. Leave no imaginary numbers in the denominator of a fraction:

a) $\dfrac{1}{i}$

b) $\dfrac{6 + 5i}{12 - 7i}$

SOLUTION 3.22

a) $\dfrac{1}{i} =$	To remove the imaginary unit from the denominator of the fraction, we multiply the numerator and denominator by i.
$\dfrac{1}{i} \cdot \dfrac{i}{i} =$	Simplify.
$\dfrac{i}{i^2} =$	Replace i^2 with -1.

$$\frac{i}{-1} =$$

Simplify the fraction by dividing by -1.

$$-i$$

b) $\dfrac{6+5i}{12-7i} =$

Multiply numerator and denominator by the conjugate of the denominator.

$$\frac{6+5i}{12-7i} \cdot \frac{12+7i}{12+7i} =$$

Multiply.

$$\frac{(6+5i)}{(12-7i)} \cdot \frac{(12+7i)}{(12+7i)} =$$

Continue.

$$\frac{(6+5i)\,(12+7i)}{(12-7i)\,(12+7i)} =$$

Multiply using FOIL.

$$\frac{72+42i+60i+35i^2}{(12)^2-(7i)^2} =$$

Simplify.

$$\frac{72+102i+35i^2}{144-49i^2} =$$

Replace i^2 with -1.

$$\frac{72+102i+35(-1)}{144-49(-1)} =$$

Simplify again.

$$\frac{72+102i-35}{144+49} =$$

Combine like terms.

$$\frac{37+102i}{193} =$$

Separate the fraction and put the imaginary unit on the side.

$$\frac{37}{193} + \frac{102}{193}i$$

The fractions will not reduce.

EXERCISE 3.5

Simplify the following complex numbers and perform the indicated operations:

1. $\sqrt{-16}$

2. $\sqrt{-36}$

3. $3 - \sqrt{-25}$

4. $2 + 3\sqrt{-49}$

5. $(3 + \sqrt{-18}) + (4 - \sqrt{-50})$

6. $(2 + 3i) + (5 - 4i) - (7 - 8i) + (6 - 5i)$

7. $3(4 + 7i) - 5(6 + 5i) - 7(7 - 8i)$

8. $(4 + 3i)(2 - 5i)$

9. $(3 + 4i)^2$

10. $(3 + 6i)^2(3 - 6i)$

11. $4(3 + 2i)(5 - 3i) + 2(3 + 4i)(2 + 3i)$

12. $\dfrac{1}{3 - 2i}$

13. $\dfrac{3}{4 - 5i}$

14. $\dfrac{2 + 3i}{2 - 3i}$

15. $\dfrac{3 - 5i}{4 - 3i}$

ANSWERS TO EXERCISE 3.5

1. $\{4i\}$

2. $\{6i\}$

3. $\{3 - 5i\}$

4. $\{2 + 21i\}$

5. $\{7 - 2i\sqrt{2}\}$

6. $\{6 + 2i\}$

7. $\{-67 + 52i\}$

8. $\{23 - 14i\}$

9. $\{-7 + 24i\}$

10. $\{135 + 270i\}$

11. $\{72 + 38i\}$

12. $\{\dfrac{3}{13} + \dfrac{2}{13}i\}$

13. $\{\dfrac{12}{41} + \dfrac{15}{41}i\}$

14. $\{-\dfrac{5}{13} + \dfrac{12}{13}i\}$

15. $\{\dfrac{27}{25} - \dfrac{11}{25}i\}$

SECTION 3.6 SOLVING QUADRATIC EQUATIONS

A quadratic equation is a second-degree equation. The standard form of a quadratic equation in one variable x is $ax^2 + bx + c = 0$ where $a \neq 0$. There are four primary methods to solve a quadratic equation: Factoring, Extraction of Roots, Completing the Square, and Quadratic Formula.

Solving Quadratic Equations by Factoring

To solve a quadratic equation by factoring, we use a property of zero.

> **Property of Zero**
> $a \cdot b = 0$ if and only if $a = 0$ or $b = 0$.

The "or" statement here is the inclusive "or". The statement is true when either $a = 0$ or $b = 0$ or both equal zero. It is false when neither a nor b equal zero. Quadratic equations that will factor can be solved by use of the property of zero. To solve a quadratic equation by factoring, we:

1. Simplify; remove parentheses and combine like terms
2. Clear of all fractions by multiplying both sides by the LCD
3. Put the equation into standard form: $ax^2 + bx + c = 0$
4. Factor completely
5. Set each factor equal to zero
6. Solve

EXAMPLE 3.23

Solve the following quadratic equation by factoring:

$$x^2 - 5x - 6 = 0.$$

SOLUTION 3.23

$x^2 - 5x - 6 = 0$ — The equation is already in standard form. Factor the expression.

$(x - 6)(x + 1) = 0$ — Use the property of zero and set each factor equal to zero and solve.

$x - 6 = 0$ or $x + 1 = 0$ — Solve the first equation.

$x - 6 = 0$ — Add +6 to both sides of the equation.

$x - 6 + 6 = 0 + 6$ — Simplify.

$x = 6$ — Solve the second equation.

or

$x + 1 = 0$ — Add −1 to both sides of the equation.

$x + 1 - 1 = 0 - 1$ — Simplify.

$x = -1$ — Write your answer as a solution set.

$\{6, -1\}$

Suppose one of the factors of a quadratic equation is $(ax + b)$. When we set the factor equal to zero, we get:

$ax + b = 0.$ To solve this equation add $-b$ to both sides of the equation.

$ax + b - b = 0 - b$ Simplify.

$ax = -b$ To solve for x, divide both sides by a.

$$\frac{ax}{a} = \frac{-b}{a}$$

If $b = 0$, then $ax = 0$ and $x = 0$. Monomial factors involving the variable x have solutions of zero. Notice that the factor $(ax + b)$ has a solution of $\frac{-b}{a}$. Anytime an equation has a linear factor in the form of $ax + b$, the root of the equation is the opposite of b divided by the coefficient of the variable a. That is, the factor $(2x + 3)$ has a root of $x = -\frac{3}{2}$ and the factor $(5x - 7)$ has a root of $x = +\frac{7}{5}$. The following theorem becomes helpful in solving quadratic equations by factoring.

> **Linear Factor Theorem:** For $a \neq 0$,
>
> if $ax + b = 0$, then $x = \dfrac{-b}{a}$.

If we use the linear factor property with factor of $(2x + 3)(5x - 7) = 0$, then

$$x = \frac{-(3)}{2}, \frac{-(-7)}{5} \quad \text{or} \quad \left\{\frac{-3}{2}, \frac{7}{5}\right\}$$

Solving quadratic equations by factoring requires that the equation be in standard form. The following examples must be put into standard form before they can be solved.

EXAMPLE 3.24

Solve the following quadratic equation by factoring:

$12x^2 - 16x = 9x - 12.$

SOLUTION 3.24

$12x^2 - 16x = 9x - 12$

To solve this equation, we must put the equation into standard form. Get all of the non-zero terms on one side and zero on the other side. Add $-9x$ and $+12$ to both sides of the equation.

$12x^2 - 16x - 9x + 12 = 9x - 12 - 9x + 12$ Simplify.

$12x^2 - 25x - 12 = 0$ Factor the expression.

$(4x - 3)(3x - 4) = 0$ Use the linear factor theorem and solve for x.

$x = \dfrac{3}{4}$ or $\dfrac{4}{3}$ Put the solutions into set notation.

$\{\dfrac{3}{4}, \dfrac{4}{3}\}$

When solving equations, we should first simplify the equation and clear of fractions before attempting to factor the equation.

EXAMPLE 3.25

Solve the following quadratic equation by factoring:
$(x - 7)(x - 8) = 6$.

SOLUTION 3.25

$(x - 7)(x - 8) = 6$ We must first simplify the equation.

$x^2 - 15x + 56 = 6$ Put the equation into standard form. Add −6 to both sides.

$x^2 - 15x + 56 - 6 = 6 - 6$ Simplify.

$x^2 - 15x + 50 = 0$ Factor the equation.

$(x - 5)(x - 10) = 0$ Set each factor equal to zero and solve.

$x = 5$ or 10 Write the answer as a solution set.

$\{5, 10\}$

EXERCISE 3.6

Solve the following quadratic equations by factoring:

1. $3x^2 - 4x + 1 = 0$

2. $8x^2 - 14x - 15$

3. $14x^2 + 22x = 12$

4. $12x^2 + 17x + 6 = 0$

5. $10x^2 - 21x = 49$

6. $6x^2 + x - 35 = 0$

7. $35x^2 - 43x = -12$

8. $33x^2 - 112x - 33 = 0$

ANSWERS TO EXERCISE 3.6

1. $\{\frac{1}{3}, 1\}$ 2. $\{\frac{5}{2}, \frac{-3}{4}\}$

3. $\{\frac{3}{7}, -2\}$ 4. $\{\frac{-2}{3}, \frac{-3}{4}\}$

5. $\{\frac{-7}{5}, \frac{7}{2}\}$ 6. $\{\frac{7}{3}, \frac{-5}{2}\}$

7. $\{\frac{3}{7}, \frac{4}{5}\}$ 8. $\{\frac{11}{3}, \frac{-3}{11}\}$

Solving Quadratic Equations by Extraction of Roots

To solve a quadratic equation by the extraction of roots, use the definition of square roots.

$$\sqrt{x^2} = |x|$$

If $\sqrt{x^2} = a$ then $|x| = a$. We solved absolute value equations earlier. If $|x| = a$, then $x = a$ or $x = -a$. This gives the theorem.

Theorem:

If $\sqrt{x^2} = a$ then $x = a$ or $x = -a$.

The answers of $x = a$ or $x = -a$ are often written as one statement $x = \pm a$. Thus, if $x^2 = a$ then $x = \sqrt{a}$ or $-\sqrt{a}$ which is sometimes written as $x = \pm\sqrt{a}$. Extraction of roots can be used anytime there is a perfect square involving the variable on one side of the equation. In standard form, a quadratic equation looks like this

$$ax^2 + bx + c = 0.$$

If the coefficient of the first-degree term in x (the coefficient b in standard form) is zero, extraction of roots is the best method to use to solve quadratic equations. Use the following rule to solve an equation by extraction of roots:

1. Simplify (Remove parentheses and combine like terms).
2. Clear of all fractions (Multiply both sides by the LCD).
3. Put into standard form (Get all terms on one side of the equation and zero on the other side).
4. If the coefficient of the first degree term in x is zero, isolate the x^2 term on one side of the equation.

5. Take the square root of both sides of the equation. When you take the square root of both sides of an equation, the answer is both the positive and negative square root $(\pm\sqrt{}\,)$.
6. Standardize the radicals and simplify your answers.

EXAMPLE 3.26

Solve for x by use of extraction of roots: $x^2 - 25 = 0$.

SOLUTION 3.26

$x^2 - 25 = 0$ This equation may be solved by factoring. Let's first solve it by factoring. Factor the equation.

$(x + 5)(x - 5) = 0$ Set each factor equal to zero and solve.

$x = 5$ or -5

The instructions indicate to solve by extraction of roots. Let's now solve by extraction of roots.

$x^2 - 25 = 0$ This equation may also be solved by extraction of roots since the first degree term involving x is missing. Solve the equation for x^2. Isolate the x^2 on one side of the equation by itself. Add $+25$ to both sides of the equation.

$x^2 - 25 + 25 = 0 + 25$ Simplify.

$x^2 = 25$ Take the square root of both sides of the equation. When you take the square root of both sides of an equation, your answer includes both the $\pm\sqrt{}$.

$\sqrt{x^2} = \pm\sqrt{25}$

$x = \pm 5$ Write the solutions as a solution set.

$\{-5, 5\}$

We can also take the square root of both sides of an equation if there is a perfect square involving x on one side of the equation.

EXAMPLE 3.27

Solve for x by taking the square root of both sides of the equation:
$(2x+3)^2 = 25$

SOLUTION 3.27

$(2x+3)^2 = 25$

There is a perfect square involving x on one side of the equation. Solve by extraction of roots. Take the square root of both sides of the equation. Don't forget to include the positive and the negative root of your answer.

$\sqrt{(2x+3)^2} = \pm 25$

$2x+3 = \pm 5$

Simplify.

Solve for x. Add -3 to both sides of the equation.

$2x = -3 \pm 5$

Separate the equation into two equations.

$2x = -3+5$ or $2x = -3-5$
$2x = 2$ or $2x = -8$

Simplify both equations.
Divide both sides of both equations by 2.

$\dfrac{2x}{2} = \dfrac{2}{2}$ or $\dfrac{2x}{2} = \dfrac{-8}{2}$

Simplify again.

$x = 1$ or -4

Put the answers into a solution set.

$\{-4, 1\}$

EXERCISE 3.7

1. $3x^2 - 27 = 0$
2. $5x^2 - 45 = 80$
3. $(2x+3)^2 = 64$
4. $x^2 - 28 = 0$
5. $4x^2 - 48 = 0$
6. $4x^2 + 16 = 0$
7. $x^2 + 27 = -9$
8. $3(x-4)^2 = 36$
9. $2(3x+5)^2 - 6 = 42$
10. $3(2x-5)^2 + 36 = 0$

ANSWERS TO EXERCISE 3.7

1. $\{3, -3\}$

2. $\{5, -5\}$

3. $\{\dfrac{11}{2}, \dfrac{-5}{2}\}$

4. $\{-2\sqrt{7}, 2\sqrt{7}\}$

5. $\{-2\sqrt{3}, 2\sqrt{3}\}$

6. $\{2i, -2i\}$

7. $\{6i, -6i\}$

8. $\{4 - 2\sqrt{3}, 4 + 2\sqrt{3}\}$

9. $\{\dfrac{-5 + 2\sqrt{6}}{3}, \dfrac{-5 - 2\sqrt{6}}{3}\}$

10. $\{\dfrac{5 + 2i\sqrt{3}}{2}, \dfrac{5 - 2i\sqrt{3}}{2}\}$

Solving Quadratic Equations by Completing the Square

When quadratic equations will not factor and you cannot solve them by extraction of roots, then you can make the expression involving the variable into a perfect square trinomial. A perfect square is an expression which has a rational square root. A perfect square trinomial factors into a $(ax + b)^2$.

EXAMPLE 3.28

Are the following numbers and expressions perfect squares?
a) 1296
b) $x^2 - 4x + 4$
c) $9x^2 + 30x + 25$

SOLUTION 3.28

a) 1296   Prime factor 1296.
    $2 \cdot 648$
    $2 \cdot 2 \cdot 324$
    $2 \cdot 2 \cdot 2 \cdot 162$
    $2 \cdot 2 \cdot 2 \cdot 2 \cdot 81 = 2 \cdot 2 \cdot 2 \cdot 2 \cdot 9 \cdot 9 = 2 \cdot 2 \cdot 2 \cdot 2 \cdot 3 \cdot 3 \cdot 3 \cdot 3$

Put the expression into power notation.

$2^4 \cdot 3^4 = (2^2 \cdot 3^2)^2 = (36)^2$

Since 1296 can be written as $(ax + b)^2$, it is a perfect square and

$\sqrt{36^2} = 36$

b) $x^2 - 4x + 4$

$(x - 2)(x - 2) = (x - 2)^2$

Factor the expression. The expression factors into $(ax + b)^2$, hence it is a perfect square and

$$\sqrt{(x-2)^2} = |x-2|$$

c) $9x^2 + 30x + 25$ Factor the expression.
    $(3x+5)(3x+5) = (3x+5)^2$ Since it factors into $(\;\;)^2$,
                                        it is a perfect square and

$$\sqrt{(3x+5)^2} = |3x+5|$$

It is easy to tell if a trinomial is a perfect square. A perfect square trinomial must have a positive first term and a positive last term. The middle term may be either positive or negative. In the previous example, notice that the first term is a perfect square $(9x^2)$ and the last term is also a perfect square (25). The middle term of the trinomial must equal two times the square root of the first term times the square root of the last term. $(2 \cdot \sqrt{9x^2} \cdot \sqrt{25} = 2 \cdot 3x \cdot 5 = 30x)$ To determine if a trinomial is a perfect square, take 2 times the square root of the first term and the square root of the last term. If this product equals either ± the middle term of the trinomial, then the trinomial is a perfect square.

EXAMPLE 3.29

Determine if the following trinomial is a perfect square:
$4x^2 + 12x + 9$

SOLUTION 3.29

$4x^2 + 12 + 9$ To see if the trinomial is a
                               perfect square, take 2 times
                               the square root of the first
                               term times the square root of
                               the last term.

$$2 \cdot \sqrt{4x^2} \cdot \sqrt{9} = 2 \cdot 2x \cdot 3 = 12x$$

$4x^2 + 12x + 9$ is a perfect square.
If the coefficient of the first term is one (the first term of the trinomial is x^2), then it is easy to see if the trinomial is a perfect square.

EXAMPLE 3.30

Determine if the following trinomial is a perfect square. $x^2 - 16x + 64$

SOLUTION 3.30

$x^2 - 16x + 64$
We know that the square root of x^2 is x. To see if a trinomial that begins with x^2 is a perfect square, take 2 times x times the square root of the last

term.
$$2 \cdot x \cdot \sqrt{64} = 2 \cdot x \cdot 8 = 16x$$
Since the middle term of the trinomial is $-16x$, the trinomial is a perfect square. It is unnecessary to take the square root of x^2 since in the completion of the square, we will always take its value to be x. All that is necessary is to take the square root of the last term and double it. If this equals the coefficient of the middle term, then the trinomial is a perfect square.

In the first chapter we found that to factor a trinomial which is a perfect square, all we have to do is take the square root of the first term, the square root of the last term, keep the sign of the middle term of the trinomial and write them as a binomial squared.

EXAMPLE 3.31

Factor the following perfect square:
$$x^2 - 4x + 4$$

SOLUTION 3.31

$$x^2 - 4x + 4$$

To factor the trinomial into a perfect square, we must first check to see that the trinomial is a perfect square. Take two times x times the square root of the last term.

$$2 \cdot x \cdot \sqrt{4} = 4x$$

This product is the middle term of the trinomial, so the trinomial factors into a perfect square .

$$(\sqrt{x^2} - \sqrt{4})^2 = (x-2)^2$$

Now let's look at the expression
$$x^2 - 8x + 5.$$
We wish to make the trinomial factor as a perfect square. To factor the trinomial into a perfect square, the middle term of the trinomial must be the square root of the last term times two. The last term of the trinomial must be a perfect square which is one-half times the coefficient of the middle term squared. Make the expression $x^2 - 8x + 5$ into a perfect square.

$$x^2 - 8x + 5$$

Multiply one-half times the coefficient of the middle term.

$$\frac{1}{2}(-8) = -4$$

Square that number.

$$(-4)^2 = 16$$

For the trinomial to be a

perfect square, the number term must be 16. If we had $x^2 - 8x + 16$, we would have a perfect square. We cannot add 16 to an expression, but we can add 16 if we also subtract 16.

$$(x^2 - 8x + 5) + 16 - 16$$

Remove the parentheses. Use the commutative and associative properties to associate the +16 with the trinomial.

$$x^2 - 8x + 16 + 5 - 16$$

Put parentheses around the trinomial.

$$(x^2 - 8x + 16) - 11$$

Factor the trinomial into a perfect square.

$$(x - 4)^2 - 11$$

EXAMPLE 3.32

Add and subtract an appropriate number to make the trinomial into a perfect square and a number term.

a) $x^2 + 12x + 32$

b) $x^2 - 6x + 7$

c) $x^2 + 5x - 3$

SOLUTION 3.32

a) $x^2 + 12x + 32$

Multiply $\frac{1}{2}$ times 12.

$$\frac{1}{2} \cdot 12 = 6$$

Square that value.

$$(6)^2 = 36$$

Add and subtract 36 from the original expression.

$$x^2 + 12x + 32 + 36 - 36$$

Associate the +36 with the x^2 and x terms.

$$x^2 + 12x + 36 + 32 - 36$$

Put parentheses around the $x^2 + 12x + 36$ and simplify.

$$(x^2 + 12x + 36) - 4$$

Factor the trinomial into a perfect square.

$$(x + 6)^2 - 4$$

b) $x^2 - 6x + 7$

Multiply $\frac{1}{2}$ times –6.

$$\frac{1}{2} \cdot (-6) = -3$$

Square that value.

$$(-3)^2 = 9$$

Add and subtract 9 from the original expression.

$$x^2 - 6x + 7 + 9 - 9$$

Associate the +9 with the x^2 and x terms.

$$x^2 - 6x + 9 + 7 - 9$$

Put parenthesis around the $x^2 - 6x + 9$ and simplify.

$$(x^2 - 6x + 9) - 2$$

Factor the trinomial into a perfect square.

$$(x - 3)^2 - 2$$

c) $\quad x^2 + 5x - 3$

Multiply $\frac{1}{2}$ times +5.

$$\frac{1}{2} \cdot (5) = \frac{5}{2}$$

Square that value.

$$\left(\frac{5}{2}\right)^2 = \frac{25}{4}$$

Add and subtract $\frac{25}{4}$ from the original expression.

$$x^2 + 5x - 3 + \frac{25}{4} - \frac{25}{4}$$

Associate the $+\frac{25}{4}$ with the x^2 and x terms.

$$x^2 + 5x + \frac{25}{4} - 3 - \frac{25}{4}$$

Put parenthesis around the $x^2 + 5x + \frac{25}{4}$ a simplify.

$$\left(x^2 + 5x + \frac{25}{4}\right) - \frac{37}{4}$$

Factor the trinomial into a perfect square.

$$\left(x + \frac{5}{2}\right)^2 - \frac{37}{4}$$

The question becomes "What good does this do in solving a quadratic equation?" To solve a quadratic equation by completing the square, use the following rules:

1. Simplify—remove parentheses and combine like terms.
2. Clear of all fractions by multiplying both sides by the LCD.
3. Put the equation into standard form. $ax^2 + bx + c = 0$
4. Add $-c$ to both sides of the equation.
5. To solve by completing the square, the coefficient of x^2 must be equal to 1, so divide both sides by the coefficient "a" (the coefficient of x^2).
6. Multiply $\frac{1}{2}$ times the coefficient "b", square that value, and add it to both sides.
7. The trinomial is now a perfect square, so factor the trinomial into a

perfect square and simplify the left hand side of the equation.

8. Use extraction of roots to solve the equation. Take the square root of both sides of the dquation. **Don't forget the** $\pm$.

9. Solve for the variable.

The following example may help to clarify the above rules.

EXAMPLE 3.33

Solve the following quadratic equation by completing the square:
$x^2 - 4x - 5 = 0$

SOLUTION 3.33

$x^2 - 4x - 5 = 0$	This equation can be solved by factoring. Factor the trinomial.
$(x - 5)(x + 1) = 0$	Set each factor equal to zero and solve.
$x = 5, 1$	

We now need to solve the same quadratic equation by completing the square.

$x^2 - 4x - 5 = 0$	The equation is simplified, it does not contain any fractions, and it is in standard form. Add 5 to both sides of the equation.
$x^2 - 4x - 5 + 5 = 0 + 5$	The coefficient of x^2 is 1. Multiply $\frac{1}{2}$ times (–4).
$\frac{1}{2} \cdot (-4) = -2$	Square that value.
$(-2)^2 = 4$	Add it to both sides of the equation.
$x^2 - 4x + 4 = 5 + 4$	Factor the trinomial into a perfect square and simplify the left-hand side of the equation.
$(x - 2)^2 = 9$	Take the square root of both sides of the equation. Remember the $\pm$.
$\sqrt{(x - 2)^2} = \pm\sqrt{9}$	Simplify.
$x - 2 = \pm 3$	Add +2 to both sides of the equation.
$x - 2 + 2 = 2 \pm 3$	Simplify and separate into two equations.
$x = 2 + 3 \quad \text{or} \quad x = 2 - 3$	Compute the values of x.
$x = 5, -1$	Write the solutions in a

solution set.

$\{-1, 5\}$

EXERCISE 3.8

Solve the following quadratic equations by completing the square.

1. $x^2 - 5x = -4$

2. $3x^2 = 2x + 1$

3. $2x^2 - 5x - 3 = 0$

4. $x^2 - 5x + 7 = 0$

5. $3x^2 - 6x - 9 = 0$

6. $4x^2 - 3x + 2 = 0$

7. $8x^2 - 30x - 27 = 0$

8. $6x^2 + 11ax + 4a^2 = 0$

9. $3x^2 - 2x - 7 = 0$

10. $x^2 - 5ix + 6 = 0$

ANSWERS TO EXERCISE 3.8

1. $\{1, 4\}$

2. $\{\frac{-1}{3}, 1\}$

3. $\{\frac{-1}{2}, 3\}$

4. $\{\frac{5 + i\sqrt{3}}{2}, \frac{5 - i\sqrt{3}}{2}\}$

5. $\{-1, 3\}$

6. $\{\frac{3 + i\sqrt{23}}{8}, \frac{3 - i\sqrt{23}}{8}\}$

7. $\{\frac{-3}{4}, \frac{9}{2}\}$

8. $\{\frac{-4a}{3}, \frac{a}{2}\}$

9. $\{\frac{1 + \sqrt{22}}{3}, \frac{1 - \sqrt{22}}{3}\}$

10. $\{3i, 2i\}$

Solving Quadratic Equations by the Formula

Completing the square can be used to solve all types of quadratic equations. If we solve the equation $ax^2 + bx + c = 0$, we will find a formula for all quadratic equations and can use the formula instead of completing the square. Solve the following quadratic equation by completing the square:

$$ax^2 + bx + c = 0$$
Add $-c$ to both sides of the equation.

$$ax^2 + bx + c - c = 0 - c$$
Simplify.

$$ax^2 + bx = -c$$
Divide each term on both sides by a.

$$\frac{a}{a}x^2 + \frac{b}{a}x = \frac{-c}{a}$$
Simplify again.

$$x^2 + \frac{b}{a}x = \frac{-c}{a}$$
Multiply $\frac{1}{2}$ times $\left(\frac{b}{a}\right)$.

$$\frac{1}{2} \cdot \left(\frac{b}{a}\right) = \frac{b}{2a}$$
Square it.

$$\left(\frac{b}{2a}\right)^2 = \frac{b^2}{4a^2}$$
Add it to both sides.

$$x^2 + \frac{b}{a}x + \frac{b^2}{4a^2} = \frac{-c}{a} + \frac{b^2}{4a^2}$$
Factor the trinomial into a perfect square.

$$\left(x + \frac{b}{2a}\right)^2 = \frac{-c}{a} + \frac{b^2}{4a^2}$$
Add the fractions on the right-hand side.

$$\left(x + \frac{b}{2a}\right)^2 = \frac{b^2 - 4ac}{4a^2}$$
Take the square root of both sides of the equation. Do not forget the $\pm$. Standardize the radicals.

$$\sqrt{\left(x + \frac{b}{2a}\right)^2} = \pm\sqrt{\frac{b^2 - 4ac}{4a^2}}$$

$$x + \frac{b}{2a} - \frac{b}{2a} = -\frac{b}{2a} \pm \frac{\sqrt{b^2 - 4ac}}{2a}$$
Simplify one more time.

$$x = \frac{-b}{2a} \pm \frac{\sqrt{b^2 - 4ac}}{2a} \quad (a \neq 0)$$
Combine the two fractions.

$$x = \frac{-b \pm \sqrt{b^2 - 4ac}}{2a}$$

The solution obtained represents a formula which will solve all quadratic equations which are written in standard form. Given a quadratic

equation in standard form
$$ax^2 + bx + c = 0 \quad \text{where } a \neq 0, \text{ the solutions are}$$

$$x = \frac{-b \pm \sqrt{b^2 - 4ac}}{2a}$$

This expression is referred to as the ***Quadratic Formula***. This formula will solve any quadratic equation in standard form no matter what a, b and c represents as long as $a \neq 0$. To use this formula you must be very careful to substitute values into the formula correctly. If you substitute a wrong value or substitute a value incorrectly, your answer will definitely be wrong. Here are some steps that might help you to use the formula correctly.

1. Simplify the equation.
2. Clear of all fractions. The formula will handle fractional coefficients, but it is much simpler to use integer values in the quadratic formula.
3. Put the equation into standard form. $(ax^2 + bx + c = 0, a \neq 0)$
4. Label a, b, and c. That is, write down $a = (?)$, $b = (?)$ and $c = (?)$. When using the quadratic formula to solve an equation, most errors occur from replacements of wrong values for a, b, or c.
5. Substitute a, b, and c into the quadratic equation using parentheses (check the following examples).
6. Compute the value of the expression under the radical $(\sqrt{})$.
7. Standardize the radical.
8. If the radical is a perfect square, simplify the numerator. If the numerator is not a perfect square, factor the numerator, if possible, to see if the fraction may be reduced.
9. Reduce the fraction if possible.

EXAMPLE 3.34

Solve the following quadratic equation by the use of the quadratic formula:
$$3x^2 - 5x = 2$$

SOLUTION 3.34

$3x^2 - 5x = 2$	Put the equation into standard form. Add -2 to both sides.
$3x^2 - 5x - 2 = 2 - 2$	Simplify.
$3x^2 - 5x - 2 = 0$	Label a, b, and c.
$a = 3, b = -5, c = -2$	Substitute a, b, and c into the quadratic formula. Use parentheses to avoid errors with the positive and

$$x = \frac{-(-5) \pm \sqrt{(-5)^2 - 4(3)(-2)}}{2(3)}$$

negative numbers.
Compute under the radical.

$$x = \frac{5 \pm \sqrt{25 + 24}}{6} = \frac{5 \pm \sqrt{49}}{6}$$

Standardize the radical and simplify.

$$x = \frac{5 \pm 7}{6} = \frac{12}{6}, \frac{-2}{6}$$

Reduce the answers and put into a solution set.

$$\{2, -\frac{1}{3}\}$$

The formula may be used on all types of quadratic equations. Some equations may have complex answers or even complex coefficients.

EXAMPLE 3.35

Solve the following quadratic equation by use of the quadratic formula:
$x^2 + 6x + 13 = 0$

SOLUTION 3.35

$x^2 + 6x + 13 = 0$

This equation is in standard form. Label a, b, and c.

$a = 1, b = 6, c = 13$

Substitute a, b, and c into the quadratic formula. Use parentheses to avoid errors. Compute under the radical.

$$x = \frac{-(6) \pm \sqrt{(6)^2 - 4(1)(13)}}{2(1)}$$

$$x = \frac{-6 \pm \sqrt{36 - 52}}{2} = \frac{-6 \pm \sqrt{-16}}{2}$$

Standardize the radical.

$$x = \frac{-6 \pm 4i}{2}$$

Factor the numerator.

$$x = \frac{2(-3 \pm 2i)}{2}$$

Divide the common factor of 2.

$$x = -3 \pm 2i$$

Write as two solutions into a solution set.

$$\{-3 + 2i, -3 - 2i\}$$

The expression under the radical sign $(b^2 - 4ac)$ is called the discriminate of the quadratic formula. It is called the discriminate because it discriminates the type of answers which are obtained when using the formula. That is,

1) If $b^2 - 4ac > 0$, we have two real and different solutions. If $b^2 - 4ac$

is a perfect root, we get two different rational solutions. If it is not a perfect root, we get two distinct irrational solutions.

2) If $b^2 - 4ac = 0$, we get one real solution.
3) If $b^2 - 4ac < 0$, we get two imaginary solutions.

Checking the discriminate before solving the equation can be helpful to inform you of the type of answers you will obtain. It is also helpful in the sense that after we substitute a, b, and c into the quadratic formula, the first thing we do is compute under the radical. If we have determined the value of the discriminate before we use the formula, the expression under the radical has already been computed and does not need to be computed again. In some countries, the Greek letter Δ is used instead of the discriminate. That is $\Delta = b^2 - 4ac$. The quadratic formula now appears like this:

Given $ax^2 + bx + c = 0$ and $\Delta = b^2 - 4ac$, then the value of x is:

$$x = \frac{-b \pm \sqrt{\Delta}}{2a}.$$

Notice that the formula is the same, but the discriminate is required to be solved before the formula can be used.

The quadratic formula may be used to solve quadratic equations in more than one variable. These equations are called quadratic literal equations.

EXAMPLE 3.36

Solve the following quadratic equation for the indicated variable by use of the quadratic formula.
a) $x^2 - 4xy + 3y^2 = 0$ (Solve for x.)
b) $x^2 - 4xy + 3y^2 = 0$ (Solve for y.)

SOLUTION 3.36

a) $x^2 - 4xy + 3y^2 = 0$ (Solve for x.) — The equation is in standard form. Label a, b, and c. Since we are solving for x, the variable y is used like a constant in the formula.

$a = 1, b = -4y, c = 3y^2$ — Substitute a, b, and c into the quadratic formula using parentheses.

$$x = \frac{-(4y) \pm \sqrt{(-4y)^2 - 4(1)(3y^2)}}{2(1)}$$

Calculate the expression under the radical.

$$x = \frac{4y \pm \sqrt{16y^2 - 12y^2}}{2} = \frac{4y \pm \sqrt{4y^2}}{2}$$

Standardize the radical.

$$x = \frac{4y \pm 2y}{2}$$

Combine like terms in the

$$x = \frac{6y}{2}, \frac{2y}{2}$$

numerator and simplify.
Reduce the fractions.

$$x = 3y, y$$
$$\{3y, y\}$$

Write the solutions in a
solution set.

b) $x^2 - 4xy + 3y^2 = 0$ (Solve for y.)

Since we are solving for y,
the variable x is treated like
a constant in the formula.
Rewrite the equation in
standard form for the
variable y.

$$3y^2 - 4xy + x^2 = 0$$
$$a = 3, b = -4x, c = x^2$$

Label a, b, and c.
Substitute a, b, and c into the
quadratic formula using
parentheses.

$$y = \frac{-(-4x) \pm \sqrt{(-4x)^2 - 4(3)(x^2)}}{2(3)}$$

Calculate the expression
under the radical.

$$y = \frac{4x \pm \sqrt{16x^2 - 12x^2}}{6} = \frac{4x \pm \sqrt{4x^2}}{6}$$

Standardize the radical.

$$y = \frac{4x \pm 2x}{6}$$

$$y = \frac{6x}{6}, \frac{2x}{6}$$

Combine like terms in the
numerator and simplify.
Reduce the fractions.

$$y = x, \frac{x}{3}$$

Write the solutions in a
solution set.

$$\{x, \frac{x}{3}\}$$

EXERCISE 3.9

Solve the following quadratic equations for x by use of the quadratic formula.

1. $x^2 + 4x - 2 = 0$

2. $9x^2 - 6x + 2 = 0$

3. $6x^2 - 11x - 5 = 0$

4. $x^2 - 7x + 13 = 0$

5. $x^2 - xy - 2y^2 = 0$

6. $2x^2 - ix + 3 = 0$

7. $x^2 - 5ix - 6 = 0$

8. $x^2 - 8y + 6x + 17 = 0$

9. $x^2 - 4y^2 + 2x - 16y - 19 = 0$

10. $x^2 + 2xy + y^2 - 4x = 0$

ANSWERS TO EXERCISE 3.9

1. $\{-2 + \sqrt{6}, -2 - \sqrt{6}\}$

2. $\{\frac{1+i}{3}, \frac{1-i}{3}\}$

3. $\{\frac{11 + \sqrt{241}}{12}, \frac{11 - \sqrt{241}}{12}\}$

4. $\{\frac{7 + i\sqrt{3}}{2}, \frac{7 - i\sqrt{3}}{2}\}$

5. $\{2y, y\}$

6. $\{\frac{3i}{2}, -i\}$

7. $\{-3i, -2i\}$

8. $\{\ 3 + 2\sqrt{2y - 2}, -3 - 2\sqrt{2y - 2}\}$

9. $\{-1 + 2\sqrt{y^2 + 4y + 5}, -1 - 2\sqrt{y^2 + 4y + 5}\}$

10. $\{-y + 2 + 2\sqrt{1 - y}, -y + 2 - 2\sqrt{1 - y}\}$

SECTION 3.7 POLYNOMIAL AND RATIONAL INEQUALITIES

In the last section we solved quadratic equations. Now we will look at polynomial and rational inequalities. Remember that a quadratic expression is a type of polynomial. In this section, we will solve inequalities of the form:
$$2x^2 - 3x - 5 > 0, \quad x^3 - x^2 - 4x + 4 \leq 0, \quad \text{and} \quad \frac{x^2 - 3x - 4}{x - 2} \leq 0.$$

The best way to solve a polynomial or rational inequality is to graph the solution on a number line.

Quadratic Inequalities

Solving quadratic inequalities is much like solving quadratic equations. The big difference is that the solutions must be found using the number line.

EXAMPLE 3.37

Solve the following quadratic inequality for x:

a) $x^2 - 5x - 6 \leq 0$

SOLUTION 3.37

a) $x^2 - 5x - 6 \leq 0$

To solve a polynomial inequality, we must first find the zeros of the polynomial. That is, we must solve it as if it was an equality. Solving a polynomial that is quadratic can be done by any of the methods of solving a quadratic equation. Solving by use of factoring and the quadratic formula are, however, the quickest methods. Factor the polynomial to find its roots.

$(x - 6)\,(x + 1) \leq 0$ Set each factor equal to zero and solve. The roots of the polynomial are $x = 6$ and -1.

Plot the roots on a number line. Since the original inequality is ≤, we plot the roots as points (•) on the number line. If the expression had been <, we would have plotted the roots as a circle (∘). The point indicates that it is part of the graph. The circle indicates that the point is the location where the graph starts, but it is not part of the graph.

The two roots have broken the number line into three regions; the region to the left of −1 ($x < -1$), the region between −1 and 6 ($-1 < x < 6$), and the region to the right of 6 ($x > 6$). Since the only points where $x^2 - 5x - 6 = 0$ are $x = -1$ and 6, all other point values of x make $x^2 - 5x - 6 \neq 0$. This means, that at all other values of x except $x = -1$ and 6, $x^2 - 5x - 6 < 0$ or $x^2 - 5x - 6 > 0$. If just one point in each region makes $x^2 - 5x - 6 < 0$ or $x^2 - 5x - 6 > 0$, then all points in that region do the same because the polynomial expression cannot change from positive to negative unless it first becomes zero.

In factored form, $x^2 - 5x - 6 \leq 0$ is $(x - 6)(x + 1) \leq 0$. Let's make a table to follow the value of the expression. In the table, put the factors and the expression on the side of the table and the regions along the top.

	$x < -1$	$-1 < x < 6$	$x > 6$
$(x + 1)$			
$(x - 6)$			
$(x + 1)(x - 6)$			

Now go along the $(x + 1)$ row in the table and determine if $(x + 1)$ is positive or negative in each of the three regions.

	$x < -1$	$-1 < x < 6$	$x > 6$
$(x + 1)$	−	+	+
$(x - 6)$			
$(x + 1)(x - 6)$			

Now go down the $(x - 6)$ column and do the same thing.

	$x < -1$	$-1 < x < 6$	$x > 6$
$(x + 1)$	−	+	+
$(x - 6)$	−	−	+
$(x + 1)(x - 6)$			

Now complete the table by establishing the signs of $(x + 1)(x - 6)$ by using the signs of the individual factors.

	$x < -1$	$-1 < x < 6$	$x > 6$
$(x + 1)$	−	+	+
$(x - 6)$	−	−	+
$(x + 1)(x - 6)$	+	−	+

We are looking for $(x + 1)(x - 6) \leq 0$. The table indicates that $(x + 1)(x - 6) < 0$ when $-1 < x < 6$. Since the original inequality is ≤ 0, we include the end points in our solution. We get the solution of $-1 \leq x \leq 6$. When we

write our answer as a solution set, we get the solution set
$\{x| -1 \le x \le 6\}$.

EXAMPLE 3.38

Solve the following quadratic inequalities for *x*:

a) $4x^2 - 12x + 9 \le 0$

b) $16x^2 + 40x + 25 < 0$

SOLUTION 3.38

a) $4x^2 - 12x + 9 \le 0$ Factor the polynomial.

　　 $(2x - 3)(2x - 3) \le 0$ Set each factor equal to zero.
                                                     In this problem there is only
                                                     one root, $x = 3/2$. Plot the
                                                     root on the number line.

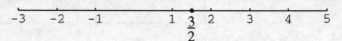

The one root has broken the number line into two regions; the region to
the left of $\frac{3}{2}$ $(x < \frac{3}{2})$ and the region to the right of $\frac{3}{2}$ $(x > \frac{3}{2})$. Make a
table.

	$x < \frac{3}{2}$	$x > \frac{3}{2}$
$(2x - 3)$		
$(2x - 3)$		
$(2x - 3)(2x - 3)$		

Now go down the three rows of the table and determine the positive or
negative values in the table.

	$x < \frac{3}{2}$	$x > \frac{3}{2}$
$(2x - 3)$	−	+
$(2x - 3)$	−	+
$(2x - 3)(2x - 3)$	+	+

We are looking for $(2x - 3)(2x - 3) \le 0$. The table indicates that

$(2x - 3)(2x - 3)$ is always positive except where it is zero at $x = 3/2$. This means that no region is negative. When $x = 3/2$, the expression $(2x - 3)(2x - 3) = 0$. So the solution set is only $x = 3/2$.

$$\{x|\, x = \frac{3}{2}\}.$$

Interval notation is not possible in this problem because we have only one single value of x that makes the inequality true.

b) $16x^2 + 40x + 25 < 0$ Factor the polynomial.

     $(4x + 5)\,(4x + 5) < 0$ Set each factor equal to zero. In this problem there is only one root, $x = -5/4$. Plot the root on the number line.

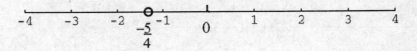

The one root has broken the number line into two regions; the region to the left of $-\frac{5}{4}$ $(x < -\frac{5}{4})$ and the region to the right of $-\frac{5}{4}$ $(x > -\frac{5}{4})$. Make a table.

	$x < -\frac{5}{4}$	$x > -\frac{5}{4}$
$(4x + 5)$		
$(4x + 5)$		
$(4x + 5)(4x + 5)$		

Now go down the three rows of the table and determine when it is positive or negative.

	$x < -\frac{5}{4}$	$x > -\frac{5}{4}$
$(4x + 5)$	−	+
$(4x + 5)$	−	+
$(4x + 5)(4x + 5)$	+	+

We are looking for $(4x + 5)(4x + 5) < 0$. The table indicates that $(4x + 5)(4x + 5)$ is always positive except where it is zero at $x = -\frac{5}{4}$. This means no region is negative. When $x = -\frac{5}{4}$, the expression $(4x + 5)(4x + 5) = 0$, but the original inequality does not allow $x = -\frac{5}{4}$. So it is not a solution. In this case there are no solutions to the inequality, so the solution set is the empty set.

$$\varnothing = \{\ \}$$

Polynomial Inequalities

Solving polynomial inequalities requires finding the roots of the polynomials.

EXAMPLE 3.39

Solve the following polynomial inequality for x.
a) $x^3 - 4x^2 - 5x \leq 0$

SOLUTION 3.39

a) $x^3 - 4x^2 - 5x \leq 0$ Factor the expression.
     $x(x - 5)(x + 1) \leq 0$ Set each factor equal to zero and solve. The roots of the polynomial are $x = 0$, $x = 5$, and -1. Plot the roots on a number line.

The three roots have broken the number line into four regions; the region to the left of -1 ($x < -1$), the region between -1 and 0 ($-1 < x < 0$), the region between 0 and 5 ($0 < x < 5$) and the region to the right of 5 ($x > 5$). Make a table to cover all of these regions. Put the factors and the expressions on the side of the table and the regions along the top.

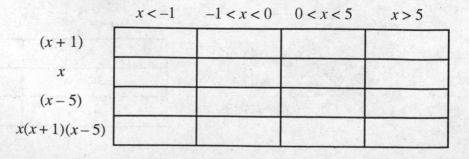

	$x < -1$	$-1 < x < 0$	$0 < x < 5$	$x > 5$
$(x + 1)$				
x				
$(x - 5)$				
$x(x + 1)(x - 5)$				

Fill in the positive and negative signs for each factor and each region in the table.

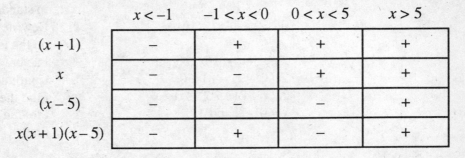

	$x < -1$	$-1 < x < 0$	$0 < x < 5$	$x > 5$
$(x + 1)$	−	+	+	+
x	−	−	+	+
$(x - 5)$	−	−	−	+
$x(x + 1)(x - 5)$	−	+	−	+

We are looking for $x(x + 1)(x - 5) \leq 0$. The table indicates that $x(x + 1)(x - 5)$ is negative when $x < -1$ or $0 < x < 5$. Since the original inequality is ≤ 0, we include the end points in our solution. When we write our answer as a solution set, we get the solution set $\{x \mid x \leq -1 \text{ or } 0 \leq x \leq 5\}$.

Rational Inequalities

A rational inequality is an inequality containing rational (fractional) expressions. Rational inequalities are much different than rational equations. In an equation like this

$$\frac{x + 4}{x} = \frac{x}{2}$$

we clear of the fraction by multiplying both sides of the equation by the LCD $(2x)$. With rational inequalities, however, we cannot multiply the equation by $2x$. $2x$ is a variable expression which can be positive, negative, or zero. We are not allowed to multiply an equation or inequality by zero, but if we multiply an inequality by a negative number, the inequality reverses and if we multiply by a positive number, the inequality stays the same.

Let's solve the inequality $\dfrac{x + 4}{x} \geq \dfrac{x}{2}$ in two ways.

1) $\dfrac{x + 4}{x} \geq \dfrac{x}{2}$ Multiply both sides of the inequality by a positive number. We can clear of the fractions by multiplying both sides not by the LCD, but by the $(\text{LCD})^2$. The LCD raised to the second power is always positive. Multiply both sides by $4x^2$.

$(4x)^2 \cdot \dfrac{x + 4}{x} \geq (4x)^2 \cdot \left(\dfrac{x}{2}\right)$ Simplify.

$\dfrac{4x^2(x + 4)}{x} \geq \dfrac{4x^2(x)}{2}$ Reduce the fractions.

$$4x(x + 4) \geq 2x^3$$ Simplify again.

$$4x^2 + 16x \geq 2x^3$$ We get a higher degree polynomial inequality. Rewrite in standard form.

$$0 \geq 2x^3 - 4x^2 - 16x$$ Rewrite with the expression on the left-hand side.

$$2x^3 - 4x^2 - 16x \leq 0$$ Factor.

$$2x(x^2 - 2x - 8) \leq 0$$ Continue factoring.

$$2x(x - 4)(x + 2) \leq 0$$ Find the roots.

$$x = 0, -2, \text{ and } 4$$ Plot the roots on the number line.

Build a table for the four regions of the graph.

	$x < -2$	$-2 < x < 0$	$0 < x < 4$	$x > 4$
$(x + 2)$				
$2x$				
$(x - 4)$				
$2x(x + 2)(x - 4)$				

Now go down the table and determine the sign of each factor for the different regions.

	$x < -2$	$-2 < x < 0$	$0 < x < 4$	$x > 4$
$(x + 2)$	−	+	+	+
$2x$	−	−	+	+
$(x - 4)$	−	−	−	+
$2x(x + 2)(x - 4)$	−	+	−	+

We are looking for $2x(x + 2)(x - 4) \leq 0$. The table indicates that $2x(x + 2)(x - 4)$ is negative when $x < -2$ or $0 < x < 4$. Since the original inequality is ≤ 0, we include the end points in our solution. Write the answer in a solution set.

$$\{x \mid x \leq -2 \text{ or } 0 < x \leq 4\}.$$

A second way to do this problem is a bit simpler. The second way does not clear of the fraction.

2) $\dfrac{x+4}{x} \geq \dfrac{x}{2}$ Add $-\dfrac{x}{2}$ to both sides of the equation.

$\dfrac{x+4}{x} - \dfrac{x}{2} \geq \dfrac{x}{2} - \dfrac{x}{2}$ Simplify.

$\dfrac{x+4}{x} - \dfrac{x}{2} \geq 0$ Add the two fractions on the left-hand side. The LCD is $2x$.

$\dfrac{2 \cdot (x+4)}{2x} - \dfrac{x \cdot x}{2x} \geq 0$ Add the fractions.

$\dfrac{2x + 8 - x^2}{2x} \geq 0$ Put the numerator into ascending powers.

$\dfrac{8 + 2x - x^2}{2x} \geq 0$ Factor both the numerator and the denominator.

$\dfrac{(4-x)(2+x)}{2x} \geq 0$ Simplify.

The values of x that make the numerator or denominator equal to zero are called the **critical numbers** or **critical values** of x. Find the critical values of x for the fraction.

$$x = 0, -2, \text{ and } 4.$$

Notice that the critical values of x and the roots in the first method of solving the inequality are identically the same. Plot the critical values on a number line.

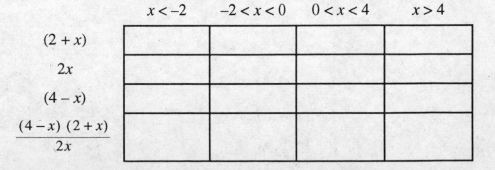

Build a table for the four regions of the graph and the factors of the numerator and denominator and the fraction itself.

	$x < -2$	$-2 < x < 0$	$0 < x < 4$	$x > 4$
$(2 + x)$				
$2x$				
$(4 - x)$				
$\dfrac{(4-x)(2+x)}{2x}$				

Now go down the table and determine the sign of each factor for the different regions.

	$x < -2$	$-2 < x < 0$	$0 < x < 4$	$x > 4$
$(2 + x)$	$-$	$+$	$+$	$+$
$2x$	$-$	$-$	$+$	$+$
$(4 - x)$	$+$	$+$	$+$	$-$
$\dfrac{(4 - x)\,(2 + x)}{2x}$	$+$	$-$	$+$	$-$

Our table does not appear the same as in the last problem, we are looking for $\dfrac{(4 - x)\,(2 + x)}{2x} \geq 0$. The table indicates that $\dfrac{(4 - x)\,(2 + x)}{2x}$ is positive when $x < -2$ or $0 < x < 4$. Since the original inequality is ≥ 0, we include the end points in our solution. Write the answer in a solution set.

$\{x \mid x \leq -2 \text{ or } 0 < x \leq 4\}$.

In interval notation, we get $(-\infty, -2] \cup [0, 4]$. Notice that both methods of solving the inequality give the same solution. You may do the following problems either way, but we will do them only by the method of fractions in this book.

EXERCISE 3.10

Solve the following inequalities for x:

1. $x^2 + x - 6 \geq 0$

2. $3x^2 - 5x + 2 < 0$

3. $6x^2 - 13x - 5 \leq 0$

4. $x^3 - 4x^2 - 5x \geq 0$

5. $x^3 - x^2 - 8x + 4 < 0$

6. $x^3 - 3x^2 - x + 3 > 0$

7. $7x^2 - 6x^3 > -3x$

8. $\dfrac{x - 1}{x + 2} > 0$

9. $\dfrac{x}{2} + \dfrac{2}{x} \le 2$

10. $\dfrac{2}{x-1} \ge \dfrac{1}{5}$

11. $\dfrac{x^2 - x - 6}{x^2 - 1} \le 0$

12. $\dfrac{1}{x^2} + \dfrac{2}{x-3} \ge 0$

ANSWERS TO EXERCISE 3.10

1. $\{x \mid x \le -3 \text{ or } x \ge 2\}$ 2. $\{x \mid \dfrac{2}{3} \le x \le 1\}$

3. $\{x \mid +-\dfrac{2}{3} \le x \le 5\}$ 4. $\{x \mid -1 \le x \le 0 \text{ or } x \ge 5\}$

5. $\{x \mid x < -2 \text{ or } 1 < x < 2\}$ 6. $\{x \mid -1 < x < 1 \text{ or } x > 3\}$

7. $\{x \mid x < -\dfrac{1}{3} \text{ or } 0 < x < \dfrac{3}{2}\}$ 8. $\{x \mid x < -2 \text{ or } x > 1\}$

9. $\{x \mid x < 0\}$ 10. $\{x \mid 1 < x \le 11\}$

11. $\{x \mid -2 \le x < 1 \text{ or } 1 < x \le 3\}$

12. $\{x \mid \dfrac{3}{2} \le x < 0 \text{ or } 0 < x \le 1 \text{ or } x > 3\}$

RADICAL EQUATIONS

A radical equation is an equation which contains a radical expression (root). Solving a radical equation requires raising both sides of an equation to a power to eliminate the radical. There is, however, a problem in squaring both sides of an equation. For example, the equation $x = 2$ is a first degree equation and has only one solution. If you square both sides of this equation you get $x^2 = 4$. This equation is a quadratic equation which has two solutions ($x = \pm 2$). When you square both sides of an equation, you sometimes get **extraneous answers** or **extraneous roots**. Extraneous roots are extra answers which do not make the original equation true.

$x^2 = 4$ has answers of 2 and –2, but the original equation,

$x = 2$ has only one solution.

When you raise both sides of an equation to a power, the solution set of the new equation will contain all of the solutions to the original equation, but may contain extra answers. That is, the solution set of the original equation is a subset of the solution set of the equation when you square both sides.

Extraneous answers only occur when you raise both sides of the equation to an even power. If you raise both sides to the 3rd, 5th, 7th, . . . power you will *not* gain extraneous roots. You may gain extraneous roots, however, when you raise both sides to the 2nd, 4th, 6th, . . . power. The reason for this is quite simple.

$$(-a)^{even} = (+a)^{even}; \ (-a)^{odd} \neq (+a)^{odd}$$

When you raise both sides of an equation to an even power, you must check the solutions for extraneous roots.

To solve radical equations use the following rules:
1. Simplify the equation.
2. Clear of all fractions.
3. Isolate the most complicated appearing radical on one side of the equation.
4. Raise both sides of the equation to the same power as the index of the radical (i.e., square both sides if a square root, cube both sides if a cube root, and so forth). When there is more than one radical expression, you may have to raise both sides to a power more than one time.
5. Solve the equation.
6. Check for extraneous roots. Check the solutions in the original equation when you raise both sides to an even power.

EXAMPLE 3.40

Solve the following equations for x:
a) $\sqrt{x} + 3 = 5$
b) $3x + 2 = \sqrt{6x + 4}$

SOLUTION 3.40

a) $\sqrt{x} + 3 = 5$ Isolate the radical on one side of the equation. Add -3 to both sides of the equation.

$\sqrt{x} + 3 - 3 = 5 - 3$ Simplify.
$\sqrt{x} = 2$ Square both sides of the equation.

$(\sqrt{x})^2 = (2)^2$ Simplify again.
$x = 4$ Check your answer to see if it is an extraneous root.

Check:
$\quad x = 4$
$\quad \sqrt{4} + 3 \overset{?}{=} 5$
$\quad 2 + 3 = 5$ The solution is correct.
The solution set is $\{4\}$.

b) $3x + 2 = \sqrt{6x + 4}$ The radical is already isolated, so square both sides of the equation. When you square the sides of an equation, you must square the sides, not the terms.

$(3x + 2)^2 = (\sqrt{6x + 4})^2$ Simplify.

Remember how to square a binomial. A binomial is squared by the following property:

$$(a + b)^2 = a^2 + 2ab + b^2$$

When we square a square root, the radical is eliminated.

$9x^2 + 12x + 4 = 6x + 4$ Add $-6x$ and -4 to both sides.

$9x^2 + 12x + 4 - 6x - 4 = 6x + 4 - 6x - 4$

Simplify again.

$9x^2 + 6x = 0$ The equation is a quadratic equation. Solve by factoring.

$3x(3x + 2) = 0$ Set each factor equal to zero and solve.

$x = 0, -\dfrac{2}{3}$ Check the solutions for extraneous roots.

Check:

$x = 0$

$3 \cdot 0 + 2 \stackrel{?}{=} \sqrt{6 \cdot 0 + 4}$

$0 + 2 \stackrel{?}{=} \sqrt{0 + 4}$

$2 = 2$

The first solution checks. Now check the second solution.

$x = -\dfrac{2}{3}$

$3 \cdot -\dfrac{2}{3} + 2 \stackrel{?}{=} \sqrt{6 \cdot -\dfrac{2}{3} + 4}$

$-2 + 2 \stackrel{?}{=} \sqrt{-4 + 4}$

$0 = 0$ Both solutions check. There are no extra roots.

The solution set is $\{-\dfrac{2}{3}, 0\}$.

EXERCISE 3.11

Solve the following radical equations.

1. $\sqrt{x + 5} = 8$

2. $\sqrt{x + 2} - 3 = 7$

3. $\sqrt[3]{x+2} + 4 = 6$

4. $\sqrt{x-4} + \sqrt{x} = 2$

5. $\sqrt{2x-5} = \sqrt{3x-11}$

ANSWERS TO EXERCISE 3.11

1. $\{9\}$
2. $\{98\}$
3. $\{6\}$
4. $\{4\}$
5. $\{6\}$

SECTION 3.8 EQUATIONS QUADRATIC IN FORM

A quadratic equation is a second degree equation. The standard form of a quadratic equation is

$$ax^2 + bx + c = 0$$

A quadratic equation can be expressed as (1) a trinomial or (2) where the highest power of the variable and the middle power are half powers of each other. Any quadratic equation can be solved by one of the methods we learned in Section 3.6. The quadratic formula can be used to solve other types of equations. Equations which can be written as trinomials where the highest power of the variable and the middle power of the variable are half powers of each other can be solved by the methods used to solve quadratic equations. The following equations are what are called **quadratic in nature** or **quadratic in form**. Equations which are quadratic in nature or form can be solved by any of the methods used to solve quadratic equations.

EXAMPLE 3.41

Solve the following by the methods used to solve quadratic equations.

a) $x^4 - 3x^2 - 4 = 0$

b) $x^6 - 9x^3 + 8 = 0$

c) $x - \sqrt{x} - 2 = 0$

d) $x^{2/3} - 3x^{1/3} - 4 = 0$

SOLUTION 3.41

a) $x^4 - 3x^2 - 4 = 0$

This is not a quadratic equation, but it is quadratic in form. The highest power and the middle power of x are half of each other. Let's solve this equation by factoring.

$$(x^2 - 4)(x^2 + 1) = 0$$

Solve for x^2 by setting each factor equal to zero and solving.

$$x^2 = 4 \text{ or } x^2 = 1$$

We can now solve for x by using extraction of roots.

Remember, when you take the square root of both sides of an equation, you must include both the positive and the negative of the square.

$$\sqrt{x^2} = \pm\sqrt{4} \quad \text{or} \quad \sqrt{x^2} = \pm\sqrt{-1}$$

Simplify.

$$x = \pm 2 \text{ and } x = \pm i$$

Separate the solutions and write them in a solution set.

$$\{-2, 2, -i, i\}$$

b) $\quad x^6 - 9x^3 + 8 = 0$

This is an equation which is quadratic in form. Solve by factoring.

$$(x^3 - 8)(x^3 - 1) = 0$$

Continue factoring as differences of cubes.

$$(x - 2)(x^2 + 2x + 4)(x - 1)(x^2 + x + 1) = 0$$

Set each factor equal to zero.

Factor 1:
$$x - 2 = 0$$
$$x = 2$$

Factor 2:
$$x^2 + 2x + 4 = 0$$

Solve by use of the quadratic formula.

$$a = 1, b = 2, \text{ and } c = 4$$

Substitute a, b, and c into the formula.

$$x = \frac{-2 \pm \sqrt{2^2 - 4(1)(4)}}{2}$$

Compute under the ratical.

$$x = \frac{-2 \pm \sqrt{4 - 16}}{2}$$

Continue simplifying under the radical.

$$x = \frac{-2 \pm \sqrt{-12}}{2}$$

Factor -12 and remove the perfect roots.

$$x = \frac{-2 \pm \sqrt{-1 \cdot 1 \cdot 3}}{2}$$

Remove the -1 and 4.

$$x = \frac{-2 \pm 2i\sqrt{3}}{2}$$

Factor out the common factor of 2.

$$x = \frac{2(-1 \pm i\sqrt{3})}{2}$$

Divide the common factor

of 2.

$$x = -1 \pm i\sqrt{3}$$

Separate the solutions into two solutions.

$$x = -1 + i\sqrt{3}, -1 - i\sqrt{3}$$

Factor 3:

$$x - 1 = 0$$
$$x = 1$$

Factor 4:

$$x^2 + x + 1 = 0$$

Solve by use of the quadratic formula.

$$a = 1, b = 1 \text{ and } c = 1$$

Substitute a, b, and c into the quadratic formula.

$$x = \frac{-1 \pm \sqrt{1^2 - 4(1)(1)}}{2}$$

Compute under the radical.

$$x = \frac{-1 \pm \sqrt{1 - 4}}{2}$$

Continue simplifying under the radical.

$$x = \frac{-1 \pm \sqrt{-3}}{2}$$

Remove the negative from under the radical.

$$x = \frac{-1 \pm i\sqrt{3}}{2}$$

Separate the answers.

$$x = \frac{-1 + i\sqrt{3}}{2}, \frac{-1 - i\sqrt{3}}{2}$$

Write the solutions in a solution set.

$$\left\{2, 1, -1 + i\sqrt{3}, -1 - i\sqrt{3}, \frac{-1 + i\sqrt{3}}{2}, \frac{-1 - i\sqrt{3}}{2}\right\}$$

c) $x - \sqrt{x} - 2 = 0$

If we put the $\sqrt{x}$ into power notation, we get a trinomial equation.

$$x - x^{1/2} - 2 = 0$$

This equation is quadratic in form. The highest power and middle powers are half powers of each other. This equation will factor.

$$(x^{1/2} - 2)(x^{1/2} + 1) = 0$$

Set each factor equal to zero.

$$x^{1/2} - 2 = 0 \quad \text{or} \quad x^{1/2} + 1 = 0$$
$$x^{1/2} = 2 \text{ and } x^{1/2} = -1$$

Solve.

Replace $x^{1/2}$ with radical expression.

$$\sqrt{x} = 2 \text{ and } \sqrt{x} = -1$$

Solve.

First equation:

$$\sqrt{x} = 2$$

Square both sides.

$$(\sqrt{x})^2 = 2^2$$
$$x = 4$$

Simplify.
Check the answer by substituting into equation 1 to see if it is an extraneous root.

Check:
$$x = 4_?$$
$$\sqrt{4} \overset{?}{=} 2$$
$$2 = 2$$

Square both sides.
The solution checks.

Second equation:
$$\sqrt{x} = -1$$

The equation $\sqrt{x} = -1$ has no solutions. $\sqrt{x}$ cannot equal a negative number.

The solution set is $\{4\}$.

d) $x^{2/3} - 3x^{1/3} - 4 = 0$

This is a trinomial equation that is quadratic in nature.

Solve by factoring
$$(x^{1/3} - 4)(x^{1/3} + 1) = 0$$

Set each factor equal to zero.

$$x^{1/3} - 4 = 0 \quad \text{or} \quad x^{1/3} + 1 = 0$$

Solve both equations.

First equation:
$$x^{1/3} - 4 = 0$$
$$x^{1/3} = 4$$

Add +4 to both sides.
Raise both sides to the third power.

$$(x^{1/3})^3 = 4^3$$
$$x = 64$$

Simplify.
This solution does not need to be checked since we raised both sides to an odd power.

Second equation:
$$x^{1/3} + 1 = 0$$

Add −1 to both sides of the equation.

$$x^{1/3} = -1$$

Cube both sides of the equation.

$$(x^{1/3})^3 = (-1)^3$$
$$x = -1$$

Simplify.
The solution again does not need to be checked since we raised both sides to an odd power.

The solution set is $\{64, -1\}$

EXERCISE 3.12

Solve the following by using the methods of solving quadratic equations.
1. $x^4 - 8x^2 + 15 = 0$

2. $x^4 - 3x^2 = 4$

3. $x - 10x^{1/3} + 9 = 0$

ANSWERS TO EXERCISE 3.12

1. $\{2, -2\}$
2. $\{2, -2, i, -i\}$
3. $\{1, 81\}$

4

Graphs and Functions

SECTION 4.1 CARTESIAN PLANE

In the last chapter, we solved equations in one variable. If there was more than one variable, then we solved the equation for one variable in terms of the other variable or variables. In this chapter, we will find numerical solutions to equations in more than one variable. The equation

$$2x + 3y = 6$$

has infinitely many solutions. Solutions to equations in two variables are paired answers. We write the solutions as ordered pairs. The procedure is to write the pair in parenthesis (x, y) where the first component of the pair represents the first variable in alphabetical order and the second component of the pair represents the second variable in alphabetical order. If the equation was $2a + 3b = 6$, then the ordered pairs would be (a, b). Since we cannot write all of the solutions to equations in two variables, we will have to graph them. To graph the solutions which have paired answers, we will need a **real number** plane. The real number plane is called the **rectangular plane, coordinate plane**; or the **Cartesian plane**, named after the mathematician Descartes. The Cartesian plane is formed by intersecting two number lines at a right angle.

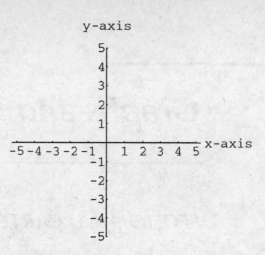

Figure 4.1

The horizontal number line is called the *x*-axis (**abscissa**) and the vertical number line is called the *y*-axis (**ordinate**). The location where the two number lines intersect is called the **origin**. The two number lines break the number plane or Cartesian plane into four **quadrants.**

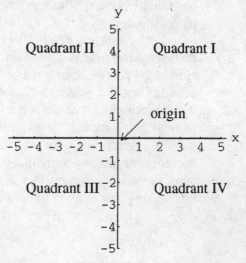

Figure 4.2

The quadrants are numbered counterclockwise I, II, III, and IV. To plot the point $P(3, 5)$, we start at the origin and locate the number 3 on the horizontal axis and draw a vertical line passing through 3. We then find the number 5 on the vertical axis and draw a horizontal line passing through the 5 on the vertical axis. The point $P(3, 5)$ is found at the intersection of the vertical and horizontal lines.

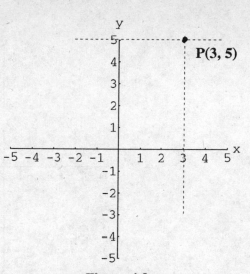

Figure 4.3

Notice the points *P*, *Q*, *R*, and *S* plotted on Figure 4.4. See how the horizontal and vertical lines intersect.

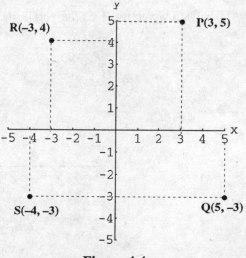

Figure 4.4

EXAMPLE 4.1

Plot the indicated points on the Cartesian plane:
A(3, –1), *B*(–4, 3), *C*(–6, –2), and *D*(5, –3)

SOLUTION 4.1

A(3, –1), *B*(–4, 3), *C*(–6, –2), and *D*(5, –3)
To plot point *A*, we start at 3 on the *x*-axis and draw a vertical line.

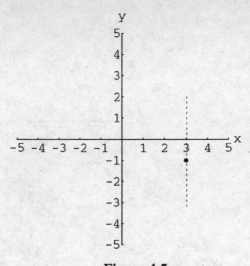

Figure 4.5

Then we go to –1 on the *y*-axis and draw a vertical line.

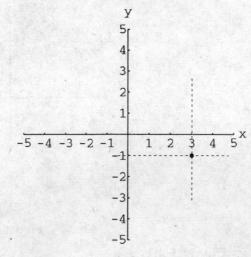

Figure 4.6

The intersection of the horizontal and vertical lines is the point *A*.

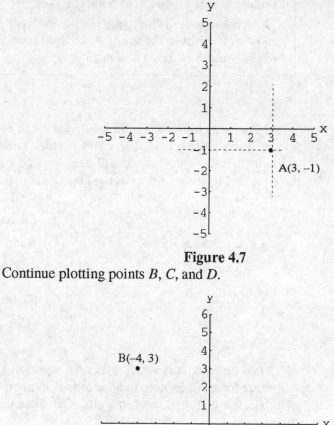

Figure 4.7

Continue plotting points *B*, *C*, and *D*.

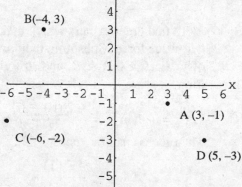

Figure 4.8

The real ordered pairs (*a*, *b*) can be graphed on the Cartesian plane and the Cartesian plane contains ordered pairs in the form of (*a*, *b*). We thus have a **one-to-one correspondence** between the set of real ordered pairs (*a*, *b*) and the points on the Cartesian plane. A one-to-one correspondence between the ordered pairs and the points on the Cartesian plane implies for each point there is only one ordered pair and for each ordered pair there is only one point. Thus we have what is called a one-to-one correspondence between the real ordered pairs and the points of the plane. This brings us to the Fundamental Theorem of Analytic Geometry.

> **Fundamental Theorem of Analytic Geometry:**
> There is a one-to-one correspondence between the points in a plane
> and the elements in the set of all ordered pairs in the form of (a, b)
> where a and b are real numbers.

Graphing by Plotting Point by Point

The solutions to the equation $2x + 3y = 6$ can be graphed on the Cartesian plane by finding values of x and y which make the equation true and graphing them on the Cartesian plane. To find ordered pair solutions to the equation, it becomes easiest to solve the equation for the variable y.

$2x + 3y = 6$ Add a $-2x$ to both sides of the equation.

$2x + 3y - 2x = 6 - 2x$ Simplify.

$3y = -2x + 6$ Divide both sides by 3.

$\dfrac{3y}{3} = \dfrac{-2x + 6}{3}$ Simplify again.

$y = \dfrac{-2x + 6}{3}$

To find ordered pairs which make the equation true, choose any numerical value for x. Substitute them into the equation and calculate the value of y. Let $x = 0, 1, 2, 3$, and so forth. Calculate the corresponding values for y.

Let $x = 0$, then $y = \dfrac{-2(0) + 6}{3} = \dfrac{0 + 6}{3} = 2$.
The ordered pair becomes $(0, 2)$.

Let $x = 1$, then $y = \dfrac{-2(1) + 6}{3} = \dfrac{-2 + 6}{3} = \dfrac{4}{3}$.

The solution becomes $(1, \dfrac{4}{3})$.

Let $x = 2$, then $y = \dfrac{-2(2) + 6}{3} = \dfrac{-4 + 6}{3} = \dfrac{2}{3}$.

The solution becomes $(2, \dfrac{2}{3})$.

Once more, let $x = 3$, then $y = \dfrac{-2(3) + 6}{3} = \dfrac{-6 + 6}{3} = 0$

The solution becomes (3, 0).

Plot the ordered pairs on the Cartesian plane.

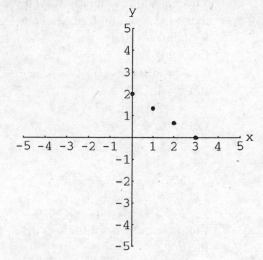

Figure 4.9

Notice that the points appear to fall into a straight line. Draw a straight line through the points.

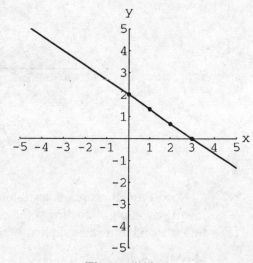

Figure 4.10

From the graph you can see why $2x + 3y = 6$ is called a **linear equation**. The graph of the line is the solution set of the equation and the solution set of the equation is the graph of the line.

EXAMPLE 4.2

Graph the following linear equation by plotting points: $y = 3x - 2$

SOLUTION 4.2

$y = 3x - 2$

This equation is already solved for y. Find four or five ordered pairs that make the equation true. Let $x = 0, 1, 2, 3,$ and 4 and calculate the corresponding y values.

Let $x = 0$.

$y = 3(0) - 2 = 0 - 2 = -2$ The solution is $(0, -2)$.

Let $x = 1$.

$y = 3(1) - 2 = 3 - 2 = 1$ The solution is $(1, 1)$.

Let $x = 2$.

$y = 3(2) - 2 = 6 - 2 = 4$ The solution is $(2, 4)$.

Let $x = 3$.

$y = 3(3) - 2 = 9 - 2 = 7$ The solution is $(3, 7)$.

Let $x = 4$.

$y = 3(4) - 2 = 12 - 2 = 10$ The solution is $(4, 10)$.

Plot at least three of these ordered pairs on the Cartesian plane and graph the line.

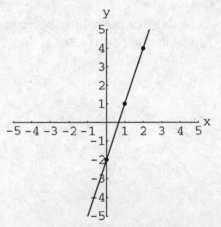

Figure 4.11

Not all equations graph a straight line. Find the solution set of the following equation by finding some of the ordered pairs that make the equation true and draw the graph as best you can.

EXAMPLE 4.3

$y = x^2 - 1$

SOLUTION 4.3

$y = x^2 - 1$

The equation is already solved for y. Let $x = -2, -1, 0, 1,$ and 2. We have chosen positive and negative values of x to give a better representation of the graph.

Let $x = 0$.
$$y = (0)^2 - 1 = 0 - 1 = -1$$ The ordered pair is $(0, -1)$.
Let $x = 1$
$$y = (1)^2 - 1 = 1 - 1 = 0$$ The ordered pair is $(1, 0)$.
Let $x = 2$
$$y = (2)^2 - 1 = 4 - 1 = 3$$ The ordered pair is $(2, 3)$.
Let $x = -1$
$$y = (-1)^2 - 1 = 1 - 1 = 0$$ The ordered pair is $(-1, 0)$.
Let $x = -2$
$$y = (-2)^2 - 1 = 4 - 1 = 3$$ The ordered pair is $(-2, 3)$.

Graph these points on a Cartesian plane.

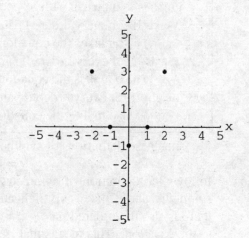

Figure 4.12

Draw the curve passing through these points.

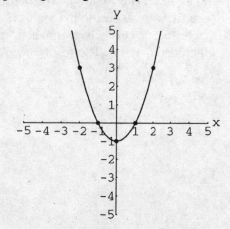

Figure 4.13

This graph is called a **parabola**. An equation in the form $y = ax^2 + bx + c$ where a, b, c are constants and $a \neq 0$ will graph a parabola. We will graph parabolas more extensively later in this chapter.

Symmetry

Look at the graph of $y = x^2 - 1$ (Figure 4.13). This graph is said to be *symmetric with respect to the y-axis*. That is, if this graph is rotated 180° (one-half turn) about the y-axis, the appearance of the graph is identically the same as the original graph. Similarly, if a graph is rotated 180° about the x-axis and the curve appears exactly the same as the original graph, then the graph is *symmetric with respect to the x-axis*.

Symmetry

A graph is symmetric with respect to the:

1. **x-axis** if for every ordered pair (x, y) that makes the equation true, $(x, -y)$ also makes the equation true.
2. **y-axis** if for every ordered pair (x, y) that makes the equation true, $(-x, y)$ also makes the equation true.
3. **origin** if for every ordered pair (x, y) that makes the equation true, $(-x, -y)$ also makes the equation true.

Using these definitions of symmetry, let's check to see that
$$y = x^2 - 1$$
follows the definition of symmetry about the y-axis. The definition of symmetry about the y-axis indicates that for every ordered pair (x, y), there is also the ordered pair $(-x, y)$. The ordered pair $(2, 3)$ is a solution to the equation. This means that if $y = x^2 - 1$ is symmetric with respect to the y-axis, then $(-2, 3)$ must also be a solution to the equation. Notice that $(-2, 3)$ is a solution. The definition does not say that a graphs is symmetric with respect to the y-axis if one ordered pair works. The definition says that a curve is symmetric only if every ordered pair (x, y) also included $(-x, y)$. The test to see if a graph is symmetric with respect to

one of the axis is as follows:

> **Theorem: Test for Symmetry**
> 1. If x is replaced by $-x$ and the equation remains equivalent to the original equation, then the equation is symmetric with respect to the **y-axis**.
> 2. If y is replaced with $-y$ and the equation remains equivalent to the original equation, then the equation is symmetric with respect to the **x-axis**.
> 3. If both x and y are replaced with $-x$ and $-y$ and the equation remains equivalent to the original equation, then the equation is symmetric with respect to the **origin**.

EXAMPLE 4.4

Check for symmetry with respect for the x-axis, y-axis, and the origin.
$$x^2 + y^2 = 25$$

SOLUTION 4.4
$$x^2 + y^2 = 25$$

Testing for symmetry with respect to the x-axis, we replace y with $-y$.
$$x^2 + (-y)^2 = 25$$
$$x^2 + y^2 = 25$$

The equation is exactly the same. The equation is symmetric with respect to the x-axis. Testing for symmetry with respect tot he y-axis, we replace x with $-x$.
$$(-x)^2 + y^2 = 25$$
$$x^2 + y^2 = 25$$

The equation is exactly the same. Therefore, the equation is also symmetric with respect to the y-axis. Testing for symmetry with respect to the origin, we replace both x and y with $-x$ and $-y$.
$$(-x)^2 + (-y)^2 = 25$$
$$x^2 + y^2 = 25$$

The equation is exactly the same. The equation is likewise symmetric with respect to the origin.

Distance Between Points

The formula for the distance between two points comes from the Pythagorean Theorem. Pythagoras proved that the sum of the squares of the sides of a right triangle is equal to the hypotenuse squared.

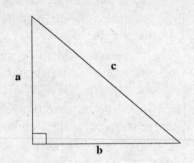

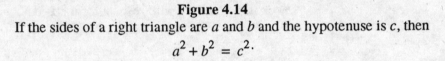

Figure 4.14

If the sides of a right triangle are a and b and the hypotenuse is c, then

$$a^2 + b^2 = c^2.$$

Let $P_1(x_1, y_1)$ and $P_2(x_2, y_2)$ be two points on the Cartesian plane with d the distance between them.

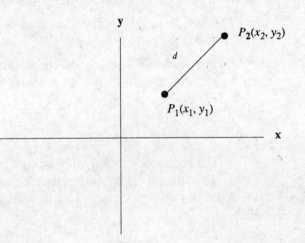

Figure 4.15

Construct a right triangle drawing a horizontal line through P_1 and a vertical line through P_2. Label the vertex at the right angle P_3. Then P_3 has coordinates (x_2, y_1). The sides of the triangle are vertical and horizontal lines. The length of the horizontal side is $|x_2 - x_1|$ and the length of the vertical side is $|y_2 - y_1|$.

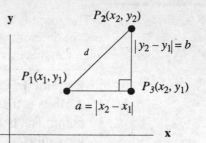

Figure 4.16

$$d^2 = a^2 + b^2$$
$$d^2 = (|x_2 - x_1|)^2 + (|y_2 - y_1|)^2.$$

Since the distance $|x_2 - x_1|$ and $|y_2 - y_1|$ are squared, we do not need the absolute value signs.

$$d^2 = (x_2 - x_1)^2 + (y_2 - y_1)^2$$

We want the distance, not the distance squared, so take the square root of both sides. Distance cannot be negative, we do not need the $\pm$.

$$\sqrt{d^2} = \sqrt{(x_2 - x_1)^2 + (y_2 - y_1)^2}$$
$$d = \sqrt{(x_2 - x_1)^2 + (y_2 - y_1)^2}$$

EXAMPLE 4.5

Find the distance between the following points: (3, 4) and (−1, 1).

SOLUTION 4.5

Given the distance formula $d = \sqrt{(x_2 - x_1)^2 + (y_2 - y_1)^2}$. With the ordered pairs we have, let (x_1, y_1) be (3, 4) and (x_2, y_2) be (−1, 1). Substitute the numerical values into the formula. Use parentheses to avoid errors.

$$d = \sqrt{((-1) - (3))^2 + ((1) - (4))^2}$$ Calculate inside of parentheses.
$$d = \sqrt{(-4)^2 + (-3)^2}$$ Square each term.
$$d = \sqrt{16 + 9}$$ Add the values.
$$d = \sqrt{25}$$ Standardize the radical.
$$d = 5$$

Circles

The formula for the distance between two points is helpful in solving several different types of problems like those in the last section. The distance formula can also be used to determine other types of equations.

> **Definition: Circle**
> A **circle** is the set of all points in a plane equidistant from a fixed point. The fixed point is called the **center** and the distance is called the **radius**.

Let the point (h, k) be the center of a circle with radius equal to r.

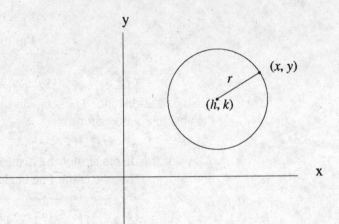

Figure 4.17

The equation of the circle is the set of all points (x, y) such that

$$\sqrt{(x-h)^2 + (y-k)^2} = r \quad (r > 0)$$

Since $r > 0$, we can square both sides and get equivalently

$$(x-h)^2 + (y-k)^2 = r^2 \quad (r > 0)$$

Theorem:. Standard Form of a Circle

1. The standard form of the circle with radius r ($r > 0$) and center (h, k):

$$(x-h)^2 + (y-k)^2 = r^2$$

2. The standard form of the circle with radius r ($r > 0$) and center $(0, 0)$:

$$x^2 + y^2 = r^2$$

EXAMPLE 4.6

Write the equation of the circle in both standard form and expanded form with:

a) Center at the origin and radius $r = 6$.

b) Center at the $(-3, 4)$ and passes through the origin.

SOLUTION 4.6

a) Center at the origin and radius $r = 6$.

   The standard form of a circle with center at the origin is $x^2 + y^2 = r^2$. Since $r = 6$, we get

$$x^2 + y^2 = 6^2$$
$$x^2 + y^2 = 36$$

   The equation in expanded form is $x^2 + y^2 - 6 = 0$.

b) Center at the $(-3, 4)$ and passes through the origin.

   To write the equation of a circle we need both the center and the radius. Let's construct the information given. Plot the center and the origin. Draw a circle with $(-3, 4)$ as its center passing through the origin.

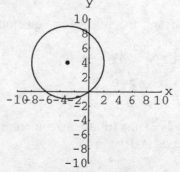

Figure 4.18

To find the equation of the circle, we need both the center and the radius. We were given the center, but we must find the radius of the circle. The radius is the distance between the center and any point on the circle. The origin is on the circle. Use the distance formula to find the radius.

$$r = \sqrt{((-3)-0)^2 + (4-0)^2}$$

$$r = \sqrt{(-3)^2 + (4)^2}$$

$$r = \sqrt{9+16}$$

$$r = \sqrt{25}$$

$$r = 5$$

Now using the standard form of a circle, write the equation of the circle with center $(-3, 4)$ and radius $r = 5$.

$$(x-(-3))^2 + (y-4)^2 = (5)^2 \qquad \text{Simplify.}$$
$$(x+3)^2 + (y-4)^2 = 25 \qquad \text{Expand.}$$

$$x^2 + 6x + 9 + y^2 - 8y + 16 = 25 \qquad \text{Add } -25 \text{ to both sides and}$$
$$\qquad\qquad\qquad\qquad\qquad\qquad\qquad \text{simplify.}$$

$$x^2 + y^2 + 6x - 8y = 0$$

EXERCISE 4.1

Plot the following points. Plot each problem on a separate Cartesian plane:

1. $A(2, 3)$, $B(-1, 5)$, $C(-3, -4)$, and $D(5, -1)$

2. $A(-5, -4)$, $B(-3, 5)$, $C(3, -1)$, and $D(6, 3)$

3. $A\left(\dfrac{1}{2}, \dfrac{3}{2}\right)$, $B\left(-\dfrac{2}{3}, 5\dfrac{1}{2}\right)$, $C\left(-2\dfrac{3}{4}, -4\dfrac{5}{6}\right)$, and $D\left(2\dfrac{2}{3}, -1\dfrac{1}{4}\right)$

Graph the following equations by plotting enough points to draw the graph:

4. $y = 4x - 3$

5. $xy = 6$

6. $y^2 = x + 4$

Check the following equations for symmetry with respect to the x-axis, y-axis and the origin.

7. $x^2 - y + 3 = 0$

8. $x^2 + y^2 = 16$

9. $y = x^4 - x^2$

Use the distance formula to solve the following problems.

10. Find the distance between $(-3, 5)$ and $(5, -7)$.

11. Find x so that the distance between $(x, 5)$ and $(3, -7)$ is 13.

Write the equations of the following circles in expanded form (General Form):

12. Center at $(3, -4)$ with radius $r = 4$.

13. Center at origin passing through the point $(2, 3)$.

Write the following circles in standard form. Find the center, the radius, and graph.

ANSWERS TO EXERCISE 4.1

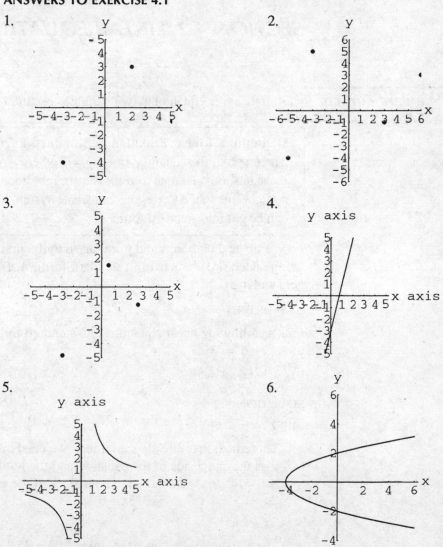

7. $\{y\text{-axis}\}$

8. $\{x\text{-axis}, y\text{-axis}, \text{origin}\}$

9. $\{y\text{-axis}\}$

10. $\{4\sqrt{13}\}$

11. $\{-2, 8\}$

12. $\{x^2 + y^2 - 6x + 8y + 9 = 0\}$

13. $\{x^2 + y^2 - 13 = 0\}$

SECTION 4.2 LINEAR EQUATIONS

Standard Form of a Linear Equation

A first degree equation in two variables is called a linear equation.

> **Definition: Linear Equation in Standard Form**
> The graph of the equation $Ax + By = C$ where A, B and C are constants, not all equal to zero, is a straight line. Any graph of a straight line in the Cartesian coordinate system has an equation that can be put into standard form.

In a linear equation, x and y are raised to the first power and x and y are being added or subtracted. In standard form, A, B and C should be integers and $A \geq 0$.

EXAMPLE 4.7

Put the following linear equations into standard form:

a) $2x - 6 = 3y$

b) $y = -\dfrac{1}{2}x + 3$

SOLUTION 4.7

a) $2x - 6 = 3y$

This equation is already simplified. We need to get the variables x and y on the same side of the equation and the number term on the opposite side. Add $-3y$ and $+6$ to both sides of the equation.

$2x - 6 - 3y + 6 = 3y - 3y + 6$ Simplify.

$2x - 3y = 6$

The equation is in standard form with $A = 2$, $B = -3$ and $C = 6$.

b) $y = -\dfrac{1}{2}x + 3$

Multiply both sides of the equation by 2 to clear of the fraction.

$2 \cdot y = 2 \cdot (-\dfrac{1}{2}x + 3)$ Simplify.

$2y = -x + 6$ Add $+x$ to both sides of the equation.

$2y + x = -x + 6 + x$ Simplify.

$x + 2y = 6$

The equation is in standard form with $A = 1$, $B = 2$, and $C = 6$.

The graph of a linear equation is a straight line. Any equation which can be written into the standard form of a linear equation will graph a straight line. And any equation in the Cartesian coordinate system with a graph that is a straight line has an equation that can be written in standard form. To graph a linear equation, we need to plot only enough points to be certain that we do not make a mistake in graphing. Two points are enough to graph a line provided that we do not make a mistake in finding these points or in graphing them. If a line crosses the x and y axis at two different points these two points can be used to graph the line. The points where the line intersects the x- and the y- axis are called the **x- and y-intercepts**. Some lines, however, do not cross both axis and some lines pass through the origin which means there is only one intercept. If the line does not have two different intercepts, then plot the graph using points other than the intercepts. If the line does have two different x- and y-intercepts, graph the line by plotting the intercepts. The method of graphing a line using the x- and y-intercepts is called the **intercept method** of graphing straight lines.

Slope of a Line

The slope of a line is defined as the change in y divided by the change in x. Using the letter m to represent the slope of a line, we get

$$m = \frac{\text{change in } y}{\text{change in } x}.$$

This is sometimes written as

$$m = \frac{\Delta y}{\Delta x}.$$

The symbol Δ is the capital Greek letter delta and stands for "change in." To the mathematician, the change between two values can be found by taking their difference. Let $P_1(x_1, y_1)$ and $P_2(x_2, y_2)$ be two different points. The change in y (Δy) is found by subtracting the y coordinates $(y_2 - y_1)$ and the change in x (Δx) is found by subtracting the x

coordinates $(x_2 - x_1)$. The formula for the slope becomes

$$m = \frac{y_2 - y_1}{x_2 - x_1}.$$

A straight line can be graphed using only one point and the slope.

EXAMPLE 4.8

Graph the line:

a)   passing through the point (2, 3) with a slope of $m = \frac{1}{2}$.

b)   passing through the point (–3, 5) with a slope of $m = -\frac{3}{2}$.

SOLUTION 4.8

a)   passing through the point (2, 3) with a slope of $m = \frac{1}{2}$.

Visualize lines passing through the point (2, 3). There are infinitely many lines which can pass through this point, but there is only one line that can pass through this point with a slope of $m = \frac{1}{2}$. The slope is defined as the change in y divided by the change in x. Our slope $m = \frac{1}{2}$ has $\Delta y = 1$ and $\Delta x = 2$. From the point (2, 3) we know, change y by 1 and change x by 2. Since both of these changes are positive, this means to start at the point (2, 3) and go one unit up and 2 units to the right and locate a second point on the line. Draw a line through these two points.

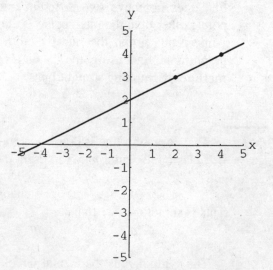

Figure 4.19

b)   passing through the point (–3, 5) with a slope of $m = -\frac{3}{2}$.

The slope of this line is $m = -\frac{3}{2}$. The negative in front of the slope needs to become part of the fraction. Rewrite $m = -\frac{3}{2}$ as $m = \frac{-3}{2}$.

It is always best to have fractions in their standard form. Start at the point (–3, 5) and move down 3 and to the right 2 and graph a point. Draw the line between these points.

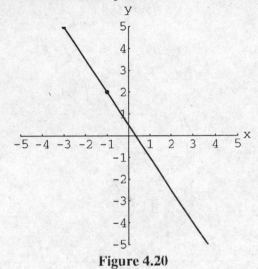

Figure 4.20

Slope-Intercept Form of a Straight Line

The equation $2x - 3y = 6$ has x- and y-intercepts of (3, 0) and (0, –2). If we find the slope of this line using these points we get,

$$m = \frac{-2 - 0}{0 - 3} = \frac{-2}{-3} = \frac{2}{3}.$$

Now solve the equation for y.

$2x - 3y = 6$	Add $-2x$ to both sides of the equation.
$2x - 3y - 2x = -2x + 6$	Simplify.
$-3y = -2x + 6$	Divide both sides by -3.
$\dfrac{-3y}{-3} = \dfrac{-2x}{-3} + \dfrac{6}{-3}$	Simplify again.
$y = \dfrac{2}{3}x - 2$	

Notice that the coefficient of x is $\frac{2}{3}$. $\frac{2}{3}$ is also the slope ($m = \frac{2}{3}$). This is not a coincidence. When we solve an equation for y in terms of x, the coefficient of x is always the slope of the equation. Notice also that the number term is –2. The y-intercept is (0, –2). This is also no coincidence. When a linear equation is solved for y in terms of x, the number term is the y-intercept.

The standard form of a linear equation is
$$Ax + By = C.$$
Solve this equation for y in terms of x.

$Ax + By = C$ — Add $-Ax$ to both sides of the equation.

$Ax + By - Ax = -Ax + C$ — Simplify.

$By = -Ax + C$ — Divide both sides by B ($B \neq 0$).

$\dfrac{By}{B} = \dfrac{-Ax + C}{B}$ — Simplify.

$y = \dfrac{-Ax + C}{B}$ — Separate the fraction into two fractions.

$y = \dfrac{-A}{B}x + \dfrac{C}{B}$ — When an equation is solved for the variable y, the coefficient of x is the slope $(m = \dfrac{-A}{B})$ and the line crosses the y-axis at $(0, \dfrac{C}{B})$.

If we use the letter m for the slope and b for the y-intercept, we get an equation

$$y = mx + b$$

The equation is known as the **slope-intercept form** of a straight line. All linear equations, except vertical lines, can be solved for y in terms of x.

EXAMPLE 4.9

Put the following equation into slope-intercept form. Find the slope, the y-intercept, and graph the line:

a) $2x + 3y = 6$

SOLUTION 4.9

a) $2x + 3y = 6$ — Solve the equation for y. Add $-2x$ to both sides of the equation.

$2x + 3y - 2x = -2x + 6$ — In slope intercept form the term involving x is written first. It is best to add the $-2x$ in front of the $+6$. Simplify the equation.

$$3y = -2x + 6$$

Divide both sides by 3 by dividing each term by 3.

$$\frac{3y}{3} = \frac{-2x}{3} + \frac{6}{3}$$

Simplify again.

$$y = \frac{-2}{3}x + 2$$

The slope of the line m is the coefficient of x. $m = \frac{-2}{3}$. The y-intercept is the number term. The y-intercept is $(0, 2)$. To graph the line we start at 2 on the y-axis and go down 2 and right 3. Graph the line.

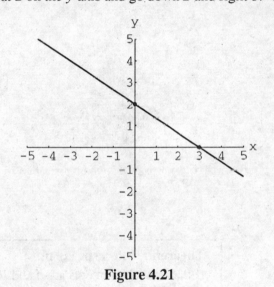

Figure 4.21

Special Forms of the Straight Line

When we first started graphing linear equations, we graphed them by using the intercept method. We let $x = 0$ and solved for y and let $y = 0$ and solved for x. The standard form of the linear equation is:

$$Ax + By = C.$$

Let $x = 0$.

$A(0) + By = C$	Simplify.
$By = C$	Divide both sides by B.
$\dfrac{By}{B} = \dfrac{C}{B}$	Simplifying the y-intercept is $\dfrac{C}{B}$.

Let $y = 0$.

$Ax + B(0) = C$	Simplify.
$Ax = C$	Divide both sides by A.

$$\frac{Ax}{A} = \frac{C}{A}$$ The x-intercept is $\frac{C}{A}$.

From standard form the x and y intercepts are

$$(\frac{C}{A}, 0) \quad \text{and} \quad (0, \frac{B}{A}).$$

The standard form of the linear equation is
$$Ax + By = C.$$
Take this equation and divide both sides by C.

$$\frac{Ax}{C} + \frac{By}{C} = \frac{C}{C}$$ If we simplify, we get:

$$\frac{A}{C}x + \frac{B}{C}y = 1$$ Notice that the coefficients of x and y are the reciprocals of the x and y intercepts. If we let $a = \frac{A}{C}$ and $b = \frac{B}{C}$, we could write the equation as:

$$\frac{1}{a}x + \frac{1}{b}y = 1$$ If we simplify, we get:

$$\frac{x}{a} + \frac{y}{b} = 1.$$ This equation is known as the **intercept form** of the straight line.

Theorem: Intercept Form

If the x and y intercepts are a and b, then the equation of the line is

$$\frac{x}{a} + \frac{y}{b} = 1.$$

EXAMPLE 4.10

Put the following into intercept form and indicate the x-intercept and the y-intercept:
a) $2x = 3y + 6$
b) $3x + 4y = 12$
c) $3x + 5y = 8$

SOLUTION 4.10

a) $2x = 3y + 6$ To put an equation into intercept form it must first be in standard form. Add $-3y$ to both sides. Simplify.

$$2x - 3y = 3y + 6 - 3y$$

$$2x - 3y = 6$$

In intercept form the equation must be equal to 1. Divide each term by 6. Simplify.

$$\frac{2x}{6} - \frac{3y}{6} = \frac{6}{6}$$

$$\frac{x}{3} + \frac{y}{-2} = 1$$

In intercept form the divisor of x is the x-intercept and the divisor of y is the y-intercept. 3 is the x intercept and -2 is the y-intercept. In intercept form the terms involving x and y must be added.

b) $3x + 4y = 12$

In intercept form the equation must equal 1. Divide each term by 12. Simplify.

$$\frac{3x}{12} + \frac{4y}{12} = \frac{12}{12}$$

$$\frac{x}{4} + \frac{y}{3} = 1$$

4 is the x-intercept and 3 is the y-intercept.

c) $3x + 5y = 8$

Divide each term by 8.

$$\frac{3x}{8} + \frac{5y}{8} = \frac{8}{8}$$

Simplify.

$$\frac{3}{8}x + \frac{5}{8}x = 1$$

In intercept form, the x and y intercepts are the divisors of x and y. Rewrite as $\frac{3}{8}x$ and $\frac{5}{8}y$ as division problems.

$$\frac{3}{8} \cdot x = x \div \frac{8}{3} \quad \frac{5}{8} \cdot x = x \div \frac{8}{5}$$

$$\frac{x}{\frac{8}{3}} + \frac{y}{\frac{8}{5}} = 1$$

$\frac{8}{3}$ is the x-intercept and $\frac{8}{5}$ is the y-intercept.

Another important form of the straight line is the point-slope form of the line. This equation allows us to write the equation of a straight line when we know at least one point and the slope.

Theorem: Point-Slope Form

Given a line containing the point (x_1, y_1) with slope m, the equation of the line is

$$y - y_1 = m(x - x_1)$$

EXAMPLE 4.11

Write an equation of the line in standard form with integer coefficients:

a) passes through the point (3, 5) and with a slope $m = -2$.

b) passes through the point (–4, 7) and with a slope $m = \dfrac{2}{3}$.

SOLUTION 4.11

a) The line passing through the point (3, 5) with a slope $m = -2$ can be found using the point slope form of the straight line.

$$y - y_1 = m(x - x_1)$$

In this form, x_1 and y_1 are the x and y coordinate of the given point and m is the slope. The x and y in the equation are the x and y variables of the linear equation. Substitute x, y and m into the point-slope form.

$y - 5 = -2(x - 5)$	Simplify.
$y - 5 = -2x + 10$	We want to keep the coefficient of x positive, so add $+2x$ to both sides of the equation.
$y - 5 + 2x = -2x + 10 + 2x$	Simplify again.
$2x + y - 5 = 10$	Add $+5$ to both sides of the equation.
$2x + y = 15$	

b) The line passing through the point (–4, 7) with slope $m = \dfrac{2}{3}$ can be found using the point-slope form of the straight line.

$$y - y_1 = m(x - x_1)$$

Substitute into the point-slope form.

$y - 7 = \dfrac{2}{3}(x - (-4))$	Simplify.
$y - 7 = \dfrac{2}{3}(x + 4)$	Distribute the $\dfrac{2}{3}$.
$y - 7 = \dfrac{2}{3}x + \dfrac{2}{3} \cdot 4$	Simplify.
$y - 7 = \dfrac{2}{3}x + \dfrac{8}{3}$	Clear of the fraction by multiplying both sides by 3.
$3(y - 7) = 3\left(\dfrac{2}{3}x + \dfrac{8}{3}\right)$	Simplify again.
$3y - 21 = 2x + 8$	Add $-3y$ and -8 to both sides of the equation.
$3y - 21 - 3y - 8 = 2x + 8 - 3y - 8$	Simplify.
$-29 = 2x - 3y$	Rewrite the equation with the x and y terms on the left-hand side using the property

of symmetry.

$2x - 3y = -29$

The point-slope form of a straight line is primarily used to find the equation of a line when you know a point and the slope. If you know two points, you can find the slope. Remember that

$$m = \frac{y_2 - y_1}{x_2 - x_1}$$

We combine the point-slope form with the slope formula, we get the two-point form of the straight line.

Theorem: Two Point Form

Given a line passing through the points (x_1, y_1) and (x_2, y_2), the equation of the line is

$$y - y_1 = \frac{(y_2 - y_1)}{(x_2 - x_1)} \cdot (x - x_1)$$

EXAMPLE 4.12

Write the equations of the line:
a) passing through (−2, 3) and (3, 7).
b) passing through (4, −2) and (2, 5).
c) passing through $(\frac{1}{2}, \frac{1}{4})$ and $(1\frac{1}{2}, 3\frac{3}{4})$.

SOLUTION 4.12

a) Write the equations of the line passing through (−2, 3) and (3, 7). Substitute the values of the ordered pairs into the point-slope formula.

$y - 3 = \frac{7 - 3}{3 - (-2)}(x - (-2))$	Simplify.
$y - 3 = \frac{4}{5}(x + 2)$	Multiply both sides by 5.
$5(y - 3) = 5 \cdot \frac{4}{5}(x + 2)$	Simplify.
$5y - 15 = 4(x + 2)$	Use the distributive property and distribute the 4.
$5y - 15 = 4x + 8$	Add −5y and −8 to both sides of the equation.
$5y - 15 - 5y - 8 = 4x + 8 - 5y - 8$	Simplify.
$-23 = 4x - 5y$	Rewrite the equation.
$4x - 5y = -23$	

b) Write the equations of the line passing through (4, –2) and (2, 5). Substitute the values of the ordered pairs into the point-slope formula.

$$y - (-2) = \frac{5 - (-2)}{2 - 4}(x - 4)$$ Simplify.

$$y + 2 = \frac{7}{-2}(x - 4)$$ Multiply both sides by –2.

$$-2(y + 2) = -2 \cdot \frac{7}{-2}(x - 4)$$ Simplify.

$$-2y - 4 = 7(x - 4)$$ Use the distributive property and distribute the 7.

$$-2y - 4 = 7x - 28$$ Add +2y and +28 to both sides of the equation.

$$-2y - 4 + 2y + 28 = 7x - 28 + 2y + 28$$ Simplify.
$$24 = 7x + 2y$$ Rewrite the equation.
$$7x + 2y = 24$$

c) Write the equations of the line passing through $(\frac{1}{2}, \frac{1}{4})$ and $(1\frac{1}{2}, 3\frac{3}{4})$. Substitute the values of the ordered pairs into the point-slope formula.

$$y - \frac{1}{4} = \frac{3\frac{3}{4} - \frac{1}{4}}{1\frac{1}{2} - \frac{1}{4}}(x - \frac{1}{2})$$ Simplify.

$$y - \frac{1}{4} = \frac{2\frac{1}{2}}{1\frac{1}{4}}(x - \frac{1}{2})$$ Simplify the complex fraction.

$$y - \frac{1}{4} = \frac{\frac{5}{2}}{\frac{5}{4}}(x - \frac{1}{2})$$

$$y - \frac{1}{4} = 2(x - \frac{1}{2})$$ Use the distributive property and distribute the 2.

$$y - \frac{1}{4} = 2x - 1$$ Multiply both sides of the equation by 4.

$$4(y - \frac{1}{4}) = 4 \cdot (2x - 1)$$ Simplify again.

$$4y - 1 = 8x - 4$$ Add –4y and +4 to both sides of the equation.

$$4y - 1 - 4y + 4 = 8x - 4 - 4y + 4$$ Simplify.

$$3 = 8x - 4y \qquad \text{Rewrite the equation.}$$
$$8x - 4y = 3$$

Parallel and Perpendicular Lines

> **Definitions: Parallel and Perpendicular Lines**
> Given two lines L_1 and L_2 with slope of m_1 and m_2 respective,
> 1. $L_1 \| L_2$ (L_1 is parallel to L_2) if and only if $m_1 = m_2$
> and
> 2. $L_1 \perp L_2$ (L_1 is perpendicular to L_2) if and only if $m_1 \cdot m_2 = -1$

Parallel lines have the same slope. If we put two parallel lines into slope-intercept form, the only difference between their equations will be the y-intercept. The definition of perpendicular lines indicates that the slopes of perpendicular lines multiply together to equal -1. When two numbers multiply to equal $+1$, the numbers are reciprocals. If two numbers multiply to equal -1, then the two numbers are negative reciprocals of each other.

EXAMPLE 4.13

a) Find the slope of the line parallel to the line through the points $(-4, 5)$ and $(6, -3)$.
b) Find the slope of the line perpendicular to the line through the points $(-2, 4)$ and $(3, -4)$.
c) Find the slope of a line parallel to the line $2x - 3y = 6$.

SOLUTION 4.13

a) Find the slope of the line parallel to the line through the points $(-4, 5)$ and $(6, -3)$.
Parallel lines have the same slope. If we find the slope of the line through the points $(-4, 5)$ and $(6, -3)$, the slope of a parallel line will be the same. Use the slope formula to find the slope.

$$m = \frac{y_2 - y_1}{x_2 - x_1} = \frac{(-3) - (5)}{(6) - (-4)} = \frac{-8}{10} = \frac{-4}{5}$$

The slope of the line passing through the two points is $m = \frac{-4}{5}$. The slope of a line parallel to this line is also $m = \frac{-4}{5}$.

b) Find the slope of the line perpendicular to the line through the points $(-2, 4)$ and $(3, -4)$.
Perpendicular lines have negative reciprocal slopes. Find the slope of the line through $(-2, 4)$ and $(3, -4)$.

$$m = \frac{(-4) - (4)}{(3) - (-2)} = \frac{-8}{5}$$

The slope of the line through the two points is $\dfrac{-8}{5}$. The slope of a perpendicular line is the negative reciprocal of $\dfrac{-8}{5}$. A perpendicular line has $m = \dfrac{5}{8}$ as its slope.

c) Find the slope of a line parallel to the line $2x - 3y = 6$.

To find the slope of the line $2x - 3y = 6$, we need to put the equation into slope-intercept form. The slope-intercept form of a linear equation requires us to solve the equation for y.

$2x - 3y = 6$	Add $-2x$ to both sides of the equation.
$2x - 3y - 2x = -2x + 6$	Simplify.
$-3y = -2x + 6$	Divide both sides by -3.
$\dfrac{-3y}{-3} = \dfrac{-2x + 6}{-3}$	Simplify.
$y = \dfrac{2x}{3} - \dfrac{6}{3}$	
$y = \dfrac{2}{3}x - 2$	

Remember that the slope of a line which is written in slope-intercept form is the coefficient of x. In our equation, $m = \dfrac{2}{3}$. Parallel lines have the same slopes, so the slope of a line parallel to our line is $m = \dfrac{2}{3}$.

EXERCISE 4.2

Graph the line that passes through the points:

1. $(3, 4)$ and $(5, 7)$.

2. $(-2, 4)$ and $(-5, 8)$.

3. $(3.5, -2.4)$ and $(3.75, -2.9)$.

Graph the following lines by using the intercept method:

4. $2x - 3y = 6$

5. $3x + 4y = 12$

6. $2x + 5y = 7$

Graph the lines:

7. $x = -2$

8. $y = 3$

9. $2(x - 3) = 2(x + y)$

Find the slope of the line passing through the points:

10. (3, 4) and (5, 7).

11. (−2, 4) and (−5, 8)

12. (3, −2) and (6, −8)

Put the following equations into slope-intercept form:

13. $3x - 4y = 12$

14. $5x + 2y = 10$

Write in standard form with integer coefficients the equation of the line:

15. with $m = 2$ and passing through the point (2, 3).

16. with $m = -\dfrac{2}{3}$ and passing through the point (−2, 4).

17. with $m = \dfrac{5}{3}$ and passing through the point (−3, −5).

Write in standard form with integer coefficients the equation of the line passing through the points:

18. (3, 4) and (5, 7)

19. (−2, 4) and (−5, 8)

20. (3, −2) and (6, −5)

Write in standard form with integer coefficients the equation of the line:

21. passing through the point (2, 3) and parallel to the line $2x - 3y = 3$.

22. passing through the point (−1, 4) and parallel to the line $x + 2y = 5$.

23. passing through the point (2, 3) and perpendicular to the line $2x - 3y = 3$.

24. passing through the point (−1, 4) and perpendicular to the line $x + 2y = 5$.

ANSWERS TO EXERCISE 4.2

1.

2.

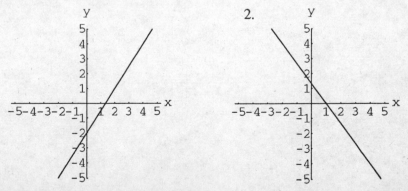

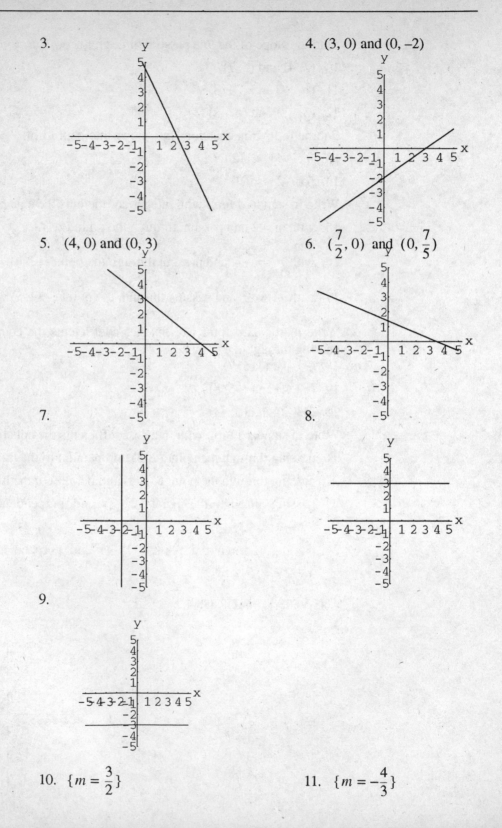

3.

4. (3, 0) and (0, –2)

5. (4, 0) and (0, 3)

6. $(\frac{7}{2}, 0)$ and $(0, \frac{7}{5})$

7.

8.

9.

10. $\{m = \frac{3}{2}\}$

11. $\{m = -\frac{4}{3}\}$

12. $\{m = -2 \text{ or } m = -\dfrac{2}{1}\}$

13. $\{y = \dfrac{3}{4}x - 3\}$

14. $\{y = -\dfrac{1}{6}x + 2\}$

15. $\{2x - y = 1\}$

16. $\{2x + 3y = 8\}$

17. $\{5x - 3y = 0\}$

18. $\{3x - 2y = 1\}$

19. $\{4x + 3y = 4\}$

20. $\{x + y = 1\}$

21. $\{2x - 3y = -5\}$

22. $\{x + 2y = 8\}$

23. $\{3x + 2y = 12\}$

24. $\{2x - y = -6\}$

SECTION 4.3 RELATIONS AND FUNCTIONS

Relations

We have been working with first degree equations in two variables. The solutions to these equations are sets of ordered pairs. We graphed the ordered pairs on the Cartesian Plane and found the graph was a straight line. A linear equation, like $2x - y = 6$, forms a relationship between x and y. If we solve this equation for y, we get $y = 2x - 6$. The values of y are related to x by taking 2 times the value of x and subtracting 6. If we solve the same equation for x, we get $x = \dfrac{y + 6}{2}$. The solution for x is related to y by taking y and adding 6 and then dividing that sum by 2. The linear equation $y = 2x - 6$ forms what is called a **mathematical relation**.

Definition:
1. A **relation** is a rule or mapping between two sets. The rule indicates how the element of the two sets are related.
2. A **relation** is any set of ordered pairs.
3. A **relation** is an equation or inequality in two variables.

The set of all possible replacements for the first component is called the **domain** and the set of all possible values of the second component is called the **range**.

EXAMPLE 4.14

Do the following form relations according to the definition of relations?
a) To each family there corresponds an address.

b) To each tree there corresponds a set of leaves.

c) A person and his/her pets.

SOLUTION 4.14

a) To each family there corresponds an address.

   We are examining the set of families which have addresses and not looking at the set of homeless families. This is a relation. To each family there is a rule which corresponds an address to the family. The rule could be house address or post office box, but the family has an address where they live or get their mail.

b) To each tree there corresponds a set of leaves.

   This is a relation. A tree grows leaves. Each tree has a particular type of leaf. There is a rule of genetics which indicates the tree and kind of leaves it will produce.

c) A person and his/her pets.

   This is a relation. People and their pets definitely form an ownership bond or relation.

EXAMPLE 4.15

a) Given $\{(1, 2), (2, 4), (3, 6), (4, 5)\}$, state the domain and the range of the relation and indicated how the first and second components are related.

b) Given $\{(0, 0), (1, 1), (2, 4), (3, 9), (4, 16)\}$, state the domain and the range of the relation and indicate the relationship between the first and second components.

SOLUTION 4.15

a) Given $\{(1, 2), (2, 4), (3, 6), (4, 5)\}$, state the domain and the range of the relation and indicate how the first and second components are related.

   The domain of the relation is the set D of all of the first components. For this relationship, $D = (1, 2, 3, 4\}$. The range is the set R of all second components. In our relation, $R = \{2, 4, 6, 8\}$. In the given relationship, the second component is the first component multiplied by 2 $(y = 2x)$.

b) Given $\{(0, 0), (1, 1), (2, 4), (3, 9), (4, 16)\}$, state the domain and the range of the relation and indicate the relationship between the first and second components.

   The domain of the relation is the set $D = \{0, 1, 2, 3, 4\}$. The range is the set $R = \{0, 1, 4, 9, 16\}$. The relationship between x and y is that the second component is the first component squared $(y = x^2)$.

EXAMPLE 4.16

Find five ordered pairs which make the following relation true:
$2x + 5y = 12$

SOLUTION 4.16

$2x + 5y = 12$
The domain of this relation is the set of all real numbers. Domains may be given as restricted values or may be restricted by division by zero or square roots of negative numbers. This equation is unrestricted so the domain of this relation is the set of all real numbers. Choose values for x or y and calculate the relation. To find ordered pairs, it is easiest to first solve the equation for y.

$2x + 5y = 12$ Add $-2x$ to both sides of the equation.

$2x + 5y - 2x = 12 - 2x$ Simplify.

$5y = 12 - 2x$ Divide both sides by 5.

$\dfrac{5y}{5} = \dfrac{12 - 2x}{5}$ Simplify again.

$y = \dfrac{12 - 2x}{5}$

Let $x = 0, 1, 2, 3$, and 4 and calculate y.

$$\left\{ \left(0, \frac{12}{5}\right), (1, 2), \left(2, \frac{8}{5}\right), \left(3, \frac{6}{5}\right), \left(4, \frac{4}{5}\right) \right\}$$

Functions

Functions are special types of relations.

Definition:

1. A **function** is a rule or a mapping between two sets such that for each element in the domain there corresponds one and only one element in the range.
2. A **function** is a set of ordered pairs such that for each element in the domain of the function there is one and only one element in the range.
3. A **function** is an equation in two variables such that for each value from the domain there corresponds one and only one value from the range.
4. A **function** is a graph on the Cartesian Plane such that no vertical line intersects the graph in more than one location.

A variation of the definition is:

A **function** is a set of ordered pairs, no two of which have the same first component and different second components.

If we think of a function as a relation between x and y, we can say:

A **function** is a set of ordered pairs such that for each x in the domain there is one and only one y in the range.

A function is similar to the operations of arithmetic. When you add, subtract, multiply, or divide any two numbers, you get one and only one answer. A function takes an element from the domain and corresponds it to one and only one element in the range.

EXAMPLE 4.17

Indicate if the following relations form functions:
a) The age of a person.
b) The fingers on your right hand.
c) The perimeter of a square.

SOLUTION 4.17

a) The age of a person.
    To each person there corresponds one and only one age. The age of a person is a functional relationship.
b) The fingers on your right hand.
    Most people have four fingers and a thumb on their right hand. If you have more than one finger on your right hand, then the fingers on your right hand do not form a functional relation.
c) The perimeter of a square.
    The formula for the perimeter of a square is 4 times the length of its side. $P = 4s$. To each square there is one and only one perimeter. The perimeter of a square forms a functional relation.

EXAMPLE 4.18

State the domain and range of the following relations and indicate if the relation is a function:
a) $\{(2, 2), (3, 4), (5, 6), (7, 5)\}$
b) $\{(1, 0), (2, 0), (5, 4), (3, 4), (4, 16)\}$

SOLUTION 4.18

a) $\{(2, 2), (3, 4), (5, 6), (7, 5)\}$
    Domain $D = \{2, 3, 5, 7\}$ and Range $R = \{2, 4, 5, 6\}$. For each first component there is one and only one second component. This relation is a function.
b) $\{(1, 0), (2, 0), (5, 4), (3, 4), (4, 16)\}$
    Domain $D = \{1, 2, 3, 4, 5\}$ and Range $R = \{0, 4, 16\}$. For each first component there is one and only one second component. This rela-

tion is a function. Notice that (1, 0) and (2, 0) have the same second component. It is acceptable for different first components to have the same second component. What is not acceptable is for the same first component to have a different second component. Think of the function like the operation of addition. $1 + 4 = 5$ and $2 + 3 = 5$. It is acceptable for different problems to have the same answers. It is not acceptable for the same problem to have different answers.

EXAMPLE 4.19

State the domain of the following graphs and indicate if the graph represents a function.

a)

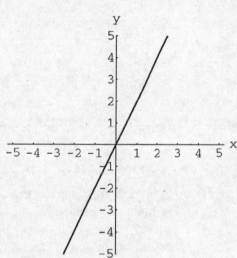

Figure 4.22

b)

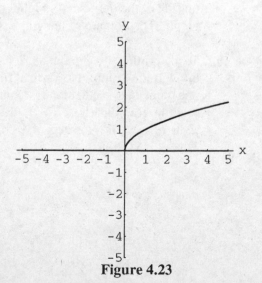

Figure 4.23

SOLUTION 4.19

a) To determine if a graph is a function, draw vertical lines through the graph. Vertical lines which do not intersect the graph put limits on the domain. Imagine vertical lines drawn through the graph.

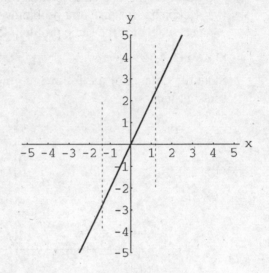

Figure 4.24

No vertical line intersects the curve more than one time, so the graph is a function. Remember that a graph on the Cartesian plane is a set of ordered pairs so the graph is a relation and also a function. The domain of the graph can be found by examining the construction of the vertical line. If vertical lines do not intersect the graph at particular points, then the places where the vertical lines do not intersect are outside of the domain. In Figure 4.24 every vertical line intersects the graph. The domain of the graph is the set of all real numbers R.

b) To determine if a graph is a function, we construct vertical lines through the graph. No vertical line intersects the graph in more than one point, so the equation is a function. The first vertical line to intersect the graph starts at $x = 1$. Every vertical line constructed to the right of $x = 1$ intersects the graph. The domain of the graph is $D = \{x \mid x \geq 1\}$.

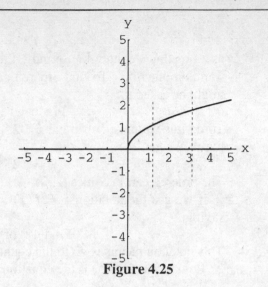

Figure 4.25

Functional Notation

By definition, a function involves the mapping of elements between two sets. Functions can be defined by mapping, sets of ordered pairs, equations, or graphs. For each element in the domain of the function there is one and only one element in the range. So that we do not always have to check to see if a relation forms a function, we use a special notation called **functional notation** to indicate when a relation is a function. We usually use letters in the alphabet starting with f and going to j, k, l, or m. We use a notation like;

    f: person $\rightarrow$ age   or

    g: $\{(1, 2), (2, 4), (3, 6)\}$ or

    h: $y = x^2 - 4$

When we see f: , g:, or h:, we know that the particular relation is a function. That is, if we see $\{(1, 2), (2, 3), (3, 4)\}$, we would have to check to see if the ordered pairs are a function. But when we see f: $\{(1, 2), (2, 3), (3, 4)\}$, we are assured by the notation that for each first component there is one and only one second component and the relation forms a function. This means for each element in the domain we are guaranteed that there is one and only one element in the range. When using equations in x and y, we often use the symbol $y = f(x)$ (read f of x or f is a function of x) to denote the function. When giving an equation like $y = x^3$, we would not know if this equation is a function without examining the equation to see if for each x there is one and only one y. When we are given an equation in the form $y = f(x) = x^3$ or just $f(x) = x^3$ we can be guaranteed by the notation that the equation is a function. It is important to remember that when you see $f(x) = x^3$, that $f(x)$ is just another representation for y.

This notation eliminates several steps in finding ordered pairs (x, y). For example, if we write

$$f:y = x^3$$

as a functional equation in x and y, the notation $(f:)$ tells us that this equation is a function. To find ordered pairs that make the equation true we might be asked to:

Find y when $x = 2$.

To do this we must substitute $x = 2$ into the equation $y = x^3$ in place of the x. We get:

$$y = (2)^3 = 8.$$

The ordered pair becomes $(2, 8)$.

If we use the notation $y = f(x) = x^3$, we can do the same thing by saying;

Find $f(2)$ or just $f(2)$.

This notation means is go to the equation $y = f(x)$ and replace the x with a 2. Remember that $f(x)$ is the equation

$$f(x) = x^3.$$

When we replace x with 2, we must do so in each location of x. That is:

$$f(2) = (2)^3 = 8 \text{ or}$$
$$f(2) = 8$$

In this notation, we can see immediately both the replacement for x and the answer for y. In the equation $f(2) = 8$, the ordered pair is $(2, 8)$.

EXAMPLE 4.20

Given $f(x) = 2x - 3$, $g(x) = x^2$ and $h(x) = 2x^2 - 3x + 1$, find:
a) $f(3)$
b) $f(2) + g(3) - h(4)$
c) $g(4) - 2 \cdot f(5) + 4 \cdot h(-2)$

SOLUTION 4.20

a) $f(3)$
    $f(x) = 2x - 3$
    $f(3) = 2(3) - 3 = 6 - 3 = 3$
    The ordered pair is $(3, 3)$.
b) $f(2) + g(3) - h(4)$
    Given $f(x) = 2x - 3$, $g(x) = x^2$ and $h(x) = 2x^2 - 3x + 1$, we want,
    $f(2) + g(3) - h(4) =$

    $[2(2) - 3] + [(3)^2] - [2(4)^2 - 3(4) + 1] =$

    $[4 - 3] + [9] - [2(16) - 12 + 1] =$

    $1 + 9 - [21] =$

    $10 - 21 = -11$

    -11 does not represent an ordered pair. It represents a calculation of different functions.

c) $g(4) - 2 \cdot f(5) + 4 \cdot h(-2)$

Given $f(x) = 2x - 3$, $g(x) = x^2$ and $h(x) = 2x^2 - 3x + 1$, find:

$g(4) - 2 \cdot f(5) + 4 \cdot h(-2)$

$[(4)^2] - 2[2(5) - 3] + 4[2(-2)^2 - 3(-2) + 1] =$

$[16] - 2[10 - 3] + 4[2(4) + 6 + 1] =$

$16 - 2[7] + 4[8 + 7] =$

$16 - 14 + 4[15] =$

$2 + 60 =$

62

EXERCISE 4.3

State the domain of the following relations and indicate if the relation is a function:

1. $\{(1, 3), (4, 7), (2, -5), (4, 8)\}$
2. $2x + y = 5$
3. $2x - y^2 = 5$

Given the following graphs, indicate the domain of the graph and tell if the graph is a function.

4.

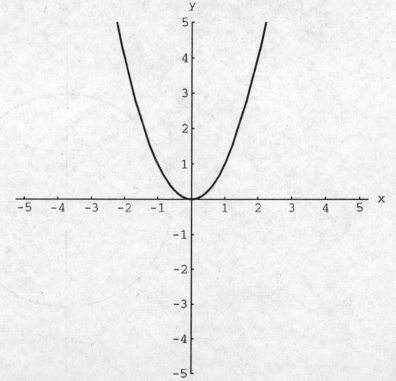

5.

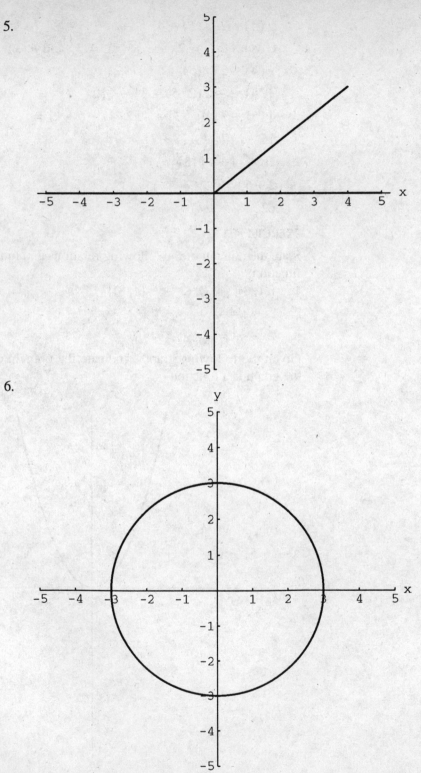

6.

Given $f(x) = 3x + 2$, $g(x) = x^2 + 2$ and $h(x) = x^2 - 1$, find

7. $g(3)$

8. $f(4)$

9. $h(-1)$

10. $h(2) - g(3)$

11. $f(3) + g(2) - h(0)$

12. $f(g(3))$

13. $g(f(2))$

14. $h(g(f(1)))$

15. $f(g(x))$

16. $g(f(x))$

Find the difference quotient for each of the following:

$$(\frac{f(x+h) - f(x)}{h})$$

17. $f(x) = 2x - 5$

18. $f(x) = x^2 + 2$

19. $f(x) = x^2 - 3x + 2$

20. $f(x) = \dfrac{1}{2x}$

21. $f(x) = \sqrt{x}$ (Hint: Rationalize the numerator using the conjugate)

22. $f(x) = \dfrac{1}{\sqrt{x}}$

ANSWERS TO EXERCISE 4.3

1. $\{D = \{1, 2, 4\}, \text{Function}\}$

2. $\{D = \{\text{all real numbers}\}, \text{Function}\}$

3. $\{D = \{x| x \geq \dfrac{5}{2}\}, \text{Not a Function}\}$

4. $\{D = \{\text{all real numbers}\}, \text{Function}\}$

5. $\{D = \{x| 0 \leq x \leq 4\}, \text{Function}\}$

6. $\{D = \{x| -3 \leq x \leq 3\}, \text{Not a function}\}$

7. $\{11\}$

8. $\{14\}$

9. $\{0\}$

10. $\{-8\}$

11. $\{18\}$

12. $\{35\}$

13. $\{66\}$

14. $\{728\}$

15. $\{3x^2 + 8\}$

16. $\{9x^2 + 12x + 6\}$

17. $\{2\}$

18. $\{2x + h\}$

19. $\{2x - 3 + h\}$

20. $\{\dfrac{-1}{2x^2 + 2xh}\}$

21. $\{\dfrac{1}{\sqrt{x+h} + \sqrt{x}}\}$

22. $\{\dfrac{-1}{x\sqrt{x+h} + (x+h)\sqrt{x}}\}$

SECTION 4.4 LINEAR, QUADRATIC AND PIECEWISE FUNCTIONS

Any function with Domain and Range consisting of real numbers can be graphed. The first component in the ordered pair is the **independent variable** x and the second component in the ordered pair is the **dependent variable** y. In functional notation, the graph of a function $f(x)$ is the same as the graph of the equation

$$y = f(x).$$

A function, like any equation, is said to be increasing, decreasing, or constant according to the following definitions:

Definition: Increasing, Decreasing, or Constant
Let f be a function with real number domain and range and let I be an interval in the domain of the function. Then
1. f **is increasing** in I, implies if $a > b$ in I, then $f(a) > f(b)$.
2. f **is decreasing** in I, implies if $a > b$ in I, then $f(a) < f(b)$.
3. f **is constant** in I, implies for all a and b in I, then $f(a) = f(b)$.

Linear Functions

Definition: Linear Function
A **linear function** is a function in the form of
$$y = f(x) = mx + b$$
where m and b are real numbers and $m \neq 0$.

From Section 4.2, we should recognize the definition of the linear function as an equation of a straight line in slope-intercept form. The domain of a linear function is the set of all real numbers and since $m \neq 0$, the range is also the set of real numbers. If $m = 0$, then the linear equation becomes a constant function $y = b$ with domain equal to the set of real numbers and the range equal to b. A linear function with a positive slope is an increasing function and a linear function with a negative slope is a decreasing function. The constant function $y = f(x) = b$ is a graph of a straight line, but is not called a linear function since $m = 0$. The graph of a linear function is a line going upward to the right (increasing) or downward to the right (decreasing). A vertical line $(x = a)$ is not a function.

EXAMPLE 4.21

Put the following linear equations into functional notation and indicate if each is an increasing linear function, a decreasing linear function or a constant.

a) $2x - 4y = 8$

b) $3(x - 5) = 2(x - y)$

c) $2(x - 5) - 5(y - 3) = 2x - 7$

SOLUTION 4.21

a) $2x - 4y = 8$

To put this equation into functional form, we must solve the equation for y.

$2x - 4y = 8$	Add $-2x$ to both sides of the equation.
$2x - 4y - 2x = -2x + 8$	Simplify.
$-4y = -2x + 8$	Divide both sides by -4.
$\dfrac{-4y}{-4} = \dfrac{-2x + 8}{-4}$	Simplify again.
$y = \dfrac{1}{2}x - 2$	

This is an increasing linear function since $m = \dfrac{1}{2} > 0$.

b) $3(x - 5) = 2(x - y)$

Simplify and solve the equation for y.

$3x - 15 = 2x - 2y$	Add $+2y$, $+15$ and $-3x$ to both sides of the equation and simplify.
$3x - 15 + 2y + 15 - 3x = 2x - 2y + 2y + 15 - 3x$	
$2y = -x + 15$	Divide both sides by 2.
$\dfrac{2y}{2} = \dfrac{-x + 15}{2}$	Simplify.
$y = -\dfrac{1}{2}x + \dfrac{15}{2}$	

This is a decreasing linear function since $m = -\dfrac{1}{2} < 0$.

c) $2(x-5) - 5(y-3) = 2x - 7$
Simplify and solve the equation for y.

$2x - 10 - 5y + 15 = 2x - 7$ Simplify.

$2x - 5y + 5 = 2x - 7$ Add $-2x$ and -5 to both sides of the equation.

$2x - 5y + 5 - 2x - 5 = 2x - 7 - 2x - 5$ Simplify.

$-5y = -12$ Divide both sides by -5.

$\dfrac{-5y}{-5} = \dfrac{-12}{-5}$ Simplify.

$y = \dfrac{12}{5}$

This is a constant function since $m = 0$.

Quadratic Functions

A linear function is a function in the form of $y = f(x) = mx + b$ $(m \neq 0)$. In a linear function the power of x is one. The highest power of a variable is called the **degree** of that variable. In functional form, $y = f(x)$ is a linear function when the degree of the independent variable is one. When the degree is two, the function is a quadratic function.

Definition: Quadratic Function
A function $y = f(x)$ is a quadratic function if
$$y = f(x) = ax^2 + bx + c$$
where a, b, and c are real numbers. $(a \neq 0)$

The domain of the function is the set of all real numbers. The range of the function and many important features can be determined by the graph of the function. Graph the function $y = x^2$ by plotting points.

$y = x^2$ Let $x = -3, -2, -1, 0, 1, 2, 3$ and find y.

$(-3, 9), (-2, 4), (-1, 1), (0, 0), (1, 1), (2, 4),$ and $(3, 9)$.

Graph these ordered pairs on a Cartesian plane.

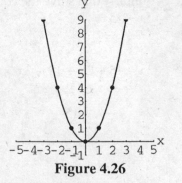

Figure 4.26

This graph is called a **parabola**. The parabola is called a conic section because its shape comes from slicing a cone parallel to one of the sides of the cone. Conic sections will be discussed in a later chapter. Any quadratic function will graph a parabola that either turns upward or downward. The place where the parabola turns is called the **vertex** or the **maximum** or **minimum point** of the parabola. It is called the maximum or minimum because if the parabola turns upward, it is the minimum value in the range. If the parabola turns downward, it is the maximum value in the range. By maximum or minimum we mean the maximum or minimum value of y. From the graph in Figure 4.26 we can find the domain and range by looking respectively at vertical and horizontal lines. If we draw vertical lines, then where the vertical lines intersect the graph will give the domain of the function. If we draw horizontal lines, then where the horizontal lines intersect the graph will give the range of the function. From the graph, the vertical lines indicate that the domain is the set of all real numbers. Horizontal lines indicate the range of the function is $\{y \mid y \geq 0\}$. This parabola has its vertex on the x-axis at $(0, 0)$.

A parabola is symmetric about a vertical line drawn through its vertex. The parabola is identical on either side of this vertical line. This vertical line is called the **axis** of the parabola or the **axis of symmetry** of the parabola. To graph a parabola, we need to find the vertex of the parabola. To do this, we must put the parabola into a special form:

$$y = f(x) = a(x-h)^2 + k$$

This form is called the **standard form** of a parabola. To obtain this form, we must complete the square. The rules for completing the square will be slightly different here than in Chapter 3 since the equation here is a function not equal to zero. To complete the square on the equation $y = x^2 - 4x + 3$ and graph the function, use the following rules:

1. Put the equation into functional form. $(y = f(x) = ax^2 + bx + c)$
2. If the coefficient of x^2 is not a 1, factor a out of the x^2 and the x terms. Leave the constant by itself.
3. Multiply $\frac{1}{2}$ times b, square it and add and subtract it from the right-hand side of the equation. Use the associative property of addition to form a trinomial and a single number term. Simplify the number term.

$y = x^2 - 4x + 3$ $\frac{1}{2}(-4) = -2$

$(-2)^2 = 4$

$y = x^2 - 4x + 4 - 4 + 3$

$y = (x^2 - 4x + 4) + (-4 + 3)$

$y = (x^2 - 4x + 4) - 1$

4.   Factor the trinomial into a perfect square.

$$y = (x^2 - 4x + 4) - 1$$
$$y = (x - 2)^2 - 1$$

Since the vertex is the maximum or minimum value of y and since $(x - 2)^2$ is always positive for real values of x, the vertex occurs when $(x - 2)^2 = 0$. This happens at $x = 2$. The y coordinate of the vertex is therefore $y = -1$, $y = -1$ is the maximum or minimum value of y in this parabola. The maximum or minimum value of a parabola is the value of the y coordinate of the vertex. It is a maximum if the parabola turns downward and a minimum if the parabola turns upward. You can determine if the parabola turns up or down by the coefficient of the x^2 term (the coefficient a). If $a > 0$, then the parabola turns upward. If $a < 0$, then the parabola turns downward. Since the coefficient of x^2 in our problem is 1, this parabola turns upward and $y = -1$ is a minimum value of y. For all real numbers x, the value of y will be ≥ -1.

$$\text{Vertex} = (2, -1)$$

In the form $y = a(x - h)^2 + k$, the vertex of the parabola is at (h, k). Be careful! Notice that the x coordinate (h) is the opposite of the number in parenthesis and the y coordinate (k) is exactly the same. In our example,

$$y = (x - 2)^2 - 1$$

the vertex was at $(+2, -1)$. The x coordinate was the opposite of the value in parenthesis and the y coordinate was exactly the same as the value outside of parenthesis. The axis of symmetry is at $x = h$. In our example the axis of symmetry is at $x = 2$. The axis of symmetry is the center of the graph. If we graph points on the right side of the axis of symmetry, there is exactly the same point on the left side of the axis. To graph a parabola, we first plot the vertex on a Cartesian plane. Label the vertex with a V so as not to confuse other plotted points with the vertex (see Figure 4.27).

The graph of every quadratic function will intersect the y axis. This point is called the y-intercept. In the form $y = ax^2 + bx + c$, the y-intercept is $(0, c)$. Our graph crosses the y-axis at $(0, 3)$. Now graph the y-intercept.

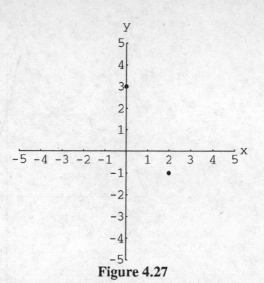

Figure 4.27

Knowing the shape of the parabola, we could easily sketch the parabola between the vertex and the y-intercept. It would be helpful, however, to plot a few more points. Other points which are helpful are the x-intercepts, if they exist. A quadratic function does not always cross the x-axis. If the vertex is above the x-axis and the parabola turns upward, there are no x-intercepts. If the vertex is below the x-axis and the parabola turns downward, there are again no x-intercepts. From our picture, however, we can see that the parabola crosses the x-axis. To find the x-intercepts, let $y = 0$ and solve the quadratic equation. Since we have completed the square to find the vertex, let's use completing the square to find the x-intercepts.

$y = (x-2)^2 - 1$	Let $y = 0$.
$0 = (x-2)^2 - 1$	Add +1 to both sides of the equation.
$0 + 1 = (x-2)^2 - 1 + 1$	Simplify.
$1 = (x-2)^2$	Take the square root of both sides of the equation. Don't forget ±.
$\pm\sqrt{1} = \sqrt{(x-2)^2}$	Simplify.
$\pm 1 = x - 2$	Add +2 to both sides of the equation.
$2 \pm 1 = x - 2 + 2$	Simplify again.
$x = 3$ or 1	

The x-intercepts are (1, 0) and (3, 0). Graph the x-intercepts on the Cartesian plane.

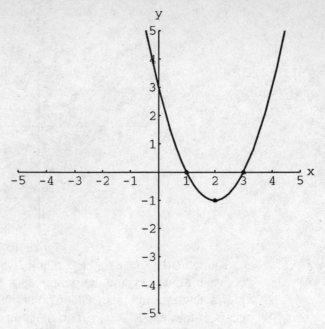

Figure 4.28

From this point, sketch the parabola by drawing the parabola through the points we have plotted.

When working with a quadratic function $y = f(x) = ax^2 + bx + c$, it is recommended to do the following:

Find the axis of symmetry.

Find the vertex.

Find the maximum or minimum value of y.

Find the y-intercept.

Find the x-intercepts, if they exist.

Find the range of the function.

Graph the parabola.

Piecewise Functions

A piecewise function is a function constructed by combining pieces of different functions over various intervals. The piecewise function

$$y = f(x) = \begin{cases} 3x & \text{if } x \le 0 \\ -2x & \text{if } x > 0 \end{cases}$$

is formed by combining the function $y = 3x$ for all values of $x \le 0$ and the function $y = -2x$ for all values of $x > 0$. To determine the ordered pairs for a given value of x, we must decide if the value of x is less than or equal to zero or greater than zero and then substitute the x into the proper piece of the function to determine the corresponding value for y.

EXAMPLE 4.22

a) Given $y = f(x) = \begin{cases} 3x & \text{if } x \leq 0 \\ -2x & \text{if } x > 0 \end{cases}$ find: $f(3)$

b) Given $y = f(x) = \begin{cases} x+4 & \text{if } x < -1 \\ x^2 & \text{if } x > -1 \end{cases}$ find: $f(2) - f(-5) + f(3)$

SOLUTION 4.22

a) $f(3)$

Since $3 > 0$, $f(3)$ is found by substituting 3 into the second piece of the equation

$$y = f(x) = \begin{cases} 3x & \text{if } x \leq 0 \\ -2x & \text{if } x > 0 \end{cases}$$

$$y = f(x) = -2x$$

$$f(3) = -2(3) = -6$$

b) $f(2) - f(-5) + f(3)$

The given function is . $y = f(x) = \begin{cases} x+4 & \text{if } x < -1 \\ x^2 & \text{if } x > -1 \end{cases}$

$f(2)$ is found using $f(x) = x^2$, since $2 > -1$.

$$f(2) = (2)^2 = 4.$$

$f(-5)$ is found using $f(x) = x + 4$.

$$f(-5) = (-5) + 4 = -1$$

$f(3)$ is found using $f(x) = x^2$.

$$f(3) = (3)^2 = 9$$

$$f(2) - f(-5) + f(3) = 4 - (-1) + 9 = 4 + 1 + 9 = 14$$

$$f(2) - f(-5) + f(3) = 14$$

EXERCISE 4.4

Graph the following linear functions:

1. $y = 3x - 2$

2. $y = -\frac{2}{3}x + 3$

3. $y = \frac{1}{2}x + 1$

Graph the following quadratic functions. List the vertex, axis of symmetry, maximum or minimum value of y, the y-intercept, and the x-intercepts if they exist.

4. $y = x^2 - 4x - 5$

5. $y = -x^2 - 2x + 3$

6. $y = 2x^2 - 4x + 4$

Given

$$y = f(x) = \begin{cases} 3x+2 & \text{if } x < -2 \\ 4x-5 & \text{if } -2 \le x \le 2 \\ x^2 & \text{if } x > 2 \end{cases}$$

find:

7. $f(3) + f(-4) - f(9)$

8. $f(1) - f(2) + f(-6)$

9. $f(-2) + f(-3) + f(8)$

10. $f(-10) - f(3) - f(5)$

ANSWERS TO EXERCISE 4.4

1. $y = 3x - 2$

2. $y = -\frac{2}{3}x + 3$

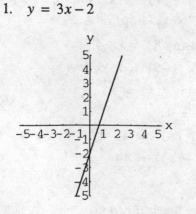

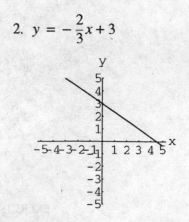

3. $y = \dfrac{1}{2}x + 1$

4. $y = x^2 - 4x - 5$

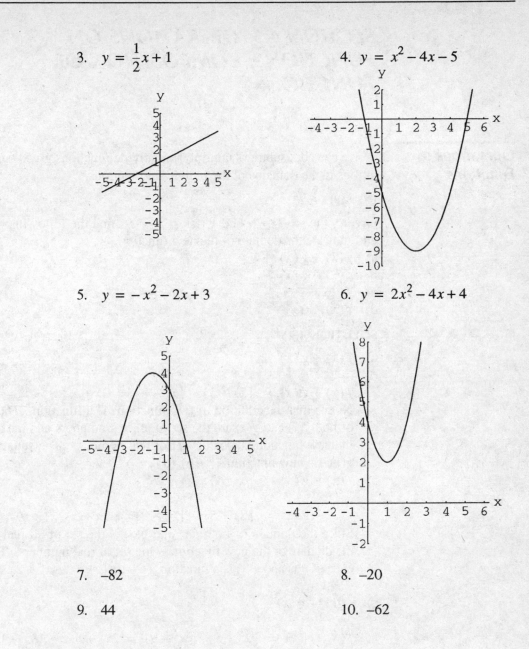

5. $y = -x^2 - 2x + 3$

6. $y = 2x^2 - 4x + 4$

7. –82

8. –20

9. 44

10. –62

SECTION 4.5 OPERATIONS ON FUNCTIONS; COMPOSITION OF FUNCTIONS

Operations of Functions

We can add, subtract, multiply, and divide functions given certain limitations in the domains of the individual functions.

EXAMPLE 4.23

Given $f(x) = 2x + 5$ and $g(x) = x^2 - 9$, find the following operations and indicate the domain of the new function.

a) $f(x) + g(x)$
b) $f(x) - g(x)$
c) $f((x) \cdot g(x))$
d) $f(x)/g(x)$

SOLUTION 4.23

a) $f(x) + g(x)$

$f(x) + g(x) = [2x + 5] + [x^2 - 9] = 2x + 5 + x^2 - 9 = x^2 + 2x - 4$
Notice that the addition of two functions is a function. The domains of both $f(x)$ and $g(x)$ are the set of all real numbers and the domain of the new function is also the set of real numbers. The sum of $f(x)$ and $g(x)$ is a new function $(f + g)(x) = x^2 + 2x - 4$.

b) $f(x) - g(x)$

$f(x) - g(x) = [2x + 5] - [x^2 - 9] = 2x + 5 - x^2 + 9 = -x^2 + 2x + 14$
Since the domain of both $f(x)$ and $g(x)$ is the set of all real numbers, the domain of the new function is the set of real numbers. The difference of $f(x)$ and $g(x)$ is a function $(f - g)(x) = -x^2 + 2x + 14$.

c) $f((x) \cdot g(x))$

$f(x) \cdot g(x) = [2x + 5] \cdot [x^2 - 9] = 2x^3 + 5x^2 - 18x - 45$
The domain of the new function is the set of real numbers, since the domain of both f and g is the set of real numbers. The product of $f(x)$ and $g(x)$ is a new function $(f \cdot g)(x) = 2x^3 + 5x^2 - 18x - 45$.

d) $f(x)/g(x)$

$f(x)/g(x) = [2x + 5]/[x^2 - 3] = \dfrac{2x + 5}{x^2 - 9}$

The domain of the new function is restricted by division. We are not allowed to divide by zero. The denominator $g(x) = x^2 - 9$ cannot equal zero. Both original functions have domains of all real numbers, so the only limits on the new function $f(x)/g(x)$ is that $g(x) \neq 0$.

$g(x) = x^2 - 9 = (x+3)(x-3) = 0$

$x \neq 3, -3$

The domain of the new function $(f/g)(x) = \dfrac{2x+5}{x^2-9}$ is the set of all real numbers excluding $x \neq \pm 3$.

When the domain of f and g is not the set of real numbers, then the domain f + g, f − g, f · g, and f/g is limited by the individual functions f and g.

Composition of Functions

The composition of functions involves the substitution of one function into another function. The composition of functions $f(x)$ and $g(x)$ (written $f \circ g(x)$ and read *"f circle g"* of x) is the combining of two functions to produce a third function by substituting the function $g(x)$ into the $f(x)$ function for the variable x.

Definition:

Given two functions f and g, the function $f \circ g(x)$ is called the composite of f and g and is defined by the equation

$$f \circ g(x) = f[g(x)].$$

The domain of $f \circ g$ is the set of all real numbers x such that x is in the domain of g and g(x) is in the domain of f.

EXAMPLE 4.24

Find $f \circ g$ and $g \circ f$ for the functions f and g and indicate the domain of $f \circ g$ and $g \circ f$:

a) $f(x) = 2x + 3$ and $g(x) = \dfrac{x}{x-1}$

b) $f(x) = x^2$ and $g(x) = \sqrt{x}$

SOLUTION 4.24

a) $f(x) = 2x + 3$ and $g(x) = \dfrac{x}{x-1}$

$f \circ g(x) = f[g(x)]$

To find $f \circ g(x)$, we substitute the expression $g(x) = (\dfrac{x}{x-1})$ into the f function for x.

$f(x) = 2x + 3$

$f[g(x)] = 2 \cdot g(x) + 3 = 2 \cdot (\dfrac{x}{x-1}) + 3 = \dfrac{2x}{x-1} + 3$

$$= \frac{2x}{x-1} + \frac{3(x-1)}{x-1} = \frac{2x}{x-1} + \frac{3x-3}{x-1} = \frac{5x-3}{x-1}$$

$$f[g(x)] = \frac{5x-3}{x-1}$$

The domain of $f \circ g(x) = f[g(x)] = \dfrac{5x-3}{x-1}$ is limited by the domains of f and g. The domain of $g(x)$ is the set $D = \{x \mid x \neq 1\}$.

$g \circ f(x) = g[f(x)]$

To find $g \circ f(x)$, we substitute the expression $f(x) = 2x+3$ into the g function for x.

$$g(x) = \frac{x}{x-1}$$

$$g[f(x)] = \frac{f(x)}{f(x)-1} = \frac{(2x+3)}{(2x+3)-1} = \frac{2x+3}{2x+3-1} = \frac{2x+3}{2x+2}$$

$$g[f(x)] = \frac{2x+3}{2x+2}$$

The domain $g \circ f(x) = g[f(x)] = \dfrac{2x+3}{2x+2}$ is limited by the domains of g and f. The domain of $f(x)$ is $D = \{x \mid x \text{ is all real numbers}\}$. The domain of $g(x)$ is the set $D = \{x \mid x \neq 1\}$. The domain of $g[f(x)]$ is the set $D = \{f(x) \mid x \neq -1\}$.

b) $f(x) = x^2$ and $g(x) = \sqrt{x}$

$f \circ g(x) = f[g(x)]$

To find $f \circ g(x)$, we substitute the expression $g(x) = (\sqrt{x})$ into the f function for x.

$f(x) = x^2$

$$f[g(x)] = [g(x)]^2 = (\sqrt{x})^2 = x$$

$$f[g(x)] = x$$

The domain of $g(x)$ is $D = \{x \mid x \geq 0\}$. The domain of $f(x)$ is the set of all real numbers. The domain of $f[g(x)]$ is the set $D = \{x \mid x \geq 0\}$. The function $y = x$ is a function of x with a domain of all real numbers. The composite of f and g is the function $f \circ g(x) = x$. Since the domain of g is the set $D = \{x \mid x \geq 0\}$. The domain of $f \circ g(x)$ is also the set $D = \{x \mid x \geq 0\}$.

$g \circ f(x) = g[f(x)]$

To find $g \circ f(x)$, we substitute the expression $f(x) = x^2$ into the g

function for x.

$$g(x) = \sqrt{x}$$

$$g[f(x)] = \sqrt{f(x)} = \sqrt{x^2} = |x|$$

(Once the domain is found, this expression can be further simplified.)

$$g[f(x)] = |x|$$

The domain of $f(x)$ is $D = \{x \mid x \text{ is all real numbers}\}$. The domain of $g(x)$ is the set $D = \{x \mid x \geq 0\}$. The domain of $g[f(x)]$ is the set $D = \{x \mid \text{all real numbers}\}$.

$$g[f(x)] = |x|$$

EXERCISE 4.5

Given the following functions, find $f + g, f - g, f \cdot g$, and f/g. Indicate the domain of each:

1. $f(x) = 2x + 3$ and $g(x) = x^2$
2. $f(x) = \sqrt{x}$ and $g(x) = 4\sqrt{x}$
3. $f(x) = x^2$ and $g(x) = x^3$
4. $f(x) = \sqrt{x+2}$ and $g(x) = \sqrt{x-1}$
5. $f(x) = \sqrt{3x+2}$ and $g(x) = \sqrt{x+3}$

Find $f \circ g$ and $g \circ f$ for each of the following and indicate the domains of each:

6. $f(x) = 2x + 3$ and $g(x) = x^2$
7. $f(x) = x + 3$ and $g(x) = 2x + 3$
8. $f(x) = 2x + 3$ and $g(x) = \dfrac{x-3}{2}$
9. $f(x) = \sqrt{x-1}$ and $g(x) = x^2 + 1$
10. $f(x) = 4x - 1$ and $g(x) = \sqrt{x}$

ANSWERS TO EXERCISE 4.5

1. $\{f + g(x) = x^2 + 2x + 3,$ all real numbers; $f - g(x) = 2x + 3 - x^2,$ all real numbers; $f \cdot g(x) = 2x^3 + 3x^2,$ all real numbers; $\dfrac{f}{g}(x) = \dfrac{2x+3}{x^2}, x \neq 0\}$

2. $\{f + g(x) = 5\sqrt{x}, x > 0; f - g(x) = -3\sqrt{x}, x \geq 0; f \cdot g(x) = 4x, x \geq 0, \dfrac{f}{g}(x) = \dfrac{1}{4}, x > 0\}$

3. $\{f+g(x) = x^2 + x^3$, all real numbers; $f-g(x) = x^2 - x^3$, all real numbers; $f \cdot g(x) = x^5$, all real numbers; $\dfrac{f}{g}(x) = \dfrac{1}{x}, x \neq 0\}$

4. $\{f+g(x) = \sqrt{x+2} + \sqrt{x-1}, x \geq 1; f-g(x) = \sqrt{x+2} - \sqrt{x-1}, x \geq 1; f \cdot g(x) = \sqrt{(x+2)(x-1)}, x \geq 1; \dfrac{f}{g}(x) = \sqrt{\dfrac{x+2}{x-1}}, x > 1\}$

5. $\{f+g(x) = \sqrt{3x+2} + \sqrt{x+3}, x \geq -\dfrac{2}{3};$

   $f-g(x) = \sqrt{3x+2} - \sqrt{x+3}, x \geq -\dfrac{2}{3};$

   $f \cdot g(x) = \sqrt{(3x+2)(x+3)}, x \geq -\dfrac{2}{3}; \dfrac{f}{g}(x) = \sqrt{\dfrac{3x+2}{x+3}}, x > -\dfrac{2}{3}\}$

6. $\{f \circ g(x) = 2x^2 + 3$, all real numbers; $g \circ f(x) = (2x+3)^2$, all real numbers$\}$

7. $\{f \circ g(x) = 2x$, all real numbers; $g \circ f(x) = 2x - 3$, all real numbers$\}$

8. $\{f \circ g(x) = x$, all real numbers; $g \circ f(x) = x$, all real numbers$\}$

9. $\{f \circ g(x) = |x|$, all real numbers; $g \circ f(x) = x, x \geq 1\}$

10. $\{f \circ g(x) = 4\sqrt{x} - 1, x \geq 0; g \circ f(x) = \sqrt{4x - 1}, x \geq \dfrac{1}{4}\}$

SECTION 4.6 INVERSE OF A FUNCTION AND INVERSE FUNCTIONS

Inverse of a Function

Many times in mathematics we are given functions with values for the independent variable and asked to find the dependent variable. For example, given the function $y = f(x) = 2x - 4$, find $f(3)$. To find $f(3)$, we take $f(x) = 2x - 4$ and replace x with 3.

$$f(3) = 2 \cdot (3) - 4 = 6 - 4 = 2.$$

So $f(3) = 2$. Suppose, however, we are given $f(x) = 2$ and we wish to find the value of x that makes $y = 2$. Let $y = 2$ and solve for x.

$y = f(x) = 2x - 4$

$2 = 2x - 4$ Add +4 to both sides of the equation.

$2 + 4 = 2x - 4 + 4$ Simplify.

$6 = 2x$ Divide both sides by 2.

$$\frac{6}{2} = \frac{2x}{2}$$ Simplify again.

$$3 = x$$

With a function like $y = f(x) = 2x - 4$, given values for x, it is relatively easy to find y. If given a value for y, it becomes more work to find the value or values of x that correspond to a particular y. Solve the equation $y = 2x - 4$ for x.

$y = 2x - 4$ Add +4 to both sides.
$y + 4 = 2x - 4 + 4$ Simplify.
$y + 4 = 2x$ Divide both sides by 2.

$$\frac{y+4}{2} = \frac{2x}{2}$$ Simplify.

$$\frac{1}{2}y + 2 = x$$ Rewrite the equation.

$$x = \frac{1}{2}y + 2$$

If we reverse or switch the variables x and y, we get a new equation. This equation is called the **inverse of the function** $y = f(x)$. To find the inverse of a function, replace the variable x with y and the variable y with x. The inverse of the function $y = f(x) = 2x - 4$ is

$$x = 2y - 4$$

When solved for y, we get

$$y = \frac{1}{2}x + 2.$$

If this equation is a function, it is called the **inverse function of $f(x)$** or the **inverse of $f(x)$** and is written $y = f^{-1}(x)$.

This equation is a function of x, so we may write

$$y = f^{-1}(x) = \frac{1}{2}x + 2$$

All functions have an inverse of the function, not all inverses of the function are functions. The inverse of a function is strictly interchanging the x and y variables. Not all of these new equations are functions of x. We will examine ways to tell if the inverse of a function is a function.

EXAMPLE 4.25

Find the inverse of each of the following functions and indicate if the inverse is a function:
a) f: $\{(2, 3), (5, 7), (-2, 5)\}$
b) f: $2x + 3y = 6$

SOLUTION 4.25

a) f: $\{(2, 3), (5, 7), (-2, 5)\}$
To find the inverse of a function, interchange the x and y components.
$\{(3, 2), (7, 5), (5, -2)\}$
Each x has one and only one y, so the inverse is a function and can be written
f^{-1}: $\{(3, 2), (7, 5), (5, -2)\}$

b) f: $2x + 3y = 6$
Switch the x and y variable.
$2y + 3x = 6$
This equation is the inverse of the function f. To see if the equation is a function, we need to solve the equation for y.

$2y + 3x = 6$	Add $-3x$ to both sides of the equation.
$2y + 3x - 3x = -3x + 6$	Simplify.
$2y = -3x + 6$	Divide both sides by 2.
$\dfrac{2y}{2} = \dfrac{-3x + 6}{2}$	Simplify again.
$y = -\dfrac{3}{2}x + 3$	

For each x there is one and only y, so the equation is a function and can be written

f^{-1}: $y = -\dfrac{3}{2}x + 3$.
This can also be written
$y = f^{-1}(x) = -\dfrac{3}{2}x + 3$.

One-to-One Functions

A function $y = f(x)$ is said to be one-to-one if for each x there is one and only one y and for each y there is one and only one x.

> **Definition: One-to-One Function**
> A function is said to be one-to-one if for each element in the range there is exactly one element in the domain.

EXAMPLE 4.26

Determine if the following functions are one-to-one:
a) f: $\{(2, 3), (5, 7), (-2, 5)\}$
b) f: $2x + 3y = 6$

c) $f: y = x^2 + 2x - 3$

SOLUTION 4.26

a) $f: \{(2, 3), (5, 7), (-2, 5)\}$
The range of this function is $R = \{3, 5, 7\}$. For each element in the range there is exactly one element in the domain. The function is one-to-one.

b) $f: 2x + 3y = 6$
The range of this function is all real numbers. For each real number in the range, there is exactly one real number in the domain. In other words, for each real number y there is one and only one value of x, so the function is one-to-one.

c) $f: y = x^2 + 2x - 3$
For the equation to be a function, for each x there is only one y. For the inverse of the function to be a function, for each y there can be only one x. Let $y = 0$ and solve for x.

$0 = x^2 + 2x - 3$	Rewrite the equation.
$x^2 + 2x - 3 = 0$	The equation is quadratic in x. Factor the equation.
$(x - 1)(x + 3) = 0$	Set each factor equal to zero and solve.

$x = 1$ and -3

There are two values of x that make $y = 0$. There are two ordered pairs that have y components of zero. They are $(1, 0)$ and $(-3, 0)$. For $y = 0$ there is more than one value of x in the domain. This function is not one-to-one.

Inverse Functions

From the examples in the preceding sections, notice that the functions with inverse functions were one-to-one and the function which did not have an inverse function was not one-to-one. This brings us to our next definition.

Definition: Inverse Functions
An inverse of the function $y = f(x)$ is a function if and only if $y = f(x)$ is a one-to-one function. Similarly;
A function $y = f(x)$ is one-to-one if and only if the inverse of $y = f(x)$ is a function.

EXAMPLE 4.27

Determine if the following functions have inverse functions:
a) $y = f(x) = 2x - 4$
b) $y = f(x) = x^2 + 4x - 3$

SOLUTION 4.27

a) $y = f(x) = 2x - 4$

To determine if $y = f(x) = x^2 - 4$ is a one-to-one function and has an inverse, we interchange the x and y variables and solve the equation for y or we can graph the function and use what is called the **horizontal line**.

$y = f(x) = 2x - 4$	Switch the x and y variables.
$x = 2y - 4$	Solve for y in terms of x.
	Add +4 to both sides.
$x + 4 = 2y - 4 + 4$	Simplify.
$x + 4 = 2y$	Divide both sides by 2.
$\dfrac{x+4}{2} = \dfrac{2y}{2}$	Simplify again.
$\dfrac{1}{2}x + 2 = y$	Rewrite the equation.
$y = \dfrac{1}{2}x + 2$	

This equation is a linear equation. All linear equations are functions except vertical lines. For each x in the domain, there is one and only one y that corresponds with each x. The inverse of $f(x)$ is a function.

$$y = f(x) = 2x - 4 \quad \text{and} \quad y = f^{-1}(x) = \frac{1}{2}x + 2$$

Another way to determine if a function is one-to-one and has an inverse is by graphing. Graph the original function $y = f(x) = 2x - 4$.

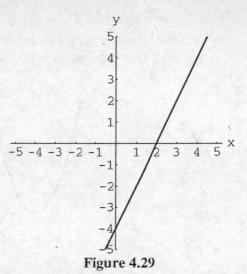

Figure 4.29

We know that this equation is a function by the vertical line test. If vertical lines drawn through the graph intersect the graph at most one point then the equation is a function. To see if a function is one-to-one, we use the **horizontal lines test**. If horizontal lines intersect the graph at most one time, then the function is a one-to-one function and its inverse is a function. Notice that no horizontal nor vertical line intersects $y = 2x - 4$ more than one time. $y = 2x - 4$ is a function and has an inverse function. Remember for every function, we can find the inverse of the function by switching the x and y variables. Not every inverse, however, is itself a function. The only functions which have inverse functions are one-to-one functions.

b) $y = f(x) = x^2 + 4x - 3$

To determine if this function has an inverse function, graph the function. The graph of this function is a parabola. Find the vertex of the parabola by completing the square.

$y = x^2 + 4x + 3$	Separate the number term and the x terms.
$y = x^2 + 4x$	$+3$
$y = x^2 + 4x + 3$	Multiply $\frac{1}{2}$ times 4, square it.
$\frac{1}{2} \cdot 4 = 2 \qquad (2)^2 = 4$	Add and subtract 4 to the right-hand side of the equation.
$y = x^2 + 4x + 4 \qquad +3 - 4$	Simplify.
$y = (x^2 + 4x + 4) \qquad -1$	Factor the trinomial into a perfect square.

$$y = (x+2)^2 - 1$$

The vertex of the parabola is at $(-2, -1)$. The y-intercept is $(0, 3)$ and the x-intercepts are at $(-1, 0)$ and $(-3, 0)$. Graph the function (Figure 4.29).

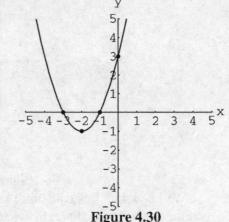

Figure 4.30

This function does not have an inverse function. Horizontal lines intersect the graph at more than one location. The inverse of $f(x)$ is not a function.

Theorem: Composite of f and f^{-1}

Suppose that $y = f(x)$ is a function with an inverse function $y = f^{-1}(x)$, then

$$(f^{-1} \circ f)(x) = x \quad \text{for all } x \text{ in the domain of } f$$

and

$$(f \circ f^{-1})(x) = x \quad \text{for all } x \text{ in the domain of } f^{-1}.$$

Increasing and Decreasing Functions

We have already discussed increasing, decreasing, and constant linear equations. The same definitions hold for functions.

Definition: Increasing and Decreasing Functions

Increasing Function

A function $y = f(x)$ is said to be increasing over the interval $[a < x < b]$, if for all c and d such that $a < c < d < b$, then $f(c) < f(d)$.

Decreasing Function

A function $y = f(x)$ is said to be decreasing over the interval $[a < x < b]$, if for all c and d such that $a < c < d < b$, then $f(c) > f(d)$.

Increasing functions are functions such that as x gets larger, y also gets larger. The bigger the x, the bigger the value of y. Decreasing functions are just the opposite, as x gets larger, y gets smaller.

EXAMPLE 4.28

Determine the intervals where the function is increasing and where it is decreasing.

a) $y = x^2$

b) $y = 4 - 2x$

SOLUTION 4.28

a) $y = x^2$

To determine the intervals where the function is increasing and decreasing, graph the function.

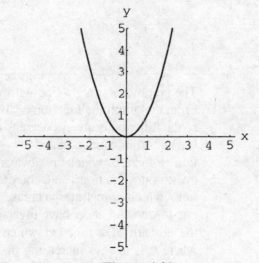

Figure 4.31

Functions are increasing when they move upward to the right and decreasing when they move downward to the right. $y = f(x) = x^2$ is moving downward to the right over the interval $(x < 0)$ and upward to the right over the interval $(x > 0)$.

$y = f(x) = x^2$

is decreasing for all $x < 0$ and increasing for all $x > 0$.

b) $y = 4 - 2x$
Graph this function.

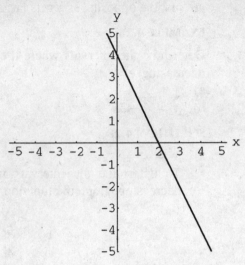

Figure 4.32

The graph is a straight line with y-intercept of 4 and slope $m = \dfrac{-2}{1}$. From the graph the function is always moving downward to the right, so the function is always decreasing. Notice that $y = f(x) = 4 - 2x$ is a one-to-one function and $y = f(x) = x^2$ is not a one-to-one function. Functions which are always increasing or always decreasing are one-to-one functions and, therefore, have inverse functions. Functions which sometimes increase and sometimes decrease are never one-to-one and never have inverse functions. If we, however, restrict the domain of a function which is not one-to-one over an interval where it is always increasing or always decreasing, then the limited function will be one-to-one and will have an inverse function over that interval.

EXERCISE 4.6

For each of the following, find the inverse of the function and indicate if the inverse of the function is a function.

1. $y = f(x) = 3x + 1$

2. $y = f(x) = x^2 - 4$

3. $y = f(x) = 2x^3$

4. $y = f(x) = \sqrt{x}$

5. $y = f(x) = \sqrt[3]{x}$

Graph the following function and indicate if the function is one-to-one. On the same graph draw the inverse of the function:

6. $y = f(x) = x + 1$

7. $y = f(x) = x^2 - 9$

8. $y = f(x) = x^3 + 1$

9. $y = f(x) = x^2 - 2x - 3$

10. $y = f(x) = x^5$

ANSWERS TO EXERCISE 4.6

1. $x = 3y + 1$, Yes, the inverse is a function.

2. $x = y^2 - 4$, No, the inverse is not a function.

3. $x = 2y^3$, Yes, the inverse is a function.

4. $x = \sqrt{y}$, Yes, the inverse is a function.

5. $x = \sqrt[3]{y}$, Yes, the inverse is a function.

6.

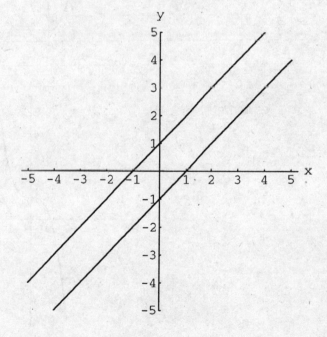

7.

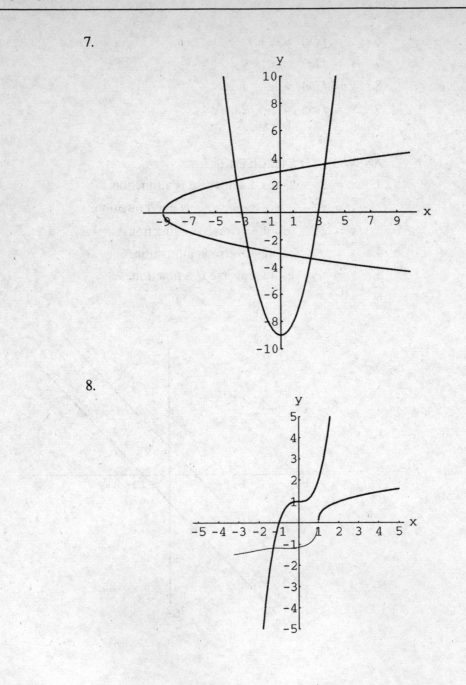

8.

9.

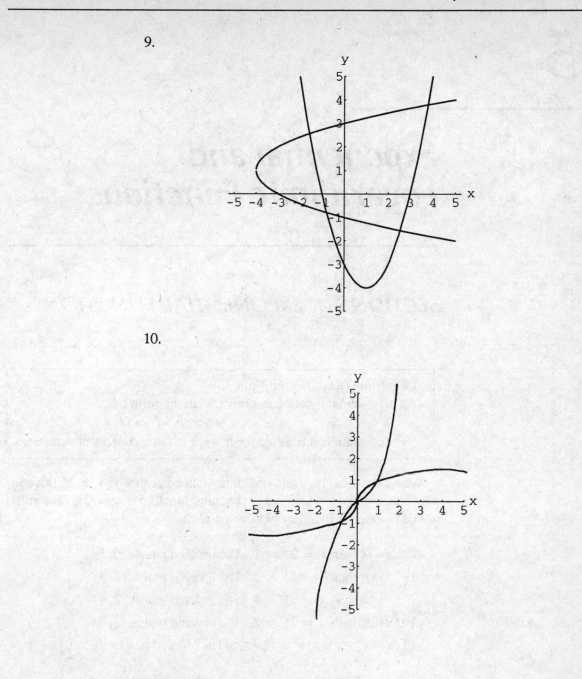

10.

5

Exponential and Logarithmic Functions

SECTION 5.1 EXPONENTIAL FUNCTIONS

> **Definition: Exponential Function**
> An exponential function is a function in the form of
> $$y = f(x) = b^x \qquad \text{where } b > 0 \text{ and } b \neq 1.$$
> b is a constant and is called the base. x is the independent variable.

We require $b > 0$ to avoid imaginary numbers. $b \neq 1$, $y = 1^x$ is a constant function $y = 1$. A typical exponential function is $y = 2^x$. The graph of this function is found by plotting points.

Let $x = 0$, then $y = 2^0 = 1$. The ordered pair is $(0, 1)$.

Let $x = 1$, then $y = 2^1 = 2$. The ordered pair is $(1, 2)$.

Let $x = 2$, then $y = 2^2 = 4$. The ordered pair is $(2, 4)$.

Let $x = 3$, then $y = 2^3 = 8$. The ordered pair is $(3, 8)$.

Let $x = -1$, then $y = 2^{-1} = \dfrac{1}{2}$. The ordered pair is $\left(-1, \dfrac{1}{2}\right)$.

Let $x = -2$, then $y = 2^{-2} = \dfrac{1}{4}$. The ordered pair is $\left(-2, \dfrac{1}{4}\right)$.

Let $x = -3$, then $y = 2^{-3} = \dfrac{1}{8}$. The ordered pair is $\left(-3, \dfrac{1}{8}\right)$.

If we plot these points, we get the graph in Figure 5.1.

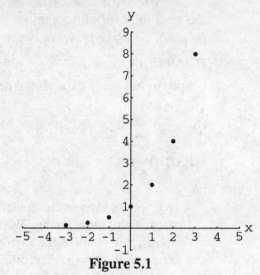

Figure 5.1

Drawing the curve through these points we get Figure 5.2.

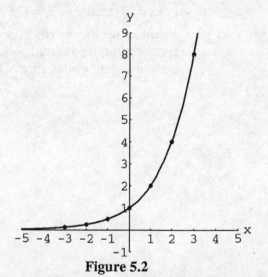

Figure 5.2

As x gets larger and larger, the values of y increase without bound. If $x = 0$, then $y = 1$. For negative values of x, the values for y get close to the x-axis. The x-axis forms what is called a horizontal **asymptote** to the curve $y = 2^x$.

Definition: Asymptote

An **asymptote** is a line whose distance from a point P on the curve to the asymptote approaches zero as the distance from the point P to the origin increases without bound.

Notice how the function moves along the *x*-axis in the second quadrant. We may think of an asymptote as a line that the curve approaches as points of the curve move away form the origin.

EXAMPLE 5.1

Graph the following exponential functions:

a) $y = 3^x$

b) $y = (\frac{1}{2})^x$

SOLUTION 5.1

a) $y = 3^x$

To graph an exponential function, we need to graph only three values of *x* and plot three points. We need to let $x = 0$, 1, and -1. These values of *x* will show us the asymptote and the direction of the curve.

Let $x = 0$, then $y = 1$. The ordered pair is (0, 1).

Let $x = 1$, then $y = 3$. The ordered pair is (1, 3).

Let $x = -1$, then $y = \frac{1}{3}$. The ordered pair is $(-1, \frac{1}{3})$

Visualize the exponential curve (Figure 5.2). The exponential has a horizontal asymptote and goes upward without bound. Now draw the curve using the points above (Figure 5.3).

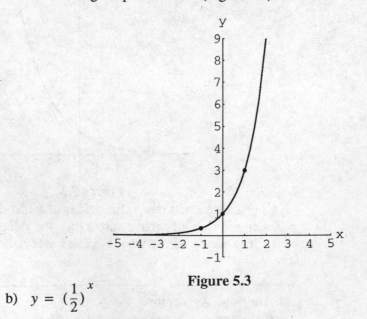

Figure 5.3

b) $y = (\frac{1}{2})^x$

Again plot the points where $x = 0$, 1, and -1.

Let $x = 0$, then $y = 1$. The ordered pair is (0, 1).

Let $x = 1$, then $y = \dfrac{1}{2}$. The ordered pair is $(1, \dfrac{1}{2})$.

Let $x = -1$, then $y = 2$. The ordered pair is $(-1, 2)$.

Visualize the exponential curve. The exponential has a horizontal asymptote and moves upward without bound (heads to infinity). Draw the curve using the points above (Figure 5.4), upward to the left and asymptotic to the x-axis to the right.

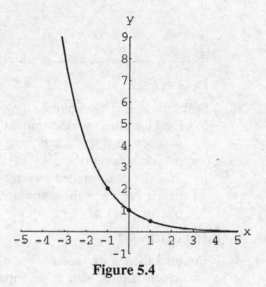

Figure 5.4

Properties of Exponential Functions:

$$y = f(x) = b^x, \text{ where } b > 0 \text{ and } b \neq 1.$$

1. The graph passes through $(0, 1)$.
2. The graph is continuous. (The graph has no holes or jumps.)
3. The x-axis is a horizontal asymptote.
4. If $b > 1$, then the function is always increasing.
5. If $0 < b < 1$, then the function is always decreasing.
6. The function is one-to-one. ($y = f(x)$ has an inverse function.)

Compound interest is an exponential function.

Compound Interest:

If a principal P is invested at an annual rate of interest r compounded n times a year, then the amount A of money in the account at the end of t years is given by

$$A = P\left(1 + \frac{r}{n}\right)^{nt}$$

EXAMPLE 5.2

Solve the following compound interest problems:

a) Find the compounded amount of money after 5 years in an account which begins with a principal of $1,500 invested at 6.5%, compounded quarterly.

b) Find the compounded amount of money after 10 years in an account which begins with a principal of $2,500 invested at 7.5%, compounded monthly.

SOLUTION 5.2

a) Find the compounded amount of money after 5 years in an account which begins with a principal of $1,500 invested at 6.5%, compounded quarterly.

To find compound interest we use the formula for compound interest

$$A = P\left(1 + \frac{r}{n}\right)^{nt}$$

where $P = 1500$, $r = 6.5\%$, $n = 4$ and $t = 5$. Our equation becomes

$$A = (1500)\left(1 + \frac{0.065}{4}\right)^{4 \cdot 5} \qquad \text{Simplify.}$$

$$A = (1500)(1 + 0.01625)^{20}$$

$$A = (1500)(1.01625)^{20} \qquad \text{Using a calculator to compute, we get}$$

$$A = (1500)(1.380419775)$$

$$A = \$2,070.63$$

b) Find the compounded amount of money after 10 years in an account which begins with a principal of $2,500 invested at 7.5%, compounded monthly.

The formula for compound interest is

$$A = P\left(1 + \frac{r}{n}\right)^{nt}$$

where $P = 2500$, $r = 7.5\%$, $n = 12$ and $t = 10$. Our equation becomes

$$A = (2500)\left(1 + \frac{0.075}{12}\right)^{12 \cdot 10} \qquad \text{Simplify.}$$

$$A = (2500)(1 + 0.00625)^{120}$$

$$A = (2500)(1.00625)^{120} \qquad \begin{array}{l}\text{Using a calculator to}\\ \text{compute, we get}\end{array}$$

$$A = (2500)(2.112064637)$$

$$A = \$5,280.16$$

Let's review some of the properties of exponents and introduce two new properties of exponential equations.

Properties of Exponents:

For a and b positive, a and $b \neq 1$ and x and y real numbers

1. $a^x a^y = a^{x+y}$

2. $(a^x)^y = a^{xy}$

3. $(ab)^x = a^x b^x$

4. $\left(\dfrac{a}{b}\right)^x = \dfrac{a^x}{b^x}$

5. $\dfrac{a^x}{a^y} = a^{x-y}$

6. $a^x = a^y$ if and only if $x = y$.

7. For $x \neq 0$, then $a^x = b^x$ if and only if $a = b$.

EXAMPLE 5.3

Solve the following exponential equations:

a) $2^{x+1} = 2^{2x-3}$

b) $3^{2x+4} = 9^{2x-5}$

SOLUTION 5.3

a) $2^{x+1} = 2^{2x-3}$

Since the base is the same on both sides of the equation, we ignore the base and set the powers equal.

$x + 1 = 2x - 3$	Add $-x$ and $+3$ to both sides of the equation.
$x + 1 - x + 3 = 2x - 3 - x + 3$	Simplify.
$4 = x$	Rewrite the equation.
$x = 4$	

b) $3^{2x+4} = 9^{2x-5}$

The bases are not the same on both sides of the equation. Replace 9 with 3^2.

$3^{2x+4} = (3^2)^{2x-5}$	Use the property of exponents to simplify.
$3^{2x+4} = 3^{4x-10}$	The bases are now the same. Set the powers equal.
$2x + 4 = 4x - 10$	Add $-2x$ and $+10$ to both sides of the equation.
$2x + 4 - 2x + 10 = 4x - 10 - 2x + 10$	Simplify.
$14 = 2x$	Divide both sides by 2.
$\dfrac{14}{2} = \dfrac{2x}{2}$	Simplify again.
$7 = x$	Rewrite the equation.
$x = 7$	

EXERCISE 5.1

Graph the following exponential functions:

1. $y = 2^x$

2. $y = 5^x$

3. $y = (\frac{1}{5})^x$

4. $y = -2^x$

5. $y = 3^{-x}$

6. $y = 2 \cdot (2^x)$

Simplify each of the following:

7. $2^x \cdot 2^{2x+3}$

8. $3^{2x-5} \cdot 3^{5x+3}$

9. $\dfrac{4^{2x+3} \cdot 2^{2x+4}}{8}$

10. $\dfrac{3^{x+3} \cdot 9^{3x+6}}{27}$

Solve the following equations for x:

11. $3^{2x-3} \cdot 3^{2x+12} = 3^{3x}$

12. $3^{x-3} \cdot 9^x = 27$

13. $5^{x-5} \cdot 25^{x-2} = 125$

14. $2^{2x} \cdot 8^{x-1} = 16^{x+1}$

15. $k^{x-8} = (k^2)^{x-3}$

Solve the following compound interest problems:

16. Find the compounded amount of money after 3 years in an account which begins with a principal of $1,000 invested at 9.0%, compounded quarterly.

17. Find the compounded amount of money after 20 years in an account which begins with a principal of $3,500 invested at 12.0%, compounded monthly.

18. Find the compounded amount of money after 2 years in an account which begins with a principal of $12,235 invested at 5.5%, compounded monthly.

ANSWERS TO EXERCISE 5.1

1.

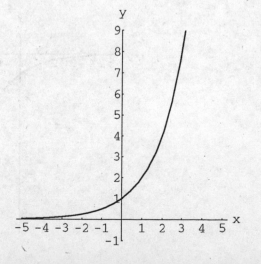

2.

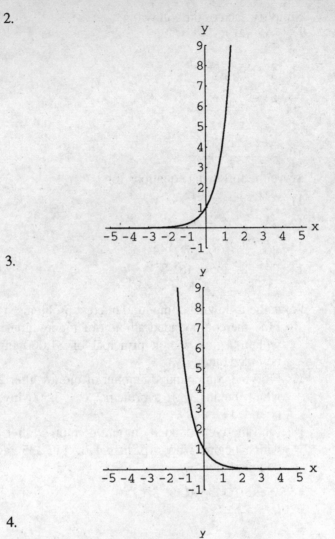

3.

4.

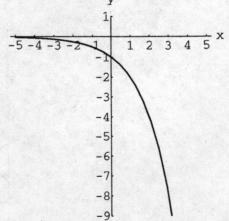

5.

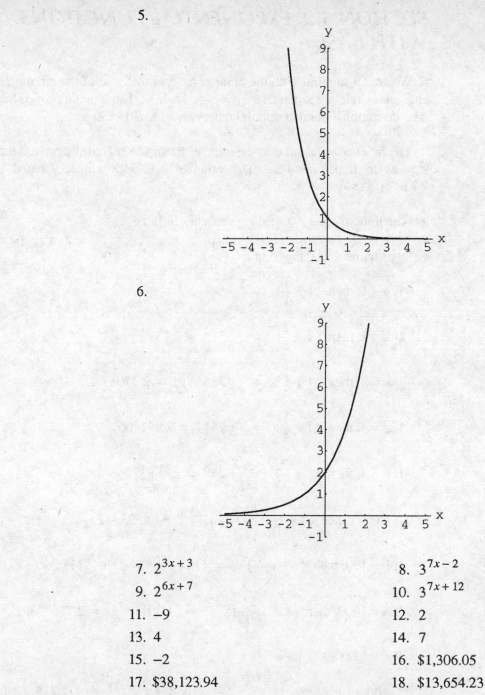

6.

7. 2^{3x+3}

8. 3^{7x-2}

9. 2^{6x+7}

10. 3^{7x+12}

11. -9

12. 2

13. 4

14. 7

15. -2

16. $\$1,306.05$

17. $\$38,123.94$

18. $\$13,654.23$

SECTION 5.2 EXPONENTIAL FUNCTIONS WITH BASE e

We are all familiar with the number π. π is the ratio of the circumference of a circle to its diameter; $\pi = \frac{C}{d}$. In 1882, Lindemann proved that π is an irrational number approximately equal to $3.14159.\ldots$

The number e is similar to the number π. In 1883, Hermite proved that e is an irrational number. The value of e is approximately equal to $2.7182818284.\ldots$

e is the limit of $\left(1 + \frac{1}{n}\right)^n$ as n approaches infinity.

Let's examine this expression $\left(1 + \frac{1}{n}\right)^n$.

If $n = 1$, then $\left(1 + \frac{1}{1}\right)^1 = 2$

If $n = 2$, then $\left(1 + \frac{1}{2}\right)^2 = (1.5)^2 = 2.25$

If $n = 3$, then $\left(1 + \frac{1}{3}\right)^3 = (1.333\ldots)^3 = 2.37037\ldots$

If $n = 4$, then $\left(1 + \frac{1}{4}\right)^4 = (1.25)^4 = 2.441406\ldots$

If $n = 5$, then $\left(1 + \frac{1}{5}\right)^5 = (1.2)^5 = 2.48832$

If $n = 10$, then $\left(1 + \frac{1}{10}\right)^{10} = (1.1)^{10} = 2.593742\ldots$

If $n = 100$, then $\left(1 + \frac{1}{100}\right)^{10} = (1.01)^{100} = 2.7048138\ldots$

If $n = 1000$, then $\left(1 + \frac{1}{1000}\right)^{1000} = (1.001)^{1000} = 2.7169239\ldots$

If $n = 1{,}000{,}000$, then

$$\left(1 + \frac{1}{1{,}000{,}000}\right)^{1000000} = (1.000001)^{1000000} = 2.718280\ldots$$

> **Definition: Exponential Function with base *e***
> For any real number *x*, the function
> $$y = f(x) = e^x$$
> is the exponential function with the base of *e*.

EXAMPLE 5.4

Graph the following exponential functions with the base of *e* (*e* = 2.7):

a) $y = e^x$

b) $y = e^{-x}$

c) $y = -e^x$

SOLUTION 5.4

a) $y = e^x$

To graph an exponential function, we need to let *x* = 0, 1, and –1.

Let *x* = 0, then *y* = 1. The ordered pair is (0, 1).

Let *x* = 1, then *y* = *e*. The ordered pair is (1, 2.7).

Let *x* = –1, then $y = \dfrac{1}{e}$. The ordered pair is (–1, 0.37).

Plot the points on the Cartesian plane and draw the curve (Figure 5.5).

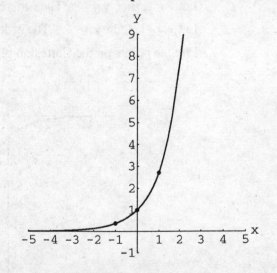

Figure 5.5

b) $y = e^{-x}$
Let *x* = 0, 1, and –1.

Let $x = 0$, then $y = 1$. The ordered pair is (0, 1).

Let $x = 1$, then $y = \dfrac{1}{e}$. The ordered pair is (1, 0.37).

Let $x = -1$, then $y = e$. The ordered pair is (−1, 2.7).

Plot the points on the Cartesian plane and draw the curve (Figure 5.6).

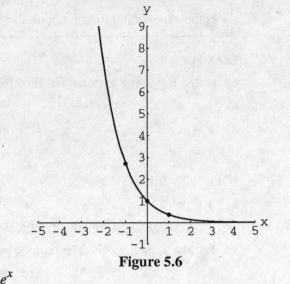

Figure 5.6

c) $y = -e^x$

Let $x = 0$, 1, and −1.

Let $x = 0$, then $y = -1$. The ordered pair is (0, −1).

Let $x = 1$, then $y = -e$. The ordered pair is (1, −2.7).

Let $x = -1$, then $y = \dfrac{1}{e}$. The ordered pair is (−1, −0.37).

Plot the points on the Cartesian plane and draw the curve (Figure 5.7).

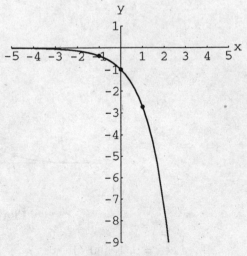

Figure 5.7

In the previous section we learned a compound interest formula

$\left[A = P\left(1 + \dfrac{r}{n}\right)^{nt} \right]$. In this formula the number of compounds per year is

a finite number n. Some banks and savings and loans are using a formula to compound interest continuously. To develop a formula to compound interest continuously, we start with the compound interest formula

$$A = P\left(1 + \frac{r}{n}\right)^{nt}$$

This is equivalent to

$$A = P\left(1 + \frac{1}{(n/r)}\right)^{(n/r)\,(rt)}$$

As n becomes infinite, the expression

$$\left[\left(1 + \frac{1}{(n/r)}\right)^{(n/r)} \right] = e.$$

The compound interest formula for interest compounded continuous is

$$A = Pe^{rt}$$

where P is the principal, r is the yearly interest rate and t is the time in years.

EXAMPLE 5.5

Find the amount of money compounded continuous for each of the following:
a) $1,500 at 6.5% for 5 years.
b) $2,500 at 7.5% for 10 years.

SOLUTION 5.5

a) $1,500 at 6.5% for 5 years.

The formula for the amount of money compounded continuous is

$A = Pe^{rt}$

Substituting the P, r and t into the formula we get

$A = (1500)\,e^{(0.065)\,(5)}$

$A = (1500)\,e^{(0.325)}$

$A = (1500)\,(1.384030646)$

$A = \$2,076.05$

If you remember, when we compounded monthly we earned $2,074.23. The difference between continuous compounding and monthly compounds is $1.82. This is not very much on an investment of $1,500, but if the investment were $1,500,000, the difference would be $1820.00.

b) $2,500 at 7.5% for 10 years.

The compound interest formula is

$$A = Pe^{rt}$$

Substituting the P, r and t into the formula we get

$$A = (2500) \, e^{(0.075)\,(10)}$$
$$A = (2500) \, e^{(0.75)}$$
$$A = (2500) \, (2.117000017)$$
$$A = \$5,292.50$$

EXERCISE 5.2

Graph the following exponential functions:

1. $y = e^x$

2. $y = (\frac{1}{e})^x$

3. $y = -e^{2x}$

4. $y = e^{-0.2x}$

5. $y = 5 \cdot (e^x)$

Graph the folowing exponential functions:

6. $y = 5e^{0.1x}$

7. $y = e^{|x|}$

8. $y = e^x + 2$

Solve the following compound interest problems:

9. Find the compounded amount of money after 3 years in an account which begins with a principal of $1,000 invested at 9.0% with continuous compounding.

10. Find the compounded amount of money after 20 years in an account which begins with a principal of $3,500 invested at 12.0% with continuous compounding.

11. Find the compounded amount of money after 2 years in an account which begins with a principal of $12,235 invested at 5.5% with continuous compounding.

ANSWERS TO EXERCISE 5.2

1.

2.

3.

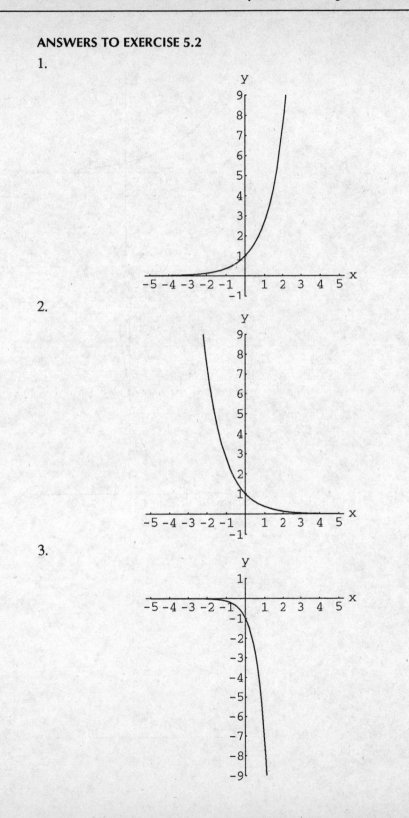

4.

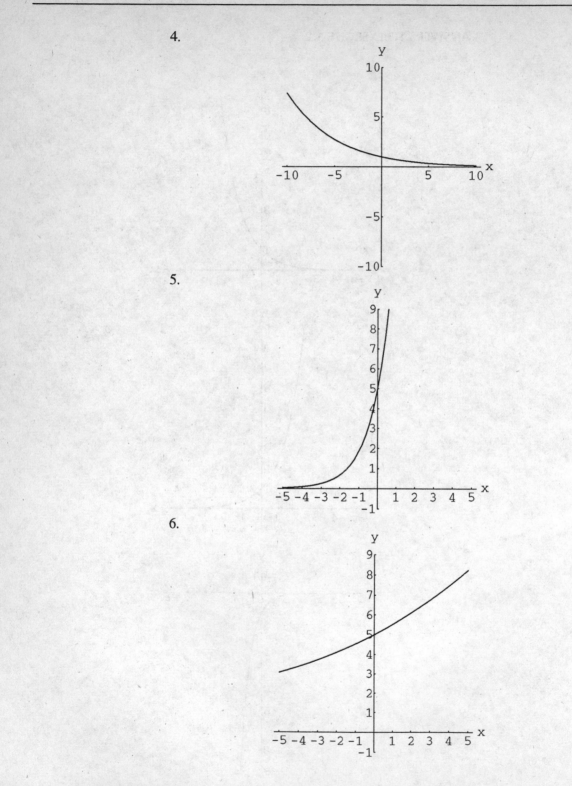

5.

6.

7.

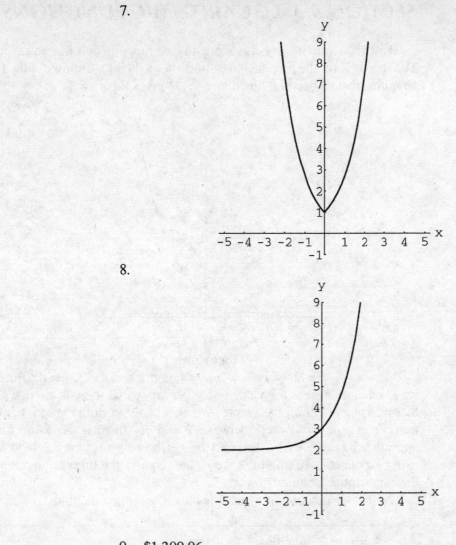

8.

9. $1,309.96
10. $38,581.12
11. $13,657.66

SECTION 5.3 LOGARITHMIC FUNCTIONS

The exponential function is a one-to-one function and has an inverse. The inverse of the exponential function is the logarithmic function. Graphing the exponential function $y = 2^x$ gives Figure 5.8.

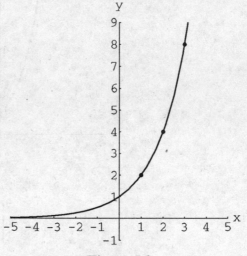

Figure 5.8

When $x = 1$, $y = 2$, when $x = 2$, $y = 4$, and when $x = 3$, $y = 8$. But for what value of x gives a y value of 5. We know that there is a value of x that makes $y = 5$ from the graph. We also know from the graph that the number of x is somewhere between 2 and 3. In fact, the value for x appears to be closer to 2. The exact answer, however, is impossible to find using exponents. To find the exact value requires the inverse function of the exponential function $y = 2^x$.

The inverse function of $x = b^y$ is the logarithmic function.

Definition: Logarithmic Function
For $b > 0$, $b \neq 1$, and $x > 0$,
$x = b^y$ is equivalent to $y = \log_b x$.

The function $y = \log_b x$ is read "y equals the log base b of x." Notice that when we say $y = \log_b x$, y is the power to which we raise the base b to equal x. The logarithm is nothing more than a power. Powers and logs are interchangeable. Try this on your calculator; enter the number 100 and hit the key marked $\boxed{\log}$. The display should read 2. This means that 2 is the power we raise 10 to to get 100.

$y = b^x$ and $x = b^y$ are inverse functions. Since $x = b^y$ and $y = \log_b x$ are equivalent then $y = b^x$ and $y = \log_b x$ are inverse functions. Figure 5.9 is the graph of $y = 2^x$. The ordered pairs (0, 1), (1, 2) and $(-1, \dfrac{1}{2})$ are on the graph.

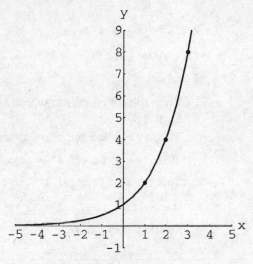

Figure 5.9

Graph the inverse of $y = 2^x$. The inverse function $x = 2^y$ reverses the ordered pairs. The points are (1, 0), (2, 1) and $(\dfrac{1}{2}, \ 1)$. Plotting these points we get Figure 5.10.

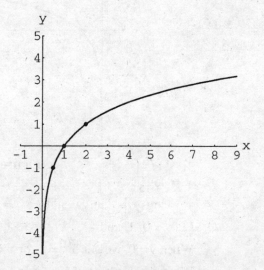

Figure 5.10

This is the graph of $y = \log_2 x$ which is the graph of $2^y = x$. To graph a logarithmic function it is easiest to pick values for y and compute the x answers.

EXAMPLE 5.6

Graph the following logarithmic functions:

a) $y = \log_3 x$

b) $y = \log_5 x$

SOLUTION 5.6

a) $y = \log_3 x$

To graph this function which is the equivalent of $3^y = x$, let $y = 0, 1,$ and -1.

When $y = 0$, we get $3^0 = x$ or $x = 1$. The ordered pair becomes $(1, 0)$.

When $y = 1$, we get $3^1 = x$ or $x = 3$. The ordered pair becomes $(3, 1)$.

When $y = -1$, we get $3^{-1} = x$ of $x = \frac{1}{3}$. The ordered pair becomes $(\frac{1}{3}, -1)$.

Graph the function.

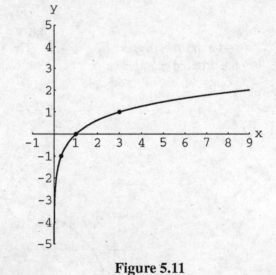

Figure 5.11

b) $y = \log_5 x$

$y = \log_5 x$ is equivalent to $5^y = x$.

Let $y = 0, 1,$ and -1.

When $y = 0$, we get $5^0 = x$ or $x = 1$. The ordered pair becomes $(1, 0)$.

When $y = 1$, we get $5^1 = x$ or $x = 5$. The ordered pair becomes $(5, 1)$.

When $y = -1$, we get $5^{-1} = x$ or $x = \frac{1}{5}$. The ordered pair becomes $(\frac{1}{5}, -1)$.

Graph the function.

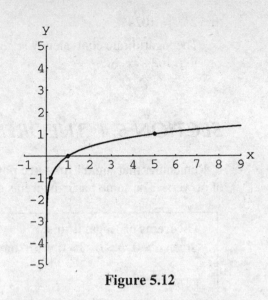

Figure 5.12

EXAMPLE 5.7

Rewrite the following exponential expressions into logarithmic equivalences:

a) $3^4 = 81$

b) $2^4 = 16$

c) $5^3 = 125$

d) $2^{10} = 1024$

SOLUTION 5.7

a) $3^4 = 81$

The exponential expression says 3 to the fourth power equals 81. The logarithmic equivalency of this expression states $4 = \log_3 81$ or $\log_3 81 = 4$.

b) $2^4 = 16$

The exponential expression says 2 to the fourth power equals 16. The logarithmic equivalency of this expression states $4 = \log_2 16$ or $4 = \log_2 16$.

c) $5^3 = 125$

The logarithmic equivalency states $3 = \log_5 125$ or $\log_5 125 = 3$.

d) $2^{10} = 1024$

The logarithmic equivalency states $10 = \log_2 1024$ or $\log_2 1024 = 10$.

SECTION 5.4 THEOREMS OF LOGARITHMS

Remember that **logarithms are powers**. Also remember the theorems of powers. The same basic theorems of powers apply to logarithms.

Theorems of Logarithms:

Given $a > 0$, $b > 0$, $x > 0$, $y > 0$, and $b \neq 1$

1. $b^{\log_b x} = x$

2. $\log_b (xy) = \log_b x + \log_b y$

3. $\log_b \left(\dfrac{x}{y}\right) = \log_b x - \log_b y$

4. $\log_b x^m = m \log_b x$

5. $\log_b \sqrt[n]{x} = \dfrac{1}{n} \log_b x$

6. $\log_b \sqrt[n]{x^m} = \dfrac{m}{n} \log_b x$

7. $\log_b a = \dfrac{1}{\log_a b}$

8. $\log_b a = \dfrac{\log_c a}{\log_c b}$

9. $\log_b 1 = 0$

10. $\log_b b = 1$

Most of these theorems we will accept without proof, but let's examine the first two theorems.

Theorem 1

$b^{\log_b x} = x$

In the expression $b^{\log_b x} = x$, let $\log_b x = a$.   The expression

$b^{\log_b x} = x$ becomes $b^a = x$. By the definition of logarithms

$$b^a = x \text{ if and only if } a = \log_b x.$$

$\log_b x = a$ and $a = \log_b x$ which says $\log_b x = \log_b x$. The conclusion is an identity and $b^{\log_b x} = x$.

Theorem 2

$$\log_b(xy) = \log_b x + \log_b y$$

We know that

$$b^{\log_b x} = x \text{ and } b^{\log_b y} = y.$$

$$xy = b^{\log_b x} \cdot b^{\log_b y}$$

To multiply a power times power, we keep the base and add the powers.

$$xy = b^{\log_b x} \cdot b^{\log_b y} = b^{\log_b x + \log_b y}$$

$$xy = b^{\log_b x + \log_b y}$$

Let $\log_b x + \log_b y = c$. When we replace $\log_b x + \log_b y$ we get

$$b^c = xy.$$

Using the definition of logarithms,

$$\log_b(xy) = c$$

$$c = \log_b x + \log_b y$$

$$\log_b(xy) = \log_b x + \log_b y.$$

The proofs of the other theorems are similar. Often we may have logs of an algebraic expression. Using the theorems, we can expand the logs into sums and differences of single logarithms. This process is known as the **expansion of logarithms**.

EXAMPLE 5.8

Expand the following logarithms into sums and differences of separate logs:

a) $\log_b\left(\dfrac{xy}{z}\right)$

b) $\log_b\left(\dfrac{2x^3 y^2}{a^2 c}\right)$

c) $\log_b\left(xy^2\sqrt{\dfrac{a^3c}{d^3}}\right)$

SOLUTION 5.8

a) $\log_b\left(\dfrac{xy}{z}\right)$

The idea of logarithms is to make difficult mathematics problems easier to compute. We know the theorems of logarithms. To expand a logarithm, we begin with the logarithm of the first number or variable in the numerator of the fraction. If the expression is not a fraction, then begin with the first number.

$\log_b x$

Now examine what is happening with x and the other numbers or variables in the problem. Since x and y are being multiplied, the logs will be added. x and z are being divided so the logs will be subtracted. Expanding the logarithm, we get

$\log_b x + \log_b y - \log_b z$.

b) $\log_b\left(\dfrac{2x^3y^2}{a^2c}\right)$

Begin with the $\log_b 2$ and expand according to what is happening to the 2 and the other terms. Do not pay attention to what is happening with x and y or a,b, and c. Look only at z and x, z and y, z and a, etc.

$\log_b 2 + 3\log_b x + 2\log_b y - 2\log_b a - \log_b c$

c) $\log_b\left(xy^2\sqrt{\dfrac{a^3c}{d^3}}\right)$

$\log_b x + 2\log_b y + \dfrac{3}{2}\log_b y + \dfrac{1}{2}\log_b c - \dfrac{3}{2}\log_b d$

Remember that roots become fractional coefficients of logarithms.

EXAMPLE 5.9

Rewrite the following into statements with a single logarithm:

a) $\log_b x + 2\log_b y - 3\log_b z$

b) $3\log_b x + 2\log_b y + \dfrac{1}{2}\log_b a - \dfrac{3}{2}\log_b c - \dfrac{5}{2}\log_b d$

SOLUTION 5.9

a) $\log_b x + 2\log_b y - 3\log_b z$

To write this statement as a single logarithm, we begin with the first log expression.

$\log_b x$

If the second term is added, we multiply the terms; if the second term is subtracted we divide the terms. Since we are adding and then subtracting, we will multiply by y and divide by z. Remember, coefficients of logarithms are powers of the terms.

$$\log_b x + 2\log_b y - 3\log_b z = \log_b\left(\frac{xy^2}{z^3}\right)$$

b) $3\log_b x + 2\log_b y + \frac{1}{2}\log_b a - \frac{3}{2}\log_b c - \frac{5}{2}\log_b d$

$$3\log_b x + 2\log_b y + \frac{1}{2}\log_b a - \frac{3}{2}\log_b c - \frac{5}{2}\log_b d = \log_b\left(x^3 y^2 \sqrt{\frac{a}{c^3 d^5}}\right)$$

EXERCISE 5.3

Find the value of the following logarithms (five decimal places) using your calculator and the base 10 logarithm:

1. $\log_5 27$

2. $\log_3 94$

3. $\log_2 233$

4. $\log_5\left(\frac{1}{2}\right)$

Expand the following logarithms into sums and differences of logs:

5. $\log_2 (x^2 y^3)$

6. $\log_5\left(\frac{x^2 y}{a^3 b^2}\right)$

7. $\log_b\left(\frac{x^4 y^5}{a^3 c^2 d^3}\right)$

8. $\log\left(\frac{x^2 y^3}{z}\sqrt{\frac{a^2 b^2 c^3}{d^5}}\right)$

9. $\log\left(x^2 y^3 \sqrt{\dfrac{ab^2}{c^3}}\right)$

10. $\log\left(\dfrac{9x}{y}\sqrt{\dfrac{xy^2}{z^3}}\right)$

Write the following logarithmic statements into statements with a single logarithm:

11. $3\log_b a - 2\log_b c - 5\log_b d$

12. $3\log_b x + 2\log_b y - 4\log_b w - 2\log_b z$

13. $2\log_b x - 3\log_b y + \dfrac{3}{2}\log_b a - \dfrac{1}{2}\log_b c + \dfrac{3}{2}\log_b d$

14. $3\log_b x - 2\log_b y + 3\log_b z + 2\log_b a - 3\log_b c - 4\log_b d$

15. $\dfrac{3}{2}\log_b x + 2\log_b y + \dfrac{1}{2}\log_b a - 3\log_b c - \dfrac{1}{2}\log_b d$

ANSWERS TO EXERCISE 5.3

1. 2.04782

2. 4.13549

3. 7.86419

4. −0.43068

5. $2\log_2 x + 3\log_2 y$

6. $2\log_5 x + \log_5 y - 3\log_5 a - 2\log_5 b$

7. $4\log_b x + 5\log_b y - 3\log_b a - 2\log_b c - 3\log_b d$

8. $2\log x + 3\log y - \log z + \log a + \log b + \dfrac{3}{2}\log c - \dfrac{5}{2}\log d$

9. $2\log x + 3\log y + \dfrac{1}{2}\log a + \log b + \dfrac{3}{2}\log c$

10. $\log 9 + \dfrac{3}{2}\log x + \dfrac{3}{2}\log y - \dfrac{3}{2}\log z$

11. $\log_2\left(\dfrac{a^3 c^2}{d^5}\right)$

12. $\log_b \left(\dfrac{x^3 y^2}{w^4 z^2} \right)$

13. $\log_b \left(\dfrac{x^2}{y^3} \sqrt{\dfrac{a^3 d^3}{c}} \right)$

14. $\log_b \left(\dfrac{x^2 z^3 a^2}{y^2 c^3 d^4} \right)$

15. $\log_b \left(\dfrac{y^2}{c^3} \sqrt{\dfrac{x^3 a}{d}} \right)$

SECTION 5.5 COMMON AND NATURAL LOGARITHMS

Logarithms can be defined using any number base. There are, however, only two bases which are in use today. These two bases are base 10 (the **common logarithms**, also known as **Briggsian logarithms**) and base e (the **natural logarithm**, also known as **Napierian logarithms**).

Logarithmic Notation	
$\log_{10} x = \log x$	**Common Logarithm**
$\log_e x = \ln x$	**Natural Logarithm**

At one time difficult calculations were performed using logarithms. Elaborate tables of logs were created and complex multiplication, division, powers, and roots could be computed by adding, subtracting, multiplying and dividing logarithms. Even today, logarithms are used to find higher roots and large powers. To do a cubic, fourth, or higher roots requires the use of logarithms. Large powers can be done by repeated multiplication, but calculators with power keys also have logarithmic keys.

EXAMPLE 5.10

Use your calculator to find the value of the following to five decimal places:
a) $\log 5$
b) $\log 382$
c) $\log 1429$

SOLUTION 5.10

a) $\log 5$

Find the log key on your calculator. With most calculators you enter the 5 then push the log key. The answer displayed is $\log 5$.

5 $\boxed{\log}$ = 0.69897

If your calculator does not display 0.69897 to five decimal places, read the book that came with your calculator to see how to use the log key.

b) $\log 382$

382 $\boxed{\log}$ = 2.58206

c) $\log 1429$

1429 $\boxed{\log}$ = 3.15503

Let's now do the same problems with the natural log key.

EXAMPLE 5.11

Use your calculator to find the value of the following to five decimal places:

a) $\ln 5$
b) $\ln 382$
c) $\ln 1429$

SOLUTION 5.11

a) $\ln 5$

5 $\boxed{\ln}$ = 1.60944

Notice that we do not get the same answer. That is because

5 $\boxed{\log}$ = 0.69897 means $10^{0.69897} = 5$ and

5 $\boxed{\ln}$ = 1.60944 means $e^{1.60944} = 5$.

b) $\ln 382$

382 $\boxed{\ln}$ = 5.94542

c) $\ln 1429$

1429 $\boxed{\ln}$ = 7.26473

Theorem 8 allows us to compute the logarithm of bases other than 10 and e. We can find the log of other bases by converting the logarithm to any new base c. The only logarithms which are available to us are logs of base 10 (**common Logarithm**) and base e (**natural logarithm**). We can find the values of unknown logarithms by using either base 10 or base e. Theorem 8 says;

$$\log_b a = \frac{\log_c a}{\log_c b}.$$

This means that $\log_2 3 = \dfrac{\log_{10} 3}{\log_{10} 2}$, that is, $\log_2 3$ can be found by using the base 10 logs.

EXAMPLE 5.12

Find the values of the following logarithms using your calculator with base 10:

a) $\log_2 5$

b) $\log_3 75$

SOLUTION 5.12

a) $\log_2 5$

To find the value of an unknown logarithm we use Theorem 8.

$$\log_b a = \frac{\log_c a}{\log_c b}$$

This theorem allows us to find the value of any logarithm using a calculator or table of any logarithm. To find the value of $\log_2 5$, we apply the theorem using base 10. When the base is smaller than the number the logarithm is greater than 1.

$$\log_2 25 = \frac{\log_{10} 25}{\log_{10} 2} = \frac{1.39794}{0.30103} = 4.664386$$

To say that

$$\log_2 25 = 4.64386$$

means that $2^{4.64386} = 25$

b) $\log_3 75 = \dfrac{\log_{10} 75}{\log_{10} 3} = \dfrac{1.87506}{0.47712} = 3.92995$

Sometimes we are given the $\log x = 1.36173$. To find the value of x, we use the inverse function keys. The inverse of the logarithm is the **antilogarithm**. The inverse of a logarithm is a power. Remember, that powers and logarithms are inverse functions.

To find $\log x = 1.36173$ on most calculators we enter 1.36173 and push the inv key and then the log key. It looks like this,

$$1.36173 \boxed{\text{inv}}\boxed{\text{log}} = .$$

In the display should be approximately 23.00011. Logarithms, like roots, which are not exact logarithms are irrational numbers; that is, they are non-terminating, non-repeating decimals. So all logarithms which are not exact have been rounded off. If we know that our original number is a whole number, then our answer will be 23.

EXAMPLE 5.13

Find the anti-logs for each of the following to the nearest whole number:

a) $\log x = 0.69897$

b) $\log x = 2.58206$

c) $\log x = 3.15503$

SOLUTION 5.13

a) $\log x = 0.69897$

   0.69897 $\boxed{\text{inv}}$ $\boxed{\text{log}}$ $= 5$

b) $\log x = 2.58206$

   2.58206 $\boxed{\text{inv}}$ $\boxed{\text{log}}$ $= 382$

c) $\log x = 3.15503$

   3.15503 $\boxed{\text{inv}}$ $\boxed{\text{log}}$ $= 1429$

You might have recognized these logs from the example where we found the logarithms. Here are some new problems.

EXAMPLE 5.14

Compute the following using logarithms:

a) 15^7

b) $\dfrac{(4.26)\,(8.74)^2\,(9.34)^3}{(5.23)^3\,(12.3)^2}$

c) $(\log 235)\,(\log 54.5)$

SOLUTION 5.14

a) 15^7

   To do this problem we could just multiply 15 times itself 7 times $(15 \cdot 15 \cdot 15 \cdot 15 \cdot 15 \cdot 15 \cdot 15 = 170,859,375)$. An easier way is by the use of logarithms. Let

   $$x = 15^7$$

   Take the log (base 10) of both sides of the equation. As long as x is non-negative we can take the logarithm of both sides of the equation.

$\log x = \log 15^7$	Simplify the log using the theorems about logs.
$\log x = 7 \cdot \log 15$	Find $\log 15$ on your calculator to 8 or 9 decimal places.
$\log x = 7 \cdot (1.176091259)$	Multiply 7 times the log 15.
$\log x = 8.232638813$	Now take the anti-log of both sides of the equation.

anti log $(\log x)$ = anti log (8.232638813)

x = anti log (8.232638813) = 8.232638813 $\boxed{\text{inv}}$ $\boxed{\text{log}}$

   = 170.859375

b) $\dfrac{(4.26)\,(8.74)^2\,(9.34)^3}{(5.23)^3\,(12.3)^2}$

Let $x = \dfrac{(4.26)\,(8.74)^2\,(9.34)^3}{(5.23)^3\,(12.3)^2}$ Take the log (base 10) of both sides of the equation.

$\log x = \log \dfrac{(4.26)\,(8.74)^2\,(9.34)^3}{(5.23)^3\,(12.3)^2}$ Simplify the logarithmic statement.

   = $(\log(4.26) + 2\log(8.74) + 3\log(9.34) - 3\log(5.23) - 2\log(12.3))$

Find the individual logarithms on your calculator to 5 decimal places.

$\log x$ = $(0.62941) + 2\,(0.94151) + 3\,(0.97035) - 3\,(0.71850) - 2\,(1.08991)$

Compute this problem.

$\log x$ = $(0.62941) + (1.88302) + (2.91105) - (2.15550) - (2.17982)$

$\log x$ = 1.08816 Now take the antilog of both sides of the equation.

anti log $(\log x)$ = anti log (1.08816)

$x = 1.08816$ $\boxed{\text{inv}}$ $\boxed{\text{log}}$ = 12.2506

Now do the same calculation on your calculator using the power key.

$\dfrac{(4.26)\,(8.74)^2\,(9.34)^3}{(5.23)^3\,(12.3)^2}$ = 12.2506

c) $(\log 235)\,(\log 54.5)$

Do not try to simplify this log statement. This is not $\log(xy)$; this is $\log x \cdot \log y$ and cannot be simplified. Strictly push is the proper numbers and logs to compute your answers.

25 $\boxed{\text{log}}$ $\boxed{x}$ 54.5 $\boxed{\text{log}}$ $\boxed{=}$

With this problem, you must push the equals key. When you enter 54.5 push the $\boxed{\text{log}}$ key what you get is the log of 54.5. When you push the $\boxed{=}$ this key completes the multiplication of the two logs and give you the final answer.

25 $\boxed{\text{log}}$ $\boxed{x}$ 54.5 $\boxed{\text{log}}$ $\boxed{=}$ 4.11711

EXERCISE 5.4

Use your calculator to find the value of the following to five decimal places:

1. $\log 574$

2. $\log 49, 300$

3. $\log 234^3$

4. $\ln 67$

5. $\ln \sqrt{12, 876}$

6. $\ln 7546^2$

Find the anti-logs for each of the following to the nearest whole number:

7. $\log x = 3.40586$

8. $\log x = 4.994607$

9. $\log x = 5.8725245$

10. $\ln x = 8.49638$

11. $\ln x = 9.438909$

12. $\ln x = 13.704089$

Compute the following using logarithms:

13. 23^4

14. $\sqrt[3]{14, 532}$

15. $\dfrac{(14.57)\,(35.79)^2}{(7.15)^3\,(3.3)^2}$

16. $(2.46)^3\,(\sqrt[4]{867, 493})$

Use a scientific calculator to perform the following logarithmic calculations to five decimal places:

17. $\dfrac{(\log 14, 526)}{(\log 3.5)}$

18. $(\ln 3.78)\,(\ln 2779)$

19. $\dfrac{\log (7.54)^3 \cdot \log (45.57)^2}{\ln (12.98)^2}$

20. $\dfrac{\ln (12.67) \cdot \ln (123.76)^2}{\ln (34.8)}$

ANSWERS TO EXERCISE 5.4

1. 2.71933	2. 4.69285
3. 7.10765	4. 4.20469
5. 4.73156	6. 17.85755
7. 2546	8. 98,766
9. 745,630	10. 4897
11. 12,568	12. 894,560
13. 279,840	14. 24.40292
15. 4.68853	16. 454.33
17. 7.650005	18. 10.54451
19. 3.92161	20. 6.89365

SECTION 5.6 EXPONENTIAL AND LOGARITHMIC EQUATIONS

Exponential Equations

An exponential equation is an equation involving a variable expression as an exponent: $3^{2x-1} = 27$.

We have already solved some exponential equations using the theorem:

$$b^x = b^y \text{ if and only if } x = y.$$

Our example equation can be solved by changing 27 to the base of 3.

$$3^{2x-1} = 27$$
$$3^{2x-1} = 3^3$$

When the bases of an exponential equation are the same, then the powers can be set equal.

$2x - 1 = 3$	Solve the equation by adding +1 to both sides.
$2x - 1 + 1 = 3 + 1$	Simplify.
$2x = 4$	Divide both sides by 2.
$\dfrac{2x}{2} = \dfrac{4}{2}$	Simplify again.
$x = 2$	

What if the bases on the different sides of the equation are not the same?

$$3^{2x-1} = 16$$

To solve this equation, we must use logarithms. Anytime we need to solve an equation with variables in an exponential expression, logarithms will allow us to remove the variable from the power.

$$3^{2x-1} = 16$$
Take the log of both sides of the equation.

$$\log 3^{2x-1} = \log 16$$
The log of a power expression becomes the coefficient of the log.

$$(2x-1)\log 3 = \log 16$$
Divide both sides by $\log 3$.

$$\frac{(2x-1)\log 3}{\log 3} = \frac{\log 16}{\log 3}$$
Simplify.

$$2x - 1 = \frac{\log 16}{\log 3}$$
Add +1 to both sides of the equation.

$$2x - 1 + 1 = \frac{\log 16}{\log 3} + 1$$
Simplify.

$$2x = \frac{\log 16}{\log 3} + 1$$
Divide both sides by 2.

$$\frac{2x}{2} = \frac{\frac{\log 16}{\log 3} + 1}{2}$$
Simplify.

$$x = \frac{\frac{\log 16}{\log 3} + 1}{2}$$
Now use your calculator to compute the answers.

$$x = 1.76186$$

To check our answer, go back to the original equation.

$$3^{2x-1} = 16$$

Let $x = 1.76186$ and replace it into the equation.

$$3^{2(1.76186)-1} \stackrel{?}{=} 16$$
Perform the indicated operation.

$$3^{3.52372-1} \stackrel{?}{=} 16$$

$$3^{2.52372} \stackrel{?}{=} 16$$

$$3^{2.52372} = 16.00001$$

EXAMPLE 5.15

Solve the following exponential equations using logarithms base 10.
Write your answer as a five place decimal:

a) $2^{3x-2} = 183$

b) $5^{7x+4} = 12,543$

SOLUTION 5.15

a) $2^{3x-2} = 183$

$2^{3x-2} = 183$	Take the log of both sides of the equation.
$\log 2^{3x-2} = \log 183$	Simplify. do not compute logs until the last steps.
$(3x-2)\log 2 = \log 183$	Divide both sides by $\log 2$.
$\dfrac{(3x-2)\log 2}{\log 2} = \dfrac{\log 183}{\log 2}$	Simplify.
$3x-2 = \dfrac{\log 183}{\log 2}$	Add $+2$ to both sides of the equation.
$3x-2+2 = \dfrac{\log 183}{\log 2} + 2$	Simplify again.
$3x = \dfrac{\log 183}{\log 2} + 2$	Divide both sides by 3.
$\dfrac{3x}{3} = \dfrac{\dfrac{\log 183}{\log 2} + 2}{3}$	Simplify.
$x = \dfrac{\dfrac{\log 183}{\log 2} + 2}{3}$	Calculate the answer with your calculator.

$x = 3.17190$

Replace the value of x back into the original equation to be certain the solution checks.

$2^{3(3.17190)-2} \overset{?}{=} 183$

$2^{9.51570-2} \overset{?}{=} 183$

$2^{7.51570} \overset{?}{=} 183$

$2^{7.51570} = 183.00002$

b) $5^{7x+4} = 12,543$

$5^{7x+4} = 12,543$ Take the log of both sides of the equation.

$\log 5^{7x+4} = \log 12,543$ Simplify. Do not compute logs until the last steps.

$(7x+4)\log 5 = \log 12543$ Divide both sides by $\log 5$.

$\dfrac{(7x+4)\log 5}{\log 5} = \dfrac{\log 12543}{\log 5}$ Simplify.

$7x+4 = \dfrac{\log 12543}{\log 5}$ Add -4 to both sides of the equation.

$7x+4-4 = \dfrac{\log 12543}{\log 5} - 4$ Simplify again.

$7x = \dfrac{\log 12543}{\log 5} - 4$ Divide both sides by 7.

$\dfrac{7x}{7} = \dfrac{\dfrac{\log 12543}{\log 5} - 4}{7}$ Simplify.

$x = \dfrac{\dfrac{\log 12543}{\log 5} - 4}{7}$ Calculate the answer with your calculator.

$x = 0.26621$

Replace the value of x back into the original equation to be certain the solution checks.

$5^{7(0.26621)+4} \overset{?}{=} 12,543$

$5^{1.86347+4} \overset{?}{=} 12,543$

$5^{5.86347} \overset{?}{=} 12,543$

$5^{5.86347} = 12,542.6600$

Logarithmic Equations

To solve logarithmic equations we need the definition of logarithms and a theorem about logarithmic equations.

> **Logarithmic Equations:**
> $$\log_b x = y \text{ if and only if } b^y = x$$
> and
> $$\log_b x = \log_b y \text{ if and only if } x = y$$

There are two basic types of log equations. One type is where a logarithm is equal to a number.

EXAMPLE 5.16

a) $\log x^3 = 9$

b) $\log_2(x^2 - 2x) = 3$

SOLUTION 5.16

a) $\log x^3 = 9$ — First simplify the logarithm.

$3\log x = 9$ — Divide both sides by 3.

$\dfrac{3\log x}{3} = \dfrac{9}{3}$ — Simplify.

$\log x = 3$ — By the definition of logs, 3 is the power you raise 10 to to get x.

$10^3 = x$ — Rewrite the equation.

$x = 1000$

For $\log_b x$, the logarithms is only defined for $b > 0$, $b \neq 1$, and $x > 0$. When solving log equations, we must check to be certain that we are taking logarithms of only positive numbers. Replace $x = 1000$ into the original equation and check your answer.

$\log x^3 = 9$

$\log(1000)^3 = 9$

$10^9 = 1000^3$

$1,000,000,000 = 1,000,000,000$

b) $\log_2(x^2 - 2x) = 3$ — 3 is the power to which we raise 2 to equal $x^2 - 2x$.

$2^3 = x^2 - 2x$ — This is a quadratic equation in x. Simplify and put into standard form.

$8 = x^2 - 2x$ Add -8 to both sides.

$8 - 8 = x^2 - 2x - 8$ Simplify.

$0 = x^2 - 2x - 8$ Factor and solve.

$0 = (x-4)(x+2)$

$x = 4, -2$

Check both answers. Let $x = 4$.

$\log_2(x^2 - 2x) = 3$

$\log_2((4)^2 - 2(4)) = 3$

$\log_2(16 - 8) = 3$

$\log_2(8) = 3$ We have the log of a positive number; $x = 4$ is acceptable.

Now check $x = -2$.

$\log_2((-2)^2 - 2(-2)) \overset{?}{=} 3$

$\log_2(4 + 4) \overset{?}{=} 3$

$\log_2(8) = 3$ Again, $x = -2$ is acceptable.

The solution set is $\{4, -2\}$. It is not necessary that x be positive. By definition, we can only take logarithms of positive numbers.

The second type of logarithmic equations involve a logarithm equal to a logarithm.

EXAMPLE 5.17

a) $\log(x-1) - \log 2 = \log 8$

b) $\log x + \log(x-2) = \log 15$

SOLUTION 5.17

a) $\log(x-1) - \log 2 = \log 8$ Write both sides of the equation as a single logarithm.

$\log \dfrac{(x-1)}{2} = \log 8$ Take the anti-log of both sides of the equation.

$\text{anti-log}\left(\dfrac{\log(x-1)}{2}\right) = \text{anti-log}(\log 8)$

The anti-log removes the log.

$$\frac{(x-1)}{2} = 8$$ Multiply both sides of the equation by 2.

$$2 \cdot \frac{(x-1)}{2} = 2 \cdot 8$$ Simplify.

$$x - 1 = 16$$ Add +1 to both sides of the equation.

$$x - 1 + 1 = 16 + 1$$ Simplify.
$$x = 17$$

Check your answer.

$$\log (x-1) - \log 2 \stackrel{?}{=} \log 8$$

$$\log (17-1) - \log 2 \stackrel{?}{=} \log 8$$

$$\log (16) - \log 2 \stackrel{?}{=} \log 8$$

$$\log \left(\frac{16}{2}\right) \stackrel{?}{=} \log 8$$

$$\log 8 = \log 8$$ The answer checks.

The solution set is $\{17\}$.

b) $\log x + \log (x-2) = \log 15$ Write both sides of the equation as a single logarithm.

$$\log x (x-2) = \log 15$$ Take the anti-log of both sides. The anti-log drops the logs.

$$x (x-2) = 15$$ Simplify.

$$x^2 - 2x = 15$$ Add –15 to both sides of the equation.

$$x^2 - 2x - 15 = 15 - 15$$ Simplify again.

$$x^2 - 2x - 15 = 0$$ Factor and solve.

$$(x - 5)(x + 3) = 0$$

$$x = 5, -3$$

Check your answers.

$$\log x + \log (x-2) \stackrel{?}{=} \log 15$$

$$\log 5 + \log (5-2) \stackrel{?}{=} \log 15$$

$$\log 5 + \log 3 \stackrel{?}{=} \log 15$$

$$\log 5 \cdot 3 \stackrel{?}{=} \log 15$$

$$\log 15 = \log 15$$ The solution checks.

Check the second solution.

$$\log(-3) + \log(-3-2) \neq \log 15$$

Solution is not possible. We cannot take the log of a negative number. The solution set is $\{5\}$.

EXERCISE 5.5

Solve the following equations. Be certain to check your answers.

1. $\log(x-4)^3 = 6$

2. $\log_5(x^2 - 4x) = 1$

3. $\log_3(x^2 - 6x) = 3$

4. $\log(4x + 8) = 2$

5. $\log_6(x-4) = 2 - \log_6(x-9)$

6. $\log(30x + 100) = 1 + 2\log x$

7. $\log(2x+7) = \log 4 - \log(2-x)$

8. $\log_7(x^2 - x - 6) - \log_7(x+2) = 1$

9. $\log x + \log(x-2) = \log 35$

10. $\log_3(2x+3) - \log_3(x-2) = 2$

11. $\log_9(x^2 - 3x - 40) - \log_9(x+5) = \dfrac{1}{2}$

12. $\log_2(\log_9 3x) = -1$

13. $\log_2 \sqrt{\dfrac{x}{2x+3}} = 0$

14. $x^{\log_2 x^3} = 8$

15. $x^{\log x^2} = 100$

16. $(\log x)^2 = \log x^2$

ANSWERS TO EXERCISE 5.5

1. $\{104\}$ 2. $\{5, -1\}$

3. $\{9, -3\}$ 4. $\{23\}$

5. $\{13\}$

6. $\{5\}$

7. $\{\frac{1}{6}\}$

8. $\{10\}$

9. $\{7\}$

10. $\{3\}$

11. $\{11\}$

12. $\{1\}$

13. $\{-3\}$

14. $\{2, \frac{1}{2}\}$

15. $\{10, \frac{1}{10}\}$

16. $\{1, 100\}$

6

Polynomial Functions: Solutions and Graphs

A polynomial expression of degree n is an expression in the form of

$$P(x) = a_n X^n + a_{n-1} X^{n-1} + a_{n-2} X^{n-2} + \dots + a_1 x^1 + a_0 \quad (a_n \neq 0)$$

where n is a whole number and a_n is a real or imaginary coefficient. Polynomial expressions do not contain division by a variable or roots of a variable. We have already solved polynomial equations of first and second degree and polynomials that were quadratic in form. In this chapter we will discuss solving and graphing polynomials of higher degree.

A **zero**, **root**, or **solution** of a polynomial is a value r, such that $P(r) = 0$. A zero of a polynomial may be real or imaginary. Given $y = P(x)$, the x-intercepts are the real zeros of the polynomial $P(x)$. The x-intercepts of $y = P(x)$ are also the real solutions or roots of the equation $P(x) = 0$.

SECTION 6.1 SYNTHETIC DIVISION

Long Division

To divide a polynomial by a polynomial we use a process similar to long division of whole numbers.

EXAMPLE 6.1

Divide the following polynomial:

$(15x^3 + 53x^2 - 30x - 8)$ by $(3x - 2)$

SOLUTION 6.1

Divide $(15x^3 + 53x^2 - 30x - 8)$ by $(3x - 2)$

Write the two polynomials under a long division sign. To divide polynmials, both the divisor and the dividend must be written in standard form. The standard form of a polynomial is written with the highest power written first in descending powers. Any missing powers must be written with coefficients of zero.

$$3x-2\overline{)15x^3 + 53x^2 - 30x - 8}$$

Divide the first term of the divisor into the first term of the dividend.

$$\begin{array}{r} 5x^2 \quad\quad\quad\quad\quad\quad \\ 3x-2\overline{)15x^3 + 53x^2 - 30x - 8} \end{array}$$

Multiply $5x^2$ times the entire divisor $(3x - 2)$ and put the product under the first two terms of the dividend (under the $15x^3 + 5x^2$).

$$\begin{array}{r} 5x^2 \quad\quad\quad\quad\quad\quad \\ 3x-2\overline{)15x^3 + 53x^2 - 30x - 8} \\ 15x^3 - 10x^2 \quad\quad\quad\quad \end{array}$$

Subtract the polynomials. To subtract polynomials, change the sign of the subtrahend and add.

$$\begin{array}{r} 5x^2 + 21x + 4 \\ 3x-2\overline{)15x^3 + 53x^2 - 30x - 8} \\ \underline{15x^3 - 10x^2} \quad\quad\quad\quad\quad \\ 63x^2 - 30x \quad\quad \\ \underline{63x^2 - 42x} \quad\quad \\ 12x - 8 \\ \underline{12x - 8} \\ 0 \end{array}$$

Bring down the $-30x$.

Now divide $3x$ into $63x^2$.

Multiply $21x$ times $(3x - 2)$.

Subtract the two polynomials. Bring down the -8.

Divide $3x$ into $12x$.

Multiply 4 times $(3x - 2)$.

Subtract.

Once the power of the dividend is less than the power of the divisor, no more division can be done. The remaining term or terms are the remainder. The remainder must be written as a fraction and added to the quotient. The remainder in this problem is zero.

The polynomial $(15x^3 + 53x^2 - 30x - 8) \div (3x - 2) = 5x^2 + 21x + 4$. Since the remainder is zero, $(3x - 2)$ is a factor of $(15x^3 + 53x^2 - 30x - 8)$. That is,

$$(3x - 2)(5x^2 + 21x + 4) = (15x^3 + 53x^2 - 30x - 8).$$

Synthetic Division

Synthetic division provides a quick way to divide polynomials by a linear factor in the form of $x - r$. The following example could be done by synthetic division if we think of $x + 2$ as $x - (-2)$.

$$\begin{array}{r} x^2 + 3 \\ x+2\overline{\smash{)}x^3 + 2x^2 + 3x + 8} \\ \underline{x^3 + 2x^2} \\ 3x + 8 \\ \underline{3x + 10} \\ 2 \end{array}$$

To do this same problem by synthetic division, take the divisor $(x + 2)$ and change the sign of the number term (change 2 to –2). Write –2 along with the numerical coefficients of the dividend as listed below.

Divisor $\underline{-2|}$ 1   2   3   8   Coefficients of dividend

Draw a line under the entire problem and bring down the first coefficient.

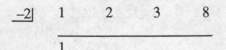

Multiply the coefficient 1 times the –2 and put that answer into the column under the positive 2.

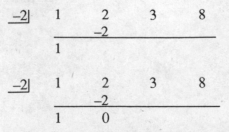

Multiply the 0 times –2 and write the value in the third column and add. Continue the process.

$$
\begin{array}{r|rrrr}
-2 & 1 & 2 & 3 & 8 \\
& & -2 & 0 & \\
\hline
& 1 & 0 & 3 &
\end{array}
$$

Multiply 3 times –2, put that in the fourth column and add.

$$
\begin{array}{r|rrrr}
-2 & 1 & 2 & 3 & 8 \\
& & -2 & 0 & -6 \\
\hline
& 1 & 0 & 3 & \underline{2}
\end{array}
$$

The 2 at the end of the third row is the remainder. The numbers 1 0 3 in the third row are the coefficients of the quotient, called the coefficients of the **depressed polynomial** or **depressed expression**. In standard form, a polynomial has one more term than its highest power. The quotient is a three-termed expression and a second degree polynomial in the form of $1x^2 + 0x + 3$ with a remainder of 2. The answer can be written as

$$ x^2 + 3 + \frac{2}{x+2}. $$

Some important characteristics of synthetic division are:
1. Synthetic division can only be used when dividing by a linear divisor in the form of $(x - r)$.
2. When dividing by $x - r$, we synthetically divide by r. If dividing by $x + r$, we rewrite the expression as $x - (-r)$ and synthetically divide by $-r$.
3. When using synthetic division, the polynomial must be in standard form. Any missing coefficients must be replaced with 0.
4. A polynomial always has one more coefficient than its highest power. If you are dividing a third degree polynomial, you must have four coefficients, a fourth degree polynomial must have five terms, and so forth.
5. The power of the quotient is one degree less than the power of the original polynomial.
6. The last number in the third row is the remainder. When dividing a polynomial by a linear factor, the remainder is always a constant.

EXAMPLE 6.2

Use synthetic division to divide the following polynomials:

a) $(5x^3 + 7x^2 - 2x - 8)$ by $(x - 2)$

b) $(4x^4 - 5x + 2x^3 - 7)$ by $(x + 3)$

SOLUTION 6.2

a) $(5x^3 + 7x^2 - 2x - 8)$ by $(x - 2)$

To synthetically divide $(5x^3 + 7x^2 - 2x - 8)$ by $(x - 2)$, write the coefficients of the dividend and divide by +2.

$$\underline{+2|} \quad \begin{array}{cccc} 5 & 7 & -2 & -8 \end{array}$$ Bring down the first term.

$$\underline{+2|} \quad \begin{array}{cccc} 5 & 7 & -2 & -8 \\ \hline 5 \end{array}$$ Multiply 5 times 2 and write the product under the 7. Add the 7 and 10.

$$\underline{+2|} \quad \begin{array}{cccc} 5 & 7 & -2 & -8 \\ & 10 & & \\ \hline 5 & 17 \end{array}$$ Continue the process.

$$\underline{+2|} \quad \begin{array}{cccc} 5 & 7 & -2 & -8 \\ & 10 & 34 & \\ \hline 5 & 17 & 32 \end{array}$$

$$\underline{+2|} \quad \begin{array}{cccc} 5 & 7 & -2 & -8 \\ & 10 & 34 & 64 \\ \hline 5 & 17 & 32 & \underline{|56} \end{array}$$

The quotient is $5x^2 + 17x + 32 + \dfrac{56}{x - 2}$.

b) $(4x^4 - 5x + 2x^3 - 7)$ by $(x + 3)$

$4x^4 + 2x^3 + 0x^2 - 5x - 7$ Put dividend into standard form.

$$\underline{-3|} \quad \begin{array}{ccccc} 4 & 2 & 0 & -5 & -7 \end{array}$$ Divide by synthetic division.

$$\underline{-3|} \quad \begin{array}{ccccc} 4 & 2 & 0 & -5 & -7 \\ & -12 & & & \\ \hline 4 & -10 \end{array}$$ Bring down the 4.

Multiply and add

$$\underline{-3|} \quad \begin{array}{ccccc} 4 & 2 & 0 & -5 & -7 \\ & -12 & 30 & -90 & 285 \\ \hline 4 & -10 & 30 & -95 & \underline{|278} \end{array}$$ Continue.

The answer is $4x^3 - 10x^2 + 30x - 95 + \dfrac{278}{x+3}$.

EXERCISE 6.1

Divide the following polynomials. Use synthetic division when possible.

1. $2x^3 - 33x + 20 + 5x^2$ by $2x - 5$
2. $14x^3 + 17x^2 + 9$ by $2x + 3$
3. $8x^3 - 5$ by $2x - 1$
4. $3x^3 - 2x + 7x^2 - 3$ by $x + 2$
5. $x^3 - 3x^2 + 3x - 5$ by $x - 1$
6. $x^4 + x^2 + 1$ by $x + 1$
7. $7x^6 - 23x^5 + 13x^4 + 54x^2 - 52x + 84$ by $x - 3$
8. $x^5 - 7x^4 - 2x - 5$ by $x - 2$
9. $x^5 - 7x^4 - 2x - 5$ by $x - 3$
10. $2x^7 - 9x^4 - 8x^3 + 4x - 1$ by $x - 2$

ANSWERS TO EXERCISE 6.1

1. $x^2 + 5x - 4$

2. $7x^2 - 2x + 3$

3. $4x^2 + 2x + 1 - \dfrac{4}{2x-1}$

4. $3x^2 + x - 4 + \dfrac{5}{x+2}$

5. $x^2 - 2x + 1 - \dfrac{4}{x-1}$

6. $x^3 - x^2 + 2x - 2 + \dfrac{3}{x+1}$

7. $7x^5 - 2x^4 + 7x^3 + 21x^2 + 117x + 299 + \dfrac{981}{x-3}$

8. $x^4 - 5x^3 - 10x^2 - 20x - 42 - \dfrac{89}{x-2}$

9. $x^4 + 3x^3 + 9x^2 + x + 3 + \dfrac{7}{x-3}$

10. $2x^6 + 4x^5 + 8x^4 + 7x^3 + 6x^2 + 12x + 28 + \dfrac{55}{x-2}$

SECTION 6.2 REMAINDER AND FACTOR THEOREMS

Division Algorithm and the Remainder Theorem

Division Algorithm:
Given a polynomial $P(x)$ of degree $n > 0$ and $x - r$, there is a unique polynomial $Q(x)$ of degree one less than $P(x)$ and a unique number R, such that
$$P(x) = (x - r) \, Q(x) + R.$$
$Q(x)$ is called the **quotient**, $(x - r)$ is the **divisor**, and R is the **remainder**.

The division algorithm guarantees every polynomial of degree one or greater can be divided by a linear factor in the form of $(x - r)$. When we divide a polynomial by $(x - r)$, we get a quotient $Q(x)$ and a remainder R. The polynomial equation becomes

$$\frac{P(x)}{(x - r)} = Q(x) + \frac{R}{(x - r)}.$$

If we multiply both sides of the equation by $(x - r)$ we get
$$P(x) = Q(x) \cdot (x - r) + R.$$

When dividing polynomials, the remainder must be one degree less than the divisor. When dividing by $(x - r)$, the remainder must be a constant.

If we let $x = r$, we get

$$P(r) = Q(r) \, (r - r) + R$$
$$P(r) = Q(r) \, (0) + R$$

$$P(r) = R$$

This is called the **remainder theorem**, which states that the value of the polynomial $P(x)$ when x is replaced by $r \, [P(r)]$ is the same as the remainder when the polynomial is divided by $(x - r)$.

Theorem 1: Remainder Theorem
If $P(x)$ is divided by $(x - r)$ until a constant remainder R is obtained, then
$$P(r) = R.$$

EXAMPLE 6.3

Evaluate the following polynomials for the given values of x by both substitution and the remainder theorem:

a) $P(x) = 3x^2 - 4x + 1$, find $P(2)$

b) $Q(x) = x^3 - 2x^2 + 4x - 5$, find $Q(3)$.

SOLUTION 6.3

a) To find the value of $P(x) = 3x^2 - 4x + 1$ when $x = 2$ substitute 2 into the polynomial for the variable x. Use parentheses when replacing a variable with a number.

$$P(2) = 3(2)^2 - 4(2) + 1$$
$$= 3(4) - 8 + 1$$
$$= 12 - 8 + 1$$
$$= 5$$
$$P(2) = 5$$

By the remainder theorem, $P(2)$ can also be found by synthetic division. Remember, we are trying to find the value when $x = 2$. This means that $x - 2 = 0$. Dividing by $x - 2$ means to synthetically divide by 2.

2⌋	3	−4	+1	Bring down the 3, multiply and add.

2⌋	3	−4	+1	Continue the process.
	3			

2⌋	3	−4	+1	Continue the process.
		+6	+4	
	3	+2	⌊+5	

The remainder is 5. By the remainder theorem $P(2) = 5$.

b) Given $Q(x) = x^3 - 2x^2 + 4x - 5$, find $Q(3)$ by replacing x with 3.

$$Q(3) = (3)^3 - 2(3)^2 + 4(3) - 5$$
$$= 27 - 2(9) + 12 - 5$$
$$= 27 - 18 + 12 - 5$$
$$= 16$$
$$Q(3) = 16$$

Find $Q(3)$ by synthetic division. Write the coefficients of the dividend and synthetically divide by 3.

$$3 \rfloor \quad 1 \quad\quad -2 \quad\quad +4 \quad\quad -5$$

Use the rules of synthetic division to find the remainder.

$$
\begin{array}{r|rrrr}
3 & 1 & -2 & +4 & -5 \\
  &   & 3 & 3 & 21 \\
\hline
  & 1 & 1 & 7 & \lfloor 16
\end{array}
$$

$Q(3) = 16$

We can use synthetic division only with linear divisors (first degree divisors) which have coefficients of one. That is, divisors in the form of $(x - r)$. We can, however, divide polynomials using synthetic division if we apply our basic laws of algebra in combination with the techniques of synthetic division. To use synthetic division on a linear divisor in the form of $ax - b$, we must think of the division as a rational expression in the form of

$$P(x) \div (ax - b) = \frac{P(x)}{(ax - b)}$$

Use the fundamental theorem of fractions and divide the numerator and the denominator by a. The linear divisor becomes $(x - \frac{a}{b})$. Now synthetically divide $P(x)$ by $\frac{b}{a}$. Once the solution is obtained, you must also divide the quotient by a.

EXAMPLE 6.4

Divide the following polynomials, using synthetic division, by factoring out the coefficient of the divisor.

a) Divide $P(x) = 3x^3 + 5x^2 - 16x - 12$ by $3x + 2$.

b) Divide $P(x) = 30x^3 - 37x^2 - 20x + 18$ by $(5x - 2)$.

SOLUTION 6.4

a) Divide $P(x) = 3x^3 + 5x^2 - 16x - 12$ by $3x + 2$.
    To use synthetic division on this problem, first divide $3x + 2$ by 3.

    The result is $\dfrac{3x + 2}{3} = x + \dfrac{2}{3}$. Now synthetically divide by $x = -\dfrac{2}{3}$.

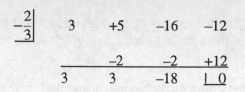

$$\begin{array}{r|rrrr} -\dfrac{2}{3} & 3 & +5 & -16 & -12 \\ & & -2 & -2 & +12 \\ \hline & 3 & 3 & -18 & \underline{}0 \end{array}$$

The quotient $3x^2 + 3x - 18$ is not the correct answer. Since we divided the divisor by 3, we must also divide the quotient by 3. The remainder is unaffected by the division by 3.

$$Q(x) = \frac{3x^2 + 3x - 18}{3} = x^2 + x - 6$$

b) Divide $P(x) = 30x^3 - 37x^2 - 20x + 18$ by $(5x - 2)$.

Divide $(5x - 2)$ by 5. We get $(x - \dfrac{5}{2})$. Synthetically divided by $\dfrac{2}{5}$.

$$\begin{array}{r|rrrr} \dfrac{2}{5} & 30 & -37 & -20 & +19 \\ & & 12 & -10 & -12 \\ \hline & 30 & -25 & -30 & \underline{}7 \end{array}$$

The actual answer becomes $P(x) = (x - \dfrac{2}{5})(30x^2 - 25x - 30) + 7$.

If we multiply the divisor by 5 and divide the quotient by 5, we get

$$P(x) = (5x - 2)(6x^2 - 5x - 6) + 7.$$

Notice how the divisor is multiplied by 5 and the quotient is divided by 5. Multiplying by 5 and dividing by 5 is the same as multiplying the polynomial by 1. The remainder is not affected by this multiplication and division.

Factor Theorem

Theorem 2: Factor Theorem

Let $P(x)$ be a polynomial; if r is a zero (root) of $P(x)$, then $(x - r)$ is a factor.

Also, if $x - r$ is a factor of $P(x)$, then r is a zero (root) of the polynomial.

When $(x - r)$ is a factor of the polynomial $P(x)$, then $P(x)$ can be written in the form of

$$P(x) = (x - r) \cdot Q(x)$$

where $Q(x)$ is the quotient upon dividing $P(x)$ by $(x - r)$. We can now use the factor theorem and synthetic division to factor polynomials.

EXAMPLE 6.5

Factor the following polynomials and find their zeros (roots):

a) $x^3 - x^2 - x + 1$

b) $2x^3 - 5x^2 - 18x + 45$

SOLUTION 6.5

a) $x^3 - x^2 - x + 1$ Group the polynomial.
    $\underline{x^3 - x^2} \ \underline{- x + 1}$ Factor each pair.

   $x^2(x - 1) - 1(x - 1)$ Factor out the common
                                                                                          binomial factor.

   $(x - 1)(x^2 - 1)$ Factor the difference of
                                                                                          squares.

   $(x - 1)(x + 1)(x - 1)$

The zeros of the polynomial are $x = -1$ and $x = 1$. $x = 1$ is called a **multiple zero (multiple root)**. The zero $x = 1$ is a multiple root since it occurs as a root 2 times.

b) $2x^3 - 5x^2 - 18x + 45$

This polynomial does not factor using the techniques learned in Chapter 1. To factor this polynomial, we must try to find a zero of the polynomial. We begin by using synthetic division with integer factors. Start with $x = 1$.

$$
\begin{array}{r|rrrr}
1\rfloor & 2 & -5 & -18 & +45 \\
  &   & 2 & -3 & -21 \\
\hline
  & 2 & -3 & -21 & \lfloor 24 \\
\end{array}
$$

$x = 1$ is not a zero of the polynomial. Divide by $x = 2$.

$$
\begin{array}{r|rrrr}
2\rfloor & 2 & -5 & -18 & +45 \\
  &   & 4 & -2 & -40 \\
\hline
  & 2 & -1 & -20 & \lfloor 5 \\
\end{array}
$$

$x = 2$ is also not a zero of the polynomial. Divide by $x = 3$.

$$
\begin{array}{r|rrrr}
3\rfloor & 2 & -5 & -18 & +45 \\
  &   & 6 & 3 & -45 \\
\hline
  & 2 & 1 & -15 & \lfloor 0 \\
\end{array}
$$

$x = 3$ is a zero of the polynomial. By the factor theorem, $(x - 3)$ is a factor. The quotient is $Q(x) = 2x^2 + x - 15$. The polynomial factors into $(x - 3)(2x^2 + x - 15)$. $Q(x)$ is a trinomial. The trinomial can now be factored into

$$(x - 3)(2x - 5)(x + 3).$$

The zeros are $x = -3, +3, \frac{5}{2}$.

The above polynomial was designed to have a zero at $x = 3$. This allowed us to find the depressed trinomial and factor it. With higher degree polynomials, we find enough zeros to get the depressed polynomial into a quadratic expression. We can then factor it as a trinomial or find the zeros by the quadratic formula.

EXERCISE 6.2

Evaluate the following polynomials by use of synthetic division.

1. Find $P(2)$ when $P(x) = 3x^2 + 5x - 7$.
2. Find $P(3)$ when $P(x) = 4x^2 - 8x + 8$.
3. Find $P(-2)$ when $P(x) = 4x^3 - 2x^2 + 5x - 9$.
4. Find $P(4)$ when $P(x) = 3x^3 + 5x^2 - 7x + 4$.
5. Find $P(-3)$ when $P(x) = 7x^4 + 3x^3 - 2x^2 + 5x - 12$.
6. Divide $P(x) = 9x^4 - 15x^3 + 13x^2 + 3x + 1$ by $(3x - 1)$ synthetically and write $P(x)$ as a product of $D(x) \cdot Q(x) + R$.
7. Divide $P(x) = x^3 - 8x - 3$ by $(x - 3)$ synthetically and write $P(x)$ as a product of $D(x) \cdot Q(x) + R$.
8. Divide $P(x) = x^4 + x^3 + 4$ by $(x + 2)$ synthetically and write $P(x)$ as a product of $D(x) \cdot Q(x) + R$.

Factor the following higher degree polynomials given the indicated zero:

9. $x^3 - 2x^2 - x + 2$; $x = -1$
10. $2x^3 - 15x^2 + 28x - 15$; $x = 5$
11. $8x^3 + 6x^2 - 29x - 30$; $x = 2$
12. $24x^3 - 14x^2 - 63x + 45$; $x = \frac{3}{2}$

ANSWERS TO EXERCISE 6.2

1. 15   2. 20
3. -59   4. 288
5. 441
6. $(3x - 1)(3x^3 - 4x^2 + 3x + 2) + 3$
7. $(x - 3)(x^2 - 3x + 1)$
8. $(x + 2)(x^3 - x^2 + 2x - 4) + 12$
9. $(x + 1)(x - 1)(x - 2)$
10. $(x - 5)(2x - 3)(x - 1)$
11. $(4x + 5)(2x + 3)(x - 2)$
12. $(4x + 3)(2x - 3)(3x - 5)$

SECTION 6.3 FUNDAMENTAL THEOREM OF ALGEBRA

> **Theorem 3: Fundamental Theorem of Algebra**
> Every polynomial $P(x)$ of degree > 0 has at least one real or imaginary zero.

Since $P(x)$ has at least one real or imaginary zero r_1, $P(x)$ can be factored into $(x - r_1) \cdot Q_1(x)$. But if $Q_1(x)$ has degree $n > 0$, then $Q_1(x)$ has at least one zero r_2 and can be factored into
$(x - r_2) \cdot Q_2(x)$. This continues until we get the **n zeros theorem**.

> **Theorem 4: *n* Zero Theorem**
> Every polynomial $P(x)$ of degree $n > 0$ can be expressed as the product of n linear factors.
> A polynomial of degree n, has exactly n zeros not necessarily distinct.

EXAMPLE 6.6

Write the following polynomial as a product of linear factors and list all of the zeros:

a) $3x^3 + 5x^2 - 58x - 40$ if $x = -5$ is a zero.

b) $x^4 - 3x^3 - 5x^2 - 3x + 4$ if $x = -1$ occurs as a zero twice.

SOLUTION 6.6

a) $3x^3 + 5x^2 - 58x - 40$ if $x = -5$ is a zero.
   -5 is a zero of the polynomial, so $(x + 5)$ is a linear factor.
   Synthetically divide by -5.

$$
\begin{array}{r|rrrr}
-5 & 3 & +5 & -58 & -40 \\
   &   & -15 & +50 & +40 \\
\hline
   & 3 & -10 & -8 & \underline{\ 0} \\
\end{array}
$$

The polynomial factors into $(x + 5)\,(3x^2 - 10x - 8)$. Now factor the trinomial.

$$(x + 5)\,(3x + 2)\,(x - 4)$$

The zeros of the polynomial are $x = -5,\ -\dfrac{2}{3},\ 4$. The polynomial is a third degree polynomial and has 3 factors.

b) $x^4 - 3x^3 - 5x^2 - 3x + 4$ if $x = -1$ occurs as a zero twice.
Synthetically divide by -1.

$-1\rfloor$	1	-3	-5	$+3$	$+4$
		-1	$+4$	$+1$	-4
	1	-4	-1	$+4$	$\lfloor 0$

Divide -1 into the depressed polynomial again.

$-1\rfloor$	1	-4	-1	$+4$
		-1	$+5$	-4
	1	-5	$+4$	$\lfloor 0$

The polynomial factors into $(x + 1) (x + 1) (x^2 - 5x + 4)$. Factor the trinomial.

$$(x + 1)^2 (x - 4) (x - 1)$$

The zeros of the polynomial are $x = -1, -1, 1, 4$. $x = -1$ is a multiple zero occuring twice.

All of the polynomials we have had thus far have had real coefficients and real zeros. Polynomials can have imaginary coefficients or imaginary zeros.

EXAMPLE 6.7

Find all of the zeros of the following polynomial and factor them:

a) $2x^3 + (-3 - 4i) x^2 + (-5 + 6i) x + 10i$ if $x = 2i$ is a zero.

b) $x^4 - 3x^3 + 9x^2 - 8x + 20$ if $x = 2i$ and $-2i$ are two of the zeros.

SOLUTION 6.7

a) $2x^3 + (-3 - 4i) x^2 + (-5 + 6i) x + 10i$ if $x = 2i$ is a zero.
Synthetically divide by $2i$.

$2i\rfloor$	2	$(-3 - 4i)$	$(-5 + 6i)$	$+10i$
		$4i$	$-6i$	$-10i$
	2	-3	-5	$\lfloor 0$

The polynomial factors into $(x - 2i) (2x^2 - 3x - 5)$. Factor the trinomial.

$$(x - 2i) (2x - 5) (x + 1)$$

The zeros are $x = 2i, \dfrac{5}{2}$, and -1.

b) $x^4 - 3x^3 + 9x^2 - 8x + 20$ if $x = 2i$ and $-2i$ are two of the zeros.
Synthetically divide by $2i$.

$2i\rfloor$	1	-3	$+9$	-8	$+20$
		$+2i$	$-4 - 4i$	$8 + 10i$	-20
	1	$-2 + 2i$	$+5 - 4i$	$+10i$	$\lfloor 0$

Divide synthetically $-2i$ into the depressed polynomial.

$$\underline{-2i} \quad \begin{array}{cccc} 1 & -2+2i & +5-4i & +10i \\ & -2i & +4i & -10i \\ \hline 1 & -2 & +5 & \underline{|\ 0} \end{array}$$

The expression factors into $(x-2i)\,(x+2i)\,(x^2-2x+5)$. The trinomial factor does not factor using the techniques of factoring. The trinomial is, however, quadratic. Find the zeros of the trinomial using the quadratic formula and factor using the factor theorem. Set the expression equal to zero and solve.

$x^2-2x+5 = 0$ Substitute a, b and c into the quadratic formula.

$a=1 \quad b=-2 \quad c=5$

The quadratic formula is $x = \dfrac{-b \pm \sqrt{b^2-4ac}}{2a}$.

$$x = \frac{-(-2) \pm \sqrt{(-2)^2 - 4\,(1)\,(5)}}{2\,(1)}$$

$$x = \frac{2 \pm \sqrt{4-20}}{2} = \frac{2 \pm \sqrt{-16}}{2} = \frac{2 \pm 4i}{2} = 1 \pm 2i$$

The zeros are $x = 2i, -2i, 1+2i$ and $1-2i$. The expression factors into $(x-2i)\,(x+2i)\,(x-1-2i)\,(x-1+2i)$.

The imaginary zeros of the expression x^2-2x+5 were found by use of the quadratic formula. The zeros are $1+2i$ and $1-2i$. These two zeros are conjugate pairs.

Theorem 5: Imaginary Zeros

Given a polynomial $P(x)$ with real coefficients, if $P(a+bi) = 0$, then $P(a-bi) = 0 \;\; (b \neq 0)$.

or

Given polynomial $P(x)$ with real coefficient, imaginary zeros, if they exist, occur in conjugate pairs.

This means that a polynomial with real coefficients must have an even number of imaginary zeros.

Theorem 6: Polynomials of Odd Degree

A polynomial of odd degree with real coefficients must have at least one real zero.

EXAMPLE 6.8

Factor the following polynomials and find all of the zeros:

a) $x^3 - 5x^2 + 12x - 8$ if $x = 2 + 2i$ is a zero.

b) $2x^4 - 15x^3 + 81x^2 - 72x - 170$ if $x = 3 + 5i$ is one of the zeros.

SOLUTION 6.8

a) $x^3 - 5x^2 + 12x - 8$ if $x = 2 + 2i$ is a zero.
Synthetically divide by $2 + 2i$.

$2 + 2i\rfloor$	1	-5	$+12$	-8
		$2 + 2i$	$-10 - 2i$	8
	1	$-3 + 2i$	$2 - 2i$	$\lfloor 0$

The polynomial has real coefficients. Imaginary roots occur in conjugate pairs. $2 - 2i$ is also a root. Synthetically divide by $2 - 2i$ into the depressed polynomial.

$2 - 2i\rfloor$	1	$-3 + 2i$	$+2 - 2i$
		$2 - 2i$	$-2 + 2i$
	1	-1	$\lfloor 0$

The polynomial factors into $(x - 2 - 2i)(x - 2 + 2i)(x + 1)$. The zeros are $x = 2 + 2i,\ 2 - 2i$, and 1.

b) $2x^4 - 15x^3 + 81x^2 - 72x - 170$ if $x = 3 + 5i$ is one of the zeros.
Synthetically divide by $3 + 5i$.

$3 + 5i\rfloor$	2	-15	$+81$	-72	-170
		$6 + 10i$	$-77 - 15i$	$87 - 25i$	$+170$
	2	$-9 + 10i$	$+4 - 15i$	$15 - 25i$	$\lfloor 0$

The polynomial has real coefficients. Since $3 + 5i$ is a root, then $3 - 5i$ is also a root. Synthetically divide $3 - 5i$ into the depressed polynomial.

$3 - 5i\rfloor$	2	$-9 + 10i$	$+4 - 15i$	$+15 - 25i$
		$6 - 10i$	$-9 + 15i$	$-15 + 25i$
	2	-3	-5	$\lfloor 0$

The depressed polynomial is $2x^2 - 3x - 5$. The polynomial factors into

$$(x - 3 - 5i)(x - 3 + 5i)(2x^2 - 3x - 5).$$

Factor the trinomial.

$$(x - 3 - 5i)(x - 3 + 5i)(2x - 5)(x + 1)$$

The roots are $x = 3 + 5i,\ 3 - 5i,\ \dfrac{5}{2}$, and -1.

EXERCISE 6.3

Find all of the roots of the following polynomials and factor:

1. $P(x) = 2x^3 - 11x^2 + 28x - 24$ if $x = 2 - 2i$ is one of the roots.

2. $P(x) = 3x^3 - x^2 + 4x + 10$ if $x = 1 + i$ is one of the roots.

3. $P(x) = 5x^4 - 10x^3 + 36x^2 - 58x + 51$ if $x = 4 - i$ is one of the roots.

4. $P(x) = x^4 - 2x^3 - 7x^2 + 18x - 18$ if $x = 1 - i$ is one of the roots.

5. $P(x) = x^4 + 3x^3 + 7x^2 + 6x + 4$ if $x = -1 - i\sqrt{3}$ is one of the roots

ANSWERS TO EXERCISE 6.3

1. $\frac{3}{2}, 2 + 2i, 2 - 2i$; Factors into $(2x - 3)(x - 2 - 2i)(x - 2 + 2i)$

2. $-\frac{5}{2}, 1 + i, 1 - i$; Factors into $(2x + 5)(x - 1 - i)(x - 1 + i)$

3. $4 - i, 4 + i, 1 + i\sqrt{2}, 1 - i\sqrt{2}$;
    Factors into $(x - 4 + i)(x - 4 - i)(x - 1 - i\sqrt{2})(x - 1 + i\sqrt{2})$

4. $3, -3, 1 - i, 1 + i$;
    Factors into $(x - 3)(x + 3)(x - 1 - i)(x - 1 + i)$

5. $-1 - i\sqrt{3}, -1 + i\sqrt{3}, \dfrac{-1 - i\sqrt{3}}{2}, \dfrac{-1 + i\sqrt{3}}{2}$; Factors into

    $(x + 1 + i\sqrt{3})(x + 1 - i\sqrt{3})(-4 + i)(x + \dfrac{1 + i\sqrt{3}}{2})(x + \dfrac{1 - i\sqrt{3}}{2})$

SECTION 6.4 FINDING THE ROOTS OF POLYNOMIALS

Descartes Rule of Signs

We know that every polynomial of degree $n > 0$ has n roots. It would be helpful to know the kinds of roots the polynomial has, and if the roots were real or imaginary. If the roots are real, it would help to know if they are positive or negative. **Descartes Rule of Signs** helps to determine the different kinds of roots.

Descartes Rule of Signs:

The number of positive (real) zeros of $P(x)$ is either equal to the number of variations in the signs of $P(x)$ or is less than that number by a positive even integer.

The number of negative (real) zeros of $P(x)$ is either equal to the number of variations in the signs of $P(-x)$ or less than that number by a positive even integer.

Imaginary zeros are neither positive nor negative. When talking about positive and negative zeros of a polynomial, it will be understood that these are for real zeros. The polynomial

$$P(x) = 4x^3 - 16x^2 + 9x + 9$$

has coefficients with the following signs: $+ - + +$

A variation in sign is when the signs of the coefficients change from positive to negative or negative to positive. In the above example, there are two variations in signs.

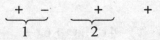

When there are two variations in signs, Descartes Rule of Signs states that there are two positive zeros or that number decreased by an even number, meaning that there are 2 or 0 positive zeros (2 or 2 decreased by 2 = 0 positive zeros).

To determine the number of negative zeros, find $P(-x)$. To find $P(-x)$ replace x with $-x$ in the polynomial.

If $P(x) = 4x^3 - 16x^2 + 9x + 9$ then
$$P(-x) = 4(-x)^3 - 16(-x)^2 + 9(-x) + 9.$$

$P(-x) = -4x^3 - 16x^2 - 9x + 9$. The signs of $P(-x)$ are

$$- \quad - \quad \underbrace{- \quad +}_{1}$$

In $P(-x)$ there is only one variation in sign. This means that there is one negative zero. Since 1 cannot be decreased by an even number, there is exactly one negative root. Putting these two parts together, the polynomial $P(x) = 4x^3 - 16x^2 + 9x + 9$ has

2 or 0 positive zeros and
1 negative zero.

Upper and Lower Bounds

Theorem 7:

Let $P(x)$ be an nth-degree polynomial with real coefficients. Divide $P(x)$ by $x - r$ using synthetic division:

1. r is an **upper bound** if $r > 0$ (r is ppsitive) and all numbers in the third row including the remainder have the same sign (all positive or all negative; zeros can be thought of as either positive or negative).

2. r is a **lower bound** if $r < 0$ (r is negative) and the numbers in the third row alternate signs (again zeros can be thought of as either positive or negative).

This theorem is called the upper and lower bound theorem. The upper and lower bounds indicate when to stop looking for zeros because numbers are too large or too small.

EXAMPLE 6.9

Find the upper positive and lower negative integer bounds for the following polynomials:

a) $5x^3 + 12x^2 - 7x - 5$

b) $x^4 - 4x^3 + x^2 + 6x + 2$

SOLUTION 6.9

a) $5x^3 + 12x^2 - 7x - 5$

To find the upper positive integer bound for the given polynomial, synthetically divide by positive integers 1, 2, 3, ...

$$
\begin{array}{r|rrrr}
\underline{1} & 5 & +12 & -7 & -5 \\
  &   & +5 & +17 & +10 \\
\hline
  & 5 & +17 & +10 & \underline{\ 5} \\
\end{array}
$$

The integer 1 is an upper bound. The third row of the synthetic division problem contains numbers that all have the same sign. Find the lower negative bounds.

$$
\begin{array}{r|rrrr}
\underline{-1} & 5 & +12 & -7 & -5 \\
  &   & -5 &   &   \\
\hline
  & 5 & +10 &   &   \\
\end{array}
$$

At this point we can stop since the first two terms in the bottom row do not alternate. Divide by –2.

$$
\begin{array}{r|rrrr}
\underline{-2} & 5 & +12 & -7 & -5 \\
  &   & -10 &   &   \\
\hline
  & 5 & +2 &   &   \\
\end{array}
$$

Divide by –3.   Stop!

$$\begin{array}{r|rrrr} -3| & 5 & +12 & -7 & -5 \\ & & -15 & +9 & -6 \\ \hline & 5 & -3 & +2 & \underline{|-11} \end{array}$$

The integer -3 is a lower integer bound since the third row of the synthetic division problem alternates positive and negative signs. All real zeros of $5x^3 + 12x^2 - 7x - 5$ fall between $-3 < x < 1$.

b) $x^4 - 4x^3 + x^2 + 6x + 2$

Begin synthetically dividing by positive integers 1, 2, 3, ...

$$\begin{array}{r|rrrrr} 1| & 1 & -4 & +1 & +6 & +2 \\ & & +1 & +21 & & \\ \hline & 1 & -3 & & & \end{array}$$

Stop! The bottom row does not contain numbers with all the same signs. Divide by 2.

$$\begin{array}{r|rrrrr} 2| & 1 & -4 & +1 & +6 & +2 \\ & & +2 & +21 & & \\ \hline & 1 & -2 & & & \end{array}$$

Notice that the bottom row does not have the same signs. Move up to a larger number. Try $x = 4$.

Divide by 4.

$$\begin{array}{r|rrrrr} 4| & 1 & -4 & +1 & +6 & +2 \\ & & +4 & +0 & +4 & +40 \\ \hline & 1 & 0 & +1 & +10 & \underline{|+42} \end{array}$$

The integer is an upper bound. Find the lower bounds. Divide by -1.

$$\begin{array}{r|rrrrr} -1| & 1 & -4 & +1 & +6 & +2 \\ & & -1 & +5 & -6 & 0 \\ \hline & 1 & -5 & +6 & 0 & \underline{|2} \end{array}$$

If we think of the zero as being negative, the signs of the bottom row alternate. -1 is a lower negative integer bound. All real zeros of $x^4 - 4x^3 + x^2 + 6x + 2$ fall between $-1 < x < 4$.

The next theorem is helpful in finding roots.

Theorem 8: If $P(x)$ is a polynomial with real coefficients and $P(a) > 0$ and $P(b) < 0$, then there is at least one real zero between a and b. Likewise, if $P(a) < 0$ and $P(b) > 0$, then there is at least one real zero between a and b.

EXAMPLE 6.10

Prove that there is at least one real root for the following polynomials between the following numbers:

a) $P(x) = x^3 - x^2 - 5x + 5$ has a root between $x = -3$ and -2.

b) $P(x) = x^4 - 2x^3 - 5x^2 + 6x + 5$ has a root between $x = 1$ and 2.

SOLUTION 6.10

a) Prove $P(x) = x^3 - x^2 - 5x + 5$ has a root between $x = -3$ and -2.
    Synthetically divide by -3.

$$
\begin{array}{r|rrrr}
-3 & 1 & -1 & -5 & +5 \\
   &   & -3 & +12 & -21 \\
\hline
   & 1 & -4 & +7 & \underline{|-16} \\
\end{array}
$$

Divide by -2.

$$
\begin{array}{r|rrrr}
-2 & 1 & -1 & -5 & +5 \\
   &   & -2 & +6 & -2 \\
\hline
   & 1 & -3 & +1 & \underline{|+3} \\
\end{array}
$$

Since $P(-3) < 0$ and $P(-2) > 0$, there is at least one zero between -3 and -2.

b) Prove $P(x) = x^4 - 2x^3 - 5x^2 + 6x + 5$ has a root between $x = 1$ and 2.
    Synthetically divide by 1.

$$
\begin{array}{r|rrrrr}
1 & 1 & -2 & -5 & +6 & +5 \\
  &   & +1 & -1 & -6 & 0 \\
\hline
  & 1 & -1 & -6 & 0 & \underline{|+5} \\
\end{array}
$$

Divide by 2.

$$
\begin{array}{r|rrrrr}
2 & 1 & -2 & -5 & +6 & +5 \\
  &   & +2 & 0 & -10 & -8 \\
\hline
  & 1 & 0 & -5 & -4 & \underline{|-3} \\
\end{array}
$$

By the theorem, since $P(1) > 0$ and $P(2) < 0$, there is at least one zero between 1 and 2.

SECTION 6.5 RATIONAL ROOT THEOREM

We now have a way to determine the number of possible positive and negative real zeros and a way to determine an interval for the real zeros using the upper and lower bound theorem. In this section, we will find a way to determine the possible rational zeros. Rational zeros are roots which are integers or fractions. They are zeros in the form of $\frac{b}{c}$ where b and c are integers, $c \neq 0$. To find rational zeros, we use the following theorem:

Theorem 9:

Let $P(x) = a_n x^n + a_{n-1} x^{n-1} + a_{n-2} x^{n-2} + \ldots + a_1 x^1 + a_0$ be a

polynomial with integer coefficients. If $P(\frac{b}{c}) = 0$ and $\frac{b}{c}$ is

irreducible, then b is a factor of a_0 and c is a factor of a_n.

This theorem states that any fractional root must be such that the numerator of the fraction is a divisor (factor) of the last term of the polynomial (the number term) and the denominator of the zero must be a divisor (factor) of the coefficient of the highest power term (first term of the polynomial).

EXAMPLE 6.11

List all of the possible rational zeros of the following polynomials:

a) $4x^3 - 3x^2 - 4x + 2$

b) $20x^3 - 9x^2 - 5x + 24$

SOLUTION 6.11

a) $4x^3 - 3x^2 - 4x + 2$

The divisors (factors) of 2 are ± 1 and ± 2. The divisors (factors) of 4 are ± 1, ± 2, and ± 4. The possible rational zeros become any fraction with a numerator of ± 1, ± 2 and a denominator of ± 1, ± 2, and ± 4.

The possible rational zeros are $\frac{\pm 1}{1}$, $\frac{\pm 2}{1}$, $\frac{\pm 1}{2}$, $\frac{\pm 2}{2}$, $\frac{\pm 1}{4}$, and $\frac{\pm 2}{4}$.

Listing all of the possible zeros becomes easy from here. The possible zeros become

$$\frac{1}{1}, \frac{-1}{1}, \frac{1}{2}, \frac{-1}{2}, \frac{1}{4}, \frac{-1}{4}, \frac{2}{1}, \frac{-2}{1}, \frac{2}{2}, \frac{-2}{2}, \frac{2}{4}, \text{ and } \frac{-2}{4}.$$

When reduced, the list of possible rational zeros is

$$1, -1, \frac{1}{2}, \frac{-1}{2}, \frac{1}{4}, \frac{-1}{4}, 2 \text{ and } -2$$

Because this list can become extremely large, short cut the list of possible rational zeros by writing the list like this
$$\frac{\pm 1, \pm 2}{1, 2, 4}.$$

From this notation, you can see each possible rational zero as you need them without actually listing each number.

b) $20x^3 - 9x^2 - 5x + 24$

The possible rational zeros are $\dfrac{\pm 1, \pm 2, \pm 3, \pm 4, \pm 6, \pm 8, \pm 12, \pm 24}{1, 2, 4, 5, 10, 20}$.

The list of all of the possible rational zeros is extensive. To actually find the zeros of a polynomial, we use Descartes Rule of Signs, the Upper and Lower Bound Theorem along with the Rational Root Theorem.

Using the theorems for Section 6.4 together with the rational root theorem, we can now begin to find rational roots (zeros) of higher degree polynomials. Here is a list of helpful rules for finding the roots of a polynomial.

Solving Higher Degree Polynomials:

1. Use Descartes Rule of Signs to determine how many positive and negative real roots are possible.
2. List the possible rational roots.
3. Begin finding integer values of $P(x)$ using synthetic division. Find $P(0)$ by substitution. Notice where $P(x)$ changes signs. Look for upper and lower bounds.
4. When one root is found, use steps 1 through 3 with the depressed expression, until the depressed expression is a quadratic expression. Set the quadratic expression equal to zero and solve by factoring or formula.

EXAMPLE 6.12

Find all zeros of the following polynomials using the rules for solving higher degree polynomials:

a) $P(x) = x^3 - x^2 - 4x + 4$

b) $P(x) = x^4 - x^3 - 13x^2 + x + 12$

SOLUTION 6.12

a) $P(x) = x^3 - x^2 - 4x + 4$

Determine the possible number of positive and negative zeros

$$P(x) = \underbrace{+ \;\; -}_{1} \; \underbrace{- \;\; +}_{2} \qquad\qquad P(-x) = \; - \; \underbrace{- \;\; +}_{1} \; +$$

There are 2 or 0 positive roots and 1 negative.

The possible rational zeros are $\dfrac{\pm 1, \pm 2, \pm 4}{1}$. Since the leading coefficient is 1, the possible rational roots are integers $\pm 1, \pm 2, \pm 4$.

Find values of $P(x)$ for the possible rational roots. Use synthetic division except when $x = 0$.

$$P(0) = 4$$

Since we are guaranteed one real negative real root, begin by using $-1, -2,$ and -4. We do not need to try -3, since -3 is not a possible rational zero.

$-1 \rfloor$	1	-1	-4	$+4$	
		-1	$+2$	$+2$	
	1	-2	-2	$\lfloor +6$	Divide by -1.

$P(-1) = 6.$

$$\underline{-2|} \quad \begin{array}{ccccc} 1 & -1 & -4 & +4 \\ & -2 & +6 & -4 \\ \hline 1 & -3 & +2 & \underline{|\,0} \end{array}$$ Divide by –2.

$P(-2) = 0.$

$x = -2$ is a zero of the polynomial. The depressed expression is $x^2 - 3x + 2$. Set it equal to zero and solve.

$x^2 - 3x + 2 = 0$ Factor.

$(x - 2)\,(x - 1) = 0$

$x = 2$ and 1

The zeros of the polynomial are $x = -2$, 1, and 2. The object of solving a higher degree polynomial is to find enough roots to get the depressed expression into quadratic form so that it can be factored or solved by the quadratic formula.

b) $P(x) = x^4 - x^3 - 13x^2 + x + 12$

Determine the possible number of positive and negative zeros.

$$P(x) = \quad \underset{1}{\underbrace{+ \quad -}} \quad \underset{2}{\underbrace{- \quad +}} \quad + \qquad P(-x) = \quad + \quad \underset{1}{\underbrace{+ \quad -}} \quad \underset{2}{\underbrace{- \quad +}}$$

The possible rational zeros are $\dfrac{\pm 1, \pm 2, \pm 3, \pm 4, \pm 6, \pm 12}{1}$. The leading coefficient is 1. The only possible real zeros must be integers. Find values of $P(x)$ for the possible rational roots.

$$P(0) = 12$$

We are not guaranteed of any real root. We can try either the positive or negative integers, but remember the upper and lower bounds. Begin by using 1, 2, 3, 4, 6, and 12.

$$\underline{1|} \quad \begin{array}{ccccc} 1 & -1 & -13 & +1 & +12 \\ & +1 & 0 & -13 & -12 \\ \hline 1 & 0 & -13 & -12 & \underline{|\,0} \end{array}$$

$P(1) = 0$. $x = 1$ is a zero of the polynomial. Descartes Rule of Signs indicated that there was 2 or 0 positive roots. Since we found one positive root, there must be another positive zero. Before trying 2, 3, 4, . . . always try the same number again. It is possible that $x = 1$ is a multiple zero. Divide 1 into the depressed expression.

$$\underline{1|} \quad \begin{array}{cccc} 1 & 0 & -13 & -12 \\ & +2 & +1 & -12 \\ \hline 1 & +1 & -12 & \underline{|-24} \end{array}$$

1 is not a multiple zero. Divide by 2.

$$\underline{2|} \quad \begin{array}{cccc} 1 & 0 & -13 & -12 \\ & +2 & +4 & -18 \\ \hline 1 & +2 & -9 & \underline{|-30} \end{array}$$

$P(2) = -30$. 2 is not a root of the polynomial. As you divide by possible rational roots, look for upper bounds. 2 is not an upper bound. Divide by 3.

$$\begin{array}{r|rrrr} 3 & 1 & 0 & -13 & -12 \\ & & +3 & +9 & -12 \\ \hline & 1 & +3 & -4 & \underline{|-24} \end{array}$$

$P(3) = -24$. 3 is not an upper bound. Divide by 4.

$$\begin{array}{r|rrrr} 4 & 1 & 0 & -13 & -12 \\ & & +4 & +16 & +12 \\ \hline & 1 & +4 & +3 & \underline{|\ 0} \end{array}$$

$P(4) = 0$. $x = 4$ is a zero of the polynomial $P(x)$. The depressed expression is a quadratic. Set the depressed expression to zero and solve.

$x^2 + 4x + 3 = 0$ Factor.

$(x + 3)(x + 1) = 0$ Set each factor equal to zero and solve.

$x = -3$ and -1

The zeros of the polynomial are $x = -3, -1, 1,$ and 4.

EXERCISE 6.4

List the possible rational zeros for each of the following:

1. $P(x) = 2x^3 - 5x^2 + 3x + 6$

2. $P(x) = 5x^3 - 3x^2 + 2x + 1$

3. $P(x) = 6x^3 + 5x^2 - 12x + 12$

4. $P(x) = 12x^4 + x^3 + 7x^2 - 3x + 16$

5. $P(x) = 36x^3 - 6x^2 + 5x + 24$

Find all of the zeros for the following polynomials.

6. $P(x) = x^3 - 6x^2 + 11x - 6$

7. $P(x) = 2x^3 - 5x^2 - x + 6$

8. $P(x) = x^4 - 3x^3 + 5x^2 + 3x - 2$

9. $P(x) = x^4 - 3x^3 + 3x^2 - 3x + 2$

10. $P(x) = 8x^5 - 12x^4 + 14x^3 - 13x^2 + 6x - 1$

ANSWERS TO EXERCISE 6.4

1. $\dfrac{\pm 1, \pm 2, \pm 3, \pm 6}{1, 2}$

2. $\dfrac{\pm 1}{1, 5}$

3. $\dfrac{\pm 1, \pm 2, \pm 3, \pm 4, \pm 6, \pm 12}{1, 2, 3, 6}$

4. $\dfrac{\pm 1, \pm 2, \pm 4, \pm 8, \pm 16}{1, 2, 3, 6, 12}$

5. $\dfrac{\pm 1, \pm 2, \pm 3, \pm 4, \pm 6, \pm 8, \pm 12, \pm 24}{1, 2, 3, 4, 6, 9, 12, 18, 36}$

6. $1, 2, 3$

7. $-1, \dfrac{3}{2}, 2$ 8. $2\,(2), 1 + i, 1 - i$

9. $1, 2, i, -i$ 10. $\dfrac{1}{2}\,(3), i, -i$

SECTION 6.6 GRAPHING POLYNOMIALS

We have already learned how to graph polynomials which are linear and quadratic. In this section, we will learn how to graph higher degree polynomials. A polynomial function with real coefficients is a continuous curve. A continuous graph is a graph that has no holes, no jumps, and no gaps in the graph of the function. To graph a polynomial function, we can plot points using synthetic division and the remainder theorem. We start by finding integer values for $P(x)$ and look for the roots of the polynomial (x-intercepts). We also need to graph the y-intercept. It is sometimes useful to plot fractional values for x.

EXAMPLE 6.13

Graph the indicated polynomial using all of the integer values of x over the indicated interval. $y = P(x) = x^3 + 4x^2 + x - 6$ from $-4 \le x \le 2$.

SOLUTION 6.13

$y = P(x) = x^3 + 4x^2 + x - 6$ from $-4 \le x \le 2$.

To graph the polynomial $y = P(x) = x^3 + 4x^2 + x - 6$ from $-4 \le x \le 2$, we need to find all of the integer values of x between $[-4, 2]$ and plot them on a Cartesian Plane. Find ordered pairs using synthetic division.

$$
\begin{array}{r|rrrr}
-4 & 1 & +4 & +1 & -6 \\
   &   & -4 & 0 & -4 \\
\hline
   & 1 & 0 & +1 & \underline{|-10} \\
\end{array}
$$

$P(-4) = -10$ and $x = -4$ is a lower bound. Divide by -3.

$$
\begin{array}{r|rrrr}
-3 & 1 & +4 & +1 & -6 \\
   &   & -3 & -3 & +6 \\
\hline
   & 1 & +1 & -2 & \underline{|0} \\
\end{array}
$$

$P(-3) = 0.$ $x = -3$ is a root of the polynomial. Divide by -2.

$$
\begin{array}{r|rrrr}
-2 & 1 & +4 & +1 & -6 \\
   &   & -2 & -4 & +6 \\
\hline
   & 1 & +2 & -3 & \underline{|0} \\
\end{array}
$$

$P(-2) = 0.$ $x = -2$ is also a root of the polynomial. Divide by -1.

$$
\begin{array}{r|rrrr}
-1 & 1 & +4 & +1 & -6 \\
   &   & -1 & -3 & +2 \\
\hline
   & 1 & +3 & -2 & \underline{|-4} \\
\end{array}
$$

$P(-1) = -4.$ $P(0)$ can be found by direct substitution. $P(0) = -6.$ $P(0)$ is the y-intercept. Divide by $x = 1$.

$$
\begin{array}{r|rrrr}
+1 & 1 & +4 & +1 & -6 \\
   &   & +1 & +5 & +6 \\
\hline
   & 1 & +5 & +6 & \underline{\ 0} \\
\end{array}
$$

$P(1) = 0$. 1 is a zero. Divide by $x = 2$.

$$
\begin{array}{r|rrrr}
+2 & 1 & +4 & +1 & -6 \\
   &   & +2 & +12 & +26 \\
\hline
   & 1 & +6 & +13 & \underline{\ 20} \\
\end{array}
$$

$P(2) = 20$. $x = 2$ is an upper bound. No value of $x > 2$ crosses the x-axis. List the ordered pairs.

$(-4, -10)$	$(-3, 0)$	$(-2, 0)$	$(-1, -4)$
$(0, -6)$	$(+1, 0)$	$(+2, 20)$	

The x-intercepts are the ordered pairs with $y = 0$ and the y-intercept is the ordered pairs with $x = 0$. Plot these points on a Cartesian Plane. The graph of a polynomial function is a smooth continuous curve. To graph the polynomial, we begin at the y-intercept and draw a curve from the y-intercept passing through the points on the graph to the x-intercepts directly to the left or right side of the y-intercepts.

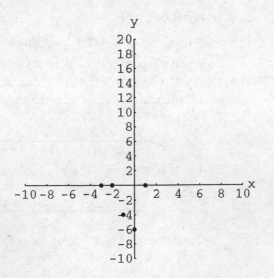

Figure 6.1

The polynomial has zeros at $x = -3, -2,$ and 1. The real zeros of a polynomial are the x-intercepts. To determine if the graph of a polynomial passes through the x-axis or stays on the same side of the x-axis, plot points on both sides of the x-intercept or look at the multiplicity of the x-intercept. From the previous section, the zeros (roots and x-intercepts) can be multiple roots.

> **Theorem 10**:
>
> Let r be a real zero of the polynomial $P(x)$ and let k be its multiplicity. The graph of the polynomial $P(x)$ will pass through the x-axis at $x = r$ if k (the multiplicity of the root r) is odd and will stay on the same side of the x-axis (not cross the x-axis) if k is even.

All of our zeros occur only one time. There are three zeros and we have three different x-intercepts. Our graph passes through all of the x-intercept. Sketch the graph through the points we have graphed. Remember that the graph passes through the x-axis at all of the x-intercepts and includes all of the points we have plotted.

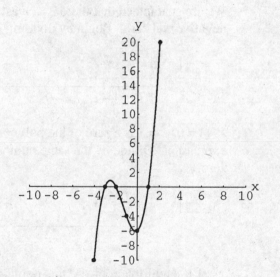

Figure 6.2

We know that the curve goes downward to the right since there are no roots to the left of –4. We also know that the graph goes upward to the right since 1 is the only positive root. The graph cannot cross the x-axis to the right of 1. Our graph is only an approximation of the true graph of $P(x)$, but the sketch of our graph gives us a good idea of the graph of the polynomial.

EXAMPLE 6.14

Graph the indicated polynomial by finding only the x-intercepts (real zeros), the y-intercept, and the information you know about polynomials. You may plot additional points if necessary:

$$P(x) = x^4 - 2x^3 - 8x^2 + 18x - 9$$

SOLUTION 6.14

$$P(x) = x^4 - 2x^3 - 8x^2 + 18x - 9$$

Determine the possible number of positive and negative zeros

$P(x) =$ $\underbrace{+ \quad -}_{1}$ $\underbrace{- \quad +}_{2}$ $\underbrace{-}_{3}$ $P(-x) = +$ $\underbrace{+ \quad -}_{1}$ $- \quad -$

There are 3 or 1 positive real zeros and 1 negative real zero.

The possible rational zeros are $\dfrac{\pm 1, \pm 3, \pm 9}{1}$.

Find the value of $P(x)$ for the rational roots. Find $P(0)$ (the y-intercept) by substitution.

  $P(0) = -9$

We are guaranteed that there is at least one positive real zero and 1 negative real zero. Begin by dividing by $x = 1$.

1⌋	1	−2	−8	+18	−9
		+1	−1	− 9	+9
	1	−1	−9	+ 9	⌊0

$P(1) = 0$. $x = 1$ is a zero of the polynomial. Divide 1 into the depressed expression. Divide by the same number again to see if 1 is a multiple zero.

1⌋	1	−1	−9	+9
		+1	0	−9
	1	0	−9	⌊0

$x = 1$ is a multiple root. At this point, $x = 1$ occurs as a zero twice. It is possible that it occurs as a zero more than two times. The depressed expression is quadratic. To find the remaining roots, set the depressed expression equal to zero and solve the quadratic equation.

$x^2 - 9 = 0$ Solve for x^2.
$x^2 = 9$ Take the square root of both
          sides. Don't forget ±.
$x = \pm\sqrt{9} = \pm 3$

The zeros are $x = 1$ (2), −3, and +3. $P(0) = -9$. Plot the roots and the y-intercept.

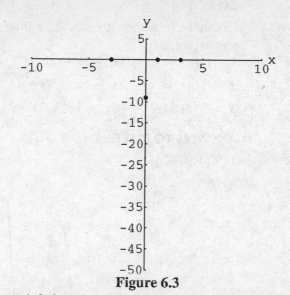

Figure 6.3

The y-intercept is below the x-axis. From the y-intercept $(0, -9)$, the graph moves upward to the x-intercepts $(-3, 0)$ and $(1, 0)$. The graph either passes through the x-intercepts or stays on the same side (does not pass through the x-axis). Since the intercept $x = 3$ is a zero which occurs only one time, the graph passes through the intercept $(-3, 0)$. The zero $x = 1$ occurs twice. The graph of the curve stays on the same side of the x-axis (bounces downward) and heads toward the intercept $(3, 0)$.

The intercept $(3, 0)$ occurs only one time, so the graph passes through this intercept and continues upward.

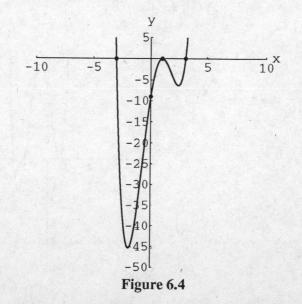

Figure 6.4

EXERCISE 6.5

Graph the following polynomials. Find all of the roots and the y-intercept.

1. $P(x) = x^3 - 2x^2 - 5x + 6$

2. $P(x) = x^4 - 3x^3 - 3x^2 + 7x + 6$

3. $P(x) = 2x^4 + 5x^3 - 5x^2 - 5x + 3$

ANSWERS TO EXERCISE 6.5

1. $\{1, 3, -2\}$

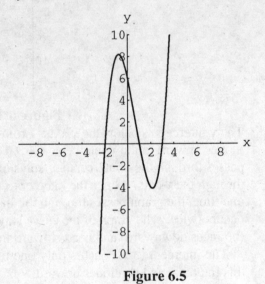

Figure 6.5

2. $\{1\,(2), 2, 3\}$

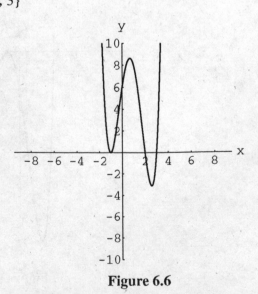

Figure 6.6

3. $\{1, -1, \dfrac{1}{2}, -3\}$

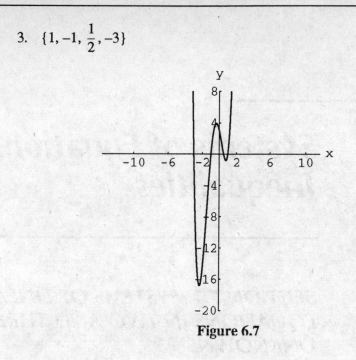

Figure 6.7

7

Systems of Equations and Inequalities

SECTION 7.1 SYSTEMS OF LINEAR EQUATIONS IN TWO AND THREE UNKNOWNS

Linear Systems in Two Variables

A **system of equations,** sometimes called a **simultaneous system of equations,** is two or more equations solved for the point or points of intersection. The solution to a system of equations involves finding a value or values (if they exist) for the variables that make all of the equations true. Linear systems of equations are systems where the highest power of any variable is 1. There are several methods that are used to solve linear system of equation:
1. Graphing
2. Substitution
3. Linear Combinations

Solutions by Graphing

We have already graphed linear equations. To solve a system of linear equations by graphing, we graph the system of equations on the Cartesian Plane and look for the point of intersection.

EXAMPLE 7.1

Solve the following linear systems of equations by graphing:

a) $2x - y = 3$
     $x + y = 3$
b) $3x + 2y = 13$
     $2x - 3y = 0$

SOLUTION 7.1

a) $2x - y = 3$
     $x + y = 3$

To graph this system of equations, solve both equations for y (put both equations into slope-intercept form).

$y = 2x - 3$ and $y = -x + 3$

Graph these equations on the Cartesian plane.

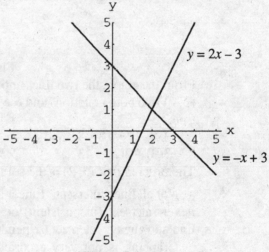

Figure 7.1

From the graph, the two lines appear to intersect at the point (2, 1). Check the solution into both equations and see if the ordered pair makes both equations true.

$2x - y = 3$ and $x + y = 3$
$2(2) - (1) = 3$ $(2) + (1) = 3$

The ordered pair (2, 1) is the point of intersection of the system of equations. A system of equations which has a finite number of solutions is called an **independent system of equations**.

b) $3x + 2y = 13$
     $2x - 3y = 0$

To graph this system of equations, solve both equations for y.

$$y = -\frac{3}{2}x + \frac{13}{2} \quad \text{and} \quad y = \frac{2}{3}x + 0$$

Graph these equations on the Cartesian plane.

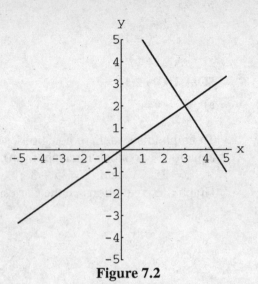

Figure 7.2

From the graph, the two lines appear to intersect at the point (3, 2). Check (3, 2) into both equations and see if the ordered pair makes both equations true.

$$3x + 2y = 13 \quad \text{and} \quad 2x - 3y = 0$$
$$3(3) + 2(2) = 13 \qquad 2(3) - 3(2) = 0$$

The ordered pair (3, 2) is the solution to the system of equations.

Not all lines intersect. Linear systems of equations may be parallel and never intersect (inconsistent) or the two lines may, in fact, be the same line and always intersect (dependent).

Graphing is not very accurate. A second way to solve a system of equations is by substitution. The method of solving systems of equations by substitution is as follows:

Solving Systems of Equations by Substitution:
1. Solve one of the equations for one of the variables.
2. Substitute that expression into the other equation for that variable.
3. Solve the equation for that variable.
4. Solve the system of equations for the other variable.

EXAMPLE 7.2

Solve the following linear systems of equations by substitution:

a) $2x + y = 8$
    $3x + y = 11$

b) $4x - 3y = 7$
    $x + 3y = -17$

SOLUTION 7.2

a) $2x + y = 8$
    $3x + y = 11$

Solve one equation for one of the variables. The second equation can easily be solved for *y*.

$y = 11 - 3x$

Substitute the expression $y = (11 - 3x)$ into the other equation for that variable.

$2x + y = 8$
$2x + (11 - 3x) = 8$

Now we have an equation in only one variable. Solve the equation for *x*.

$2x + (11 - 3x) = 8$	Simplify.
$-x + 11 = 8$	Add -11 to both sides.
$-x = -3$	Take the opposite of both sides of the equation.

$x = 3$

Solve for the other variable. Substitute $x = 3$ into either equation for the variable *x* and solve for *y*.

$2x + y = 8$
$2(3) + y = 8$
$6 + y - 8$
$y = 2$

The solution to the system of equations is (3, 2).

b) $4x - 3y = 7$
    $x + 3y = -17$

Solve one equation for one of the variables. When selecting which variable to solve for, try to choose a variable with a coefficient of 1. Solve the second equation for *x*.

$x = -17 - 3y$

Substitute the expression $x = (-17 - 3y)$ into the other equation for that variable.

$4x - 3y = 7$
$4(-17 - 3y) - 3y = 7$

Solve the equation for *y*.

$4(-17 - 3y) - 3y = 7$	Simplify.
$-68 - 12y - 3y = 7$	
$-15y - 68 = 7$	Add $+ 68$ to both sides.
$-15y = 75$	Divide both sides of the equation by -15.

$y = -5$

Solve for the other variable. Substitute $y = -5$ into either equation for the variable *y*.

$x + 3y = -17$

$$x + 3(-5) = -17$$
$$x - 15 = -17$$
$$x = -2$$

The solution to the system of equations is $(-2, -5)$.

Here are some examples of inconsistent and dependent systems solved by substitution.

EXAMPLE 7.3

Solve the following linear systems of equations by substitution.

a) $2x + 3y = 8$
    $6x + 9y = 11$

b) $2x - 4y = 6$
    $3x - 6y = 9$

SOLUTION 7.3

a) $2x + 3y = 8$
    $6x + 9y = 11$

Solve one equation for one of the variables. Solve the first equation for x.

$$2x = 8 - 3y \qquad \qquad \text{Divide both sides by 2.}$$
$$x = 4 - \frac{3}{2}y$$

Substitute the expression $x = 4 - \frac{3}{2}y$ into the other equation for that variable.

$$6\left(4 - \frac{3}{2}\right) + 9y = 11$$
$$24 - 9y + 9y = 11$$

In the process of solving the equation, the variable is eliminated from both sides of the equation. We get the equation

$$24 = 11.$$

This equation is a contradiction. That is, $24 \neq 11$. When solving a system of equations and both variables are eliminated from the equation, the system of equations is either an inconsistent system of equations (parallel lines, no solutions) or a dependent system of equations (same line, infinitely many solutions). If the variable is eliminated and the equation is a contradiction, the system is inconsistent. If the variable is eliminated and the equation is an identity, the system is dependent. This system is inconsistent. There is no solution to this system.

b) $2x - 4y = 6$
    $3x - 6y = 9$

Solve one equation for one of the variables. Solve the first equation for x.

$$2x - 4y = 6 \qquad \qquad \text{Add 4y to both sides of the}$$
$$\qquad \qquad \qquad \qquad \qquad \text{equation.}$$
$$2x = 4y + 6 \qquad \qquad \text{Divide both sides by 2.}$$

$$x = 2y + 3$$

Substitute the expression $x = 2y + 3$ into the other equation for that variable.

$$3x - 6y = 9$$
$$3(2y + 3) - 6y = 9$$
$$6y + 9 - 6y = 9$$

Again the variable drops out of the equation, but this time we get

$$9 = 9.$$

$9 = 9$ is an identity. $9 = 9$ is an equation which is always true. This means that the system of equations has infinitely many solutions. This system of equations is a dependent system (same line).

Any time all of the variables are eliminated, the system is either inconsistent (no solutions) or dependent (infinitely many solutions). There are no solutions if we get a contradiction ($3 = 4$, $0 = 5$, $-1 = 2$, . . .) and there are infinitely many solutions if we get an identity ($0 = 0$, $2 = 2$, . . .).

The disadvantage of the method of substitution is that the arithmetic involved in solving the system may become awkward. A quicker method for solving linear systems of equations is the method of **linear combinations**, sometimes called **addition-subtraction**, **addition-multiplication**, **elimination**, and **elimination by addition**. This method is called linear combinations because when you add, subtract, multiply or divide an equation by a number or numbers, you get an equivalent equation which is a linear combination of the original equation. Linear combinations requires us to eliminate one of the variables so that we can solve for the other. The method is as follows:

Solving Systems of Equations by Linear Combinations

1. Put all equations into standard form with integer coefficients. The standard form of a linear equation is $Ax + By = C$.
2. Multiply one or both of the equations by a number or numbers to get opposites in one of the variables.
3. Add the two equations together and solve.
4. Solve for the other variable.

To demonstrate the method of linear combination for solving systems of equations, we will use the same systems of equations that were solved by using the method of substitution.

EXAMPLE 7.4

Solve the following linear systems of equations by linear combinations:

a) $2x + y = 8$
   $3x + y = 11$

b) $4x - 3y = 7$
    $x + 3y = -17$

SOLUTION 7.4

a) $2x + y = 8$
    $3x + y = 11$

Both equations are already in standard form.
$$2x + y = 8$$
$$3x + y = 11$$

Multiply the first equation by -1 to get opposites in the variable y.
$$-1(2x + y = 8)$$
$$3x + y = 11$$

The system of equations becomes
$$-2x - y = -8$$
$$3x + y = 11$$

Add the two equations together. It does no good to add the two equations together unless there are opposites in one of the variables.
$$x = 3$$

Solve for the other variable. Substitute $x = 3$ into either equation for the variable x.
$$2x + y = 8$$
$$2(3) + y = 8$$
$$6 + y = 8$$
$$y = 2$$

The solution to the system of equations is $(3, 2)$.

b) $4x - 3y = 7$
    $x + 3y = -17$

Both equations are already in standard form.
$$4x - 3y = 7$$
$$x + 3y = -17$$

The y variable already has opposites.
$$4x - 3y = 7$$
$$x + 3y = -17$$

Add the two equations and solve.
$$5x = -10$$
$$x = -2$$

Solve for the other variable. Substitute $x = -2$ into either equation for the variable x.
$$x + 3y = -17$$
$$(-2) + 3y = -17$$
$$3y = -15$$
$$y = -5$$

The solution to the system of equations is $(-2, -5)$.

Linear combination will usually allow us to solve the system of equations much faster than the method of substitution.

Here are some examples of inconsistent and dependent systems solved by linear combinations.

EXAMPLE 7.5

Solve the following linear systems of equations by linear combinations:
a) $2x + 3y = 8$
   $6x + 9y = 11$
b) $2x - 4y = 6$
   $3x - 6y = 9$

SOLUTION 7.5

a) $2x + 3y = 8$
   $6x + 9y = 11$

Multiply the first equation by -3 to opposites in the variable x.

   $-3(2x + 3y = 8)$
   $6x + 9y = 11$

Simplify.

   $-6x - 9y = -24$
   $6x + 9y = 11$

Add the two equations.

   $0 = -13$

This equation is a contradiction and the system is inconsistent. There is no solution to this system of equations.

b) $2x - 4y = 6$
   $3x - 6y = 9$

We cannot multiply just one of the equations by a number unless we use a fractional number. To eliminate the variable x, multiply the first equation by the coefficient of x from the second equation and multiply the second equation by the coefficient of x from the first equation. Be certain that one of the variables has a positive coefficient and the other has a negative. To eliminate x, multiply the first equation by 3 and the second equation by -2.

   $3(2x - 4y = 6)$
   $-2(3x - 6y = 9)$

Simplify.

   $6x - 12y = 18$
   $-6x + 12y = -18$

Add the two equations.

   $0 = 0$

$0 = 0$ is an identity. There are infinitely many solutions. The lines are the same. The system of equations is dependent.

Linear Systems of Equations in Three Variables

Systems of equations can have more than two equations and two variables. For a system of equations to have a finite number of solutions, there must be exactly the same number of equations as the number of variables. A system of equations in three variables and three equations is known as a 3×3 system of equations. 3×3 systems of equations can be solved by using linear combinations.

EXAMPLE 7.6

Solve the following system of equations by linear combinations:

$$x + y + z = 6$$
$$2x - y + z = 7$$
$$x - y + 2z = 6$$

SOLUTION 7.6

$$x + y + z = 6$$
$$2x - y + z = 7$$
$$x - y + 2z = 6$$

To solve a 3×3 system of equations by linear combinations, we must eliminate one of the variables two times. If we add the first two equations, the y variable will be eliminated. If we then add the first and the third, the y variable will again be eliminated. Add the first two equations.

$$x + y + z = 6$$
$$2x - y + z = 7$$

We get

$$3x + 2z = 13$$

We now have an equation in two variables, x and z. Now, eliminate y again by adding the first and the third equations.

$$x + y + z = 6$$
$$x - y + 2z = 6$$

We get

$$2x + 3z = 12$$

We have a second equation in the same two variables. Solve this 2×2 system of equations in x and z.

$$3x + 2z = 13$$
$$2x + 3z = 12$$

Eliminate the z variable by multiplying the first equation by 3 and the second equation by -2.

$$3(3x + 2z = 13)$$
$$-2(2x + 3z = 12)$$

Simplify.

$$9x + 6z = 39$$
$$-4x - 6z = -24$$

Add the two equations.

$$5x = 15$$
$$x = 3$$

To find the solutions for y and z work backwards. First go to one of the equations in two variables and let $x = 3$ and find z.

$$3x + 2z = 13$$
$$3(3) + 2z = 13$$
$$9 + 2z = 13$$
$$2z = 13 - 9$$
$$2z = 4$$
$$z = 2$$

Now go to any of the equations in the three variables and let $x = 3$ and $z = 2$ and find y.

$$x + y + z = 6$$
$$(3) + y + (2) = 6$$
$$5 + y = 6$$
$$y = 6 - 5$$
$$y = 1$$

The solution to the 3×3 system of equations is $(3, 1, 2)$.

EXERCISE 7.1

Solve the following systems of equations by any method:

1. $4x - y = -17$
   $3x + y = -4$
2. $3x - 4y = 13$
   $2x - 5y = 18$
3. $5x + 3y = -11$
   $4x - 5y = 18$

Solve the following 3×3 systems of equations:

4. $x + y + z = 6$
   $2x - y + z = 15$
   $2x + 3y - z = 1$
5. $2x - y + 3z = 16$
   $x + 3y - z = 1$
   $3x + 2y + 4z = 31$

ANSWERS TO EXERCISE 7.1

1. $(-3, 5)$ 2. $(-1, -4)$

3. $(2, -7)$ 4. $(5, -2, 3)$

5. $(-1, 3, 7)$ 6. $(\frac{1}{3}, -\frac{1}{2})$

SECTION 7.2 SYSTEMS OF EQUATIONS AND AUGMENTED MATRICES

A **matrix** is a rectangular array of numbers enclosed in brackets. Some examples of matrices are

$$\begin{bmatrix} 8 & 7 \\ 5 & 9 \end{bmatrix} \quad \begin{bmatrix} 8 & 7 & 6 \\ 5 & 9 & 1 \\ 4 & 3 & 9 \end{bmatrix} \quad \begin{bmatrix} 2 & 7 & 8 \\ 5 & 9 & 1 \end{bmatrix} \quad \begin{bmatrix} 4 & 7 & 8 \end{bmatrix}$$

Each number inside the brackets is called an **element** of the matrix and is given a location by its position in the matrix. In the first matrix, the number 8 is in the position of row 1 and column 1 and is denoted by a_{11}. The number 7 is in the first row and the second column denoted by a_{12}. The 5 is a_{21} meaning that the number 5 is in the second row first column. The number $9 = a_{22}$. Notice that the first subscripted number indicates the row and the second subscripted number represents the column.

The coefficients of a system of equations form a rectangular array of numbers. The system of equations

$$2x + 4y = 8$$
$$3x - y = 5$$

can be represented by a matrix by taking the coefficients of x and y along with the answers to each equation. This matrix is called the **augmented matrix** for the system of equations. The augmented matrix for the above system of equations is

$$\begin{bmatrix} 2 & 4 & 8 \\ 3 & -1 & 5 \end{bmatrix}.$$

Sometimes you will see the augmented matrix with a vertical line separating the coefficients of x and y and the solutions to the equations.

$$\left[\begin{array}{cc|c} 2 & 4 & 8 \\ 3 & -1 & 5 \end{array}\right]$$

The vertical line is not necessary and is only used to separate the coefficients from the constant terms. Systems of equations can be much larger. It is not uncommon to have 6×6, 10×10 or much larger systems of equations. We use a different notation for larger systems of equations. Instead of using $x, y, z, \ldots$, we use subscripted notation for the variables.

$$2x_1 + 4x_2 = 8$$
$$3x_1 - x_2 = 5$$

Using the subscripted notation, we will never run out of variables. In subscripted notation a 2×2 system of equations looks like this:

$$a_1 x_1 + b_1 x_2 = c_1$$
$$a_2 x_1 + b_2 x_2 = c_2$$

The subscript behind the a, b and c stand for the equation. a_2 is the coefficient of the first variable in the second equation. The subscript for the variables represents which variable we are working with. x_2 represents the second variable. The general augmented matrix of a 2×2 system of equations is

$$\begin{bmatrix} a_1 & b_1 & c_1 \\ a_2 & b_2 & c_2 \end{bmatrix}.$$

When solving systems of equations by linear combinations we were allowed to:

1. Interchange any two equations.
2. Multiply any equation by a constant not equal to zero.
3. Multiply any equation by a constant and add it to any other equation.

If we apply these rules to the rows of an augmented matrix, the matrix obtained is said to be a **row-equivalent** matrix. Matrices which are row-equivalent are denoted by the symbol $\approx$. The rules to produce row-equivalent matrices are as follows:

Row-equivalent Matrices

An augmented matrix is transformed into a row-equivalent matrix whenever any of the following row operations are performed:

1. Two rows are interchanged.
2. A non zero constant is multiplied by any row.
3. A non zero constant multiplied by one row is added to another row.

When performing row operations, it is necessary to indicate which transformation is being used. We use a special notation to indicate row transformations. To indicate that two rows are being interchanged, we write $R_1 \leftrightarrow R_2$. The double headed arrow means that R_1 is being replaced by R_2 and R_2 is being replaced by R_1. The notation $kR_2 \rightarrow R_2$ means that R_2 is being multiplied by k and R_2 is being replaced by kR_2. The arrow in this notation is only directed toward R_2. This means that R_2 is being replaced by kR_2. The next notation is a bit more complicated. $kR_1 + R_2 \rightarrow R_2$. This notation means that k is multiplied by R_1 and added to R_2. The arrow is pointing toward R_2. This notation indicates R_2 is being replaced by $kR_1 + R_2$. If the notation have read $kR_1 + R_2 \rightarrow R_1$, then row 1 would have been replaced by $kR_1 + R_2$.

The following examples show how augmented matrices are useful in solving systems of equations.

EXAMPLE 7.7

Solve the following system of equations by use of augmented matrices:

$$x_1 + 3x_2 = -9$$

$$5x_1 - x_2 = 19$$

SOLUTION 7.7

$$x_1 + 3x_2 = -9$$
$$5x_1 - x_2 = 19$$

Put the coefficients and the constants into an augmented matrix.

$$\begin{bmatrix} 1 & 3 & -9 \\ 5 & -1 & 19 \end{bmatrix}$$

In using an augmented matrix to solve a system of equations, we always need to get a 1 in a_{11} (1 in the first row, first column). We already have the 1 where we need it. Now get a zero in a_{21}. Multiply -5 times row 1 and add it to row 2.

$$\begin{bmatrix} 1 & 3 & -9 \\ 5 & -1 & 19 \end{bmatrix} -5R_1 + R_2 \begin{bmatrix} 1 & 3 & -9 \\ 5_{-5} & -1_{-15} & 19_{45} \end{bmatrix} -5R_1 + R_2 \rightarrow R_2 \begin{bmatrix} 1 & 3 & -9 \\ 0 & -16 & 64 \end{bmatrix}.$$

Now get a 1 in a_{22} position. Multiply $-\dfrac{1}{16}$ times row 2.

$$-\frac{1}{16}R_2 \rightarrow R_2 \begin{bmatrix} 1 & 3 & -9 \\ 0 & 1 & -4 \end{bmatrix}$$

The object now is to get a zero in the a_{12} position. We need the 3 in the first row to become zero. Multiply the second row times -3 and add it to row 1.

$$\begin{bmatrix} 1 & 3 & -9 \\ 0 & 1 & -4 \end{bmatrix} -3R_2 + R_1 \begin{bmatrix} 0 & -3 & 12 \\ 1 & 3 & -9 \\ 0 & 1 & -4 \end{bmatrix} -3R_2 + R_1 \rightarrow R_1$$

$$\sim \begin{bmatrix} 1 & 0 & 3 \\ 0 & 1 & -4 \end{bmatrix}$$

The final matrix is equivalent to the original matrix which is equivalent to the original system of equations.

$$x_1 + 3x_2 = -9$$
$$5x_1 - x_2 = 19$$

is equivalent to

$$1x_1 + 0x_2 = 3$$
$$0x_1 + 1x_2 = -4.$$

The solutions for x_1 and x_2 are (3, –4). The matrix

$$\begin{bmatrix} 1 & 0 & 3 \\ 0 & 1 & -4 \end{bmatrix}$$

indicates that $x_1 = 3$ and $x_2 = -4$.

The method of solving systems of equations by augmented matrices is also helpful in solving inconsistent systems (no solutions) and dependent systems (infinitely many solutions).

EXAMPLE 7.8

Solve the following system of equations by use of augmented matrices:
$$3x_1 + 6x_2 = 9$$
$$2x_1 + 4x_2 = 5$$

SOLUTION 7.8

$$3x_1 + 6x_2 = 9$$
$$2x_1 + 4x_2 = 5$$

Put the coefficients and the constants into an augmented matrix.

$$\begin{bmatrix} 3 & 6 & 9 \\ 2 & 4 & 5 \end{bmatrix}$$

Get a 1 in a_{11}. Multiply $\dfrac{1}{3}$ times row 1.

$$\begin{bmatrix} 3 & 6 & 9 \\ 2 & 4 & 5 \end{bmatrix} \dfrac{1}{3} R_1 \rightarrow R_1 \begin{bmatrix} 1 & 2 & 3 \\ 2 & 4 & 5 \end{bmatrix}$$

We must get a zero in a_{21}. Multiply –2 times row 1 and add it to row 2.

$$\begin{bmatrix} 1 & 2 & 3 \\ 2 & 4 & 5 \end{bmatrix} -2R_1 + R_2 \begin{bmatrix} 1 & 2 & 3 \\ 2_{-2} & 4_{-4} & 5_{-6} \end{bmatrix} -2R_1 + R_2 \rightarrow R_2 \begin{bmatrix} 1 & 2 & 3 \\ 0 & 0 & -1 \end{bmatrix}$$

To solve an augmented matrix, we try to obtain a matrix in the form of

$$\begin{bmatrix} 1 & 0 & c_1 \\ 0 & 1 & c_2 \end{bmatrix}.$$

The solutions are $x_1 = c_1$ and $x_2 = c_2$. When we get

$$\begin{bmatrix} 1 & 0 & c_1 \\ 0 & 0 & c_2 \end{bmatrix},$$

the system has no solutions. Notice in the second row, the first two columns represent the variable columns. Also, in the second row, all of the variables were lost. The system is an inconsistent system of equations.

Solutions to systems of equations by use of augmented matrices have three possibilities:

1. $\begin{bmatrix} 1 & 0 & c_1 \\ 0 & 1 & c_2 \end{bmatrix}$ has one unique solution at c_1 and c_2.

2. $\begin{bmatrix} 1 & 0 & c_1 \\ 0 & 0 & c_2 \end{bmatrix}$ where $c_2 \neq 0$ has no solutions.

3. $\begin{bmatrix} 1 & b_1 & c_1 \\ 0 & 0 & 0 \end{bmatrix}$ has infinitely many solutions.

SECTION 7.3 SOLVING SYSTEMS OF EQUATIONS BY GAUSS-JORDAN REDUCTION METHOD

Reduced Matrix

When solving linear systems of equations by matrix methods, the object is to write the system of equations as an augmented matrix and use row operations on the matrix to obtain an equivalent matrix that can be solved easily. The equivalent matrix is called a **reduced matrix**.

Reduced Matrix

A matrix is in reduced form if:

1. Each row that contains only zeros is below any row having at least one non-zero element.
2. The leftmost non-zero element of any row is the number 1.
3. The column containing the leftmost 1 must have zeros above and below that 1.
4. The leftmost 1 in any column is to the right of the leftmost 1 of any row above that row.

EXAMPLE 7.9

The following are examples of non-reduced matrices. State which rule is not applied:

a) $\begin{bmatrix} 2 & 0 & 0 \\ 0 & 1 & 1 \end{bmatrix}$

b) $\begin{bmatrix} 1 & 0 & 0 \\ 0 & 1 & 1 \\ 0 & 0 & 1 \end{bmatrix}$

c) $\begin{bmatrix} 0 & 0 & 0 & 0 \\ 1 & 0 & 0 & 7 \\ 0 & 1 & 0 & 0 \end{bmatrix}$

d) $\begin{bmatrix} 0 & 1 & 0 \\ 1 & 0 & 0 \\ 0 & 0 & 1 \end{bmatrix}$

SOLUTION 7.9

a) 2 — The leftmost non-zero element of any row must be the number 1.
b) 3 — The column containing the leftmost 1 must have zeros above and below that 1.
c) 1 — Each row that contains only zeros is below any row having at least one non-zero element.
d) 4 — The leftmost 1 in any column is to the right of the leftmost 1 of any row above that row.

EXAMPLE 7.10

Put the following into reduced form:

a) $\begin{bmatrix} 2 & 0 & 0 \\ 0 & 1 & 1 \end{bmatrix}$

b) $\begin{bmatrix} 1 & 0 & 0 \\ 0 & 1 & 1 \\ 0 & 0 & 1 \end{bmatrix}$

c) $\begin{bmatrix} 0 & 0 & 0 & 0 \\ 1 & 0 & 0 & 7 \\ 0 & 1 & 0 & 0 \end{bmatrix}$

d) $\begin{bmatrix} 0 & 1 & 0 \\ 1 & 0 & 0 \\ 0 & 0 & 1 \end{bmatrix}$

SOLUTION 7.10

a) $\begin{bmatrix} 2 & 0 & 0 \\ 0 & 1 & 1 \end{bmatrix}$ Multiply row 1 by $\dfrac{1}{2}$.

$$\begin{bmatrix} 1 & 0 & 0 \\ 0 & 1 & 1 \end{bmatrix}$$

$$\frac{1}{2}R_1 \to R_1.$$

b) $\begin{bmatrix} 1 & 0 & 0 \\ 0 & 1 & 1 \\ 0 & 0 & 1 \end{bmatrix}$

The 1 in the second row, third column must be a zero.

$$-1R_3 + R_2 \to R_2$$

$$-1(0\ 0\ 1) + (0\ 1\ 1) \ \to \ (0\ 0\ -1) + (0\ 1\ 1) \ \to \ (0\ 1\ 0)$$

$$\begin{bmatrix} 1 & 0 & 0 \\ 0 & 1 & 0 \\ 0 & 0 & 1 \end{bmatrix}$$

c) $\begin{bmatrix} 0 & 0 & 0 & 0 \\ 1 & 0 & 0 & 7 \\ 0 & 1 & 0 & 0 \end{bmatrix}$

A row containing all zeros with non-zero elements. Interchange row one, two and three.

$$\begin{bmatrix} 0 & 0 & 0 & 0 \\ 1 & 0 & 0 & 7 \\ 0 & 1 & 0 & 0 \end{bmatrix} \quad R_1 \leftrightarrow R_2 \quad \begin{bmatrix} 1 & 0 & 0 & 7 \\ 0 & 0 & 0 & 0 \\ 0 & 1 & 0 & 0 \end{bmatrix}$$

$$\begin{bmatrix} 1 & 0 & 0 & 7 \\ 0 & 0 & 0 & 0 \\ 0 & 1 & 0 & 0 \end{bmatrix} \quad R_2 \leftrightarrow R_3 \quad \begin{bmatrix} 1 & 0 & 0 & 7 \\ 0 & 1 & 0 & 0 \\ 0 & 0 & 0 & 0 \end{bmatrix}$$

d) $\begin{bmatrix} 0 & 1 & 0 \\ 1 & 0 & 0 \\ 0 & 0 & 1 \end{bmatrix}$

Leftmost 1 in row 2 is not to the right of the left most 1 in row 1. $R_1 \leftrightarrow R_2$

$$\begin{bmatrix} 0 & 1 & 0 \\ 1 & 0 & 0 \\ 0 & 0 & 1 \end{bmatrix} \quad R_1 \leftrightarrow R_2 \quad \begin{bmatrix} 1 & 0 & 0 \\ 0 & 1 & 0 \\ 0 & 0 & 1 \end{bmatrix}$$

In the previous section, we wrote systems of equations as augmented matrices. Augmented matrices can be written as systems of equations.

EXAMPLE 7.11

Write the following augmented matrices as systems of equations:

a) $\begin{bmatrix} 1 & 2 & 3 & 6 \\ 2 & 1 & 1 & 7 \\ 4 & 3 & 9 & 37 \end{bmatrix}$

b) $\begin{bmatrix} 1 & 0 & 8 \\ 0 & 1 & 2 \end{bmatrix}$

c) $\begin{bmatrix} 1 & 0 & 0 & 4 \\ 0 & 1 & 0 & 7 \\ 0 & 0 & 1 & 2 \end{bmatrix}$

SOLUTION 7.11

a) $\begin{bmatrix} 1 & 2 & 3 & 6 \\ 2 & 1 & 1 & 7 \\ 4 & 3 & 9 & 37 \end{bmatrix}$

This augmented matrix is a three by four matrix. The system of equations is a three by three system of equations. The last column is the answer column. the system of equations is

$$x_1 + 2x_2 + 3x_3 = 6$$
$$2x_1 + x_2 + x_3 = 7$$
$$4x_1 + 3x_2 + 9x_3 = 37$$

b) $\begin{bmatrix} 1 & 0 & 8 \\ 0 & 1 & 2 \end{bmatrix}$

This matrix is in reduced matrix form. The augmented matrix is a two by two system of equations.

$$x_1 + 0x_2 = 8$$
$$0x_1 + 1x_2 = 2$$

The advantage of the reduced matrix is the coefficients of zero eliminate those variables and we get

$$x_1 = 8$$
$$x_2 = 2.$$

Note that in reduced matrix form, the column containing the 1 has its answer in the last column.

c) $\begin{bmatrix} 1 & 0 & 0 & 4 \\ 0 & 1 & 0 & 7 \\ 0 & 0 & 1 & 2 \end{bmatrix}$

The system of equations is

$$x_1 = 4$$
$$x_2 = 7$$
$$x_3 = 2$$

Gauss-Jordan Elimination

In the last example, the solutions to a system of equations when written as an augmented matrix are the numbers in the last column. The **Gauss-Jordan Elimination Method** provides a systematic way to put a matrix into reduced form and solve the system.

EXAMPLE 7.12

Solve the following system of equations by the Gauss-Jordan Elimination Method:

$x_1 + 2x_2 = 5$

$x_1 + x_2 = 3$

SOLUTION 7.12

$x_1 + 2x_2 = 5$

$x_1 + x_2 = 3$

To solve a system by Gauss-Jordan Elimination Method, we write the system as an augmented matrix.

$$\begin{bmatrix} 1 & 2 & 5 \\ 1 & 1 & 3 \end{bmatrix}$$

The object of the Gauss-Jordan Elimination Method is to get a 1 in the first row, first column.

In this system, the first row, first column already has a 1 in that position. Next, get a zero in all of the rows beneath that 1. Multiply the first row by −1 and add it to the second row $(-1R_1 + R_2 \rightarrow R_2)$.

$$\begin{bmatrix} 1 & 2 & 5 \\ 1 & 1 & 3 \end{bmatrix} -1R_1 + R_2 \rightarrow R_2 \begin{bmatrix} 1 & 2 & 5 \\ 1_{-1} & 1_{-2} & 3_{-5} \end{bmatrix} = \begin{bmatrix} 1 & 2 & 5 \\ 0 & -1 & -2 \end{bmatrix}$$

We must now get a 1 in the second row, second column. Multiply the second row by −1 $(-1R_2 \rightarrow R_2)$.

$$\begin{bmatrix} 1 & 2 & 5 \\ 0 & -1 & -2 \end{bmatrix} -1R_2 \rightarrow R_2 \begin{bmatrix} 1 & 2 & 5 \\ 0 & 1 & 2 \end{bmatrix}$$

Now we must get a zero above the 1 in the second row. Multiply −2 times row 2 and add it to row 1 $(-2R_2 + R_1 \rightarrow R_1)$.

$$\begin{bmatrix} 0 & -2 & -4 \\ 1 & 2 & 5 \\ 0 & 1 & 2 \end{bmatrix} -2R_2 + R_1 \rightarrow R_1 \begin{bmatrix} 1 & 0 & 1 \\ 0 & 1 & 2 \end{bmatrix}$$

The augmented matrix is in reduced form and the solution is $x_1 = 1$ and $x_2 = 2$.

The Gauss-Jordan Elimination Method is a systematic process for solving systems of equations. The process is as follows:

Gauss-Jordan Elimination Method
1. Get a 1 in the first row, first column.
2. Get zeros below the leftmost 1 by adding multiples of row 1.
3. Get a 1 in the second row, second column.
4. Get zeros above and below that 1 by adding multiples of row 2.
5. Continue this process until the main diagonal contains all 1 or until a row contains all zeros or all zeros except for the last entry.

Some systems of equations have infinitely many solutions; some have no solutions. When we get a row with all zeros, there are infinitely many solutions and when we get the last row to contain all zeros except for the last entry there are no solutions.

EXAMPLE 7.13

Determine if the following system of equations has infinitely many solutions or no solutions by the Gauss-Jordan Elimination Method.

$x_1 + x_2 - 3x_3 = 5$
$4x_1 + 2x_2 - x_3 = 4$
$8x_1 + 4x_2 - 2x_3 = 7$

SOLUTION 7.13

$x_1 + x_2 - 3x_3 = 5$
$4x_1 + 2x_2 - x_3 = 4$
$8x_1 + 4x_2 - 2x_3 = 7$

Write the system as an augmented matrix.

$$\begin{bmatrix} 1 & 1 & -3 & 5 \\ 4 & 2 & -1 & 4 \\ 8 & 4 & -2 & 7 \end{bmatrix}$$

There is a 1 in the upper left-hand corner. Eliminate the 4 and 8 from beneath the 1.

$$\begin{bmatrix} 1 & 1 & -3 & 5 \\ 4 & 2 & -1 & 4 \\ 8 & 4 & -2 & 7 \end{bmatrix} \quad \begin{array}{c} -4R_1 + R_2 \rightarrow R_2 \\ -4R_1 + R_3 \rightarrow R_3 \end{array} \quad \begin{bmatrix} 1 & 1 & -3 & 5 \\ 0 & -2 & 11 & -16 \\ 0 & -4 & 22 & -37 \end{bmatrix}$$

Get a 1 in the second row, second column.   Multiply the second row by $-\dfrac{1}{2}$.

$$\begin{bmatrix} 1 & 1 & -3 & 5 \\ 0 & -2 & 11 & -16 \\ 0 & -4 & 22 & -37 \end{bmatrix} \qquad -\frac{1}{2}R_2 \to R_2 \qquad \begin{bmatrix} 1 & 1 & -3 & 5 \\ 0 & 1 & -\dfrac{11}{2} & 8 \\ 0 & -4 & 22 & -37 \end{bmatrix}$$

Now get zeros in the columns above and below the 1 in the second row.

$$\begin{bmatrix} 1 & 1 & -3 & 5 \\ 0 & 1 & -\dfrac{11}{2} & 8 \\ 0 & -4 & 22 & -37 \end{bmatrix} \qquad \begin{array}{c} -1R_2 + R_1 \to R_1 \\ 4R_2 + R_3 \to R_3 \end{array} \qquad \begin{bmatrix} 1 & 0 & \dfrac{5}{2} & -3 \\ 0 & 1 & -\dfrac{11}{2} & 8 \\ 0 & 0 & 0 & -5 \end{bmatrix}$$

The last row contains all zeros except for the last element. This system of equations has no solutions.

SECTION 7.4 NON-LINEAR SYSTEMS OF EQUATIONS

In this chapter we have solved systems of equations by:
1.   Substitution
2.   Linear Combinations
3.   Augmented Matrix methods

The systems we solved have been systems of linear equations, or systems which could be made into a linear system by a linear substitution. In this section, we will solve non-linear (higher degree) systems of equations.

EXAMPLE 7.14

a) $y = x^2$
$2x + y = 15$

b) $y = x^2 - x - 3$
$x - 2y = -8$

SOLUTION 7.14

a) $y = x^2$
$2x + y = 15$

A system like this cannot be solved by linear combinations or augmented matrices. This system must be solved by substitution. To solve a system of equations by substitution, solve one of the equations for one of the variables. The first equation is already solved for y.

$$y = x^2$$

Substitute $y = x^2$ into the other equation for y.

$$2x + (x^2) = 15$$

Solve for x.

$x^2 + 2x = 15$	Get everything on one side equal to zero.
$x^2 + 2x - 15 = 0$	Factor.
$(x + 5)(x - 3) = 0$	Solve.
$x = -5$ and $x = 3$	Solve for the other variable. Substitute $x = -5$ and 3 into the equation with the lowest powers of x and y.

$$2x + y = 15$$

Let $x = -5$.

$$2(-5) + y = 15$$
$$y = 25$$

One solution is $(-5, 25)$. Now let $x = 3$.

$$2(3) + y = 15$$
$$y = 9$$

Another solution is $(3, 9)$. The solutions are $(-5, 25)$ and $(3, 9)$.

b) $y = x^2 - x - 3$
$x - 2y = -8$

The first equation is already solved for y. Substitute $y = x^2 - x - 3$ into the other equation for y.

$x - 2(x^2 - x - 3) = -8$	Simplify.
$x - 2x^2 + 2x + 6 = -8$	
$-2x^2 + 3x + 6 = -8$	Put the equation into standard form and factor.
$0 = 2x^2 - 3x - 14$	
$0 = (2x - 7)(x + 2)$	
$x = \dfrac{7}{2}$ and -2	

Substitute $x = \dfrac{7}{2}$ into $x - 2y = -8$ and solve for y.

$$\left(\frac{7}{2}\right) - 2y = -8$$

$$-2y = -8 - \frac{7}{2}$$

$$-2y = -\frac{23}{2}$$

$$y = \frac{23}{4}$$

Substitute $x = -2$ into $x - 2y = -8$.

$$(-2) - 2y = -8$$
$$-2y = -8 + 2$$
$$-2y = -6$$
$$y = 3$$

The ordered pairs are $\left(\frac{7}{2}, \frac{23}{4}\right)$ and $(-2, 3)$.

Some systems of non-linear equation may be solved by using linear combinations.

EXAMPLE 7.15

$$x^2 + y^2 = 25$$
$$3x^2 - y^2 = 11$$

SOLUTION 7.15

$$x^2 + y^2 = 25$$
$$3x^2 - y^2 = 11$$

This is not a linear system of equations. This system could be solved by substitution, but if we add the two equations, the y^2 term will drop out. Add the two equations.

$$x^2 + y^2 = 25$$
$$3x^2 - y^2 = 11$$
$$4x^2 = 36$$
$$x^2 = 9$$
$$x = \pm 3$$

Neither of these two equations are functions of x. Substitute $x = 3$ and $x = -3$ into both equations and take the ordered pairs which are common to both.

$$(3)^2 + y^2 = 25 \qquad\qquad 3(3)^2 - y^2 = 11$$
$$9 + y^2 = 25 \qquad\qquad 3(9) - y^2 = 11$$
$$y^2 = 16 \qquad\qquad 27 - y^2 = 11$$
$$y = \pm 4 \qquad\qquad 16 = y^2$$
$$\qquad\qquad\qquad y = \pm 4$$

When $x = 3$, $y = \pm 4$. The ordered pairs are $(3, 4)$ and $(3, -4)$. Now let $x = -3$.

$$(-3)^2 + y^2 = 25$$
$$9 + y^2 = 25$$
$$y^2 = 16$$
$$y = \pm 4$$

$$3(-3)^2 - y^2 = 11$$
$$3(9) - y^2 = 11$$
$$27 - y^2 = 11$$
$$16 = y^2$$
$$y = \pm 4$$

When $x = -3$, $y = \pm 4$. The ordered pairs are $(-3, 4)$ and $(-3, -4)$. The solutions to this system are $(3, 4)$, $(3, -4)$ and $(-3, -4)$. How many points of intersection can we expect in a system of equations? With polynomial equations in x and y, we can expect at most the product of the degrees of x and y (assuming they have no common factors). In our system,

$$x^2 + y^2 = 25$$
$$3x^2 - y^2 = 11$$

the degree of the first equation is 2 and the degree of the second equation is 2. The product of the degrees is 4. We can expect 4 or fewer points of intersections.

Sometimes it is necessary to use both linear combinations and substitution to solve a system of equations.

EXAMPLE 7.16

$$x^2 - 2xy + y^2 = 25$$
$$x^2 - 3xy + y^2 - 31$$

SOLUTION 7.16

$$x^2 - 2xy + y^2 = 25$$
$$x^2 - 3xy + y^2 = 31$$

This system would be extremely difficult to solve by substitution. Both equations are quadratic in x and y. To solve this system of equations, eliminate the x^2 term or the y^2 terms. Multiply the second equation by -1 and add the two equations.

$$x^2 - 2xy + y^2 = 25$$
$$-1(x^2 - 3xy + y^2 = 31)$$

Simplify.

$$x^2 - 2xy + y^2 = 25$$
$$-1x^2 + 3xy - y^2 = -31$$

Add the two equations.

$$xy = -6$$

This new equation is first degree in both x and y. Solve the new equation for y.

$$y = -\frac{6}{x}$$

Now substitute $y = -\frac{6}{x}$ into either of the original equations for y.

$$x^2 - 2xy + y^2 = 25$$
$$x^2 - 3xy + y^2 = 31$$

$$x^2 - 2x\left(-\frac{6}{x}\right) + \left(-\frac{6}{x}\right)^2 = 25 \qquad \text{Simplify.}$$

$$x^2 + 12 + \frac{36}{x^2} = 25 \qquad \text{Multiply both sides by } x^2.$$

$$x^4 + 12x^2 + 36 = 25x^2 \qquad \text{Put into standard form.}$$

$$x^4 + 12x^2 + 36 - 25x^2 = 0$$

$$x^4 - 13x^2 + 36 = 0 \qquad \text{Factor.}$$

$$(x^2 - 9)(x^2 - 4) = 0$$

$$(x + 3)(x - 3)(x + 2)(x - 2) = 0 \qquad \text{Solve.}$$

$$x = -3, -2, 2, \text{ and } 3.$$

These are the values of the points of intersection for x. We now need to solve for y. To solve for y, we want to substitute the values of x into the simplest equation involving both x and y and solve for y. The available equations are:

$$x^2 - 2xy + y^2 = 25$$

$$x^2 - 3xy + y^2 = 31$$

$$y = -\frac{6}{x}.$$

The simplest equation is $y = -\dfrac{6}{x}$.

If $x = -3$, then $y = -\dfrac{6}{(-3)} = 2$. The ordered pair is $(-3, 2)$.

If $x = -2$, then $y = -\dfrac{6}{(-2)} = 3$. The ordered pair is $(-2, 3)$.

If $x = 2$, then $y = -\dfrac{6}{(2)} = -3$. The ordered pair is $(2, -3)$.

If $x = 3$, then $y = -\dfrac{6}{(3)} = -2$. The ordered pair is $(3, -2)$.

The solutions to this system of equations are $(-3, 2)$, $(-2, 3)$, $(2, -3)$ and $(3, -2)$.

EXERCISE 7.2

Solve the following systems of equations:

1. $x^2 + y^2 = 13$

    $x - y = -1$

2. $x^2 - 2xy + y^2 = 16$

    $2x + y = 1$

3. $x^2 + y^2 = 25$

    $x^2 - y^2 = -7$

4. $x^2 + 2xy + y^2 = 4$
    $2x^2 - 3xy + 2y^2 = 64$
5. $x^2 - 2xy + y^2 = 4$
    $x^2 - 4xy + y^2 = -26$

ANSWERS TO EXERCISE 7.2

1. $\{(2, 3), (-3, -2)\}$

2. $\{\,(\frac{5}{3}, -\frac{7}{3}),\ (-1, 3)\,\}$

3. $\{(3, 4), (3, -4), (-3, 4), (-3, -4)\}$
4. $\{(2, -4), (-2, 4), (4, -2), (-4, 2)\}$
5. $\{(3, 5), (-3, -5), (5, 3), (-5, -3)\}$

SECTION 7.5 SYSTEMS OF LINEAR INEQUALITIES

Linear Inequalities   To solve a system of linear inequalities, we must first learn to solve an inequality in two variables.   Since there are infinitely many solutions to a linear inequality, we cannot list the solution set. The solution set must be found graphically.

EXAMPLE 7.17

Solve the following linear inequalities graphically:
a) $2x - y \geq 1$
b) $2x + 3y < 6$

SOLUTION 7.17

a) $2x - y \geq 1$
To solve a linear inequality, we need to change the inequality to an equality and graph the linear equation.

$2x - y = 1$ Put the equation into slope-intercept form.

$2x - 1 = y$ or

$y = \frac{2}{1}x - 1$ Plot points.

This linear equation has a slope of $m = \frac{2}{1}$ and a y-intercept of $b = -1$.

Graph the equation on the Cartesian plane. We first graph the equation in order to solve the inequality. The equation is graphed as a solid line if the inequality is ≤ or ≥. The equation is graphed as a broken line if the inequality is < or >. The original inequality is $2x - y \geq 1$, so this line is graphed as a solid line.

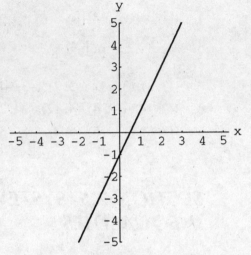

Figure 7.3

This line divides the Cartesian plane into two half-planes. One of the half-planes is $2x - y < 1$ and the other is $2x - y > 1$. Check an ordered pair in one of the two half-planes to determine if the ordered pair makes $2x - y < 1$ or $2x - y > 1$. The origin $(0, 0)$ is a good point to choose for this graph.
$$2x - y = 2(0) - (0) = 0 \text{ and } 0 < 1.$$
Since we are looking for ordered pairs where $2x - y \geq 1$, the origin is not part of our solutions set. Thus, we want the points on the side opposite of the point $(0, 0)$. Shade the half-plane on the opposite side of the origin.

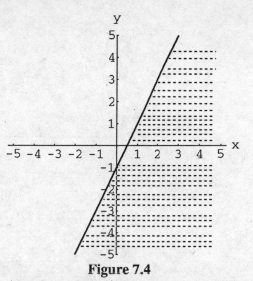

Figure 7.4

The line $2x - y = 1$ is a **boundary line** between the points which make the inequality true and those which make the inequality false. When the line is a solid line, it implies the boundary is included in the solutions set. When the line is a broken line, the boundary is not included in the solutions set.

b) $2x + 3y < 6$

Graph the linear equation $2x + 3y = 6$.

$2x + 3y = 6$	Put the equation into slope-intercept form. Add $-2x$ to both sides.
$3y = -2x + 6$	Divide both sides by 3.
$y = -\dfrac{2}{3}x + 2$	

This linear equation has a slope of $m = -\dfrac{2}{3}$ and y-intercept of $b = 2$. Graph the equation on the Cartesian plane. Graph this line as a broken line since the inequality is $<$.

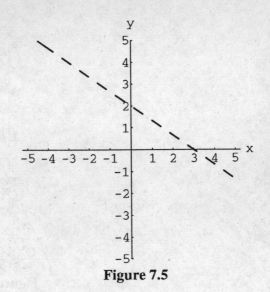

Figure 7.5

The line has divided the Cartesian plane into two half-planes. Check any point in one of the two half-plane and see if the ordered pair makes $2x + 3y < 6$. The origin $(0, 0)$ is again a good point to try.

$$2x + 3y = 2(0) + 3(0) = 0 \text{ and } 0 < 6.$$

This inequality is a true statement, so shade all points of the half-plane that are on the same side of the line as the origin.

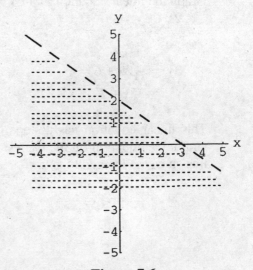

Figure 7.6

Since the line is a broken line, only those points on the shaded side of the

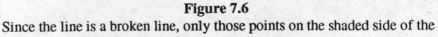

line are in the solution set.

Solving Linear Inequalities:
1. Change the inequality to an equality and graph the boundary line.
2. Choose any point on either side of the boundary line.
3. If that point makes the inequality true, shade that half of the Cartesian Plane. If that point does not make the inequality true, then shade the other half of the plane.

Systems of Linear Inequalities

To solve a system of linear inequalities, use the techniques of graphing linear inequalities.

EXAMPLE 7.18

Solve the following system of linear inequalities by graphing:
$$2x + y \leq 3$$
$$x - y \geq 0$$

SOLUTION 7.18

$$2x + y \leq 3$$
$$x - y \geq 0$$

To solve a system of inequalities, we graph both inequalities independently on the same Cartesian plane. Change both inequalities to equations.

$$2x + y = 3 \quad \text{and} \quad x - y = 0 \qquad \text{Put into slope-intercept form.}$$

$$y = -2x + 3 \quad \text{and} \quad y = 1x + 0 \qquad \text{Graph the first line.}$$

Check the origin into the original inequality and shade the proper half-plane.

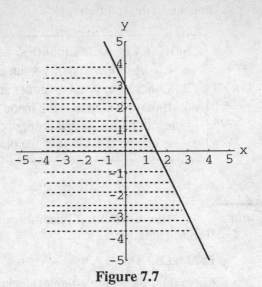

Figure 7.7

Now graph the second line on the same Cartesian Plane. While graphing the second line, ignore the fact that the first line has already been graphed. Treat the Cartesian plane as if it were completely blank.

Choose a point on either side of the line $y = x$. The origin $(0, 0)$ cannot be used to test the half-planes because $(0, 0)$ is a point of the line $y = x$. Use the point $(1, 0)$. This time, shade the side of the line that makes the second inequality true. Again, think of the Cartesian plane as completely blank except for the two sides of the second line.

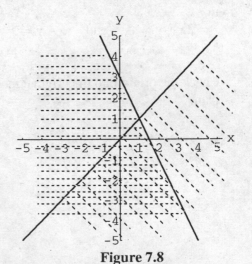

Figure 7.8

The solution set for the system of inequalities is the intersection of the two shaded regions. In our graph, it is the double-shaded region. Now reconstruct the graph with only the solution set shaded.

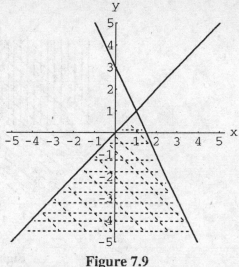

Figure 7.9

Systems of inequalities, like systems of equations, can have more than two inequalities.

EXAMPLE 7.19

Solve the following system of linear inequalities by graphing:
$x + y \leq 3$
$x \geq 0$ and $y \geq 0$

SOLUTION 7.19

$x + y \leq 3$
$x \geq 0$ and $y \geq 0$
To solve a system of inequalities, we graph all of the inequalities independently on the same Cartesian plane. Change all inequalities to equations.

$$x + y = 3, \qquad x = 0 \qquad \text{and} \qquad y = 0$$

Graph the first line and shade the side of the half-plane that makes the inequality true.

Graph the second line on the same Cartesian Plane and shade the side of the half-plane that makes that inequality true. The second line is $x = 0$. Remember from Chapter 4 that linear equations in only one variable graph a straight line running parallel to the opposite axis. The equation $x = 0$ is the y-axis. Since $x \geq 0$, we need to shade the points on the right-hand side of the y-axis.

Now graph the third line $y = 0$. Again, this is a line running parallel to the x-axis and in fact is the x-axis. We want those values of $y \geq 0$ or above the *y*-axis. Shade the region above the *y*-axis.

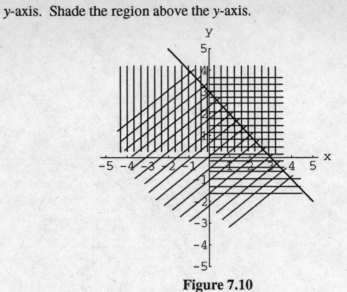

Figure 7.10

The solution set for the system of inequalities is the intersection of the three shaded regions. Here is a graph of the solution set.

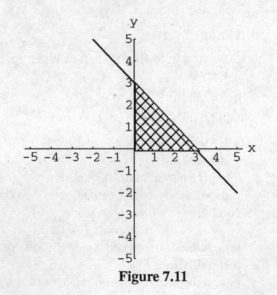

Figure 7.11

EXERCISE 7.3

Solve the following systems of inequalities by graphing:
1. $x + y \geq 4$
    $x - y \leq 2$
2. $x + y > 1$
    $x < 2$ and $y \leq 3$

3. $x > 3$ and $x < 8$
    $y \geq -2$ and $y \leq 5$
    $x - y > 2$

ANSWERS TO EXERCISE 7.3

1.

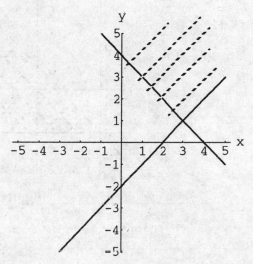

Figure 7.12

2.

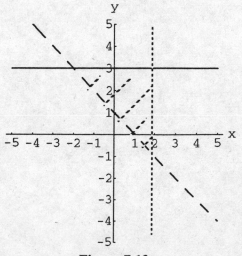

Figure 7.13

3.

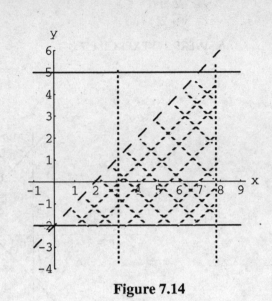

Figure 7.14

8

Sequences and Series

SECTION 8.1 SEQUENCES AND SERIES

Sequences

In Chapter 4, we studied functions and functional notation. A function is an equation in the form of

$$y = f(x)$$

such that for each x in the domain of the function there is one and only one value for y in the range of the function. Some examples of functions are:

$y = 1$ Constant function.
$y = 3x - 2$ Linear function.
$y = x^2$ Quadratic function.

In each of these functions, the domain of the function is the set of all real numbers. A **sequence** is a function where the domain of the function is the set of integers. Since the domain of a sequence is the set of integers, we use the letter n for the independent variable. That is,

$$f(n) = 3n - 2.$$

The domain of a sequence is the set of integers, but often we restrict the domain to the set of natural numbers. With restricted domains the notation can be written

$f(n) = 3n - 2$ where $n = 1, 2, 3, \ldots$
$f(1) = 1$
$f(2) = 4$
$f(3) = 7$
etc.

The sequence of numbers becomes

    $1, 4, 7, \ldots$

Functional notation still does not lend itself to the format of sequences. To better work with sequences, a special sequence notation is used.

$$a_n = 3n - 2$$

In sequence notation, the number n is understood to be a natural number and the expression a_n is the individual term of the sequence. a_1 is the first term of the sequence, a_2 represents the second term of the sequence and a_5 represents the fifth term of the sequence. a_n is called the **nth term**, or **general term** of the sequence. a_n is also the generator of the sequence. Suppose $a_n = 3n - 2$ is the general term of a sequence. The ninth term of the sequence is found by taking $a_n = 3n - 2$ and letting $n = 9$.

$$a_9 = 3(9) - 2 = 27 - 2 = 25$$
$$a_9 = 25$$

In the notation $a_n = 3n - 9$, n represents the number of the term (1st, 2nd, 3rd, etc.) and a_n is the value of the term. If we continue with our terms, we get

$$a_1 = 3(1) - 2 = 1$$
$$a_2 = 3(2) - 2 = 4$$
$$a_3 = 3(3) - 2 = 7$$
$$a_4 = 3(4) - 2 = 10$$
$$a_5 = 3(5) - 2 = 13$$
$$a_6 = 3(6) - 2 = 16$$

etc.

The terms of a sequence can be written in a sequential form as

$$a_1, a_2, a_3, a_4, ..., a_n, ...$$

or $$1, 4, 7, 10, 13, ..., 3n - 2, ...$$

If the domain of a sequence is a finite set of integers, the sequence is called a **finite sequence**. If the domain is an infinite set of integers, the sequence is called an **infinite sequence**. Some sequences have generators which are **algebraic formulas**. The algebraic formula for the above sequence is the general term of the sequence $a_n = 3n - 2$. Some sequences, however, are generated by a **recursive formula**. A recursive formula is a formula that generates the nth term by operating on the terms which precede it. A recursive formula for the above sequence is $a_n = a_{n-1} + 3$. That is, the sequence $1, 4, 7, 10, 13, ..., 3n - 2, ...$ can be found by starting at

$a_1 = 1$ and adding three to each sequential term in the sequence

$$a_2 = a_1 + 3 = (1) + 3 = 4$$
$$a_3 = a_2 + 3 = (4) + 3 = 7$$
$$a_4 = a_1 + 3 = (7) + 3 = 10$$

Recursive formulas rely on knowing a_8 to find a_9 and knowing a_{n-1} to find a_n.

EXAMPLE 8.1

List the first 5 terms of the following sequences:

a) $a_n = 5n + 1$

b) $a_n = n^2$

c) $a_n = 2 \cdot a_{n-1}$ where $a_1 = 1$

SOLUTION 8.1

a) $a_n = 5n + 1$

This sequence is generated by an algebraic formula. Let $n = 1, 2, 3, 4$, and 5 to find the first 5 terms of the sequence.

$$a_1 = 5(1) + 1 = 6$$
$$a_2 = 5(2) + 1 = 11$$
$$a_3 = 5(3) + 1 = 16$$
$$a_4 = 5(4) + 1 = 21$$
$$a_5 = 5(5) + 1 = 26$$

The sequence of numbers becomes 6, 11, 16, 21, and 26.

b) $a_n = n^2$

Let $n = 1, 2, 3, 4$, and 5 to find the first 5 terms of the sequence.

$$a_1 = (1)^2 = 1$$
$$a_2 = (2)^2 = 4$$
$$a_3 = (3)^2 = 9$$
$$a_4 = (4)^2 = 16$$
$$a_5 = (5)^2 = 5$$

The sequence of numbers becomes 1, 4, 9, 16, and 25.

c) $a_n = 2 \cdot a_{n-1}$ where $a_1 = 1$

This is a recursive formula. To find any term in the sequence, we must know the preceding term. Since we know $a_1 = 1$, we can find the first 5 terms.

$$a_1 = 1$$
$$a_2 = 2 \cdot a_1 = 2(1) = 2$$
$$a_3 = 2 \cdot a_2 = 2(2) = 4$$
$$a_4 = 2 \cdot a_3 = 2(4) = 8$$
$$a_5 = 2 \cdot a_4 = 2(8) = 16$$

The sequence of numbers becomes 1, 2, 4, 8, and 16.

Series

The summation of the terms of a sequence is called a **series**. If the sequence is finite, then the corresponding series is a **finite series**, and if the sequence is infinite, then the corresponding series is an **infinite series**.

Finite Sequence; 1, 3, 5, 7, 9   Finite Series: $1 + 3 + 5 + 7 + 9$

Infinite Sequence; 1, 4, 9, 16, ...   Finite Series: $1 + 4 + 9 + 16 + ...$

Series are often written in what is known as **sigma notation** or **summation notation**. Sigma notation uses the Greek letter sigma (Σ) to indicate a sum.

$$\sum_{k=1}^{4} a_k = a_1 + a_2 + a_3 + a_4.$$

$$\sum_{k=1}^{5} b_k = b_1 + b_2 + b_3 + b_4 + b_5.$$

If $a_k = 2k - 1$, then

$$\sum_{k=1}^{4} a_k = a_1 + a_2 + a_3 + a_4 = \sum_{k=1}^{4} (2k-1) = 1 + 3 + 5 + 7.$$

If $b_k = k^2 - 1$, then

$$\sum_{k=1}^{5} b_k = \sum_{k=1}^{5} (k^2 - 1) = 0 + 3 + 8 + 15 + 24.$$

Some sigma notations may contain so many terms that we do not wish to list them all.

$$\sum_{k=1}^{100} a_k = a_1 + a_2 + a_3 + ... + a_{99} + a_{100}.$$

If $a_k = 2k - 1$, then

$$\sum_{k=1}^{100} a_k = \sum_{k=1}^{100} (2k-1) = 1 + 3 + 5 + ... + 197 + 199.$$

In sigma notation, the series does not have to begin at $k = 1$.

$$\sum_{k=3}^{6} a_k = a_3 + a_4 + a_5 + a_6$$

$$\sum_{k=8}^{12} b_k = b_8 + b_9 + b_{10} + b_{11} + b_{12}$$

If $a_k = 2k - 1$, then

$$\sum_{k=3}^{6} a_k = \sum_{k=3}^{6} (2k - 1) = 5 + 7 + 9 + 11$$

If $b_k = k^2 - 1$, then

$$\sum_{k=8}^{12} b_k = \sum_{k=8}^{12} k^2 - 1 = 63 + 80 + 99 + 120 + 143.$$

k does not have to be positive.

$$\sum_{k=-1}^{2} a_k = a_{-1} + a_0 + a_1 + a_2.$$

$$\sum_{k=0}^{4} b_k = b_0 + b_1 + b_2 + b_3 + b_4.$$

We normally like to begin at $k = 1$. With $k = 1$, the first term of the series is found by putting 1 into the generator of the series. In sigma notation

$$\sum_{k=1}^{4} a_k$$

k is called the **summing index** or the **index**. We begin at k equal to the number below the Σ sign and end with k equal to the number at the top of the Σ sign. ,

$$\sum_{k=1}^{5} (3k + 1) = [3(1) + 1] + [3(2) + 1] + [3(3) + 1] + [3(4) + 1] + [3(5) + 1]$$

$$= 4 + 7 + 10 + 13 + 16.$$

The expression

$$\sum_{k=1}^{10} k$$

is called **sigma notation** and the series

$$1 + 2 + 3 + \ldots + 9 + 10$$

is called the **expanded form**. A series is the summation of a sequence.

EXAMPLE 8.2

Put the following sigma notation into expanded form:

a) $\displaystyle\sum_{k=1}^{5} (3k+5)$

b) $\displaystyle\sum_{k=0}^{4} (k^2+3)$

c) $\displaystyle\sum_{k=1}^{10} \left(\frac{k}{k+1}\right)$

d) $\displaystyle\sum_{k=1}^{100} (5k+1)$

SOLUTION 8.2

a) $\displaystyle\sum_{k=1}^{5} (3k+5)$

Substitute $k = 1, 2, 3, 4, 5$ and write the corresponding values as a sum. Do not add the terms together.

$$\sum_{k=1}^{5} (3k+5) = [3(1)+5] + [3(2)+5] + [3(3)+5] + [3(4)+5] + [3(5)+5]$$

$$= 8 + 11 + 14 + 17 + 20$$

b) $\displaystyle\sum_{k=0}^{4} (k^2+3)$

$$\sum_{k=0}^{4} (k^2+3) = [(0)^2+3] + [(1)^2+3] + [(2)^2+3] + [(3)^2+3] + [(4)^2+3]$$

$$= 3 + 4 + 7 + 12 + 19$$

c) $\displaystyle\sum_{k=1}^{10} (\frac{k}{k+1}) = \frac{1}{2} + \frac{2}{3} + \frac{3}{4} + \frac{4}{5} + \frac{5}{6} + ... + \frac{10}{11}$

d) $\displaystyle\sum_{k=1}^{100} (5k+1) = 6 + 11 + 16 + ... + 496 + 501$

Sometimes we may only want part of the summation of a series. The summation of only part of a series is called a **partial sum**. Partial sums are denoted using the letter s with a subscript (s_n). Find the first five partial sums for the series

$$\sum_{k=1}^{10} k = 1 + 2 + 3 + ... + 9 + 10$$

$s_1 = 1$

$s_2 = 1 + 2 = 3$

$s_3 = 1 + 2 + 3 = 6$

$s_4 = 1 + 2 + 3 + 4 = 10$

$s_5 = 1 + 2 + 3 + 4 + 5 = 15$

EXAMPLE 8.3

Find the first four partial sums for the following series:

a) $\displaystyle\sum_{k=1}^{5} (3k+5)$

b) $\displaystyle\sum_{k=1}^{100} (5k+1)$

SOLUTION 8.3

a) $\displaystyle\sum_{k=1}^{5} (3k+5)$

To find a partial sum, you must first expand the series. We did this in the last example. Now we can add the individual terms of the series.

$$8 + 11 + 14 + 17 + 20$$

$s_1 = 8$

$s_2 = 8 + 11 = 19$

$s_3 = 8 + 11 + 14 = 33$

$s_4 = 8 + 11 + 14 + 17 = 50$

b) $\displaystyle\sum_{k=1}^{100} (5k+1) = 6 + 11 + 16 + \ldots + 496 + 501$

$$s_1 = 6$$
$$s_2 = 6 + 11 = 17$$
$$s_3 = 6 + 11 + 16 = 33$$
$$s_4 = 6 + 11 + 16 + 21 = 54$$

EXAMPLE 8.4

Put the following series into sigma notation:
a) $1 + 2 + 3 + 4 + 5 + 6 + 7 + 8 + 9 + 10$
b) $2 + 4 + 6 + \ldots + 50$
c) $1 + 4 + 9 + 16 + \ldots + 144$

SOLUTION 8.4

a) $1 + 2 + 3 + 4 + 5 + 6 + 7 + 8 + 9 + 10$
The generator in this expansion is k. k varies from 1 to 10. The sigma notation is
$$\sum_{k=1}^{10} k$$

b) $2 + 4 + 6 + \ldots + 50$
The generator is $2k$. When $k = 1$ the first term is 2. The last term 50 is obtained when $k = 25$. The sigma notation is
$$\sum_{k=1}^{25} 2k$$

c) $1 + 4 + 9 + 16 + \ldots + 144$
The individual terms are the values of k^2. When $k = 1$ we get 1 and when $k = 12$ we get 144. In sigma notation the series $1 + 4 + 9 + 16 + \ldots + 144$ is
$$\sum_{k=1}^{12} k^2$$

EXERCISE 8.1

List the first five terms of the following sequences:

1. $a_n = 3n + 4$
2. $a_n = n^2 + 3$
3. $a_n = (-1)^n (2n)$

List the next four terms of each of the following:

4. $3, 7, 11, 15, \ldots$
5. $\dfrac{1}{2}, \dfrac{1}{4}, \dfrac{1}{8}, \dfrac{1}{16}, \ldots$

Expand the following sigma notation:

6. $\displaystyle\sum_{k=1}^{5} 2k + 3$

7. $\displaystyle\sum_{k=1}^{6} (-1)^k (k+1)(k+2)$

8. $\displaystyle\sum_{k=1}^{n} 5k(k+1)$

Put the following into sigma notation.

9. $1 + 4 + 9 + 16 + \ldots + 196$

10. $\dfrac{1}{2} - \dfrac{1}{4} + \dfrac{1}{6} - \dfrac{1}{8} + \ldots + \dfrac{1}{98} - \dfrac{1}{100}$

ANSWERS TO EXERCISE 8.1

1. 7, 10, 13, 16, 19   2. 4, 7, 12, 19, 28

3. –2, 4, –6, 8, –10   4. 19, 23, 27, 31

5. $\dfrac{1}{32}, \dfrac{1}{64}, \dfrac{1}{128}, \dfrac{1}{256}$ 6. $5 + 7 + 9 + 11 + 13$

7. $-6 + 12 - 20 + 30 - 42 + 56$

8. $5 \cdot 2 + 10 \cdot 3 + 15 \cdot 4 + 20 \cdot 5 + \ldots + 2n \cdot (n+1) =$
   $= 10 + 30 + 60 + 100 + \ldots + 2n \cdot (n+1)$

9. $\displaystyle\sum_{k=1}^{14} k^2$ 10. $\displaystyle\sum_{k=1}^{50} \dfrac{(-1)^{k-1}}{2k}$

SECTION 8.2 MATHEMATICAL INDUCTION

Axioms, **postulates**, and **properties** are mathematical statements that are accepted without proof. A **theorem** however, is a statement which reaches a general conclusion proposed to be true based on a certain given hypothesis (assumption). A theorem must be proved to be true to have any validity. A mathematical **proof** is a logical argument which establishes the truth of a statement. Theorems can be proven in several different ways. There is proof by;

1. a **direct** approach,
2. an **indirect** approach, and
3. **induction**.

Proof by a **direct** approach uses an argument and makes direct use of axioms, postulates, properties and other theorems to reach the given conclusion. Proof by an **indirect** approach assumes that the theorem which is being proved is false. Then by the use of axioms, postulates, properties, other theorems and the use of a direct approach, reaches a proof by contradiction. Both the direct approach and the indirect approach to mathematical proofs require what is called **deductive reasoning**. The deductive reasoning method or theory is a formal structure of proof based on a set of axioms and postulates.

Inductive reasoning, however, is a different way of proving that a theorem is true. The **principle of mathematical induction** is often denoted using the letters **PMI**. To do a proof by PMI, we need the following axiom:

Axiom of Induction:
Given N is the set of natural numbers and S a subset of N. If
1. 1 is an element of S and
2. if k is an element of S implies $(k + 1)$ is an element of S, then
3. S is equal to N.

The principle of mathematical induction uses the axiom of induction in the following way.

Fundamental Principle of Mathematical Induction (PMI)
Let $T(n)$ be a theorem associated with the positive integer n;
If 1. $T(1)$ is true, and
2. if when $T(k)$ is true implies that $T(k + 1)$ is true, then
3. $T(n)$ is true for all positive integers n.

EXAMPLE 8.5

Show that the following statement is true for $n = 1, 2,$ and 3.
$$2 + 4 + 6 + \ldots + 2n = n(n + 1)$$

SOLUTION 8.5

$$2 + 4 + 6 + \ldots + 2n = n(n + 1)$$
Let $n = 1$, then
$$2 \overset{?}{=} 1(1 + 1)$$
$$2 \overset{?}{=} 1(2)$$

$2 = 2.$
Let $n = 2$, then
$$2 + 4 \stackrel{?}{=} 2(2 + 1)$$
$$6 \stackrel{?}{=} 2(3)$$
$$6 = 6.$$
Let $n = 3$, then
$$2 + 4 + 6 \stackrel{?}{=} 3(3 + 1)$$
$$12 \stackrel{?}{=} 3(4)$$
$$12 = 12.$$

This is not a proof by induction. All we have done is show that the statement is true for $n = 1, 2,$ and 3. It would be impossible to show that the statement is true for all natural numbers by substitution. To prove that this statement is true for all numbers requires a proof by induction.

To prove a theorem by induction, use the following steps:

Steps of Proof by Mathematical Induction:
1. Prove true for $n = 1$.
2. Assume true for $n = k$. There is nothing to do in this step except to write down the original statement with n replaced by k. This is one of the most important steps in the proof. This step must be written so that we can use this step to prove Step Three.
3. Use the assumption in Step Two to prove that the statement is true for $n = k + 1$.
4. Conclude that the statement is true for all natural numbers n.

Be certain to write down each and every step when doing a proof by induction.

EXAMPLE 8.6

Prove by PMI that the following statement is true for all $n \in N$:
$$2 + 4 + 6 + \ldots + 2n = n(n + 1)$$

SOLUTION 8.6

$$2 + 4 + 6 + \ldots + 2n = n(n + 1)$$
Step 1: Prove true for $n = 1$.
$$2 \stackrel{?}{=} 1(1 + 1)$$
$$2 \stackrel{?}{=} 1(2)$$
$$2 = 2$$
The statement is true for $n = 1$.
Step 2: Assume true for $n = k$.

There is no work in this step except to replace all of the variable n in the original statement with the variable k.

$$2 + 4 + \ldots + 2k = k(k + 1)$$

This is a very important step and often overlooked. We use this step to prove step 3.

Step 3: Prove that the statement is true for $n = k + 1$, using step 2. First write down the statement to be proved.

$$2 + 4 + 6 + \ldots + 2n = n(n + 1)$$

Let $n = (k + 1)$ and substitute $(k + 1)$ into the statement.

$$2 + 4 + 6 + \ldots + 2(k + 1) \overset{?}{=} (k + 1)((k + 1) + 1)$$

Simplify.

$$2 + 4 + 6 + \ldots + 2(k + 1) \overset{?}{=} (k + 1)(k + 2)$$

Remember that this statement has not been proven. When we use the $\overset{?}{=}$ between two statements, we are trying to show that we have not yet proven the statement. The statement $2 + 4 + 6 + \ldots + 2n$ is in expanded form. n can be any positive integer. Think of

$$2 + 4 + 6 + \ldots + 2(k + 1) = 2 + 4 + 6 + \ldots + 2k + 2(k + 1).$$

Rewriting the expression, we get

$$2 + 4 + 6 + \ldots + 2k + 2(k + 1) \overset{?}{=} (k = 1)(k + 2).$$

The term just before $n = (k + 1)$ is $n = k$. In the expression

$$2 + 4 + 6 + \ldots + 2k + 2(k + 1) \overset{?}{=} (k + 1)(k + 2),$$

the sum of the first k terms is equal to $k(k + 1)$ from step 2. Replace

$$2 + 4 + 6 + \ldots + 2k$$

with

$$k(k + 1).$$

$$\underbrace{2 + 4 + 6 + \ldots + 2k}_{k(k + 1)} + 2(k + 1) \overset{?}{=} (k + 1)(k + 2)$$

With replacement, we get

$$k(k + 1) + 2(k + 1) \overset{?}{=} (k + 1)(k + 2).$$

When we factor the left-hand side, the expressions become equal.

$$(k + 1)(k + 2) = (k + 1)(k + 2)$$

When the two expressions are equal, the proof has been completed except for the conclusion. By PMI, the statement was true for $n = 1$. When true for $n = k$, the statement was true for $n = k + 1$. By PMI, the statement is true for all $n \in N$.

$$2 + 4 + 6 + \ldots + 2n = n(n + 1) \text{ for all } n \in N.$$

Step 4: Proof by induction lends itself nicely to sequences and series. PMI can also be used on other types of proofs. Here are some examples from number theory.

EXAMPLE 8.7

Prove the following by PMI: $2^n > n$

SOLUTION 8.7

$2^n > n$

Step 1: Prove true for $n = 1$.

$$2^1 > 1$$
$$2 > 1$$

The statement is true for $n = 1$.

Step 2: Assume true for $n = k$.

Replace the variable n with the variable k.

$$2^k > k$$

Step 3: Prove that the statement is true for $n = k + 1$, using step 2. Write the original statement.

$$2^n > n$$

Replace n with $(k + 1)$.

$$2^{(k+1)} \overset{?}{>} (k+1)$$

Simplify this inequality.

$$2^{(k+1)} = 2^k \cdot 2 \overset{?}{>} (k+1)$$

We know from step two that $2^k > k$. We also know that $k \geq 1$ from the principle of induction. Begin with the fact that

$2^k > k$	Multiply both sides of the inequality by 2.
$2 \cdot 2^k > 2 \cdot k$	$2k$ is equal to $k + k$.
$2 \cdot 2^k > k + k$	$2 \cdot 2^k = 2^{k+1}$
$2^{k+1} > k + k$	

We know that $k \geq k$ and $k \geq 1$, since k is a natural number. By the addition property of inequality, the sum of two larger numbers is bigger than the sum of two smaller numbers. So $k + k \geq k + 1$. By the transitive property of inequality

$$2^{k+1} > k + k \text{ and } k + k \geq k + 1 \text{ implies that}$$
$$2^{k+1} > k + 1.$$

By PMI

Step 4: $2^n > n$ for all $n \in N$.

EXERCISE 8.2

Prove by PMI that the following are true:

1. $1 + 2 + 3 + \ldots + n = \dfrac{n(n+1)}{2}$

2. $4 + 8 + 12 + \ldots + 4n = 2n(n+1)$

3. $3 + 7 + 11 + \ldots + (4n - 1) = n(2n + 1)$

4. $1 + 3 + 5 + \ldots + (2n - 1) = n^2$

5. $\dfrac{1}{2} + \dfrac{1}{2^2} + \dfrac{1}{2^3} + \ldots + \dfrac{1}{2^n} = 1 - \dfrac{1}{2^n}$

6. 3 is a factor of $4^n - 1$

7. 2 is a factor of $n^2 + 5n$

Solutions are left to the student.

SECTION 8.3 ARITHMETIC SEQUENCES AND SERIES

Arithmetic Sequences

In Section 8.1 we discussed sequences and series. A special type of sequence is called an arithmetic sequence. Here is an arithmetic sequence.

$$1, 2, 3, 4, \ldots, 100$$

An arithmetic sequence is a sequence where the difference between any two consecutive terms is always the same. This difference is called the **common difference** and is denoted by d. In the sequence

$1, 2, 3, 4, \ldots, 100$

$a_1 = 1$

$a_2 = 2$

$a_3 = 3$

$a_4 = 4$

$a_{100} = 100.$

Notice that

$a_2 - a_1 = 1$

$a_3 - a_2 = 1$

$a_4 - a_3 = 1$

and

$a_n - a_{n-1} = 1.$

Any sequence of terms where the difference between any two terms is a constant d is called an **arithmetic sequence** of numbers.

> **Arithmetic Sequence**
> A sequence
> $$a_1, a_2, a_3, a_4, ..., a_n, ...$$
> is called an **arithmetic sequence** (or **arithmetic progression**) if for all $n > 1$,
> $$a_n - a_{n-1} = d$$
> where d is the **common difference**.

EXAMPLE 8.8

Which of the following are arithmetic sequences?
a) $3, 6, 9, 12, ...$
b) $1, 2, 4, 7, 11, ...$

SOLUTION 8.8

a) $3, 6, 9, 12, ...$
    To determine if the sequence is an arithmetic sequence, subtract two consecutive terms several times. If the difference between any two consecutive terms is always the same value, then the sequence is an arithmetic sequence.
    $$6 - 3 = 3$$
    $$9 - 6 = 3$$
    $$12 - 9 = 3$$
    The sequence is arithmetic.

b) $1, 2, 4, 7, 11, ...$
    Subtract consecutive terms.
    $$2 - 1 = 1$$
    $$4 - 2 = 2$$

The difference between the second and the first terms is not the same as the difference between the third and the second terms. The sequence is not arithmetic.

Arithmetic sequences have a recursive relationship between their terms. Since $a_n - a_{n-1} = d$, then
$$a_n = a_{n-1} + d.$$
From this recursive relationship we can develop formulas about arithmetic sequences.

$a_1 = a_1$

$a_2 = a_1 + d$

$a_3 = a_2 + d = (a_1 + d) + d = a_1 + 2d$ Replace a_2 with $a_1 + d$.

$a_4 = a_3 + d = (a_1 + 2d) + d = a_1 + 3d$ Replace a_3 with $a_1 + 2d$.

If we continue with the same process, we get

$$a_n = a_1 + (n-1) \cdot d \quad \text{for all } n > 1.$$

This gives a formula for the general term of an arithmetic sequence. The general term of an arithmetic sequence can be found if we know the first term and the common difference.

General Term of an Arithmetic Sequence

If a_1 is the first term of an arithmetic sequence and d is the common difference, then the nth term of the arithmetic sequence is

$$a_n = a_1 + (n-1) \cdot d \quad \text{for all } n > 1.$$

EXAMPLE 8.9

Find the nth term (general term a_n) and the 8th term for the following arithmetic sequences:
a)   3, 6, 9, 12, . . .
b)   100, 95, 90, 85, . . .

SOLUTION 8.9

a)   3, 6, 9, 12, . . .

We are given the fact that the sequence is arithmetic. To find the nth term, we need a_1 and d.

$$a_1 = 3 \text{ and } d = 6 - 3 = 3$$
$$a_n = a_1 + (n-1)d$$
$$a_n = 3 + (n-1)3 = 3 + 3n - 3 = 3n$$

The general term for all $n \geq 1$ is

$$a_n = 3n$$

Use the general term formula to find the eighth term.

$$a_8 = 3(8) = 24$$

The nth term is $a_n = 3n$ and the eighth term is $a_8 = 24$.

b)   100, 95, 90, 85, . . .

$$a_1 = 100 \text{ and } d = 95 - 100 = -5$$
$$a_n = a_1 + (n-1)d$$
$$a_n = 100 + (n-1)(-5) = 100 - 5n + 5$$
$$= 105 - 5n$$

The general term for all $n \geq 1$ is

$$a_n = 105 - 5n$$

Use the general term formula to find the eighth term.

$$a_8 = 105 - 5(8) = 105 - 40 = 65$$

The nth term is $a_n = 105 - 5n$ and the eighth term is $a_8 = 65$.

Finite Arithmetic Series

A series is the summation of the terms of a sequence. A finite arithmetic series is the summation of the terms of a finite arithmetic sequence. Let

$$A = a_1, a_2, a_3, a_4, ..., a_n$$

be a finite arithmetic sequence. Let

$$S_n = a_1 + a_2 + a_3 + a_4 + ... + a_n$$

be an arithmetic series. Replacing each a_n with the general formula for a_n we get,

$$S_n = a_1 + [a_1 + d] + [a_1 + 2d] + [a_1 + 3d] + ...$$

$$+ [a_1 + (n-2)d] + [a_1 + (n-1)d]$$

If we reverse the order, we get

$$S_n = [a_1 + (n-1)d] + [a_1 + (n-2)d] + [a_1 + (n-3)d] + ...$$

$$+ [a_1 + d] + a_1$$

Now add the two equations, in the order given. We get

$$2S_n = [a_1 + a_1 + (n-1)d] + [a_1 + d + a_1 + (n-2)d]$$

$$+ [a_1 + 2d + a_1 + (n-3)d] + ... + [a_1 + d + a_1 + (n-2)d]$$

$$+ [a_1 + a_1 + (n-1)d]$$

Simplify.

$$2S_n = [2a_1 + (n-1)d] + [2a_1 + (n-1)d] + ... + [2a_1 + (n-1)d]$$

If we count the number of $[2a_1 + (n-1)d]$ terms, there are n of them.

$$2S_n = n[2a_1 + (n-1)d] \qquad \text{Divide both sides by 2.}$$

$$S_n = \frac{n[2a_1 + (n-1)d]}{2} \quad \text{or} \quad S_n = \frac{n}{2}[2a_1 + (n-1)d]$$

If we use our identities, we get

$$S_n = \frac{n}{2}[2a_1 + (n-1)d] = \frac{n}{2}[a_1 + a_1 + (n-1)d]$$

$$= \frac{n}{2}(a_1 + [a_1 + (n-1)d]) = \frac{n}{2}(a_1 + a_n)$$

Summation Formulas for Finite Arithmetic Series:

1. $S_n = \dfrac{n}{2}[2a_1 + (n-1)d]$

2. $S_n = \dfrac{n}{2}(a_1 + a_n)$

The first formula is used to find the sum of a finite arithmetic series when you know the first term and the common difference. The second formula is used when you know the first term and the last term.

EXAMPLE 8.10

Find the indicated finite sums of the following arithmetic series:
a) Find the sum of the first 15 terms of $4 + 8 + 12 + \ldots$

b) Find the sum of the first 57 terms of $14 + 17 + 20 + \ldots$

c) Find the sum of the first 80 terms of $\dfrac{3}{4} + \dfrac{5}{4} + \dfrac{7}{4} + \ldots$

SOLUTION 8.10

a) Find the sum of the first 15 terms of $4 + 8 + 12 + \ldots$

In the arithmetic series, we know the first term and the number of terms to be added together. We need to use the first formula. To use the first formula, we need a_1, n (the number of terms) and the common difference d. We were not given the common difference, but we can find it.

$$d = 8 - 4 = 4$$

The summation formula is $S_n = \dfrac{n}{2}[2a_1 + (n-1)d]$. Substitute $a_1 = 4$, $n = 15$ and $d = 4$ into the formula.

$$S_{15} = \frac{15}{2}[2(4) + (15-1)\cdot 4]$$

$$= \frac{15}{2}[8 + (14)\cdot 4]$$

$$= \frac{15}{2}(8 + 56)$$

$$= \frac{15}{2}(64)$$

$$= 480$$

b) Find the sum of the first 57 terms of $14 + 17 + 20 + \ldots$

Find d.

$$d = 17 - 14 = 3$$

Substitute $a_1 = 14$, $n = 57$ and $d = 3$ into the summation formula.

$$S_{57} = \frac{57}{2} [2(14) + (57 - 1) \cdot 3]$$

$$= \frac{57}{2} [28 + (56) \cdot 3]$$

$$= \frac{57}{2} (28 + 168)$$

$$= \frac{57}{2} (196)$$

$$= 5586$$

c) Find the sum of the first 80 terms of $\frac{3}{4} + \frac{5}{4} + \frac{7}{4} + \ldots$

Find d.

$$d = \frac{5}{4} - \frac{3}{4} = \frac{1}{2}$$

Substitute $a_1 = \frac{3}{4}$, $n = 80$ and $d = \frac{1}{2}$ into the summation formula.

$$S_{80} = \frac{80}{2} \left[2 \left(\frac{3}{4} \right) + (80 - 1) \cdot \frac{1}{2} \right]$$

$$= 40 \left[\frac{3}{2} + (79) \cdot \frac{1}{2} \right]$$

$$= 40 \left(\frac{3}{2} + \frac{79}{2} \right)$$

$$= 40 \left(\frac{82}{2} \right)$$

$$= 40 (41)$$

$$= 1640$$

The following is a summary of the formulas needed to solve arithmetic sequences and series.

Arithmetic Sequences and Series:

An arithmetic sequence is a sequence in the form of

$A = a_1, a_2, a_3, \ldots, a_n, \ldots$ where

$d = a_n - a_{n-1}$ for all n.

The general term of an arithmetic sequence is

$a_n = a_1 + (n-1)\,d$ for all $n \geq 1$.

The finite sum

$S_n = a_1 + a_2 + a_3 + \ldots + a_n$ can be found using either formula.

$$S_n = \frac{n}{2}\left[2a_1 + (n-1)\,d\right] \text{ or}$$

$$S_n = \frac{n}{2}\left(a_1 + a_n\right)$$

EXERCISE 8.3

Which of the following are arithmetic sequences?

1. $2, 9, 16, 23, \ldots$

2. $1, 12, 23, 34, 45, \ldots$

Find the nth term (general term) and 12th term for the following arithmetic sequences:

3. $5, 18, 31, 44, \ldots$

4. $\dfrac{1}{4}, 1, \dfrac{7}{4}, \dfrac{5}{2}, \ldots$

Find the indicated finite sums:

5. Find the sum of the first 21 terms of $5 + 8 + 11 + \ldots$

6. Find the sum of the first 37 terms of $24 + 41 + 58 + \ldots$

Find the indicated finite sum for the following arithmetic series:

7. $10 + 13 + 16 + \ldots + 67$

8. $8 + 17 + 26 + \ldots + 386$

Find the required information about each of the following arithmetic sequences and series:

9. $a_5 = 32$ and $a_{12} = 81$, find a_1 and the common difference d.

10. $a_3 = 94$, $a_{15} = 322$, find a_1, the common difference d, and S_{273}.

ANSWERS TO EXERCISE 8.3

1. Yes

2. Yes

3. $a_n = 13n - 8$, $a_{12} = 148$

4. $a_n = \frac{3}{4}n - \frac{1}{2}$, $a_{12} = \frac{17}{2}$

5. 735

6. 12,210

7. 770

8. 8,471

9. $a_1 = 4$ and $d = 7$

10. $a_1 = 56$, $d = 19$ and $S_{237} = 544,626$.

SECTION 8.4 GEOMETRIC SEQUENCES AND SERIES

Geometric Sequences

In Section 8.3 we discussed arithmetic sequences and series. Arithmetic sequences and series have a common difference between individual terms. A **geometric sequence** (or **geometric progression**) has a common ratio between two consecutive terms. Here is a geometric sequence.

$$1, 2, 4, 8, 16, \ldots$$

A geometric sequence is one where the division of any two consecutive terms is always the same value. This ratio is called the **common ratio** and is denoted by the variable r. In the sequence

$$1, 2, 4, 8, 16, \ldots$$

$$a_1 = 1$$
$$a_2 = 2$$
$$a_3 = 4$$
$$a_4 = 8$$
$$a_5 = 16$$

Notice that

$$r = \frac{a_2}{a_1} = \frac{2}{1} = 2$$

$$r = \frac{a_3}{a_2} = \frac{4}{2} = 2$$

$$r = \frac{a_4}{a_3} = \frac{8}{4} = 2$$

$$r = \frac{a_5}{a_4} = \frac{16}{8} = 2.$$

In general,

$$r = \frac{a_n}{a_n - 1} = 2.$$

Any sequence of terms where the ratio between any two consecutive terms is a constant r, is called a geometric sequence.

Geometric Sequence
A sequence

$$a_1, a_2, a_3, a_4, ..., a_n, ...$$

is called a **geometric sequence** (or **geometric progression**)
if for all $n > 1$,

$$r = \frac{a_n}{a_{n-1}}$$

where r is the **common ratio**.

EXAMPLE 8.11

Which of the following are geometric sequences?

a) $3, 9, 27, 81, ...$
b) $1, 2, 4, 7, 11, ...$

SOLUTION 8.11

a) $3, 9, 27, 81, ...$
To determine if a sequence is a geometric sequence, divide two consecutive terms several times. If the ratio between any two consecutive terms is always the same value, the sequence is a geometric sequence.

$$\frac{a_2}{a_1} = \frac{9}{3} = 3$$

$$\frac{a_3}{a_2} = \frac{27}{9} = 3$$

$$\frac{a_4}{a_3} = \frac{81}{27} = 3$$

This sequence is geometric.

b) $1, 2, 4, 7, 11, \ldots$

Divide consecutive terms.

$$\frac{a_2}{a_1} = \frac{2}{1} = 2$$

$$\frac{a_3}{a_2} = \frac{4}{2} = 2$$

$$\frac{a_4}{a_3} = \frac{7}{4} \neq 2$$

The division of the fourth term by the third term is not the same as the division of the third term by the second term. The sequence is not geometric.

Geometric sequences have a recursive relationship between terms.

Since $r = \dfrac{a_n}{a_{n-1}}$, then

$$a_n = a_{n-1} \cdot r.$$

From this recursive relationship, we can develop the following formula about geometric sequences.

$a_1 = 1$

$a_2 = a_1 \cdot r$

$a_3 = a_2 \cdot r = (a_1 \cdot r) \cdot r = a_1 \cdot r^2$ Replace a_2 with $a_1 \cdot r$.

$a_4 = a_3 \cdot r = (a_1 \cdot r^2) \cdot r = a_1 \cdot r^3$ Replace a_3 with $a_1 \cdot r^2$.

If we continue with the same process, we get

$$a_n = a_1 \cdot r^{n-1} \quad \text{for all } n \geq 1.$$

The formula for the *n*th term of a geometric sequence, if we know the first term and the common ratio, is given below.

General Term of a Geometric Sequence

If a_1 is the first term of a geometric sequence and r is the common ratio, then the *n*th term of the geometric sequence is

$$a_n = a_1 \cdot r^{n-1} \quad \text{for all natural numbers } n \geq 1.$$

EXAMPLE 8.12

Find the *n*th term (general term) and 6th term for the following geometric sequences:

a) $3, 9, 27, 81, \ldots$

b) $\dfrac{1}{2}, -\dfrac{1}{4}, \dfrac{1}{8}, -\dfrac{1}{16}, \ldots$

SOLUTION 8.12

a) $3, 9, 27, 81, \ldots$

We were given the fact that the sequence is geometric. To find the nth term, we need a_1 and r.

$$a_1 = 3 \text{ and } r = \frac{a_2}{a_1} = \frac{9}{3} = 3$$

$$a_n = a_1 \cdot r^{n-1} \qquad \qquad \text{Substitute } a_1 \text{ and } r \text{ into the formula.}$$

$$a_n = 3 \cdot (3)^{n-1} = 3 \cdot 3^{n-1} = 3^n$$

The general term for all natural numbers is

$$a_n = 3^n$$

Use the general term to find the sixth term.

$$a_6 = 3^6 = 729$$

The nth term is $a_n = 3^n$ and the sixth term is $a_6 = 729$.

b) $\dfrac{1}{2}, -\dfrac{1}{4}, \dfrac{1}{8}, -\dfrac{1}{16}, \ldots$

We know that $a_1 = \dfrac{1}{2}$. We need to find r.

$$r = \frac{a_2}{a_1} = \frac{-\dfrac{1}{4}}{\dfrac{1}{2}} = -\frac{1}{2}$$

$$a_n = a_1 \cdot r^{n-1}$$

$$a_n = \frac{1}{2} \cdot \left(-\frac{1}{2}\right)^{n-1}$$

Simplify.

$$a_n = \frac{1}{2} \cdot \left(\frac{-1}{2}\right)^{n-1}$$

$$a_n = \frac{1}{2} \cdot \left(\frac{(-1)^{n-1}}{2^{n-1}}\right)$$

$$a_n = \frac{(-1)^{n-1}}{2^n}$$

Use the general term formula to find the sixth term.

$$a_6 = \frac{(-1)^{6-1}}{2^6}$$

$$a_6 = \frac{(-1)^5}{2^6}$$

$$a_6 = \frac{-1}{64} = -\frac{1}{64}$$

The nth term is $a_n = \dfrac{(-1)^{n-1}}{2^n}$ and the sixth term is $a_6 = -\dfrac{1}{64}$.

Finite Geometric Series

A series is the summation of the terms of a sequence. A finite geometric series is the summation of the terms of a finite geometric sequence. Let

$$A = a_1, a_2, a_3, a_4, ..., a_n$$

be a finite geometric sequence. Let

$$S_n = a_1 + a_2 + a_3 + a_4 + ... + a_n$$

be the sum of a finite geometric series of n terms. Replacing each a_n with the general formula for a_n we get,

1. $S_n = a_1 + a_1 \cdot r + a_1 \cdot r^2 + a_1 \cdot r^3 + ... + a_1 \cdot r^{n-2} + a_1 \cdot r^{n-1}$

Multiply both sides of the equation by r.

2. $r \cdot S_n = a_1 \cdot r + a_1 \cdot r^2 + a_1 \cdot r^3 + a_1 \cdot r^4 + ... + a_1 \cdot r^{n-1} + a_1 \cdot r^n$

Multiply the second equation by -1.

3. $-r \cdot S_n = a_1 \cdot r - a_1 \cdot r^2 - a_1 \cdot r^3 - a_1 \cdot r^4 - ... - a_1 \cdot r^{n-1} - a_1 \cdot r^n$

Add equations 1 and 3.

$$S_n = a_1 + a_1 \cdot r + a_1 \cdot r^2 + a_1 \cdot r^3 + ... + a_1 \cdot r^{n-2} + a_1 \cdot r^{n-1}$$
$$-r \cdot S_n = a_1 \cdot r - a_1 \cdot r^2 - a_1 \cdot r^3 - a_1 \cdot r^4 - ... - a_1 \cdot r^{n-1} - a_1 \cdot r^n$$

We get

$$S - r \cdot S_n = (a_1 + a_1 \cdot r + a_1 \cdot r^2 + a_1 \cdot r^3 + ... + a_1 \cdot r^{n-2} + a_1 \cdot r^{n-1})$$

$$+ (-a_1 \cdot r - a_1 \cdot r^2 - a_1 \cdot r^3 - a_1 \cdot r^4 - ... - a_1 \cdot r^{n-1} - a_1 \cdot r^n).$$

Notice that all of the terms drop out except the first term and the last term.

$$S_n - r \cdot S_n = a_1 - a_1 \cdot r^n$$

Factor S_n from the left-hand side and a_1 from the right-hand side.

$$S_n(1-r) = a_1(1-r^n)$$

Divide both sides by $(1 - r)$.

$$S_n = \frac{a_1(1 - r^n)}{(1 - r)}$$

In the above formula, if we distribute a_1 inside of the parentheses in the numerator, we get

$$S_n = \frac{a_1 - a_1 r^n}{(1 - r)}.$$

But $a_n = a_1 \cdot r^{n-1}$ and $r \cdot a_n = a_1 r^n$. Replace $r \cdot a_n$ for $a_1 \cdot r^n$ into the formula.

$$S_n = \frac{a_1 - r \cdot a_n}{(1 - r)}$$

Summation Formulas for n Terms of a Geometric Series:

1. $S_n = \dfrac{a_1(1 - r^n)}{(1 - r)}$

2. $S_n = \dfrac{a_1 - r \cdot a_n}{(1 - r)}$

The first formula is used to find the sum of a finite geometric series of n terms when know the first term and the common ratio. The second formula is used to find the finite sum of a geometric series of n terms when you know the first term, last term, and the common ratio. In the second formula, we need to know more information to find the summation, but we do not have to raise the common ratio r to powers.

EXAMPLE 8.13

Find the indicated sums of the following geometric series:
a)   Find the sum of the first 6 terms of $1 + 4 + 16 + \ldots$
b)   Find the sum of the first 11 terms of $2 + 4 + 8 + \ldots$

SOLUTION 8.13

a)   Find the sum of the first 6 terms of $1 + 4 + 16 + \ldots$
     In this geometric series, we know the first term and the number of terms to be added together. We need to find the common ratio to be able to use the first formula for finite geometric sums.

$$r = \frac{a_2}{a_1} = \frac{4}{1} = 4$$

The summation formula is $S_n = \frac{a_1(1-r^n)}{(1-r)}$, substitute $a_1 = 1$, $n = 6$ and $r = 4$ into the formula.

$$S_6 = \frac{1(1-4^6)}{(1-4)}$$

$$= \frac{1(1-4096)}{(-3)}$$

$$= \frac{-4095}{-3}$$

$$= 1365$$

b) Find the sum of the first 11 terms of $2 + 4 + 8 + \ldots$
Find r.

$$r = \frac{a_2}{a_1} = \frac{4}{2} = 2$$

The summation formula is $S_n = \frac{a_1(1-r^n)}{(1-r)}$. Substitute $a_1 = 2$, $n = 11$ and $r = 2$ into the formula.

$$S_{11} = \frac{2(1-2^{11})}{(1-2)}$$

$$= \frac{2(1-2048)}{(-1)}$$

$$= \frac{2(-2047)}{-1}$$

$$= \frac{-4094}{-1}$$

$$= 4094$$

The following is a summary of the formulas needed to understand finite geometric sequences and series.

Geometric Sequences and Series:

A finite geometric sequence is a sequence in the form of

$$A = a_1, a_2, a_3, ..., a_n, ... \text{ where}$$

$$r = \frac{a_n}{a_n - 1} \text{ for all } n.$$

The general term of a geometric sequence is

$$a_n = a_1 \cdot r^{n-1} \text{ for all } n > 1.$$

The finite sum

$$S_n = a_1 + a_2 + a_3 + ... + a_n \text{ can be found using either formula.}$$

$$1) \quad S_n = \frac{a_1(1 - r^n)}{(1 - r)} \qquad\qquad 2) \quad S_n = \frac{a_1 - r \cdot a_n}{(1 - r)}$$

Infinite Geometric Series

It is impossible to find the sum of an infinite arithmetic series because an infinite arithmetic series always has an infinite sum. Infinite geometric series, however, sometimes have finite sums. Take the geometric series

$$A = \frac{1}{2} + \frac{1}{4} + \frac{1}{8} + \frac{1}{16} + ...$$

This series is an infinite geometric series. Find the first four partial sums.

$$S_1 = \frac{1}{2}$$

$$S_2 = \frac{1}{2} + \frac{1}{4} = \frac{3}{4}$$

$$S_3 = \frac{1}{2} + \frac{1}{4} + \frac{1}{8} = \frac{7}{8}$$

$$S_4 = \frac{1}{2} + \frac{1}{4} + \frac{1}{8} + \frac{1}{16} = \frac{15}{16}$$

Notice the pattern. The denominator is 2 raised to the power of the partial sum and the numerator is one less than the denominator.

$$S_1 = \frac{2^1 - 1}{2^1}$$

$$S_2 = \frac{2^2 - 1}{2^2} = \frac{3}{4}$$

$$S_3 = \frac{2^3 - 1}{2^3} = \frac{7}{8}$$

$$S_4 = \frac{2^4 - 1}{2^4} = \frac{15}{16}$$

The nth partial sum is

$$S_n = \frac{2^n - 1}{2^n}.$$

From this pattern, the 10th partial sum is

$$S_{10} = \frac{2^{10} - 1}{2^{10}} = \frac{1023}{1024}.$$

The 15th partial sum is

$$S_{15} = \frac{2^{15} - 1}{2^{15}} = \frac{32767}{32768}.$$

As n gets larger and larger, the partial sums get closer and closer to the number 1. As n gets infinitely larger

$$S = \frac{1}{2} + \frac{1}{4} + \frac{1}{8} + \frac{1}{16} + \dots = 1.$$

To prove that the series

$$A = \frac{1}{2} + \frac{1}{4} + \frac{1}{8} + \frac{1}{16} + \dots$$

has a sum of 1, use the summation formula for finite geometric series.

$$S_n = \frac{a_1 - a_1 \cdot r^n}{(1 - r)}$$

Separate the expression into two fractions.

$$S_n = \frac{a_1}{(1 - r)} - \frac{a_1 \cdot r^n}{(1 - r)}$$

In our problem, $a_1 = \frac{1}{2}$ and $r = \frac{1}{2}$. Substitute these values into the formula.

$$S_n = \frac{\frac{1}{2}}{(1 - \frac{1}{2})} - \frac{\frac{1}{2} \cdot (\frac{1}{2})^n}{(1 - \frac{1}{2})} \qquad \text{Simplify.}$$

$$S_n = \frac{\frac{1}{2}}{\frac{1}{2}} - \frac{\frac{1}{2} \cdot (\frac{1}{2})^n}{\frac{1}{2}}$$

$$S_n = 1 - \frac{1}{2^n}$$

As n increases in size, the value of the fraction $\dfrac{1}{2^n}$ decreases in size. As n gets infinitely larger, $\dfrac{1}{2^n}$ approaches and becomes zero. If $\dfrac{1}{2^n} = 0$, the sum

$$S_n = 1 - \frac{1}{2^n} \quad \text{and} \quad s = 1 - 0 = 1.$$

In general, the term

$$\frac{a_1 \cdot r^n}{(1 - r)} = 0$$

for all values of r such that $-1 < r < 1$. $-1 < r < 1$ means $|r| < 1$. When the ratio between any two consecutive terms of an infinite geometric series is a fractional value with absolute value less than 1, the infinite geometric series has a finite sum and the sum of the infinite geometric series is

$$S = \frac{a_1}{1 - r}$$

The Sum of Infinite Geometric Series:
Let

$$A = a_1, a_2, a_3, a_4, ..., a_n, ...$$

be an infinite geometric sequence with $|r| < 1$, then the sum of the series

$$S = a_1 + a_2 + a_3 + a_4 + ...$$

is given by the formula

$$S = \frac{a_1}{1 - r}.$$

If $|r| < 1$, the infinite geometric series has an infinite sum.

EXAMPLE 8.14

Find the sums of the following infinite geometric series:

a) $2 + 1 + \dfrac{1}{2} + \dfrac{1}{4} + \ldots$

b) $\dfrac{2}{3} + \dfrac{1}{6} + \dfrac{1}{24} + \dfrac{1}{96} + \ldots$

c) $\dfrac{5}{6} + \dfrac{5}{9} + \dfrac{10}{27} + \dfrac{20}{81} + \ldots$

SOLUTION 8.14

a) $2 + 1 + \dfrac{1}{2} + \dfrac{1}{4} + \ldots$

To find the sum of an infinite geometric series, we need a_1 and r. Find r.

$$r = \frac{a_2}{a_1} = \frac{1}{2}$$

Before we can use the infinite geometric formula, check to be certain that $|r| > 1$. Substitute a_1 and r into the infinite geometric formula for sums.

$$S = \frac{a_1}{1 - r}$$

$$S = \frac{2}{1 - \dfrac{1}{2}}$$

$$S = \frac{2}{\dfrac{1}{2}} = 4$$

The infinite geometric series $2 + 1 + \dfrac{1}{2} + \dfrac{1}{4} + \ldots$ has a sum of 4.

b) $\dfrac{2}{3} + \dfrac{1}{6} + \dfrac{1}{24} + \dfrac{1}{96} + \ldots$

Find r.

$$r = \frac{a_2}{a_1} = \frac{\dfrac{1}{6}}{\dfrac{2}{3}} = \frac{1}{4}$$

$r = \dfrac{1}{4} < 1$. Substitute a_1 and r into the infinite geometric formula for sums.

$$S = \frac{a_1}{1-r}$$

$$S = \frac{\dfrac{2}{3}}{1-\dfrac{1}{4}}$$

$$S = \frac{\dfrac{2}{3}}{\dfrac{3}{4}} = \frac{8}{9}$$

The infinite geometric series $\dfrac{2}{3} + \dfrac{1}{6} + \dfrac{1}{24} + \dfrac{1}{96} + \ldots$ has a sum of $\dfrac{8}{9}$.

c) $\dfrac{5}{6} + \dfrac{5}{9} + \dfrac{10}{27} + \dfrac{20}{81} + \ldots$

Find r.

$$r = \frac{a_2}{a_1} = \frac{\dfrac{5}{9}}{\dfrac{5}{6}} = \frac{30}{45} = \frac{2}{3}$$

$r = \dfrac{2}{3} < 1$. Substitute a_1 and r into the infinite geometric formula for sums.

$$S = \frac{a_1}{1-r}$$

$$S = \frac{\dfrac{5}{6}}{1-\dfrac{2}{3}}$$

$$S = \frac{\dfrac{5}{6}}{\dfrac{1}{3}} = \frac{15}{6} = \frac{5}{2} = 2\frac{1}{2}$$

The infinite geometric series $\dfrac{5}{6} + \dfrac{5}{9} + \dfrac{10}{27} + \dfrac{20}{81} + \ldots$ has a sum of $\dfrac{5}{2}$.

The infinite geometric series formula can be used to find the fractional value of repeating decimals.

EXAMPLE 8.15

Change the following decimal into a fraction:
$0.333\ldots$

SOLUTION 8.15

$0.333\ldots$

The decimal $0.333\ldots$ can be written as an infinite geometric series in the following way.

$$\frac{3}{10} + \frac{3}{100} + \frac{3}{1000} + \frac{3}{10000} + \cdots$$

Find r.
$$r = \frac{a_2}{a_1} = \frac{\dfrac{3}{100}}{\dfrac{3}{10}} = \frac{30}{300} = \frac{1}{10}$$

$r = \dfrac{1}{10} < 1$. Substitute a_1 and r into the infinite geometric formula for sums.

$$S = \frac{a_1}{1-r}$$

$$S = \frac{\dfrac{3}{10}}{1 - \dfrac{1}{10}}$$

$$S = \frac{\dfrac{3}{10}}{\dfrac{9}{10}} = \frac{30}{90} = \frac{1}{3}$$

The decimal $0.333\ldots = \dfrac{3}{10} + \dfrac{3}{100} + \dfrac{3}{1000} + \dfrac{3}{10000} + \cdots$ has a value

of $\dfrac{1}{3}$. Of course you already knew that $0.333\ldots = \dfrac{1}{3}$. Try this one.

EXERCISE 8.4

Which of the following are geometric sequences?

1. $5, 10, 20, 40, \ldots$
2. $1, 4, 9, 16, 25, \ldots$

3. 1, 2, 4, 7, 11, . . .

4. $\dfrac{1}{3}, \dfrac{5}{9}, \dfrac{25}{27}, \ldots$

Find the nth term (general term) and 5th term for the following geometric sequences:

5. $\dfrac{1}{8}, \dfrac{1}{4}, \dfrac{1}{2}, 1, \ldots$

6. 2, 10, 50, 250, . . .

7. 1, –2, 4, –8, . . .

8. $\dfrac{2}{3}, \dfrac{1}{3}, \dfrac{1}{6}, \dfrac{1}{12}, \ldots$

Find the indicated finite sums of the following geometric series:

9. Find the sum of the first 12 terms of $5 + 10 + 20 + \ldots$

10. Find the sum of the first 7 terms of $2 + 6 + 18 + \ldots$

11. Find the sum of the first 5 terms of $21 + 84 + 336 + \ldots$

12. Find the sum of the first 80 terms of $\dfrac{1}{3} + \dfrac{1}{6} + \dfrac{1}{18} + \ldots$

13. $3 + 6 + 12 + \ldots + 384$

14. $8 + 24 + 72 + \ldots + 1944$

15. $1 + \dfrac{1}{5} + \dfrac{1}{25} + \ldots + \dfrac{1}{625}$

Find the sum of the following infinite geometric series:

16. $3 + \dfrac{3}{2} + \dfrac{3}{4} + \ldots$

17. $5 - 1 + \dfrac{1}{5} - \dfrac{1}{25} + \ldots$

18. $3 + 2 + \dfrac{4}{3} + \dfrac{8}{9} + \ldots$

Change the following decimals to fractions:

19. $0.555 \ldots$

20. $0.656565 \ldots$

ANSWERS TO EXERCISE 8.4

1. Yes

2. No

3. No

4. Yes

5. $a_n = \dfrac{1}{2^{n+2}}, a_7 = \dfrac{1}{512}$

6. $a_n = 2(5)^{n-1}$, $a_7 = 31,250$

7. $a_n = (-2)^{n-1}$, $a_7 = 64$

8. $a_n = \dfrac{1}{3 \cdot 2^{n-2}}$, $a_7 = \dfrac{1}{96}$

9. 20,475

10. 2,186

11. 7,161

12. $\dfrac{2047}{3072}$

13. 765

14. 2,912

15. $\dfrac{781}{625}$

16. 6

17. $\dfrac{25}{6}$

18. 9

19. $\dfrac{5}{9}$

20. $\dfrac{65}{99}$

SECTION 8.5 BINOMIAL THEOREM

Factorials

For a positive integer $n \geq 2$, **n factorial**, denoted $n!$, is the product of all of the positive integers less than or equal to n. **Zero factorial** (0!) is defined to be equal to 1 (0! = 1) and **one factorial** (1!) is also defined to be 1 (1! = 1). Here are some of the factorials.

$$0! = 1$$
$$1! = 1$$
$$2! = 2 \cdot 1 = 2$$
$$3! = 3 \cdot 2 \cdot 1 = 6$$
$$4! = 4 \cdot 3 \cdot 2 \cdot 1 = 24$$
$$5! = 5 \cdot 4 \cdot 3 \cdot 2 \cdot 1 = 120$$
$$\vdots$$
$$n! = n \cdot (n-1) \cdot (n-2) \cdot \ldots \cdot 3 \cdot 2 \cdot 1$$

Factorial expressions can build upon each other. Each factorial can be found by multiplying the last factorial by the next consecutive positive integer.

$$1! = 1$$

$$2! = 2 \cdot 1! = 2 \cdot 1$$

$$3! = 3 \cdot 2! = 3 \cdot 2 \cdot 1! = 3 \cdot 2 \cdot 1 = 6$$

$$4! = 4 \cdot 3! = 4 \cdot 3 \cdot 2! = 4 \cdot 3 \cdot 2 \cdot 1! = 4 \cdot 3 \cdot 2 \cdot 1 = 24$$

$$5! = 5 \cdot 4! = 5 \cdot 4 \cdot 3! = 5 \cdot 4 \cdot 3 \cdot 2! = 5 \cdot 4 \cdot 3 \cdot 2 \cdot 1!$$
$$= 5 \cdot 4 \cdot 3 \cdot 2 \cdot 1 = 120$$

$$n! = n \cdot (n-1)! = n \cdot (n-1) \cdot (n-2)!$$
$$= n \cdot (n-1) \cdot (n-2) \cdot \ldots \cdot 3 \cdot 2 \cdot 1$$

EXAMPLE 8.16

Compute the following factorials:

a) 7!

b) 9!

c) 12!

SOLUTION 8.16

a) 7!

In factorial statements, we multiply all of the consecutive positive integers beginning at the given positive integer and ending at 1. Factorial statements of fractions are not defined.

$$7! = 7 \cdot 6 \cdot 5 \cdot 4 \cdot 3 \cdot 2 \cdot 1 = 5040$$

b) 9!

$$9! = 9 \cdot 8 \cdot 7 \cdot 6 \cdot 5 \cdot 4 \cdot 3 \cdot 2 \cdot 1$$
$$= 9 \cdot 8 \cdot 7! = 9 \cdot 8 \cdot 5040 = 362,880$$

c) 12!

$$12! = 12 \cdot 11 \cdot 10 \cdot 9 \cdot 8 \cdot 7 \cdot 6 \cdot 5 \cdot 4 \cdot 3 \cdot 2 \cdot 1$$
$$= 12 \cdot 11 \cdot 10 \cdot 9! = 12 \cdot 11 \cdot 10 \cdot 362,880$$
$$= 479,001,600$$

Notice how quickly factorial statements get large. Factorial statements can be added, subtracted, multiplied, and divided like any other mathematical statements.

EXAMPLE 8.17

Simplify the following factorial statements:

a) $\dfrac{5!}{4!}$

b) $\dfrac{7! \cdot 3!}{5! \cdot 2!}$

c) $\dfrac{12!}{7! \cdot 5!}$

SOLUTION 8.17

a) $\dfrac{5!}{4!}$

Factorials can be treated using their numerical values.

$$\frac{5!}{4!} = \frac{120}{24} = 5$$

When dividing factorial statements, however, it is often better to expand the factorials and divide common factors. With large factorials, this method is usually much easier.

$$\frac{5!}{4!} = \frac{5 \cdot 4 \cdot 3 \cdot 2 \cdot 1}{4 \cdot 3 \cdot 2 \cdot 1} = \frac{5 \cdot \cancel{4} \cdot \cancel{3} \cdot \cancel{2} \cdot \cancel{1}}{\cancel{4} \cdot \cancel{3} \cdot \cancel{2} \cdot \cancel{1}} = 5$$

It is still easier not to expand each factorial. Factorial statements in the numerator can be divided with the same factorial statement in the denominator as long as the numerator and denominator are in factored form. Factorial statements can also be broken into smaller factors by definition. That is,

$$5! = 5 \cdot 4!.$$

The above statement becomes,

$$\frac{5!}{4!} = \frac{5 \cdot 4!}{4!} = \frac{5 \cdot \cancel{4!}}{\cancel{4!}} = 5.$$

b) $\dfrac{7! \cdot 3!}{5! \cdot 2!}$

Take the larger factorial statement in the numerator and expand it until you get the same factorial in the denominator. Do this again with the next larger factorial statement. Divide the common factorials.

$$\frac{7! \cdot 3!}{5! \cdot 2!} = \frac{7 \cdot 6 \cdot 5! \cdot 3 \cdot 2!}{5! \cdot 2!} = \frac{7 \cdot 6 \cdot \cancel{5!} \cdot 3 \cdot \cancel{2!}}{\cancel{5!} \cdot \cancel{2!}} = 7 \cdot 6 \cdot 3 = 126$$

c) $\dfrac{12!}{7! \cdot 5!}$

Expand the factorials in the numerator and denominator until common factorials are obtained.

$$\frac{12! \cdot 9!}{7! \cdot 5! \cdot 8!} = \frac{12 \cdot 11 \cdot 10 \cdot 9 \cdot 8! \cdot 9 \cdot 8 \cdot 7!}{7! \cdot 5! \cdot 8!}$$

$$= \frac{12 \cdot 11 \cdot 10 \cdot 9 \cdot \cancel{8!} \cdot 9 \cdot 8 \cdot \cancel{7!}}{\cancel{7!} \cdot 5! \cdot \cancel{8!}}$$

$$= \frac{12 \cdot 11 \cdot 10 \cdot 9 \cdot 9 \cdot 8}{5!} \qquad \text{Now expand 5!}$$

$$= \frac{12 \cdot 11 \cdot 10 \cdot 9 \cdot 9 \cdot 8}{5 \cdot 4 \cdot 3 \cdot 2 \cdot 1} \qquad \begin{array}{l}\text{Divide common factors and} \\ \text{multiply.}\end{array}$$

$$= \frac{12 \cdot 11 \cdot \overset{2}{\cancel{10}} \cdot \overset{3}{\cancel{9}} \cdot 9 \cdot \cancel{8}}{\cancel{5} \cdot \cancel{4} \cdot \cancel{3} \cdot \cancel{2} \cdot 1} = 12 \cdot 11 \cdot 2 \cdot 3 \cdot 9 = 7128$$

Combinatorial

Factorial statements become very important when working in statistics. Factorials are also important when working with a combination of two numbers. The symbols often used for combinations are:

1. $\dbinom{n}{r}$

2. ${}_nC_r$

3. C_r^n

4. $C(n, r)$

These symbols are called combinatorial symbols and are used to define a relation between two non-negative integers n and r. A statement like $\dbinom{n}{r}$ is defined as follows.

Combinatorial Definition:
For two non-negative integers n and r such that $0 \leq r \leq n$

$$\binom{n}{r} = \frac{n!}{(n-r)! \cdot r!}$$

EXAMPLE 8.18

Compute each of the following combinations:

a) $\binom{5}{3}$

b) $\binom{7}{4}$

SOLUTION 8.18

a) $\binom{5}{3}$

By definition,

$$\binom{5}{3} = \frac{5!}{(5-3)! \cdot 3!}.$$

Simplify.

$$\frac{5!}{2! \cdot 3!}$$

Expand the factorials.

$$\frac{5 \cdot 4 \cdot 3!}{2 \cdot 1 \cdot 3!}$$

Divide common factorials.

$$\frac{5 \cdot 4 \cdot \cancel{3!}}{2 \cdot 1 \cdot \cancel{3!}} = \frac{5 \cdot 4}{2 \cdot 1}$$

Divide common factors.

$$\frac{5 \cdot 4}{2 \cdot 1} = 10$$

$$\binom{5}{3} = 10$$

b) $\binom{7}{4}$

By definition,

$$\binom{7}{4} = \frac{7!}{(7-4)! \cdot 4!}.$$

Simplify.

$$\frac{7!}{3! \cdot 4!}$$

Expand the factorials.

$$\frac{7 \cdot 6 \cdot 5 \cdot 4!}{4! \cdot 3 \cdot 2 \cdot 1}$$

Divide common factorials.

$$\frac{7 \cdot 6 \cdot 5 \cdot \cancel{4!}}{\cancel{4!} \cdot 3 \cdot 2 \cdot 1}$$

Simplify.

$$\frac{7 \cdot 6 \cdot 5}{3 \cdot 2 \cdot 1}$$

Divide common factors.

$$\frac{7 \cdot \cancel{6} \cdot 5}{\cancel{3} \cdot \cancel{2} \cdot 1} = 7 \cdot 5 = 35$$

$$\binom{7}{4} = 35$$

Binomial Expansion

The combination formula becomes very important when raising binomials to powers. We have already taken and expanded certain binomials.

$$(x+y)^0 = 1$$

$$(x+y)^1 = x+y$$

$$(x+y)^2 = (x+y)(x+y) = x^2 + 2xy + y^2$$

and

$$(x+y)^3 = (x+y)(x+y)(x+y) = (x^2 + 2xy + y^2)(x+y)$$

$$= x^3 + 3x^2y + 3xy^2 + y^3$$

To raise binomials to higher powers by multiplication requires a tedious amount of work. The expansion of a binomial, however, forms a pattern. Look at $(x+y)^3$.

$$(x+y)^3 = x^3 + 3x^2y + 3xy^2 + y^3$$

Notice that the expression begins with x having the power of 3. The power of x continually decreases by 1.

$$x^3 \qquad x^2 \qquad x^1 \qquad x^0$$

The powers of y increase by 1.

$$y^0 \qquad y^1 \qquad y^2 \qquad y^3$$

Also, notice that in any of the terms in the polynomial, the powers of x and y always add together to equal the power of 3. The coefficients of the terms are equal to $\binom{n}{r}$ where $n = 3$ and r is the power of the variable y.

$$(x+y)^3 = \binom{3}{0}x^3 + \binom{3}{1}x^2y + \binom{3}{2}xy^2 + \binom{3}{3}y^3$$

Compute these combinations and make certain that they give the correct values.

$$\binom{3}{0} = \frac{3!}{(3-0)! \cdot 0!} = \frac{3!}{3! \cdot 0!} = \frac{\cancel{3!}}{\cancel{3!} \cdot 1} = 1$$

$$\binom{3}{1} = \frac{3!}{(3-1)! \cdot 1!} = \frac{3!}{2! \cdot 1!} = \frac{3 \cdot 2!}{2! \cdot 1!} = \frac{3 \cdot \cancel{2!}}{\cancel{2!} \cdot 1} = 3$$

$$\binom{3}{2} = \frac{3!}{(3-2)! \cdot 2!} = \frac{3!}{1! \cdot 2!} = 3 \qquad \text{This expression is the same as the second.}$$

$$\binom{3}{3} = \frac{3!}{(3-3)! \cdot 3!} = \frac{3!}{0! \cdot 3!} = 1 \qquad \text{This is the same as the first.}$$

Binomial Theorem:
For $n \, \varepsilon \, N$

$$(a+b)^n = \binom{n}{0}a^n + \binom{n}{1}a^{n-1}b + \binom{n}{2}a^{n-2}b^2 + \dots$$

$$+ \binom{n}{n-1}ab^{n-1} + \binom{n}{n}b^n.$$

EXAMPLE 8.19

Raise the following binomials to the power indicated using the binomial theorem:

a) $(x+y)^4$

b) $(a+b)^5$

SOLUTION 8.19

a) $(x+y)^4$

By use of the binomial theorem, we get

$$(x+y)^4 = \binom{4}{0}x^4 + \binom{4}{1}x^{4-1}y + \binom{4}{2}x^{4-2}y^2 + \binom{4}{3}xy^{4-1} + \binom{4}{4}y^4$$

Simplify.

$$(x+y)^4 = \binom{4}{0}x^4 + \binom{4}{1}x^3y + \binom{4}{2}x^2y^2 + \binom{4}{3}xy^3 + \binom{4}{4}y^4$$

Compute the coefficients.

$$\binom{4}{0} = \frac{4!}{(4-0)!\cdot 0!} = \frac{4!}{4!\cdot 0!} = \frac{\cancel{4!}}{\cancel{4!}\cdot 1} = 1$$

$$\binom{4}{1} = \frac{4!}{(4-1)!\cdot 1!} = \frac{4!}{3!\cdot 1!} = \frac{4\cdot 3!}{3!\cdot 1!} = \frac{4\cdot\cancel{3!}}{\cancel{3!}\cdot 1} = 4$$

$$\binom{4}{2} = \frac{4!}{(4-2)!\cdot 2!} = \frac{4!}{2!\cdot 2!} = \frac{4\cdot 3\cdot 2!}{2!\cdot 2\cdot 1} = \frac{4\cdot 3\cdot\cancel{2!}}{\cancel{2!}\cdot 2} = \frac{12}{2} = 6$$

$$\binom{4}{3} = \frac{4!}{(4-3)!\cdot 3!} = \frac{4!}{1!\cdot 3!} = 4 \quad \text{(Same as 2nd)}$$

$$\binom{4}{4} = \frac{4!}{(4-4)!\cdot 4!} = \frac{4!}{0!\cdot 4!} = 1 \quad \text{(Same as 1st)}$$

$$(x+y)^4 = x^4 + 4x^3y + 6x^2y^2 + 4xy^3 + y^4$$

b) $(a+b)^5$

Expand by use of the binomial theorem.

$$(a+b)^5 = \binom{5}{0}a^5 + \binom{5}{1}a^4b + \binom{5}{2}a^3b^2 + \binom{5}{3}a^2b^3 + \binom{5}{4}ab^4 + \binom{5}{5}b^5$$

Compute the coefficients.

$$\binom{5}{0} = \frac{5!}{(5-0)!\cdot 0!} = \frac{5!}{5!\cdot 0!} = \frac{\cancel{5!}}{\cancel{5!}\cdot 1} = 1$$

$$\binom{5}{1} = \frac{5!}{(5-1)!\cdot 1!} = \frac{5!}{4!\cdot 1!} = \frac{5\cdot 4!}{4!\cdot 1!} = \frac{5\cdot\cancel{4!}}{\cancel{4!}\cdot 1} = 5$$

$$\binom{5}{2} = \frac{5!}{(5-2)!\cdot 2!} = \frac{5!}{3!\cdot 2!} = \frac{5\cdot 4\cdot 3!}{3!\cdot 2\cdot 1} = \frac{5\cdot 4\cdot\cancel{4!}}{\cancel{4!}\cdot 2} = \frac{20}{2} = 10$$

$$\binom{5}{3} = \frac{5!}{(5-3)!\cdot 3!} = \frac{5!}{2!\cdot 3!} = 10 \quad \text{(Same as 3rd)}$$

$$\binom{5}{4} = \frac{5!}{(5-4)! \cdot 4!} = \frac{5!}{1! \cdot 4!} = 5 \quad \text{(Same as 2nd)}$$

$$\binom{5}{5} = \frac{5!}{(5-5)! \cdot 5!} = \frac{5!}{0! \cdot 5!} = 1 \quad \text{(Same as 1st)}$$

$$(a+b)^5 = a^5 + 5a^4b + 10a^3b^2 + 10a^2b^3 + 5ab^4 + b^5$$

EXAMPLE 8.20

Expand the following binomial without using the combinatorial symbol:
a) $(a+b)^3$

b) $(a+b)^4$

SOLUTION 8.20

a) $(a+b)^3$

$$(a+b)^3 = \frac{3!}{3! \cdot 0!}a^3 + \frac{3!}{2! \cdot 1!}a^2b + \frac{3!}{1! \cdot 2!}ab^2 + \frac{3!}{0! \cdot 3!}b^3$$

Compute the coefficients.

$$\frac{3!}{3! \cdot 0!} = \frac{3!}{3! \cdot 1} = 1$$

$$\frac{3!}{2! \cdot 1!} = \frac{3 \cdot 2!}{2! \cdot 1!} = \frac{3 \cdot 2!}{2! \cdot 1} = 3$$

$$\frac{3!}{1! \cdot 2!} = 3 \qquad\qquad \text{This expression is the same as the second.}$$

$$\frac{3!}{0! \cdot 3!} = 1 \qquad\qquad \text{This is the same as the first.}$$

$$(a+b)^3 = a^3 + 3a^2b + 3ab^2 + b^3$$

b) $(a+b)^4$

$$(a+b)^4 = \frac{4!}{4! \cdot 0!}a^4 + \frac{4!}{3! \cdot 1!}a^3b + \frac{4!}{2! \cdot 2!}a^2b^2 + \frac{4!}{1! \cdot 3!}ab^3 + \frac{4!}{0! \cdot 4!}b^4$$

Compute the coefficients. Notice how the first and the last terms, the second and next to the last term, etc. have exactly the same factorial statements. We never need to compute all of the coefficients of a binomial expansion. When x and y reverse powers, the coefficients remain the same. That is, a^2b^3 has the same coefficient as a^3b^2. We only need to compute half of the coefficients and use symmetry to know the value of the remaining terms.

$$\frac{4!}{4! \cdot 0!} = \frac{4!}{4! \cdot 1} = 1$$

$$\frac{4!}{3! \cdot 1!} = \frac{4 \cdot 3!}{3! \cdot 1!} = \frac{4 \cdot 3!}{3! \cdot 1} = 4$$

$$\frac{4!}{2! \cdot 2!} = \frac{4 \cdot 3 \cdot 2!}{2! \cdot 2 \cdot 1} = \frac{4 \cdot 3 \cdot 2!}{2! \cdot 2} = \frac{12}{2} = 6$$

$$\frac{4!}{1! \cdot 3!} = 4$$

$$\frac{4!}{0! \cdot 4!} = 1$$

Write the expanded binomial.

$$(a+b)^4 = a^4 + 4a^3b + 6a^2b^2 + 4ab^3 + b^4$$

Using these patterns, we can find coefficients of individual terms without expanding the whole binomial.

EXAMPLE 8.21

Find the coefficient of the indicated term of the following expansions:

a)   Given $(a+b)^8$, find the coefficient of the a^3b^5.

b)   Given $(2a+b)^9$, find the coefficient of the a^4b^5.

c)   Given $(a-3b)^{12}$, find the coefficient of the a^5b^7.

SOLUTION 8.21

a)   Given $(a+b)^8$, find the coefficient of the a^3b^5.

The numerator of the factorial of the coefficient is the sum of the two powers. The denominator is the product of the individual factorials of the two powers.

$$\frac{8!}{3! \cdot 5!} a^3 b^5$$

Notice the coefficient:

$$\underbrace{\frac{8!}{3!5!}}_{} \longleftarrow (3+5) \text{ sum of powers}$$

power of y.

$$\frac{8 \cdot 7 \cdot 6 \cdot 5!}{3 \cdot 2 \cdot 1 \cdot 5!} a^3 b^5$$

power of x.

$$\frac{8 \cdot 7 \cdot 6 \cdot 5!}{3 \cdot 2 \cdot 1 \cdot 5!} a^3 b^5$$

$$56a^3 b^5$$

b) Given $(2a+b)^9$, find the coefficient of the a^4b^5.

To find the coefficient of a^4b^5, the variable a is replaced by $2a$ in the binomial theorem.

$$\frac{9!}{4! \cdot 5!}(2a)^4 b^5$$

$$\frac{9 \cdot 8 \cdot 7 \cdot 6 \cdot 5!}{4 \cdot 3 \cdot 2 \cdot 1 \cdot 5!}(16)\,a^4 b^5$$

$$\frac{9 \cdot \overset{2}{\cancel{8}} \cdot 7 \cdot \cancel{6} \cdot \cancel{5!}}{\cancel{4} \cdot \cancel{3} \cdot \cancel{2} \cdot 1 \cdot \cancel{5!}}(16)\,a^4 b^5$$

$$126\,(16)\,a^4 b^5$$

$$2016 a^4 b^5$$

c) Given $(a-3b)^{12}$, find the coefficient of the a^5b^7.

The variable b is replaced by $(-3b)$ in the binomial theorem.

$$\frac{12!}{5! \cdot 7!}a^5(-3b)^7$$

$$\frac{12 \cdot 11 \cdot 10 \cdot 9 \cdot 8 \cdot 7!}{5 \cdot 4 \cdot 3 \cdot 2 \cdot 1 \cdot 7!}a^5(-2187)\,b^7$$

$$\frac{12 \cdot 11 \cdot \overset{1}{\cancel{10}} \cdot \overset{3}{\cancel{9}} \cdot \overset{2}{\cancel{8}} \cdot \cancel{7!}}{\cancel{5} \cdot \cancel{4} \cdot \cancel{3} \cdot \cancel{2} \cdot 1 \cdot \cancel{7!}}a^5(-2187)\,b^7$$

$$792 a^5(-2187)\,b^7$$

$$-1732104 a^5 b^7$$

The expansion of binomials has several patterns which should be noted:

Patterns to Binomial Expansions:

1. A binomial $(a+b)^n$ has $n+1$ terms (the binomial has one more term than the power).
2. The power of the variable a decreases by powers of 1 and the power of the variable b increases by powers of 1.
3. In any term, the sum of the powers of both a and b add to be n.
4. The coefficient of any term $a^{n-m}b^m$ is given by the expression

$$\frac{n!}{(n-m)! \cdot m!}.$$

EXERCISE 8.5

Simplify the following:

1. $11!$

2. $8!$

3. $\dfrac{7!}{4!}$

4. $\dfrac{9! \cdot 5!}{3! \cdot 6!}$

Compute each of the following combinations:

5. $\dbinom{8}{3}$

6. $\dbinom{11}{8}$

Raise the following binomial to the power indicated using the binomial theorem:

7. $(x+y)^6$

8. $(a+b)^9$

9. $(2a+3b)^3$

10. $(5x-4y)^4$

Find the coefficient of the indicated term of the following expansions:

11. $(a+b)^8$ find the coefficient of the a^4b^4

12. $(2x-5y)^9$ find the coefficient of the x^3y^6

13. $(5a+3b)^{12}$ find the coefficient of the a^4b^8

ANSWERS TO EXERCISE 8.5

1. $39{,}916{,}800$ 2. $40{,}320$

3. 210 4. $10{,}080$

5. 56 6. 165

7. $x^6 + 6x^5y + 15x^4y^2 + 20x^3y^3 + 15x^2y^4 + 6xy^5 + y^6$

8. $(a+b)^9 = a^9 + 9a^8b + 36a^7b^2 + 84a^6b^3 + 126a^5b^4 + 126a^4b^5$
$\qquad\qquad + 84a^3b^6 + 36a^2b^7 + 9ab^8 + b^9$

9. $8a^3 + 36a^2b + 54ab^2 + 27y^3$

10. $625x^4 - 2000x^3y + 2400x^2y^2 - 1280xy^3 + 256y^4$

11. $70a^4b^4$

12. $10{,}500{,}000x^3y^6$

13. $2{,}029{,}809{,}375\,a^4b^8$

9

Topics in Geometry

SECTION 9.1 CONIC SECTION

In Chapter 4, we discussed first and second degree equations in two variables. A first degree equation in the form of

$$Ax + By = C$$

where A, B, and C are not all zero is called a linear equation. Every linear equation will graph a straight line when graphed on a Cartesian Plane. A second degree equation in the form of

$$y = ax^2 + bx + c$$

where a does not equal zero is a quadratic equation in functional form. Every quadratic function will graph a parabola when graphed on the Cartesian Plane. The quadratic function is first degree in y and second degree in x. In this chapter, we will discuss the graphs of second degree equations in two variables in the form of

$$Ax^2 + Cx^2 + Dx + Ey + F = 0$$

where A and C are not both zero. Graphs of this type of equation are called **conic sections** or just **conics**. To understand the graphs of the conics, we need to define a **right circular cone**. A right circular cone is the geometrical figure formed by a fixed straight line L and a fixed point V on L. The surface generated by all straight lines passing through V making a constant angle θ with L is a **right circular cone**. L is called the **axis** of the cone and V is called the **vertex** or **apex** of the cone. The two parts of the cone separated by the vertex are called **nappes**.

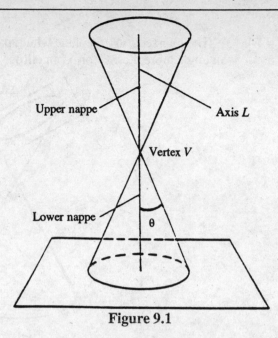

Figure 9.1

Conic sections are the curves of a plane which are formed by the inter-section of a plane and a right circular cone. An intersection of a plane which passes through a nappe of the cone perpendicular to the axis forms a **circle**.

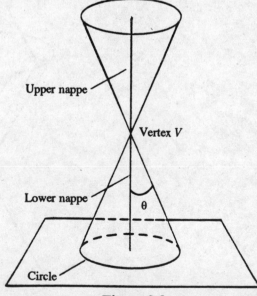

Figure 9.2

The intersection of a plane which passes through a nappe of the cone at an angle more than θ forms an **ellipse**.

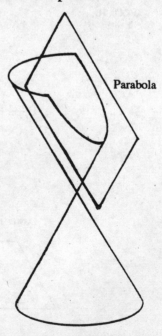

Figure 9.3

The intersection of a plane which passes through a nappe of the cone parallel to a side of the cone forms a **parabola**.

Figure 9.4

The intersection of a plane which passes through a nappe of the cone parallel to the axis of the cone forms a **hyperbola**.

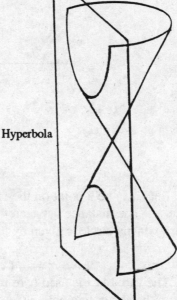

Hyperbola

Figure 9.5

In all of these cases, it is assumed that the plane does not pass through the vertex of the cone. If the plane passes through the vertex of the cone, the intersection is a point, a straight line, or two straight lines. The graph of the parabola was discussed in Chapter 4, so only the circle, ellipse, and hyperbola will be discussed here.

SECTION 9.2 CIRCLE

Definition:
A circle is the set of all of points P in a plane equidistant from a given point. The given point is the **center** and the distance is the **radius**.

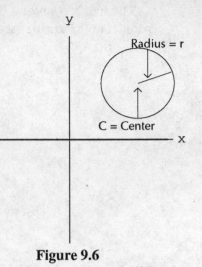

Figure 9.6

Let (x, y) be a point on the circle and let (h, k) be the center of the circle.   The distance between the center of the circle (h, k) and any point (x, y) on the circle is given by the distance formula

$$r = \sqrt{(x-h)^2 + (y-k)^2}.$$

The variable r is used here instead of the variable d, since the distance from the center to a point is the radius. If we square both sides, the equation becomes

$$r^2 = (x-h)^2 + (y-k)^2.$$

This equation is the standard form of the circle. In standard form, the center of the circle C is (h, k) and the radius is r. Be careful! Notice, in standard form, the center is at (h, k) and h and k have the opposite signs as the h and k in standard form. In standard form the radius is squared. The circle,

$$(x-3)^2 + (y+2)^2 = 4$$

has its center at $(3, -2)$ with a radius of 2.

EXAMPLE 9.1

Find the center and radius of the following circle and graph:

$$x^2 + y^2 = 16$$

SOLUTION 9.1

$$x^2 + y^2 = 16$$

The standard form of a circle is

$$(x-h)^2 + (y-k)^2 = r^2.$$

When the only terms are x^2 and y^2, the expression can be written

$$(x-0)^2 + (y-0)^2 = r^2.$$

A circle in the form of

$$x^2 + y^2 = r^2$$

is a circle with center at the origin and radius of r. The circle

$$x^2 + y^2 = 16$$

is a circle with center at (0, 0) and radius of $r = \sqrt{16} = 4$.

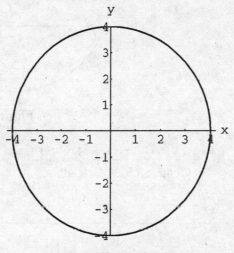

Figure 9.7

EXAMPLE 9.2

Find the center and radius of the following circles and graph:

a) $(x+2)^2 + (y-1)^2 = 9$

b) $(x-5)^2 + (y-3)^2 = 4$

SOLUTION 9.2

a) $(x+2)^2 + (y-1)^2 = 9$

In standard form, the center of the circle is the opposite of the +2 and −1 and the radius is the square root of 9.

Center: (−2, 1)   Radius: $\sqrt{9} = 3$

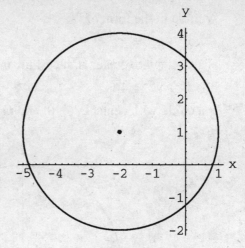

Figure 9.8

b) $(x-5)^2 + (y-3)^2 = 4$

   Center: $(5, 3)$ Radius: $\sqrt{4} = 2$

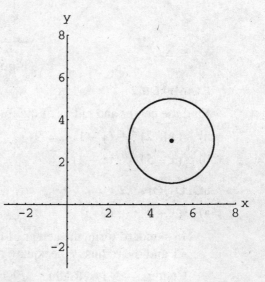

Figure 9.9

EXAMPLE 9.3

Write the equation of the circle in standard form with the given center and radius:

Center $C = (2, 4)$ and radius $r = 3$

SOLUTION 9.3

Center $C = (2, 4)$ and radius $r = 3$
The standard form of a circle is

$$(x - h)^2 + (y - k)^2 = r^2.$$

The equation of the circle with center $C = (2, 4)$ and radius $r = 3$ is

$$(x - 2)^2 + (y - 4)^2 = 3^2.$$
$$(x - 2)^2 + (y - 4)^2 = 9$$

If we combine like terms and clear of fractions, the equation of circle in **general form** is

$$Ax^2 + Ay^2 + Dx + Ey + F = 0$$

where $A \neq 0$. Notice, a circle in general form has the same coefficient for x^2 and y^2. Since the coefficients of x^2 and y^2 are the same, neither can be zero. If one was zero then the other would also have to be zero and the equation would be a straight line, not a circle.

EXAMPLE 9.4

Write the equation of the circle in general form with the given center and radius:

a) Center $C = (-5, 7)$ and radius $r = 2$.

b) Center $C = (3, -4)$ and radius $r = 9$.

SOLUTION 9.4

a) Center $C = (-5, 7)$ and radius $r = 2$.

The standard form of a circle is

$$(x - h)^2 + (y - k)^2 = r^2.$$

The equation of the circle with center $C = (-5, 7)$ and radius $r = 2$ is

$(x + 5)^2 + (y - 7)^2 = 2^2.$ Remove parentheses and

$x^2 + 10x + 25 + y^2 - 14y + 49 = 4$ simplify to get the equation

$x^2 + y^2 + 10x - 14y + 49 + 25 - 4 = 0$ in general form.

$x^2 + y^2 + 10x - 14y + 60 = 0$

b) Center $C = (3, -4)$ and radius $r = 9$.

The equation of the circle with center $C = (3, -4)$ and radius $r = 9$ is

$(x - 3)^2 + (y + 4)^2 = 9^2.$ Remove parentheses and

$x^2 - 6x + 9 + y^2 + 8y + 16 = 81$ simplify.

$x^2 + y^2 - 6x + 8y + 9 + 16 - 81 = 0$

$x^2 + y^2 - 6x + 8y - 56 = 0$

A circle in general form must be put into standard form to find the center and the radius of the circle. To do this, we must use the technique of completing the square.

EXAMPLE 9.5

a) Find the center and radius of the following circle and graph:

$$x^2 + y^2 - 2x + 4y - 4 = 0$$

b) Write the equation of the circle in general form with:

Center $C = (-2, 3)$ and passing through the point $(1, 7)$.

SOLUTION 9.5

a) $x^2 + y^2 - 2x + 4y - 4 = 0$

To find the center of the circle and the radius, put the equation into standard form. To change this equation into standard form, we must complete the square in both x and y. Use the associative and commutative properties of addition and get the x and y terms together. Get the number term on the other side of the equation.

$$x^2 - 2x + \quad + y^2 + 4y + \quad = 4$$

To complete the square in x, the coefficient of x^2 must equal 1. In this problem, the coefficient of x^2 does equal 1. Now multiply $\frac{1}{2}$ times the coefficient of x, square it and add it to both sides.

$$x^2 - 2x + \quad + y^2 + 4y + \quad = 4$$

$$\frac{1}{2} \cdot (-2) = -1; \quad (-1)^2 = 1 \qquad \text{Add 1 to both sides of the equation.}$$

$$x^2 - 2x + 1 + y^2 + 4y = 4 + 1$$

Factor and simplify.

$$(x - 1)^2 + (y + 2)^2 = 9.$$

Do the same thing to the y terms.

$$\frac{1}{2} \cdot (4) = 2; \quad (2)^2 = 4 \qquad \text{Add 4 to both sides of the equation.}$$

$$x^2 - 2x + 1 + y^2 + 4y + 4 = 4 + 1 + 4$$

In standard form, the center is the opposite of the (-1) and $(+2)$ and the radius is the square root of 9.

Center: $(1, -2)$ Radius: $\sqrt{9} = 3$

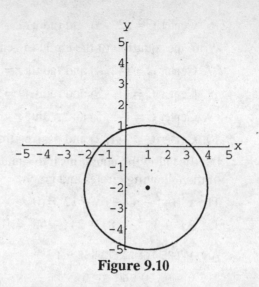

Figure 9.10

b) Center $C = (-2, 3)$ and passing through the point $(1, 7)$.

To find the equation of a circle in general form, start with the equation of a circle in standard form. To write an equation in standard form, we need both the center and the radius. The center is at $(-2, 3)$ and the circle passes through the point $(1, 7)$. The distance from the center to any point on the circle is the radius. Use the distance formula to find the distance between the center and the point $(1, 7)$.

$$d = \sqrt{(1-(-2))^2} = \sqrt{(3)^2 + (4)^2} = \sqrt{9+16} = \sqrt{25} = 5$$

The equation of the circle with center $C = (-2, 3)$ and radius $r = 5$ is

$(x+2)^2 + (y-3)^2 = 5^2$.   Remove parentheses and simplify.

$$x^2 + 4x + 4 + y^2 - 6y + 9 = 25$$
$$x^2 + y^2 + 4x - 6y + 4 + 9 - 25 = 0$$
$$x^2 + y^2 + 4x - 6y - 12 = 0$$

EXERCISE 9.1

Find the center and radius of the following circles and graph:

1. $x^2 + y^2 = 36$

2. $(x-1)^2 + (y+3)^2 = 16$

3. $(x+2)^2 + (y-5)^2 = 10$

Put the equation of the given circles in standard form:

4. Center $C = (3, 1)$ and radius $r = 2$

5. Center $C = (-1, 5)$ and radius $r = 5$

6. Center $C = (2, -3)$ and radius $r = \sqrt{7}$

Write the equation of the circle in general form:

7. Center $C = (-2, 4)$ and radius $r = 3$

8. Center $C = (1, -3)$ and radius $r = 5$

9. Center $C = (-5, 5)$ and radius $r = \sqrt{12}$

10. Center $C = (-1, 2)$ and passing through the point $(2, 6)$

Put the following equations into standard form. Find the center and radius of the following circles and graph:

11. $x^2 + y^2 - 4x + 6y - 12 = 0$

12. $3x^2 + 3y^2 - 18x + 24y + 48 = 0$

ANSWERS TO EXERCISE 9.1

1. $C = (0, 0)$ and $r = 6$

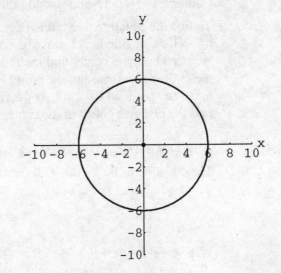

Figure 9.11

2. $C = (1, -3)$ and $r = 4$

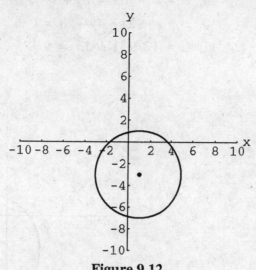

Figure 9.12

3. $C = (-2, 5)$ and $r = \sqrt{10}$

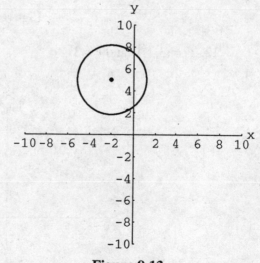

Figure 9.13

4. $(x - 3)^2 + (y - 1)^2 = 4$
5. $(x + 1)^2 + (y - 5)^2 = 25$
6. $(x - 2)^2 + (y + 3)^2 = 7$
7. $x^2 + y^2 + 4x - 8y + 16 = 0$

8. $x^2 + y^2 - 2x + 6y - 15 = 0$

9. $x^2 + y^2 + 10x - 10y + 38 = 0$

10. $x^2 + y^2 + 2x - 4y - 20 = 0$

11. $C = (2, -3)$ and $r = 5$

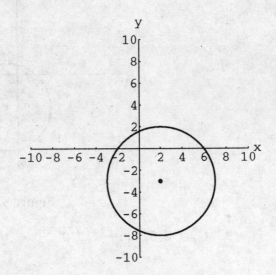

Figure 9.14

12. $C = (3, -4)$ and $r = 3$

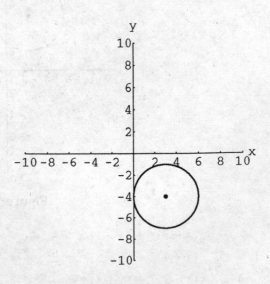

Figure 9.15

SECTION 9.3 ELLIPSE

> **Definition:**
> An **ellipse** is the set of all points P in a plane such that the sum of the distance of P from two fixed points in the plane is a constant. The fixed points F and F' are called **foci** (each point is a **focal point** or **focus**). The midpoint of the segment joining the foci is the **center**.

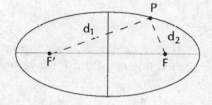

$d_1 + d_2$ = Positive constant

Figure 9.16

The segment passing through the foci and intersection of the ellipse is the **major axis**. The segment passing through the center perpendicular to the major axis is the **minor axis**. The end points of the major axis are called **vertices**. The end points of the minor axis are called **covertices**. Let the ellipse be centered at the origin and let the foci be $(c, 0)$ and $(-c, 0)$.

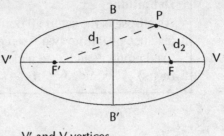

V' and V vertices
B' and B covertices
F' = (−c, 0) and F = (c, 0), c > 0

Figure 9.17

Let d_1 be the distance from the point $P(x, y)$ and $F(c, 0)$ and let d_2 be the distance from $P(x, y)$ and $F'(-c, 0)$.

$$d_1 = \sqrt{(x-c)^2 + (y-0)^2} = \sqrt{(x-c)^2 + y^2}$$

$$d_2 = \sqrt{(x-(-c))^2 + (y-0)^2} = \sqrt{(x+c)^2 + y^2}$$

The sum of the distances from the foci to the point P must be greater than the distance between the two foci.

$$d(F, P) + d(F', P) > d(F, F')$$

$$d_1 + d_2 > 2c.$$

Let $2a > 2c$ and let

$$d_1 + d_2 = 2a.$$

$\sqrt{(x-c)^2 + y^2} + \sqrt{(x+c)^2 + y^2} = 2a$ Add $-d_2$ to both sides.

$\sqrt{(x-c)^2 + y^2} = 2a - \sqrt{(x+c)^2 + y^2}$ Square both sides.

$(\sqrt{(x-c)^2 + y^2})^2 = (2a - \sqrt{(x+c)^2 + y^2})^2$

Simplify.

$(x-c)^2 + y^2 = 4a^2 - 4a\sqrt{(x+c)^2 + y^2} + (x+c)^2 + y^2$

Simplify.

$x^2 - 2cx + c^2 + y^2 = 4a^2 - 4a\sqrt{(x+c)^2 + y^2} + x^2 + 2cx + c^2 + y^2$

Isolate the radical onto one side of the equation and simplify.

$$4a\sqrt{(x+c)^2+y^2} = 4a^2+4cx \qquad \text{Divide both sides by 4.}$$

$$a\sqrt{(x+c)^2+y^2} = a^2+cx \qquad \text{Square both sides again.}$$

$$a^2(x+c)^2+a^2y^2 = a^4+2a^2cx+c^2x^2$$
$$\text{Square the binomial.}$$

$$a^2x^2+2a^2cx+a^2c^2+a^2y^2 = a^4+2a^2cx+c^2x^2$$

Get the x and y terms on the left-hand side.

$$a^2x^2-c^2x^2+a^2y^2 = a^4-a^2c^2 \qquad \text{Factor.}$$

$$(a^2-c^2)x^2+a^2y^2 = a^2(a^2-c^2)$$

Divide both sides by $a^2(a^2-c^2)$. $a^2 \neq 0$ and $(a^2-c^2) \neq 0$.

$$\frac{x^2}{a^2}+\frac{y^2}{a^2-c^2} = 1 \qquad \text{Let } b^2 = a^2-c^2.$$

$$\frac{x^2}{a^2}+\frac{y^2}{b^2} = 1$$

This is the **standard form** of an ellipse with center at $(0, 0)$ and foci at $(c, 0)$ and $(-c, 0)$ where $b^2 = a^2-c^2$. To graph this ellipse, calculate ordered pairs. Let $y = 0$ and solve for x.

$$\frac{x^2}{a^2} = 1$$

$$x^2 = a^2$$

$$x = \pm a$$

The ordered pairs are $(a, 0)$ and $(-a, 0)$. These two points are the end points of the major axis (vertices). To graph the vertices of the ellipse move in the x direction, 'a' units to the right of the center and 'a' units to the left of the center, and graph the vertices. Let $x = 0$ and solve for y.

$$\frac{y^2}{b^2} = 1$$

$$y^2 = b^2$$

$$y = \pm b$$

The ordered pairs are $(0, b)$ and $(0, -b)$. These two points are the end points of the minor axis (covertices). To graph the covertices move in the y direction 'b' units up from the center and 'b' units down from the center, and graph the covertices. Now, graph the ellipse.

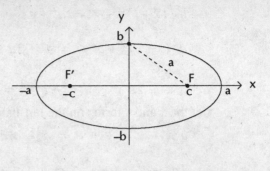

$$c > 0$$

Figure 9.18

Notice the length of the major axis is $2a$ and the length of the minor axis is $2b$. The standard form of an ellipse with center at the origin is

$$\frac{x^2}{a^2} + \frac{y^2}{b^2} = 1.$$

To graph an ellipse in standard form

$$\frac{x^2}{a^2} + \frac{y^2}{b^2} = 1,$$

from the origin $(0, 0)$, move to left by 'a' units and move to the right by 'a' units and graph these points. From the origin $(0, 0)$, move down by 'b' units and then move up by 'b' units and graph these points. We then draw the ellipse around these points.

If the foci are on the y-axis, then the equation becomes

$$\frac{y^2}{a^2} + \frac{x^2}{b^2} = 1.$$

In this equation, from the origin move 'a' units up and down and move 'b' units left and right. The major axis still has the length of $2a$ and the minor axis still has the length of $2b$. The vertices are $(0, a)$ and $(0, -a)$. The covertices are $(b, 0)$ and $(-b, 0)$.

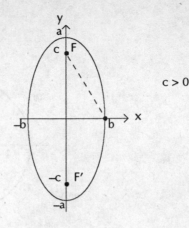

Figure 9.19

When graphing an ellipse, the important idea is that you move in the x direction by the square root of the number under the x^2 term and you move in the y direction by the square root of the number under the y^2 term. The larger of the two numbers $2a$ or $2b$ represents the length of the major axis and the smaller of the two numbers represents the length of the minor axis.

EXAMPLE 9.6

Graph the following ellipses. Find the length of the major and minor axis. Find the coordinates of the vertices and the covertices:

a) $\dfrac{x^2}{25} + \dfrac{y^2}{16} = 1$

b) $\dfrac{x^2}{4} + \dfrac{y^2}{9} = 1$

SOLUTION 9.6

a) $\dfrac{x^2}{25} + \dfrac{y^2}{16} = 1$

The standard form of an ellipse centered at the origin is

$$\frac{x^2}{a^2} + \frac{y^2}{b^2} = 1,$$

where $a^2 > b^2$. This ellipse has its center at the origin. $25 > 16$ so $a^2 = 25$ and $b^2 = 16$ and $a = 5$ and $b = 4$.

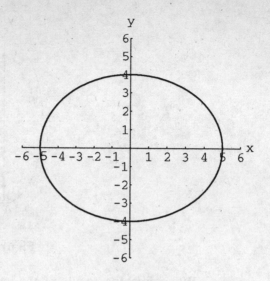

Figure 9.20

The length of the major axis is $2a = 10$ units and the length of the minor axis is $2b = 8$ units. The end points of the major axis are the vertices which are $(5, 0)$ and $(-5, 0)$. The end points of the minor axis are the covertices which are $(0, 4)$ and $(0, -4)$.

b) $\dfrac{x^2}{4} + \dfrac{y^2}{9} = 1$

The number under the y^2 term is greater than the number under the x^2 term, so the ellipse is elongated in the y direction. The standard form of an ellipse elongated in the y direction is

$\dfrac{y^2}{a^2} + \dfrac{x^2}{b^2} = 1$, where $a^2 > b^2$.

Rewrite the equation into this form.

$\dfrac{y^2}{9} + \dfrac{x^2}{4} = 1$

The ellipse has its center at the origin with $a^2 = 9$ and $b^2 = 4$, so $a = 3$ and $b = 2$.

The length of the major axis is $2a = 6$ units and the length of the minor axis is $2b = 4$ units. The end points of the major axis are the vertices at $(0, 3)$ and $(0, -3)$. The end points of the minor axis are the covertices at $(2, 0)$ and $(-2, 0)$.

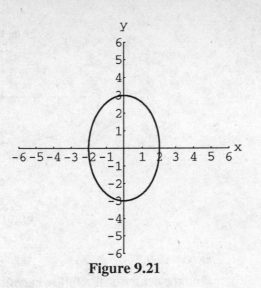

Figure 9.21

The standard form of an ellipse with center at (h, k) is

$$\frac{(x-h)^2}{a^2} + \frac{(y-k)^2}{b^2} = 1$$

with major in the x direction. From the center (h, k), move 'a' units left and right and 'b' units up and down. The vertices are at $(h \pm a, k)$ and the covertices are at $(h, k \pm b)$. The length of the major axis is still $2a$ and the length of the minor axis is $2b$.

When the ellipse is elongated in the y direction the equation becomes

$$\frac{(y-k)^2}{a^2} + \frac{(x-h)^2}{b^2} = 1.$$

Remember the center is still at (h, k). From the center (h, k), move 'a' units up and down and 'b' units left and right. The vertices are at $(h, k \pm a)$ and the covertices are at $(h \pm b, k)$. The length of major axis is $2a$ and the length of the minor axis is $2b$.

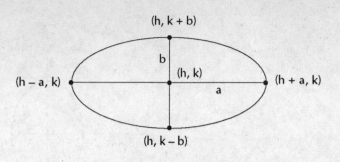

Figure 9.22

EXAMPLE 9.7

Find the center of the following ellipse and graph. Find the length of the major axis and the length of the minor axis. Find the coordinates of the vertices and the coordinates of the covertices:

$$\frac{(x-2)^2}{9} + \frac{(y-1)^2}{4} = 1$$

SOLUTION 9.7

$$\frac{(x-2)^2}{9} + \frac{(y-1)^2}{4} = 1$$

This ellipse has its center at $(2, 1)$. Since $9 > 4$, it is elongated in the x direction with $a^2 = 9$ and $b^2 = 4$, so $a = 3$ and $b = 2$.

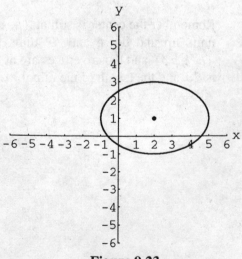

Figure 9.23

The length of the major axis is $2a = 6$ units and the length of the minor axis is $2b = 4$ units. The end points of the major axis are the vertices at $(2 + 3, 1)$ and $(2 - 3, 1)$ which are $(5, 1)$ and $(-1, 1)$. The end points of the minor axis are the covertices at $(2, 1 + 2)$ and $(2, 1 - 2)$ or $(2, 3)$ and $(2, -1)$.

Remember the general form of a circle is
$$Ax^2 + Ay^2 + Dx + Ey + F = 0.$$
The general form of an ellipse is
$$Ax^2 + Cy^2 + Dx + Ey + F = 0.$$
The only difference between the general form of the circle and the ellipse is that a circle must have the same coefficients of x^2 and y^2. In the ellipse, however, the coefficients of x^2 and y^2 (A and C) are different (not equal).

EXAMPLE 9.8

Put the following ellipse into standard form. Find the center of the ellipse and graph. Find the lengths of the major and minor axis. Find the coordinates of the vertices and covertices:

$9x^2 + 16y^2 + 36x + 96y + 36 = 0$

SOLUTION 9.8

$9x^2 + 16y^2 + 36x + 96y + 36 = 0$
Associate the x terms and the y terms.

$9x^2 + 18x + \quad + 16y^2 + 96y + \quad = -36$
Factor 9 out of the x terms and 16 from the y terms.

$9(x^2 + 4x + \quad) + 16(y^2 + 6y + \quad) = -36$ Complete the square.

$$\frac{1}{2} \cdot 4 = 2 \qquad \frac{1}{2} \cdot 6 = 3$$

$$(2)^2 \qquad\qquad (3)^2$$
$$4 \qquad\qquad\quad 9$$

Add 4 and 9 inside of the parentheses.

$9(x^2 + 4x + 4) + 16(y^2 + 6y + 9) = -36$

Add $4 \cdot 9$ and $9 \cdot 16$ to the other side of the equation.

$9(x^2 + 4x + 4) + 16(y^2 + 6y + 9) = -36 + 36 + 144$

$9(x^2 + 4x + 4) + 16(y^2 + 6y + 9) = 144$

Factor.

$9(x + 2)^2 + 16(y + 3)^2 = 144$ Divide both sides by 144.

$$\frac{(x + 2)^2}{16} + \frac{(y + 3)^2}{9} = 1$$

The center of the ellipse is at (–2, –3). The ellipse is elongated in the x direction.

$$a^2 = 16 \quad \text{and} \quad b^2 = 9$$

$$a = 4 \quad \text{and} \quad b = 3$$

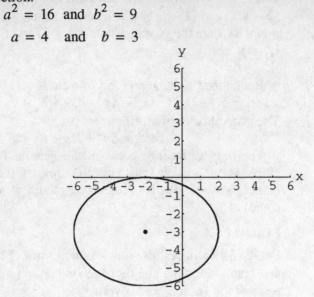

Figure 9.24

The length of the major axis is $2a = 8$ units and the length of the minor axis is $2b = 6$ units. The end points of the major axis are the vertices at (–2 + 4, –3) and (–2 – 4, –3) or (2, –3) and (–6, –3). The end points of the minor axis are the covertices at (–2, –3 + 3) and (–2, –3 – 3) or (–2, 0) and (–2, –6).

EXERCISE 9.2

Find the center of the following ellipses and graph. Find the length of the major axis and the length of the minor axis. Find the coordinates of the vertices and the coordinates of the covertices:

1. $\dfrac{x^2}{25} + \dfrac{y^2}{9} = 1$

2. $\dfrac{(x-1)^2}{16} + \dfrac{(y+2)^2}{25} = 1$

3. $\dfrac{(x+2)^2}{9} + \dfrac{(y-1)^2}{16} = 1$

Put the following ellipses into standard form. Find the center of the ellipse and graph. Find the length of the major axis and the length of the minor axis. Find the coordinates of the vertices and covertices:

4. $4x^2 + 9y^2 - 16x - 54y + 61 = 0$

Write the equation of the ellipse in both standard form and general form:

5. with center at $(2, 3)$, $a = 4$ and $b = 2$ elongated in the x direction.
6. with center at $(-1, 4)$, length of major axis is 16, length of minor axis is 10 and elongated in the y direction.
7. with vertices at $(7, 3)$ and $(-3, 3)$ and one covertice at $(2, 5)$.

ANSWERS TO EXERCISE 9.2

1. Center: $(0, 0)$; Length of Major Axis: $2a = 10$; Length of Minor Axis: $2b = 6$; Vertices: $(5, 0)$ and $(-5, 0)$; Covertices: $(0, 3)$ and $(0, -3)$

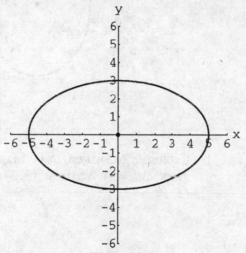

Figure 9.25

2. Center: $(1, -2)$; Length of Major Axis: $2a = 10$; Length of Minor Axis: $2b = 8$; Vertices: $(1, 3)$ and $(1, -7)$; Covertices: $(5, -2)$ and $(-3, -2)$

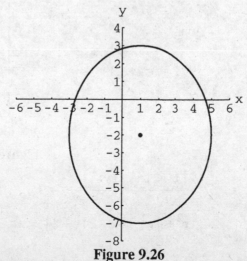

Figure 9.26

3. Center: (–2, 1); Length of Major Axis: $2a = 8$; Length of Minor Axis: $2b = 6$; Vertices: (–2, 5) and (–2, –3) Covertices: (1, 1) and (–5, 1)

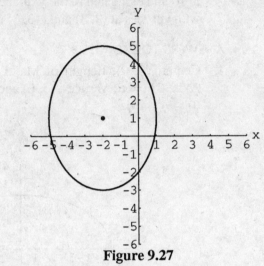

Figure 9.27

4. Center: (2, 3); Length of Major Axis: $2a = 6$; Length of Minor Axis: $2b = 4$; Vertices: (5, 3) and (–1, 3); Covertices: (2, 5) and (2, 1)

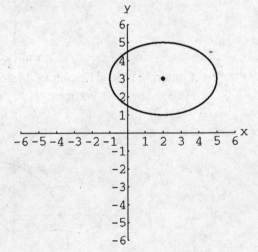

Figure 9.28

5. $\dfrac{(x-2)^2}{16} + \dfrac{(y-3)^2}{4} = 1$

    $x^2 + 4y^2 - 4x - 24y + 24 = 0$

6. $\dfrac{(y+1)^2}{64} + \dfrac{(x-4)^2}{25} = 1$

    $64x^2 + 25y^2 + 128x - 200y - 1136 = 0$

7. $\dfrac{(x-2)^2}{25} + \dfrac{(y-3)^2}{9} = 1$

    $9x^2 + 25y^2 - 36x - 150y + 36 = 0$

SECTION 9.4 HYPERBOLA

Definition:

A **hyperbola** is the set of all points P in a plane such that the absolute value of the difference of the distance of a point $P(x, y)$ on the hyperbola to two fixed points is a constant. The fixed points F and F' are called the **foci** (or **focal points** or **focus**). The intersection points of the line passing through the foci are the **vertices** V and V' (each point is a **vertex**). The line segment with the foci as its endpoints is called the **transverse axis**. The midpoint of the transverse axis is the **center** of the hyperbola.

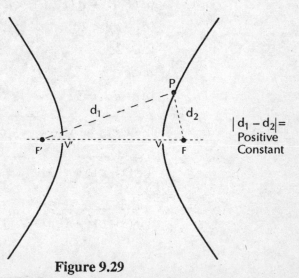

Figure 9.29

Like the ellipse, it is best to let the constant difference be $2a$, where $a > 0$. Let d_1 be the distance from the point $P(x, y)$ and $F(c, 0)$ and let d_2 be the distance from $P(x, y)$ and $F'(-c, 0)$ with the x-axis as the transverse axis.

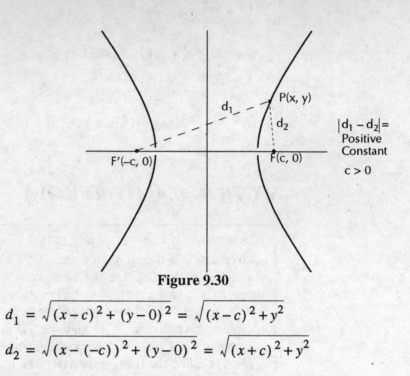

Figure 9.30

$$d_1 = \sqrt{(x-c)^2 + (y-0)^2} = \sqrt{(x-c)^2 + y^2}$$

$$d_2 = \sqrt{(x-(-c))^2 + (y-0)^2} = \sqrt{(x+c)^2 + y^2}$$

The difference of the distances from the foci to the point P must be less than the distance between the two foci.

$$|d(F, P) - d(F', P)| < d(F, F')$$

$$|d_1 - d_2| < 2c$$

$$2a < 2c$$

$$a < c$$

$$|d_1 - d_2| = 2c$$

$$\left| \sqrt{(x-c)^2 + y^2} - \sqrt{(x+c)^2 + y^2} \right| = 2a \quad \text{Square both sides.}$$

$$\left(\sqrt{(x-c)^2 + y^2} - \sqrt{(x+c)^2 + y^2} \right)^2 = (2a)^2$$
$$\text{Simplify.}$$

$$\left(\sqrt{(x-c)^2 + y^2} \right)^2 - 2\sqrt{[(x-c)^2 + y^2][(x+c)^2 + y^2]}$$
$$+ \left(\sqrt{(x+c)^2 + y^2} \right)^2 = 4a^2$$

$$(x-c)^2 + y^2 - 2\sqrt{[(x-c)^2 + y^2][(x+c)^2 + y^2]} + (x+c)^2 + y^2$$
$$= 4a^2$$

$$x^2 - 2cx + c^2 + y^2 - 2\sqrt{[(x-c)^2 + y^2][(x+c)^2 + y^2]}$$

$$+ x^2 + 2cx + c^2 + y^2 = 4a^2$$

$$2x^2 + 2c^2 + 2y^2 - 4a^2 = 2\sqrt{[(x-c)^2 + y^2][(x+c)^2 + y^2]}$$

Divide both sides by 2.

$$x^2 + c^2 + y^2 - 2a^2 = \sqrt{[(x-c)^2 + y^2][(x+c)^2 + y^2]}$$

Square both sides again.

$$(x^2 + c^2 + y^2 - 2a^2)^2 = \left(\sqrt{[(x-c)^2 + y^2][(x+c)^2 + y^2]}\right)^2$$

Simplify.

$$(x^2 + c^2 + y^2 - 2a^2)^2 = [(x-c)^2 + y^2][(x+c)^2 + y^2]$$

$$(x^2 + c^2 + y^2 - 2a^2)^2 = [x^2 - 2cx + c^2 + y^2][x^2 + 2cx + c^2 + y^2]$$

$$x^4 - 4a^2x^2 - 4a^2y^2 - 4a^2c^2 + 4a^4 + y^4 + 2c^2y^2 + 2c^2x^2 + 2x^2y^2 + c^4$$

$$= x^4 - 2c^2x^2 + 2x^2y^2 + c^4 + y^4 + 2c^2y^2$$

$$-4a^2x^2 - 4a^2y^2 - 4a^2c^2 + 4a^4 + 2c^2x^2 = -2c^2x^2$$

Get the x and y terms on one side.

$$4c^2x^2 - 4a^2x^2 - 4a^2y^2 = 4a^2c^2 - 4a^4 \quad \text{Divide both sides by 4.}$$

$$c^2x^2 - a^2x^2 - a^2y^2 = a^2c^2 - a^4 \qquad \text{Factor common factors.}$$

$$x^2(c^2 - a^2) - a^2y^2 = a^2(c^2 - a^2)$$

Divide both sides by $a^2(c^2 - a^2)$. This is permitted since a^2 and $(c^2 - a^2)$ are not zero. Also a^2 and $(c^2 - a^2)$ are both positive from the original conditions.

$$\frac{x^2}{a^2} - \frac{y^2}{c^2 - a^2} = 1$$

Let $b^2 = c^2 - a^2$.

$$\frac{x^2}{a^2} - \frac{y^2}{b^2} = 1$$

This is the equation in standard form of a hyperbola with center at the origin and foci on the x axis. Notice that the standard form of the hyperbola and the standard form of the ellipse are exactly the same except that in the hyperbola the $\dfrac{x^2}{a^2}$ and $\dfrac{y^2}{b^2}$ are subtracted and in the ellipse they are added.

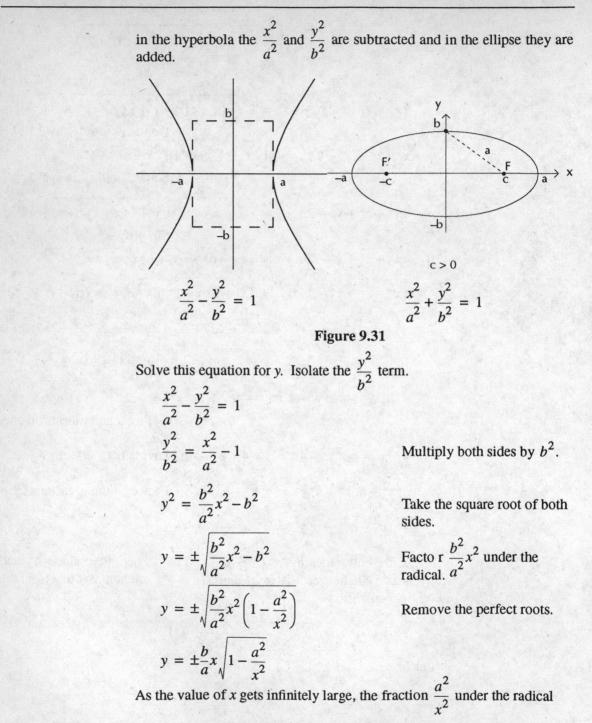

$$\frac{x^2}{a^2} - \frac{y^2}{b^2} = 1 \qquad\qquad \frac{x^2}{a^2} + \frac{y^2}{b^2} = 1$$

Figure 9.31

Solve this equation for y. Isolate the $\dfrac{y^2}{b^2}$ term.

$$\frac{x^2}{a^2} - \frac{y^2}{b^2} = 1$$

$$\frac{y^2}{b^2} = \frac{x^2}{a^2} - 1 \qquad\qquad\qquad \text{Multiply both sides by } b^2.$$

$$y^2 = \frac{b^2}{a^2}x^2 - b^2 \qquad\qquad\qquad \text{Take the square root of both sides.}$$

$$y = \pm\sqrt{\frac{b^2}{a^2}x^2 - b^2} \qquad\qquad \text{Facto r } \frac{b^2}{a^2}x^2 \text{ under the radical.}$$

$$y = \pm\sqrt{\frac{b^2}{a^2}x^2\left(1 - \frac{a^2}{x^2}\right)} \qquad \text{Remove the perfect roots.}$$

$$y = \pm\frac{b}{a}x\sqrt{1 - \frac{a^2}{x^2}}$$

As the value of x gets infinitely large, the fraction $\dfrac{a^2}{x^2}$ under the radical

goes to zero. As the denominator of a fraction gets larger the fraction gets smaller. As x gets large

$$y = \pm \frac{b}{a} x \sqrt{1 - \frac{a^2}{x^2}}$$

approaches

$$y = \pm \frac{b}{a} x \sqrt{1}$$

which equals

$$y = \pm \frac{b}{a} x.$$

$y = \pm \frac{b}{a} x$ means $y = \frac{b}{a} x$ and $y = -\frac{b}{a} x.$

These two equations are linear equations which are important to the graph of the hyperbola. These two lines are called **asymptotes** of the graph of the hyperbola. As points of the hyperbola move away from the vertices, the points of the hyperbola approaches these lines (asymptotes).

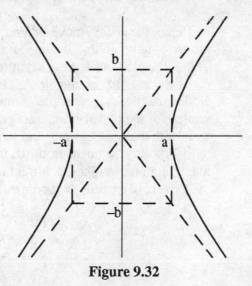

Figure 9.32

The standard form of a hyperbola with center at the origin and the transverse axis along the y-axis is

$$\frac{y^2}{a^2} - \frac{x^2}{b^2} = 1.$$

The relationship between a, b, and c is the same as before $(b^2 = c^2 - a^2)$, except the asymptotes are $y = \pm \frac{a}{b} x.$

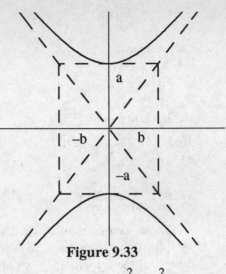

Figure 9.33

A good way to graph the hyperbola $\dfrac{x^2}{a^2} - \dfrac{y^2}{b^2} = 1$ is to start at the cen-

ter. From the center, move 'a' units to the left and right of the center and move 'b' units up and down. Draw a rectangle as in the above figure. This rectangle is called the **asymptote rectangle**. The diagonals of this rectangle are the asymptotes. Draw the diagonals of this rectangle. Notice that the diagonals pass through the center of the hyperbola. The vertices of the hyperbola are the points $(a, 0)$ and $(-a, 0)$. The line segment with the vertices $(a, 0)$ and $(-a, 0)$ as its end points is the **transverse axis**. The line segment from $(0, b)$ and $(0, -b)$ is called the **conjugate axis**. From the vertices, construct the hyperbola by drawing the graph of the hyperbola towards the asymptotes.

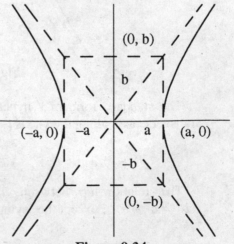

Figure 9.34

Standard Equations of a Hyperbola:

1. $\dfrac{x^2}{a^2} - \dfrac{y^2}{b^2} = 1$ Transverse Axis along the x-Axis.

   Foci: $(c, 0)$ and $(-c, 0)$

   Vertices: $(a, 0)$ and $(-a, 0)$

   $b^2 = c^2 - a^2$

   Length of Transverse Axis: $2a$

   Length of Conjugate Axis: $2b$

   Equations of Asymptotes: $y = \dfrac{b}{a}x$ and $y = -\dfrac{b}{a}x$

2. $\dfrac{y^2}{a^2} - \dfrac{x^2}{b^2} = 1$ Transverse Axis along the y-Axis.

   Foci: $(0, c)$ and $(0, -c)$

   Vertices: $(0, a)$ and $(0, -a)$

   $b^2 = c^2 - a^2$

   Length of Transverse Axis: $2a$

   Length of Conjugate Axis: $2b$

   Equations of Asymptotes: $y = \dfrac{a}{b}x$ and $y = -\dfrac{a}{b}x$

EXAMPLE 9.9

Draw the graph of the following hyperbola. Draw the asymptote rectangle and the asymptotes. Give the coordinates of the vertices and the equations of the asymptotes.

$$\frac{x^2}{4} - \frac{y^2}{9} = 1$$

SOLUTION 9.9

$$\frac{x^2}{4} - \frac{y^2}{9} = 1.$$

The center of the hyperbola is (0, 0). Since the x^2 term is positive, the transverse axis is along the x axis. $a^2 = 4$ so $a = 2$. $b^2 = 9$ so $b = 3$. Draw the asymptote rectangle and draw the asymptotes.

The vertices are (2, 0) and (–2, 0).

The asymptotes are $y = \frac{3}{2}x$ and $y = -\frac{3}{2}x$. Draw the hyperbola.

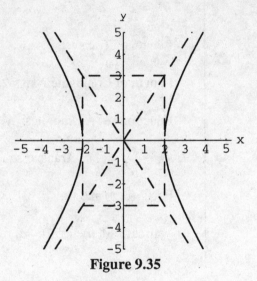

Figure 9.35

If the hyperbola has its center at the (h, k), the standard form for the hyperbola with transverse axis in the x direction is

$$\frac{(x-h)^2}{a^2} - \frac{(y-k)^2}{b^2} = 1.$$

The center of the hyperbola is at (h, k) and the vertices are at $(h, k \pm a)$. The asymptotes are

$$y - k = \pm\frac{a}{b}(x-h).$$

Standard Equations of a Hyperbola:

1. $\dfrac{(x-h)^2}{a^2} - \dfrac{(y-k)^2}{b^2} = 1$ Transverse Axis along the x-Axis.

Foci: $(h+c, k)$ and $(h-c, k)$

Vertices: $(h+a, k)$ and $(h-a, k)$

$b^2 = c^2 - a^2$

Length of Transverse Axis: $2a$

Length of Conjugate Axis: $2b$

Equations of Asymptotes: $y - k = \dfrac{b}{a}(x-h)$ and
$$y - k = -\dfrac{b}{a}(x-h)$$

2. $\dfrac{(y-k)^2}{a^2} - \dfrac{(x-h)^2}{b^2} = 1$ Transverse Axis along the y-Axis.

Foci: $(h, k+c)$ and $(h, k-c)$

Vertices: $(h, k+a)$ and $(h, k-a)$

$b^2 = c^2 - a^2$

Length of Transverse Axis: $2a$

Length of Conjugate Axis: $2b$

Equations of Asymptotes: $y - k = \dfrac{a}{b}(x-h)$ and
$$y - k = -\dfrac{a}{b}(x-h)$$

EXAMPLE 9.10

Draw the graphs of the following hyperbolas. Draw the asymptote rectangle and the asymptotes. Give the coordinates of the vertices and the equations of the asymptotes.

a) $\dfrac{(x-1)^2}{9} - \dfrac{(y-2)^2}{4} = 1$

b) $\dfrac{(y-4)^2}{25} - \dfrac{(x+1)^2}{4} = 1$

SOLUTION 9.10

a) $\dfrac{(x-1)^2}{9} - \dfrac{(y-2)^2}{4} = 1$

The center of the hyperbola is $(1, 2)$. Since the x^2 term is positive, the transverse axis is in the x direction. $a^2 = 9$ so $a = 3$. $b^2 = 4$ and $b = 2$. The vertices are $(4, 2)$ and $(-2, 2)$. The asymptotes are $y - 2 = \dfrac{2}{3}(x-1)$ and $y - 2 = -\dfrac{2}{3}(x-2)$. Simplify the equations of the asymptotes.

$$2x - 3y = -4 \text{ and } 2x + 3y = 10$$

Draw the asymptote rectangle, the asymptotes, and the hyperbola.

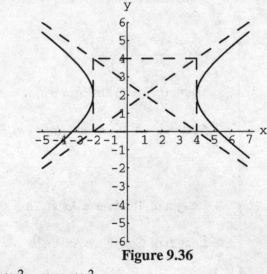

Figure 9.36

b) $\dfrac{(y-4)^2}{25} - \dfrac{(x+1)^2}{4} = 1$

The center of the hyperbola is $(4, -1)$. Since the y^2 term is positive, the transverse axis is in the y direction. $a^2 = 25$ and $a = 5$. $b^2 = 4$ and $b = 2$. The vertices are $(4, 4)$ and $(4, -6)$. The equations of the asymptotes are $y - 4 = \dfrac{5}{2}(x+1)$ and $y - 4 = -\dfrac{5}{2}(x+1)$. Simplify the equations of the asymptotes.

$$5x - 2y = -13 \text{ and } 5x + 2y = 3$$

Draw the asymptote rectangle, the asymptotes, and the hyperbola.

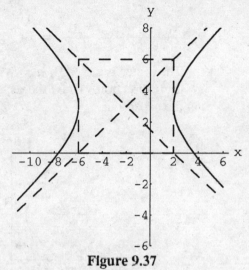

Figure 9.37

The general form of the conic sections is

$$Ax^2 + Cy^2 + Dx + Ey + F = 0.$$

If A and C have opposite signs, then the conic section is a hyperbola or a point.

EXAMPLE 9.11

Put the following hyperbolas into standard form and graph:

a) $4x^2 - 9y^2 - 16x + 54y - 101 = 0$

b) $9x^2 - 4y^2 + 54x - 40y + 17 = 0$

SOLUTION 9.11

a) $4x^2 - 9y^2 - 16x + 54y - 101 = 0$

To put the equation into standard form, complete the square. Commute and associate the x and y terms.

$$4x^2 - 16x \quad - 9y^2 + 54y \quad = 101$$

Factor 4 from the x terms and –9 from the y terms.

$$4(x^2 - 4x \quad) - 9(y^2 - 6y \quad) = 101$$

$$\frac{1}{2} \cdot (-4) = -2 \qquad \frac{1}{2} \cdot (-6) = -3$$

$$(-2)^2 = 4 \qquad (-3)^2 = 9$$

Add 4 and 9 inside of the parentheses and $4 \cdot 4 = 16$ and $-9 \cdot 9 = -81$ to the left-hand side of the equation.

$$4(x^2 - 4x + 4) - 9(y^2 - 6y + 9) = 101 + 16 - 81$$

Simplify and factor.

$$4(x-2)^2 - 9(y-3)^2 = 36$$ Divide both sides by 36.

$$\frac{(x-2)^2}{9} - \frac{(y-3)^2}{4} = 1$$

The center is at (2, 3), $a = 3$ and $b = 2$. The transverse axis is in the x direction. Draw the asymptote rectangle, the asymptotes, and the hyperbola.

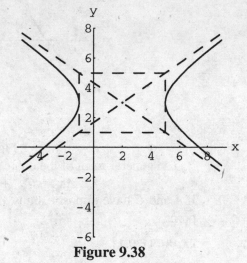

Figure 9.38

b) $9x^2 - 4y^2 + 54x - 40y + 17 = 0$

Associate the x and y terms and complete the square.

$$9x^2 + 54x \quad - 4y^2 - 40y \quad = -17$$

Factor 9 from the x terms and –4 from the y terms.

$$9(x^2 + 6x \quad) - 4(y^2 + 10y \quad) = -17$$

$$\frac{1}{2} \cdot (6) = 3 \quad \frac{1}{2} \cdot (10) = 5$$

$$(3)^2 = 9 \quad (5)^2 = 25$$

Add 9 and 25 inside of the parentheses and 81 and –100 to the left-hand side of the equation.

$$9(x^2 + 6x + 9) - 4(y^2 + 10y + 25) = -17 + 81 - 100$$

Simplify and factor.

$$9(x+3)^2 - 4(y+5)^2 = -36$$ Divide both sides by –36 and write the positive term first.

$$\frac{(y+5)^2}{9} - \frac{(x+3)^2}{4} = 1$$

The center is at $(-3, -2)$, $a = 3$ and $b = 2$. This time the transverse axis is in the y direction. Draw the asymptote rectangle, the asymptotes, and the curve.

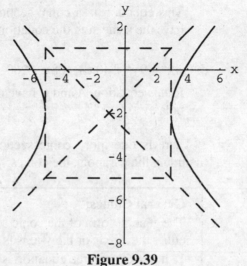

Figure 9.39

General Conics:

The general form of the conic sections which turn with respect to either the x-axis or the y-axis is $Ax^2 + Cy^2 + Dx + Ey + F = 0$.

1. If $A = C$, then the equation is a circle, point, or no graph.
2. If $A \neq C$, but both are positive or both negative, then the equation is an ellipse, point, or no graph.
3. If A and C have different signs, then the equation is a hyperbola or a point.

EXAMPLE 9.12

Name the graph of the following equations. Assume that all graphs form conic sections:

a) $2x^2 + 2y^2 - 8x + 10y + 18 = 0$

b) $9x^2 + 4y^2 + 54x - 32y + 109 = 0$

c) $4x^2 - 9y^2 + 40x + 108y - 260 = 0$

SOLUTION 9.12

a) $2x^2 + 2y^2 - 8x + 10y + 18 = 0$

The equation is assumed to be a conic section. Since A and C are equal, the equation is an equation of a circle.

b) $9x^2 + 4y^2 + 54x - 32y + 109 = 0$

This equation is a conic section. Since A and C are not equal, but have the same sign the equation graphs as an ellipse.

c) $4x^2 - 9y^2 + 40x + 108y - 260 = 0$

In this equation, A and C have opposite signs, the equation is a hyperbola.

There is one more conic section. The parabola is a conic section. Including the parabola, the conics sections are:

General Conics:

The general form of the conic sections which turn with respect to either the x-axis or the y-axis is $Ax^2 + Cy^2 + Dx + Ey + F = 0$.

1. If $A = C$, then the equation is a circle, point, or no graph.
2. If $A = 0$ or $C = 0$ but not both, then the equation is a parabola.
3. If $A \neq C$, but both are positive or both negative, then the equation is an ellipse, point, or no graph.
4. If A and C have different signs, then the equation is a hyperbola or a point.

EXERCISE 9.3

Draw the graph of the following hyperbolas. Draw the asymptote rectangle and the asymptotes. Give the coordinates of the vertices and the equations of the asymptotes.

1. $\dfrac{x^2}{16} - \dfrac{y^2}{25} = 1$

2. $\dfrac{y^2}{4} - \dfrac{x^2}{16} = 1$

3. $\dfrac{(x-7)^2}{25} - \dfrac{(x+4)^2}{49} = 1$

Put the following hyperbolas into standard form and graph:

4. $9x^2 - 4y^2 - 36x - 8y - 4 = 0$

5. $16x^2 - 25y^2 + 96x + 100y + 444 = 0$

6. $4x^2 - y^2 + 16x + 10y + 315 = 0$

Name the graph of the following equations. Put the equation into standard form and graph. Label all important parts of the graph (center, vertices, covertices, length of the major axis, length of the minor axis, length of the transverse axis, and equation of the asymptotes):

7. $x^2 + 4y^2 - 4x + 40y + 68 = 0$

8. $9x^2 + 9y^2 + 54x - 36y + 108 = 0$

9. $9x^2 - 16y^2 + 36x + 96y + 36 = 0$

ANSWERS TO EXERCISE 9.3

1. Center: $(0, 0)$; Vertices: $(4, 0)$ and $(-4, 0)$

   Asymptotes: $y = \dfrac{5}{4}x$ and $y = -\dfrac{5}{4}x$

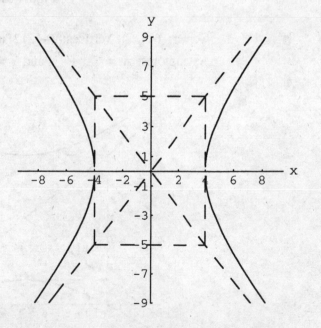

Figure 9.40

2.   Center: (0, 0); Vertices: (0, 2) and (0, –2)
     Asymptotes: $y = \dfrac{1}{2}x$ and $y = -\dfrac{1}{2}x$

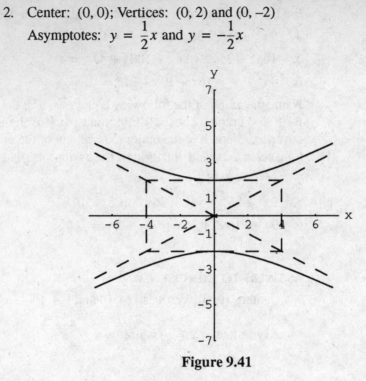

Figure 9.41

3.   Center: (–4, 7); Vertices: (–4, 12) and (–4, 2)
     Asymptotes: $y = \dfrac{5}{7}x + \dfrac{69}{7}$ and $y = -\dfrac{5}{7}x + \dfrac{29}{7}$

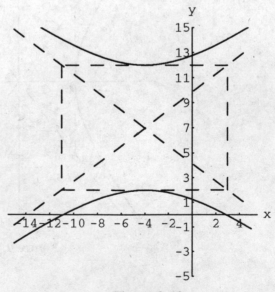

Figure 9.42

4. $\dfrac{(x-2)^2}{4} - \dfrac{(y+1)^2}{9} = 1$

Center: $(2, -1)$; Vertices: $(4, -1)$ and $(0, -1)$

Asymptotes: $y = \dfrac{3}{2}x - 4$ and $y = -\dfrac{3}{2}x + 2$

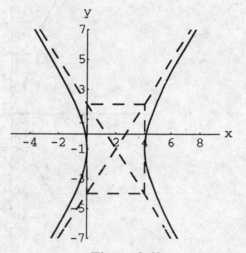

Figure 9.43

5. $\dfrac{(y+2)^2}{16} - \dfrac{(x+3)^2}{25} = 1$

Center: $(-3, -2)$; Vertices: $(-3, 2)$ and $(-3, -6)$

Asymptotes: $y = \dfrac{4}{5}x + \dfrac{22}{5}$ and $y = -\dfrac{4}{5}x - \dfrac{2}{5}$

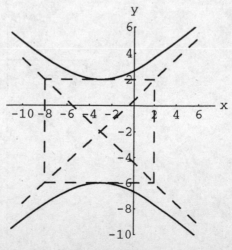

Figure 9.44

6. $\dfrac{(y-5)^2}{324} - \dfrac{(x+2)^2}{81} = 1$

Center: $(-2, 5)$; Vertices: $(-2, 23)$ and $(-2, -13)$

Asymptotes: $y = 2x + 9$ and $y = -2x + 1$

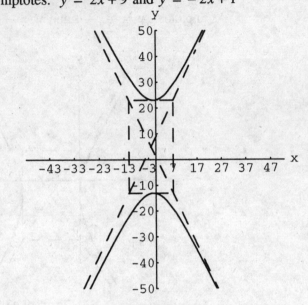

Figure 9.45

7. $\dfrac{(x-2)^2}{36} + \dfrac{(y+5)^2}{9} = 1$ The equation is an ellipse.

Center: $(2, -5)$; Length of Major Axis: $2a = 12$; Length of Minor Axis: $2b = 6$; Vertices: $(8, -5)$ and $(-4, -5)$; Covertices: $(2, -2)$ and $(2, -8)$

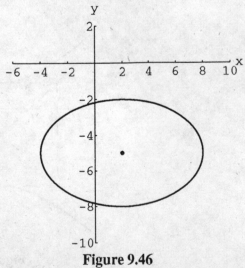

Figure 9.46

8. $(x+3)^2 + (y-2)^2 = 1$ The equation is a circle.

Center: $(-3, 2)$; Radius: 1

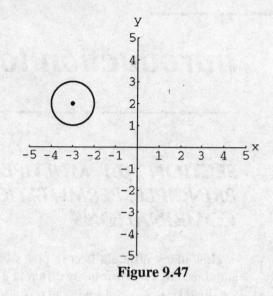

Figure 9.47

9. $\dfrac{(y-3)^2}{9} - \dfrac{(x+2)^2}{16} = 1$ The equation is a hyperbola.

Center: $(-2, 3)$; Vertices: $(-2, 6)$ and $(-2, 0)$

Asymptotes: $y = \dfrac{3}{4}x + \dfrac{3}{2}$ and $y = -\dfrac{3}{4}x + \dfrac{9}{2}$

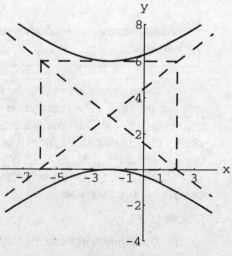

Figure 9.48

10

Introduction to Probability

SECTION 10.1 MULTIPLICATION PRINCIPLE, PERMUTATIONS AND COMBINATIONS

How many different license plates can be made using three numbers and three letters? How many different 3 digit numbers can be made using the digits 0, 1, 2, 3 and 4 without repeating any digit? These questions can be answered using the **multiplication principle** (also known as the **fundamental principle of counting**).

Definition: Multiplication Principle

If two events Q_1 and Q_2 can be performed in order in N_1 and N_2 mutually exclusive ways respectively, then there are

$$N_1 \cdot N_2$$

possible combined outcomes of the first event followed by the second event.

Two or more events are said to be **mutually exclusive** if the occurrence of any one precludes the occurrence of all the others. For example, when a coin is tossed, the outcome is a head or a tail. If a head is obtained, it precludes the possibility of the tail occurring. By the multiplication principle, if there are $N_1, N_2, N_3, ..., N_n$ mutually exclusive ways for the events $Q_1, Q_2, Q_3, ..., Q_n$ to happen, then there are $N_1 \cdot N_2 \cdot N_3 \cdot ... \cdot N_n$ number of possible outcomes.

EXAMPLE 10.1

a) In how many ways can the letters A, B and C be used to make two-letter code words?

b) How many four digit numbers can be made using the digits 1, 2 and 3?

SOLUTION 10.1

a) In how many ways can the letters *A*, *B* and *C* be used to make two-letter code words?

A two-letter code word using the letters *A*, *B* and *C* looks like this

$$\underline{\quad ? \quad} \cdot \underline{\quad ? \quad}$$

where *A*, *B*, or *C* can be put in the first location or the second location. It is often helpful to make a tree diagram to list all of the possible outcomes. A tree diagram for this problem looks like this:

If we count the number of two-letter code words, there are nine. We can also determine the number of code words using the multiplication principle. A two-letter code word is a word in the form of

$$\underline{\quad ? \quad} \cdot \underline{\quad ? \quad}$$

where three letters can go into the first location and three letters can also go into the second location.

$$\underline{\quad 3 \quad} \cdot \underline{\quad 3 \quad} = 9$$

b) How many four digit numbers can be made using the digits 1, 2 and 3?

A tree diagram would be extremely large for this problem. To find the number of possible four digit numbers that can be made using the digits 1, 2 and 3, use the multiplication principle. There are three digits that can be used as the first number. Since we are allowed to repeat digits, there are also three digits that can be used as the second, third and fourth locations of the number. The multiplication principle tells us that the number of possible three digit numbers that can be made using the digits 1, 2 and 3 are

$$3 \cdot 3 \cdot 3 \cdot 3 = 81.$$

EXAMPLE 10.2

How many four digit numbers can be made using the digits 1, 2, 3, and 4 without repeating any digit?

SOLUTION 10.2

How many four digit numbers can be made using the digits 1, 2, 3, and 4 without repeating any digit?

There are 4 digits which can be used as the first digit. After one of the digits 1, 2, 3, or 4 has been used for the first digit, there are three digits left for the second digit since we are not allowed to repeat the first digit. Once the first and second digits have been chosen, there are two digits which can be used in the third location and only one that can be used as the last digit of the four digit number. By the multiplication principle, there are

$$4 \cdot 3 \cdot 2 \cdot 1 = 24$$

four digit numbers which can be written using the digits 1, 2, 3, and 4 without repeating any digit.

Permutations

There are six people standing in line. In how many different ways can these six people line up? By the multiplication principle, the solution is
$$6 \cdot 5 \cdot 4 \cdot 3 \cdot 2 \cdot 1 = 720 \text{ or } 6!.$$
The above arrangement or ordering is called a **permutation**. A permutation is an ordering of n objects taken r at a time. The above permutation is a permutation of six people taken six at a time. Suppose that not all of the six people stand in line at the same time. Suppose that only three of the six people stand in line. The number of permutations of six people taken three at a time (written $_nP_r$) is
$$_6P_3 = \underbrace{6 \cdot 5 \cdot 4}_{3} = 120.$$

Other notations for permutations are $P_{n,\,r}$, $P(n, r)$, and P_r^n. Notice how we multiply three numbers together starting at 6 and descending by one until there is a multiplication problem using three numbers. Permutations are only defined when n and r are whole numbers and $r \leq n$. Permutations of fractional and decimal numbers are not defined.

Theorem: Permutations of n objects taken r at a time
The number of permutations of n objects taken r at a time is
$$_nP_r = \underbrace{n \cdot (n-1) \cdot (n-2) \cdot \ldots \cdot (n-r+1)}_{r \text{ factors}}$$
or
$$_nP_r = \frac{n!}{(n-r)!} \quad \text{where } 0 \leq r \leq n.$$

It should be noted that

1. $_nP_0 = \dfrac{n!}{(n-0)!} = \dfrac{n!}{n!} = 1$

2. $_nP_n = \dfrac{n!}{(n-n)!} = \dfrac{n!}{0!} = \dfrac{n!}{1} = n!$

EXAMPLE 10.3

Find

a) $_5P_2$

b) $_7P_3$

c) $_8P_4$

d) $_5P_5$

SOLUTION 10.3

a) $_5P_2 = \dfrac{5!}{(5-2)!} = \dfrac{5!}{3!} = \dfrac{5 \cdot 4 \cdot 3 \cdot 2 \cdot 1}{3 \cdot 2 \cdot 1} = 5 \cdot 4 = 20$

$_5P_2 = 5 \cdot 4 = 20$

b) $_7P_3 = \dfrac{7!}{(7-3)!} = \dfrac{7!}{4!} = \dfrac{7 \cdot 6 \cdot 5 \cdot 4!}{4!} = 7 \cdot 6 \cdot 5 = 210$

$_7P_3 = 7 \cdot 6 \cdot 5 = 210$

c) $_8P_4 = 8 \cdot 7 \cdot 6 \cdot 5 = 1680$

d) $_5P_5 = 5 \cdot 4 \cdot 3 \cdot 2 \cdot 1 = 120$

EXAMPLE 10.4

a) From a group of 15 people, in how many ways can we select a president, vice-president, secretary and treasurer?

b) College students must take English, Mathematics, History, Science, Health, and Physical Education to fulfill graduation requirements. In how many different ways can Mary make her schedule if she takes exactly four of these courses?

c) There are 10 horses in a race. In how many different ways can they place first, second, and third?

SOLUTION 10.4

a) From a group of 15 people, in how many ways can we select a president, vice-president, secretary and treasurer?

The selection of president, vice-president, secretary and treasurer is a permutation of events. There are 15 people who can be chosen for president. Once the president is chosen there are 14 people who can be chosen for vice-president. Since the same person cannot be two of the officers, this problem is solved by a permutation of 15 people being chosen 4 at a time.

$$_{15}P_4 = 15 \cdot 14 \cdot 13 \cdot 12 = 32,760$$

There are 37,760 different ways that the officers of the group can be chosen.

b) College students must take English, Mathematics, History, Science, Health, and Physical Education to fulfill graduation requirements. In how many different ways can Mary make her schedule if she takes exactly four of these courses?

The selection of a class schedule is a permutation. Mary has 6 classes to choose from for her first class. Once Mary chooses her first class, she then has five classes she can pick for her next class, etc. Mary's schedule is a permutation of 6 classes taken four at a time.

$$_6P_4 = 6 \cdot 5 \cdot 4 \cdot 3 = 360$$

There are 360 different ways that Mary can choose four of the six classes that meet the graduation requirements.

c) There are 10 horses in a race. In how many different ways can they place first, second, and third?

The winning of a horse race is a permutation. In this race, there are ten horses which take three places.

$$_{10}P_3 = 10 \cdot 9 \cdot 8 = 720$$

There are 720 different ways which the horses can place first, second and third.

Combination

How many different committees of three people can be chosen from a group of four people? Let A, B, C, and D represent the four people in the group. Below is a list of all of the possible groupings of four people taken three at a time:

ABC	ABD	ACB	ACD	ADB	ADC
BAC	BAD	BCA	BCD	BDA	BDC
CAB	CAD	CBA	CBD	CDA	CDB
DAB	DAC	DBA	DBC	DCA	DCB

This list represents the number of permutations of 4 objects taken three at a time.

$$_4P_3 = 4 \cdot 3 \cdot 2 = 24$$

When selecting a committee of three people, order is not important. The committees *ABC* and *ACB* are really the same committee. It is not important if *A* is selected first, *B* second and *C* third or *A* first, *C* second and *B* third. *ABC* and *ACB* are still the same committee. To find the number of committees of three people which can be selected from a group of four people, duplicate committees must be thrown away. *ABC* is the first committee listed. Go through the list and throw away all other groups that contain *A*, *B* and *C*.

ABC	*ABD*	*ACB*	*ACD*	*ADB*	*ADC*
BAC	*BAD*	*BCA*	*BCD*	*BDA*	*BDC*
CAB	*CAD*	*CBA*	*CBD*	*CDA*	*CDB*
DAB	*DAC*	*DBA*	*DBC*	*DCA*	*DCB*

Now all duplicate committees of *ABC* have been removed. Remove duplicates of committee *ABD*.

ABC	*ABD*	*ACB*	*ACD*	*ADB*	*ADC*
BAC	*BAD*	*BCA*	*BCD*	*BDA*	*BDC*
CAB	*CAD*	*CBA*	*CBD*	*CDA*	*CDB*
DAB	*DAC*	*DBA*	*DBC*	*DCA*	*DCB*

Remove duplicates of *ACD*.

ABC	*ABD*	*ACB*	*ACD*	*ADB*	*ADC*
BAC	*BAD*	*BCA*	*BCD*	*BDA*	*BDC*
CAB	*CAD*	*CBA*	*CBD*	*CDA*	*CDB*
DAB	*DAC*	*DBA*	*DBC*	*DCA*	*DCB*

Remove duplicates of *BCD*.

ABC	*ABD*	*ACB*	*ACD*	*ADB*	*ADC*
BAC	*BAD*	*BCA*	*BCD*	*BDA*	*BDC*
CAB	*CAD*	*CBA*	*CBD*	*CDA*	*CDB*
DAB	*DAC*	*DBA*	*DBC*	*DCA*	*DCB*

At this point, all committees have been thrown away except *ABC*, *ABD*, *ACD* and *BCD*. There are only four committees of three people which can be made from a group of four. If the order of objects is not important, then duplicates must be thrown away. The combination formula for *n* objects taken *r* at a time is given below.

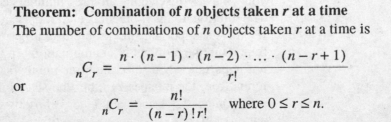

Theorem: Combination of *n* objects taken *r* at a time

The number of combinations of *n* objects taken *r* at a time is

$$_nC_r = \frac{n \cdot (n-1) \cdot (n-2) \cdot \ldots \cdot (n-r+1)}{r!}$$

or

$$_nC_r = \frac{n!}{(n-r)!\,r!} \quad \text{where } 0 \le r \le n.$$

Other notations used for the combinations of n taken r at a time include $C_{n,\,r}$, $C(n,r)$, C_r^n and $\binom{n}{r}$. When using the combination formula, the order that the object is chosen is not important. We have used the combination formula before when expanding binomials.

EXAMPLE 10.5

Find:

a) $\binom{5}{3}$

b) $\binom{9}{6}$

c) $\binom{11}{3}$

SOLUTION 10.5

a) $\binom{5}{3} = \dfrac{5!}{(5-3)!\,3!} = \dfrac{5!}{2!3!} = \dfrac{5\cdot 4\cdot 3!}{2\cdot 1\cdot 3!} = \dfrac{20}{2} = 10$

b) $\binom{9}{6} = \dfrac{9!}{(9-6)!\,6!} = \dfrac{9!}{3!6!} = \dfrac{9\cdot 8\cdot 7\cdot 6!}{3\cdot 2\cdot 1\cdot 6!} = \dfrac{504}{6} = 84$

c) $\binom{11}{3} = \dfrac{11!}{(11-3)!\,3!} = \dfrac{11!}{8!3!} = \dfrac{11\cdot 10\cdot 9\cdot 8!}{8!\cdot 3\cdot 2\cdot 1} = \dfrac{990}{6} = 165$

EXAMPLE 10.6

a) Three numbers are chosen from a group of ten numbers. What are your chances of selecting all three numbers correctly?

b) In how many ways can a committee of 5 people be selected from a faculty of 55 people?

c) Determine the number of ways five papers can be chosen from a group of 20 papers?

d) In the California lotto drawing, a contestant selects 6 of 53 numbers. In how many different ways can 6 of 53 numbers be chosen?

SOLUTION 10.6

a) Three numbers are chosen from a group of ten numbers. What are your chances of selecting all three numbers correctly?
    The solution to this problem is either a permutation or a combination. If order is important, the problem is a permutation. If order is not important, the problem is a combination. In this problem, the order is not important when selecting three numbers. The number 123 is different from the number 213, but the selection 1, 2 and 3 is the same selection as if 2, 1 and then 3 were chosen. The problem is a combination of 10 numbers chosen 3 at a time

$$\binom{10}{3} = \frac{10!}{(10-3)!3!} = \frac{10!}{7!3!} = \frac{10 \cdot 9 \cdot 8 \cdot 7!}{7! \cdot 3 \cdot 2 \cdot 1} = \frac{720}{6} = 120$$

b) In how many ways can a committee of 5 people be selected from a faculty of 55 people?

This is a combination. The committee *ABCDE* is the same committee as *EDCAB*.

$$\binom{55}{5} = \frac{55!}{(55-5)!5!} = \frac{55!}{50!5!} = \frac{55 \cdot 54 \cdot 53 \cdot 52 \cdot 51 \cdot 50!}{50! \cdot 5 \cdot 4 \cdot 3 \cdot 2 \cdot 1}$$

$$= 3,478,761$$

c) Determine the number of ways five papers can be chosen from a group of 20 papers?

Suppose that an English teacher decides to read five papers from a class of 20 students. It does not matter if your paper is chosen first or last. If your paper is among the five chosen, then it will be read. Order is not important, so this problem is a combination.

$$\binom{20}{5} = \frac{20!}{(20-5)!5!} = \frac{20!}{15!5!} = \frac{20 \cdot 19 \cdot 18 \cdot 17 \cdot 16 \cdot 15!}{15! \cdot 5 \cdot 4 \cdot 3 \cdot 2 \cdot 1}$$

$$= 15,504$$

d) In the California lotto drawing, a contestant selects 6 of 53 numbers. In how many different ways can 6 of 53 numbers be chosen?

It does not matter if your numbers are chosen by the lottery in the same order you selected them. If you pick the numbers 4, 7, 15, 27, 35 and 53 and the lotto selects 15, 27, 53, 35, 4 and 7, you still win. This problem is a combination of 53 numbers taken 6 at a time.

$$\binom{53}{6} = \frac{53!}{(53-6)!6!} = \frac{53!}{47!6!} = \frac{53 \cdot 52 \cdot 51 \cdot 50 \cdot 49 \cdot 48 \cdot 47!}{47! \cdot 6 \cdot 5 \cdot 4 \cdot 3 \cdot 2 \cdot 1}$$

$$= 22,957,480$$

There are almost 23 million ways in which 6 numbers can be chosen from a group of 53. Your chances of winning the California lottery is one out of 22,957,480.

EXERCISE 10.1

Use the multiplication principle of counting to solve the following problems:

1. In how many ways can the letters *A*, *B*, *C*, *D* and *E* be used to make three-letter code words? It is acceptable to repeat a letter.
2. How many four digit numbers can be made using the digits 1, 2, 3, 4 and 5?
3. How many differenc license plates can be made using one number, three letters and then three numbers?

4. In how many ways can the letters A, B, C, D and E be used to make four-letter code words if no letter is repeated more than one time?

5. How many five digit numbers can be made using the digits 1, 2, 3, 4, 5, 6 and 7 without repeating any of the digits?

Evaluate the following permutations:

6. $_6P_3$

7. $_9P_2$

8. $_{11}P_4$

9. $_6P_4$

10. $_{13}P_8$

11. From a group of 25 people, in how many ways can we select a president, vice-president, secretary and treasurer?

12. There are 8 horses in a race. In how many different ways can they place first, second, and third?

13. In how many ways can 5 pictures be hung in a row on a wall in an art gallery?

14. On a vacation, you wish to visit five of the 22 national parks. If the order of the trip matters, in how many different ways can you plan your vacation?

15. There are 10 different roads between your house and school. On any day, in how many different ways can you go to and from school without driving the same road twice.

Evaluate the following combinations:

16. $\begin{pmatrix} 7 \\ 2 \end{pmatrix}$

17. $\begin{pmatrix} 9 \\ 5 \end{pmatrix}$

18. $\begin{pmatrix} 11 \\ 7 \end{pmatrix}$

19. $\begin{pmatrix} 12 \\ 5 \end{pmatrix}$

20. $\begin{pmatrix} 21 \\ 7 \end{pmatrix}$

21. Four numbers are chosen from a group of 20 numbers. What are your chances of selecting all four numbers correctly?

22. In how many ways can a committee of 3 people be selected from a group of 15 people?

23. In the California little lotto drawing, a contestant selects 6 numbers from 1 to 39. In how many different ways can these six numbers be chosen?

ANSWERS TO EXERCISE 5.1

1. 125	2. 625
3. 175,760,000	4. 120
5. 2,520	6. 120
7. 72	8. 7,920
9. 360	10. 51,891,840
11. 303,600	12. 336
13. 120	14. 3,160,080
15. 90	16. 21
17. 126	18. 330
19. 792	20. 116,280
21. 4,845	22. 455
23. 3,262,623	

SECTION 10.2 SAMPLE SPACES AND PROBABILITY

In mathematics, the term experiment can be used for several different situations. In this book, the term **experiment** will mean an act or process leading to specific outcomes. An **outcome** is the result obtained from the experiment. Some experiments will not yield with certainty the same results no matter how many times the experiment is conducted. A **random experiment** is an act or process that leads to a single outcome that cannot be predicted with certainty. Random experiments include tossing a coin, rolling of dice, or drawing numbers from the lottery. In the remainder of this book, when the word experiment is used, it will imply random experiment.

Associated with the word outcome and experiment are sample spaces and events. The set of all possible outcomes in an experiment is called the **sample space**. Sample space is usually denoted by the letter S. In the toss of a single coin, the sample space is either a head or a tail ($S = \{H, T\}$). In the roll of a die (a cube with the sides numbered 1 through 6), the sample space is $S = \{1, 2, 3, 4, 5, \text{or } 6\}$. If we toss two coins, the sample space is $S = \{HH, HT, TH, TT\}$. To be a sample space the following three criteria must be upheld.

> **Definition of a Sample Space**
> The set of outcomes in an experiment is called the **Sample Space**
> designated by S if all three of the following hold true:
> 1. All of the outcomes are defined and in the set S.
> 2. The experiment must lead to one of the outcomes in S.
> 3. No two outcomes can occur at the same time.

To determine a sample space, we often us a tree diagram listing the set of
all possible outcomes. Suppose that we toss three coins. A tree diagram
for the tossing of three coins is given below.

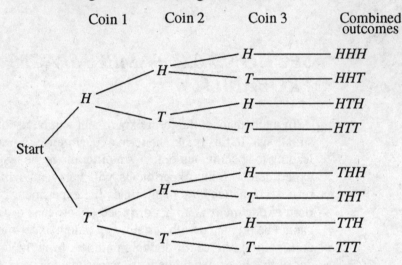

From the tree diagram, the sample space for tossing three coins is
$$S = \{HHH, HHT, HTH, HTT, THH, THT, TTH, TTT\}.$$
In a given sample space, we define an event (denoted by the letter E) to be
a subset of S. A **simple event** is an event with only one element. $E =$
$\{HHH\}$ is a simple event. If the event E has more than one element, then
E is called a **compound event**. The event $E = \{HHH, TTT\}$ is a compound event.

EXAMPLE 10.7

Find the sample space for each of the following using a tree diagram:
a) The sexes of the children (B-boy, G-girl) in a family having two chil-
    dren.
b) True-False answers to a three-question quiz.

SOLUTION 10.7

a) The sexes of the children (*B*-boy, *G*-girl) in a family having two children.

To answer this question, we must first consider all of the possible situations one at a time. To start, the first child can be either a boy or a girl. Once the first child is born, the second child again has only two choices, boy or girl. Below is a tree diagram for the sample space of the sexes of children in a family having two children.

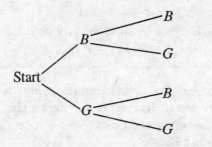

$$S = \{BB, BG, GB, GG\}$$

b) True-False answers to a three-question quiz.

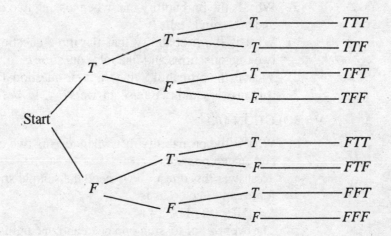

The sample space is $S = \{TTT, TTF, TFT, TFF, FTT, FTF, FFT, FFF\}$. There are 8 different possiblities of outcomes in a sample space of this size.

Probability of an Event

The probability of an event happening requires the definition of a probability function for a simple event.

Probability Function for Simple Events

Given a sample space $S = \{e_1, e_2, e_3, ..., e_n\}$ of n simple events denoted e_i. To each event we assign a real number $P(e_i)$ that is called the probability of the event e_i. The probability of the even e_i [denoted $P(e_i)$] must satisfy the following two conditions:

1. $0 \le P(e_i) \le 1$ and

2. The sum of all of the probabilities of events $e_1, e_2, e_3, ..., e_n = 1$
   $$P(e_1) + P(e_2) + P(e_3) + ... + P(e_n) = 1.$$

The probability of an event happening is assigned a fractional value from zero to one inclusive. If n is the number of events in sample space S and m is the number of times event e_i occurs, then the probability of event e_i happening is

$$P(e_i) = \frac{m}{n}.$$

EXAMPLE 10.8

Find the following probabilities:

a)   What is the probability that when tossing two coins, one coin is heads and one coin is tails?

b)   What is the probability that the three-question True-False quiz had two true questions and one false question?

c)   What is the probability that the four-question True-False quiz had two true answers and two false answers?

SOLUTION 10.8

a)   What is the probability that when tossing two coins, one coin is heads and one coin is tails?
     To answer this question we need the sample space. The sample space for tossing two coins is
     $S = \{HH, HT, TH, TT\}$
     The event e_i of tossing one head and one tail is

$$P(e_1) = \frac{1 \text{ head and 1 tail}}{\text{total number of events}} = \frac{2}{4} = \frac{1}{2} = 0.5$$

b)   What is the probability that the three-question True-False quiz had two true questions and one false question?
     The solution space for the three-question True-False quiz is
     $S = \{TTT, TTF, TFT, TFF, FTT, FTF, FFT, FFF\}$. This was found in a previous example. The event of having 2 true and 1 false is

$E = \{TTF, TFT, FTT\}$. The probability of having answers of two true and one false is

$$P(e_1) = \frac{2 \text{ true and 1 false}}{\text{total number of events}} = \frac{3}{8} = 0.375$$

c) What is the probability that the four-question True-False quiz had two true answers and two false answers?

The sample space for the four-question True-False quiz is
$S = \{TTTT, TTTF, TTFT, TTFF, TFTT, TFTF, TFFT, TFFF, FTTT, FTTF, FTFT, FTFF, FFTT, FFTF, FFFT, FFFF\}$. This was also found in a previous example. $E = \{TTFF, TFTF, TFFT, FTTF, FTFT, FFTT\}$. The probability of having answers of two true and one false is

$$P(e_1) = \frac{2 \text{ true and 2 false}}{\text{total number of events}} = \frac{6}{16} = \frac{3}{8} = 0.375$$

The steps needed to find the probability of an event are as follows:

Steps for Finding the Probability of an Event
1. Set up the sample space S for the experiment.
2. Find the number of times the event happens.
3. Determine the total number of events in the sample space.
4. Probability of event e_i happening is

$$P(e_i) = \frac{\text{number of times event } e \text{ happens}}{\text{total number of events}}.$$

EXAMPLE 10.9

Determine the following probabilities:
a) What is the probability of drawing a king from a deck of 52 cards?
b) What is the probability of drawing a king or queen from a deck of 52 cards?
c) What is the probability of drawing a ten or higher from a deck of 52 cards?
d) What is the probability of drawing a diamond from a deck of 52 cards?

SOLUTION 10.9

a) What is the probability of drawing a king from a deck of 52 cards?
There are four kings in a deck of 52 cards.

$$P(e_k) = \frac{4 \text{ kings}}{\text{total number of events}} = \frac{4}{52} = \frac{1}{13}$$

b) What is the probability of drawing a king or queen from a deck of 52 cards?
    There are 4 kings and 4 queens in a deck of 52 cards.

$$P(e_{k,q}) = \frac{4 \text{ kings or } 4 \text{ queens}}{\text{total number of events}} = \frac{8}{52} = \frac{2}{13}$$

c) What is the probability of drawing a ten or higher from a deck of 52 cards?
    There are 4 tens, 4 jacks, 4 queens, 4 kings, and 4 aces. There are 20 cards which are 10 or higher.

$$P(e) = \frac{20}{52} = \frac{5}{13}$$

d) What is the probability of drawing a diamond from a deck of 52 cards?
    There are four suits in a deck of 52 cards. The suits are diamonds, hearts, spades, and clubs. There are 13 cards in each suit so there are 13 diamonds.

$$P(e_d) = \frac{13}{52} = \frac{1}{4} = 0.25$$

EXERCISE 10.2

Find the probability of each of the following:
 1. The probability of a family having two children of opposite sex.
 2. The probability of a family of three children having 2 boys and one girl.
 3. The probability of a family of three children having 2 boys and one girl in that order.
 4. The probability of a family of three children having all three boys.
 5. The probability of a family of three children having at least 1 boy.

Use the table of the sample space for the rolling of dice to answer the following probabilities:
 6. What is the probability of rolling a sum of 1?
 7. What is the probability of rolling a sum of 2?
 8. What is the probability of rolling a sum of at least 5?
 9. What is the probability of rolling a sum of less than 5?
10. What is the probability of rolling a sum of 6, 7 or 8?
11. What is the probability of rolling a sum between 4 and 7 inclusive?
12. What is the probability of rolling a sum between 4 and 7 exclusive?
13. What is the probability of rolling a sum of 2 (snake eyes)?
14. What is the probability of rolling a double (both die have the same number)?

15. What is the probability of rolling a sum greater than 7?

Using a true deck of 52 cards, answer the following probabilities:

16. What is the probability of drawing a card smaller than 5 (count the ace as less than 5)?
17. What is the probability of drawing a card smaller than 3 or bigger than a jack (count the ace as smaller or larger, but not both)?
18. What is the probability of drawing a red card?
19. What is the probability of drawing a heart or an ace?
20. What is the probability of drawing a black card or a number less than 6?

ANSWERS TO EXERCISE 10.2

1. $\dfrac{1}{2} = 0.5$

2. $\dfrac{3}{8} = 0.375$

3. $\dfrac{1}{8} = 0.125$

4. $\dfrac{1}{8} = 0.125$

5. $\dfrac{7}{8} = 0.875$

6. $\dfrac{0}{36} = 0.000$

7. $\dfrac{1}{36} = 0.02777\ldots$

8. $\dfrac{30}{36} = \dfrac{5}{6} = 0.8333\ldots$

9. $\dfrac{6}{36} = \dfrac{1}{6} = 0.1666\ldots$

10. $\dfrac{16}{36} = \dfrac{4}{9} = 0.444\ldots$

11. $\dfrac{18}{36} = \dfrac{1}{2} = 0.5$

12. $\dfrac{9}{36} = \dfrac{1}{4} = 0.25$

13. $\dfrac{1}{36} = 0.02777\ldots$

14. $\dfrac{6}{36} = \dfrac{1}{6} = 0.1666\ldots$

15. $\dfrac{15}{36} = \dfrac{5}{12} = 0.41666\ldots$

16. $\dfrac{16}{52} = \dfrac{4}{13}$

17. $\dfrac{16}{52} = \dfrac{4}{13}$

18. $\dfrac{26}{52} = \dfrac{1}{2} = 0.5$

19. $\dfrac{16}{52} = \dfrac{4}{13}$

20. $\dfrac{34}{52} = \dfrac{17}{26}$

Index

G

Gauss-Jordan elimination method, solving systems of equations by, 314–316
General term
  arithmetic sequence, 346–347
  of geometric sequence, 353
  of sequence, 332
General trinomials, 21, 29–30
Geometric progression, 351, 352
Geometric sequences, 351–355
  general term of, 353
Geometric series
  finite, 355–358
  infinite, 358–365
  summation formulas for *n* terms of, 356
Geometry
  circle, 166–170, 379, 381–390
  conic section, 378–381
  ellipse, 380, 391–403
  hyperbola, 381, 403–421
Geometry problems, linear equations in, 97–100
Graphing
  cartesian plane in, 153–158
  circles in, 166–170
  distance between points, 163–165
  by plotting point-by-point, 153–158, 158–162
  polynomials, 289–295
  solving linear system of equation by, 296–298
  symmetry in, 162–163
Grouping, 30–32
  1 by 3, 21, 31–32
  3 by 1, 21, 31–32
  2 by 2, 21, 30–31

H

Horizontal line, 214
  test for, 215
Hyperbola, 381, 403–421
  definition, 403
  standard equations of a, 409, 411

I

Identities, 2, 80, 88–89
Imaginary number, 112
Imaginary unit, 111, 112
Imaginary zeros, 278
In-between inequalities, 102–104
Increasing functions, 196, 216–221
Independent system of equations, 297
Independent variable, 196

Index, 335–336
Indirect approach, proof by, 340
Induction, axiom of, 340
Inequalities. *See also* Linear inequalities
  absolute, 109–111
  polynomial, 140–141
  quadratic, 136–140
  rational, 141–145
Infinite geometric series, 358–365
  sum of, 360–365
Infinite sequence, 332
Infinite series, 334
Integer, 1
Integer exponents, 46
  multiplying and dividing with negative, 48–50
  multiplying and dividing with positive, 47–48
  simplifying, that include addition or subtraction, 51–52
  theorems of, 46
Intercept form, 176–177
Intercept method, 171
Inverse, of a function, 210–212
Inverse functions, 213–216, 240–241
Irrational numbers, 1

L

Least common denominators, 5–7
Like radical expressions, 76
Like terms, 9
  combining, 10
Line(s)
  parallel, 181–185
  perpendicular, 181–185
  slope-intercept form of a straight, 173–175
  slope of, 171–173
  special forms of straight, 175–181
Linear combinations, solving linear systems of equations by, 301–303
Linear equations, 81, 89–90, 159, 378
  age problems, 91–92
  distance-rate-time, 92–94
  geometry problems, 97–100
  mixture problems, 96–97
  money problems, 95–96
  number problems, 90–91
  parallel lines, 181–185
  perpendicular lines, 181–185
  slope-intercept form of a straight line, 173–175
  slope of a line, 171–173
  special forms of the straight line, 175–181
  standard form of, 170–171
Linear factor theorem, 118

Linear functions, 196–198
Linear inequalities, 100, 321–325
  graphing, 325–328
  properties of, 100
  solving, 101–104, 325
Linear systems of equations, in three variables, 304–305
Linear systems in two variables, 296
  solutions by graphing, 296–298
  solutions by linear combinations, 301–303
  solutions by substitution, 298–301
Logarithmic equations, 258–263
Logarithmic functions, 240–244
  definition of, 240
Logarithmic notation, 249
Logarithms
  common and natural, 249–255
  expansion of, 245–247
  theorems of, 244–249
Long division, 264–266
Lower bound, 282–284

M

Major axis, 391
Mathematical induction, 339–344
  fundamental principle of, 340–341
  steps of proof by, 341–344
Mathematical relation, 185
Matrix
  augmented, 306–310
  definition of, 306
  reduced, 310–313
  row-equivalent, 307
Maximum point, 199
Members, 1
Minimum point, 199
Minor axis, 391
Mixture problems, linear equations in, 96–97
Money problems, linear equations in, 95–96
Monomial factors, common, 21–22
Monomials, 11
Multiple zero (multiple root), 274
Multiplication
  of conjugate pairs, 17
  distributive property of, over addition, 2, 14
  of exponential expressions with negative exponents, 48–50
  of exponential expressions with positive exponents, 47–48
  of fractions, 4
  of polynomials, 14–17
  of rational expressions, 36–38
  of terms, 10
Multiplication principle, 422–424